Territory, time and state is a study of long-term archaeological history in the remote and beautiful upland Valley of Gubbio within the Umbrian Apennines of Italy. The aim of the work is to understand a human landscape that is well defined by the natural constraints of this mountainous region.

The authors have developed a multi-disciplinary approach to study the human and physical characteristics of the valley from the palaeolithic to the medieval period. They integrate the analysis of a unique text (the Iguvine Tables) with excavation, field survey and environmental reconstruction to provide a synthesis of current knowledge. They break boundaries of time and tradition which are normally compartmentalised between different scholars. Although the linkage is sometimes controversial, it is always stimulating.

The book has two major focuses: the first is on the Bronze Age landscape where spectacular sites and finds have contributed very significantly to our knowledge of pre-state Italy; and the second is on the identity and character of the early city-state of Gubbio and its incorporation into the Roman world.

Territory, time and state

TERRITORY, TIME *and* STATE

The archaeological development of the Gubbio Basin

edited by
CAROLINE MALONE *and*
SIMON STODDART

with contributions from Francesco Allegrucci, Catherine Backway, Edoardo Biondi, Gillian Clark, Mauro Coltorti, Peter Finke, Rachel Fulton, Jenny Harding, Rupert Housley, Christopher Hunt, Dorica Manconi, James McVicar, Timothy Reynolds, Mirjam Schomaker, Rene Sewuster, Jan Sevink, Erik van Waveren, Nicholas Whitehead, James Whitley and John Wilkins.

CAMBRIDGE
UNIVERSITY PRESS

Published by the Press Syndicate of the University of Cambridge
The Pitt Building, Trumpington Street, Cambridge CB2 1RP
40 West 20th Street, New York, NY 10011–4211, USA
10 Stamford Road, Oakleigh, Melbourne 3166, Australia

First published 1994

Printed in Great Britain at the University Press, Cambridge

A catalogue record for this book is available from the British Library

Library Congress cataloguing in publication data

Territory, time and state: the archaeological development of the
Gubbio Basin / edited by Caroline Malone and Simon Stoddart; with
contributions from Francesco Allegrucci . . . [*et al.*].
    p.   cm.
ISBN 0 521 35568 0
1. Gubbio Region (Italy) – Antiquities. 2. Excavations (Archaeology)
– Italy – Gubbio Region. 3. Man, Prehistoric – Italy – Gubbio
region. 4. Eugubine Tables. I. Malone, Caroline. II. Stoddart,
Simon. III. Allegrucci, Francesco.
DG975.G8T47   1994
945.6'51 – dc20   93–8122   CIP

ISBN 0 521 35568 0 hardback

CONTENTS

ILLUSTRATIONS

TABLES

ACKNOWLEDGEMENTS

It is difficult to make proper acknowledgement to all who have aided the writing of this book and the fieldwork that lies behind it. A few must be given special mention, whilst we have also attempted to credit others in the listings below.

A first debt must be acknowledged to David Whitehouse who encouraged us to initiate the Gubbio project, building on the work he had started on the Rocca Posteriore.

A major debt is owed to Roberto Abbondanza who was instrumental in transforming the project from a rescue excavation into a properly funded regional project.

We would like to thank Professor Graeme Barker, Professor Lord Colin Renfrew and Professor H. Wright for their advice and support in developing the project.

British Olivetti and Olivetti SpA gave invaluable assistance in providing computers and technical assistance both in Italy and England. This allowed much more efficient data analysis from the outset.

Technical and financial support was provided by the following institutions (in alphabetical order): The Azienda di Soggiorno e Turismo per l'Eugubino, British Academy, the British Museum Conservation and Radiocarbon laboratories, the British School at Rome, the Casa di Riposo, Via Cavour, the Comune di Gubbio (especially Paolo Barboni and Mauro Tomarelli), the Comunità montana dell'Alto Chiascio (especially Francesco Allegrucci), the Crowther Beynon Fund (Cambridge), the Gorwin Radiocarbon laboratory of the University of Cambridge (Dr Roy Switsur) the Emslie Horniman Fund of the Royal Anthropological Institute (London), the Istituto d'Arte (Gubbio), the Istituto Quinquennio Sperimentale (Gubbio), Magdalene College (Cambridge), the National Geographic Society (Washington, DC, USA) (NGS grants #2931-84, #3487-87), the Ospedale di Gubbio (Dipartimento di Radiologia–for X-rays), the Oxford University Radiocarbon Accelerator Unit, the Prehistoric Society, the Provincia di Perugia, the Regione dell'Umbria (Ortofotocarte and finance), the Society of Antiquaries, the Soprintendenza archeologica per l'Umbria (especially Prof.ssa Anna Feruglio, Dorica Manconi and Maria Cristina De Angelis), Trinity Hall (Cambridge).

Further invaluable assistance was given by Pino Angeletti, Silvana Biagarelli, Laura Bonomi Ponzi, Mauro Broggi, Ubaldo Casoli, C. Cattuto, Bruno Cenni, Girolamo Clementi, Alganesc Fessaha, Nello Fumaria, Leandro Galli, Franco Gavirati, Donatello Magaldi, Piero Meloni, Franco Mezzanotte, Ivana Minelli, Franco Pedrotti, John Penney, Signor Pippitone, A. Raspi, Maria Franca Raspi, Bruno Ronchi, A. Solazzi, Mario Stirati, Maria Vispi and Ruth Whitehouse.

Section 2.1 was undertaken with CNR funds allocated to Professore G. Ficcarelli and Dottore M. Coltorti. We are grateful to the CNR for financing the printing of Fig. 2.10.

The excavation and survey teams consisted of the following: Elizabeth Allan, Tim Allen, Patrizia Anconetani, Steven Ashley, Andrew Atter, Sarah Austin, Jan Auton, Ramone Avallone, Catherine Backway, Alexia Ballance, Elisabeth Bannan, Graeme Barker, Judith Barton, Sarah Bates, Stefania Bavastro, Laura Bear, Christopher Bell, Marco Bettelli, Andrew Blackstock, Paul Blinkhorn, Bridget Brehm, Jody Brown, Craig Burrell, Fiona Burtt, Lydia Cahill, J. Campbell, Gregory Campbell, Simona Capecci, Corrado Cencetti, Christopher Chippindale, Sally Churchyard, Giuseppe Cilla, Teresa Clay, Roger Colten, David Cook, Lisa Cook, Gerry Corti, Dom Corti, V. Craig, Janine Crawley, James Cunningham, Vanessa Darnborough, Simon Dearsley, Catherine Dench, Felicity Devlin, Randolph Donahue, David Dunlop, Jane Elder, Joseph Elders, Peter Finke, Paul Flavell, Sharon Fleming, Barry Flood, Colum Fordham, Jacqueline Foster, Debbie Foster, Richard Fowler, Mary Fraser, Peter Freeman, Rachel Fulton, Caroline Gait, Helen Gilhooly, Paul Godfrey, Robert Hall, Jenny Harding, Susanna Hawkins, Mike Heaton, Edward Herring, Valerie Higgins, Andrew Hoaen, Loretta Hogan, Rupert Housley, Sally Howard, Gillian Hunt, Patrizia Ianantuono, Bridget Ibbs, Yvonne Jenkins, Matthew Johnson, Matthew Jones, Simon Kaner, Sheila King, John Kitchin, Brona Langton, Lisa Larsson, Anna Louise Lawrence, Michael Lester, Avi Levine, Kris Lockyear, Helen Loney, Helen Macdonald, Tim Malim, Caroline Malone, Michele Matteini Chiari, Anna McCord, Helen McDonald, Jackie McInley, Gillian McIntyre, James McVicar, Mikolai Melnyczek, Brigid Menin, Sarah Milliken, Giles Morris, Louise Mount, Lynda Mulvin, Betty Naggar, Paolo Negri, Susannah Noy-Scott, Gavin Oulton, Alan Palmer,

Helen Patterson, John Patterson, John Pitt, Daniel Reed, Tim Reynolds, Isobel Rodgers, Roy Rushbrooke, Annabel Russell, R. Ryan, Mirjam Schomaker, Rene Sewuster, Louise Simpson, Anthony Sinclair, Robin Skeates, David Smith, Thyrza Smith, Lawrence Smith, David Smith, Helen Smith, Ruth Soames, Marcus Soanes, Allan Southworth, Nigel Spivey, Kenneth Stoddart, Simon Stoddart, Sarah Taylor, Alison Taylor, Jeremy Thoday, Hope Thorp, Rozalyn Todd, Judith Toms, David Trinchero, David Tucker, Victoria Twist, Erik van Waveren, Iain Wanstall, Sarah Watkins, Marylyn Whaymond, Pippa White, Nicholas Whitehead, Sarah Whitehouse, James Whitley, Peter Winsor, James Woodman, Richard Woolley, Sarah Wyles, Jeremy Youle.

The writing of the text took much co-ordination. A number of individuals painstakingly assisted the editorial corrections. We would particularly like to thank Steven Ashley and Nicholas Whitehead for helping us in this regard. Dr Christopher Hunt made valuable comments on sections 2.1, 2.2 and 4.1. Professore Mauro Coltorti made valuable comments on section 2.3. Sebastian Payne made valuable comments on section 2.4. Judith Toms made valuable comments on an earlier draft of section 4.3 and 4.4. Dottoressa Caloi provided invaluable information on fauna from comparable sites in central Italy. Dr Robin Skeates kindly provided comparative radiocarbon dates for the Bronze Age and Dottore Francesco di Gennaro kindly checked our knowledge of the standard dates of the central Italian Bronze Age. Bryan Ward-Perkins kindly commented on Chapter 7.

We are grateful for identifications of floral remains by John Giorgi, of human bone by Valerie Higgins, fish bones by Andrew Jones, small animal bones by Geraldine Barber and charcoal by Maisie Taylor, and would like to thank Steven Ashley, Caroline Gait, Sue Grice, Caroline Malone and John Wymer for the finished drawings.

We are indebted to Dottore Franco Gavirati for permission to reproduce photographs of the Iguvine Tables (Plate 5.1), and to Mauro Coltorti for Plate 2.2.

1 INTRODUCTION

The Valley of Gubbio, in the remote Apennine mountains of central Italy (Figs. 1.1 and 1.2), is the setting for an intriguing paradox. Despite its remoteness, Gubbio produced during state formation the famous Iguvine Tables. These Tables, more properly described as a set of seven bronze tablets, were inscribed with scripts that purport to describe the extensive ritual practices and transactions of the ancient city of Ikuvium. However, in spite of the importance of the Tables as one of the longest inscriptions in the ancient Mediterranean world, there has never been much complementary archaeology to provide an historical background. A principal aim of the volume is to provide an archaeological context for this self-contained valley, so that the imaginative topographical maps of the ancient city provided by some scholars (Devoto 1974; Costantini 1970; Micalizzi 1988) can be replaced by more solidly based, if not always quite as elaborate, reconstructions of the Gubbio landscape. We offer a perspective expressed in terms of time and space. Landscape replaces topography.

This temporal and spatial context is not perceived in the narrow sense of contemporary politics and society but in the wider sense of the *longue durée* (Braudel 1972). The valley has provided a well-defined geographic focus over many millennia and it is the long-term processes that are outlined and analysed in this volume. Histories of *événements* abound for the development of the Gubbio Valley (Menichetti 1987), but it is not our intention to duplicate these here. The aim of the volume is to provide the missing element: the long-term and yet varied trajectories of development from the Palaeolithic to the medieval period.

If the intention of the volume is to provide an even coverage of millennia, it has to be emphasised that certain periods are represented better than others. Following the enhancement of knowledge of the valley during the Gubbio Project (1983–7), particular detail can be found in this volume on the Neolithic, Bronze Age and Roman settlement and early Archaic ritual. The potential research biases contributing to this picture are considered immediately below. The more important geomorphological biases are considered later (Chapter 2). However, the prominence

of these periods remains even though these potential distortions have been considered.

The primary research aim has been to provide an understanding of the prehistoric origins of the Gubbio Valley and more particularly the pre-state context of the settlement nucleation that was to become the urban centre of Gubbio itself. It was in the Bronze Age (particularly from *c.* 1200 BC) that major changes took place in the settlement organisation of the valley which made the site of modern Gubbio the primary focus of the human landscape until the present day. Why did this take place? What was the attraction of this central place? How did the territory and region relate to this central place? These are questions which remain central to the research presented in this volume.

1.1 Regional studies in Italy

The present project, focused on the Gubbio Basin, is very much part of a long tradition of topographical and regional research initiated by individuals such as Thomas Ashby at the end of the nineteenth century (Ashby 1927). Central Italy has seen the development of a series of studies, such as the South Etruria research project, started by Ashby, and brilliantly re-developed by John Ward-Perkins in the three decades following the last war (Kahane *et al.* 1968). Stimulated partly by the example of Ward-Perkins, British, Italian, American, Canadian, Dutch and Swedish scholars (Potter 1979; Barker and Lloyd 1991; Celuzza and Regoli 1982; Dyson 1978) have developed this tradition of regional study. This ranges across a very broad timescale from prehistoric to the medieval, with much emphasis on the most evident remains of the Roman period.

Studies of naturally defined regions, particularly valleys, have become a feature of recent years (Barker in preparation). The naturally defined nature of a valley or basin gives a control and coherence to fieldwork that can be difficult to achieve in undifferentiated terrain. Thus the Gubbio Project was conceived as a study in the same tradition, focused on a well-defined territory which intermittently developed its own cultural and political identity.

1

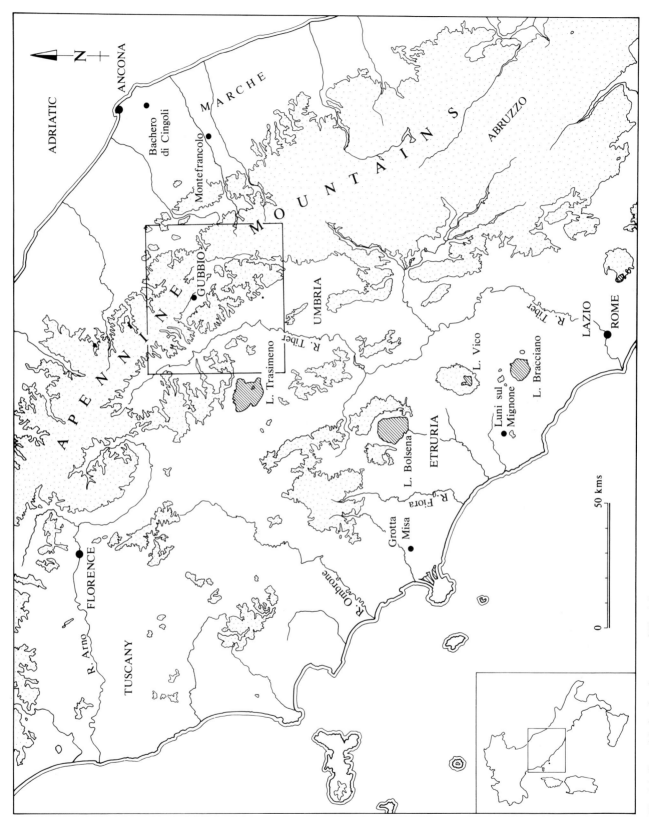

Fig. 1.1 Central Italy, showing area of Fig. 1.2

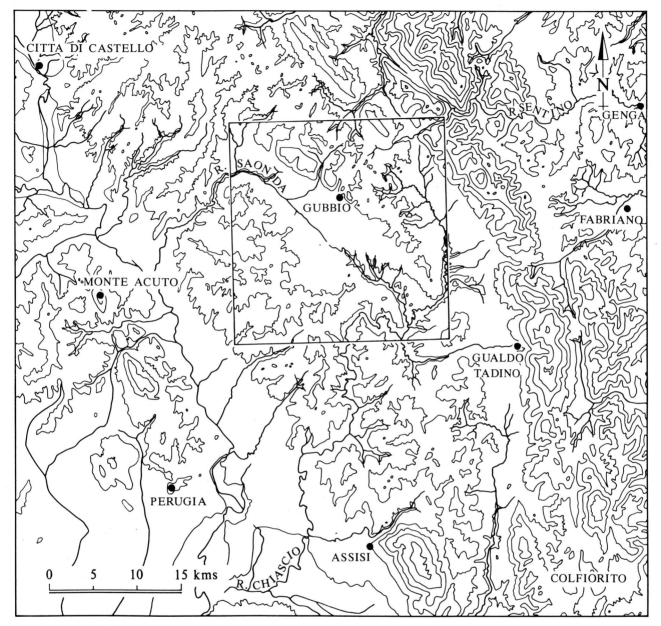

Fig. 1.2 The location of the Valley of Gubbio, showing area of Fig. 1.3 and subsequent survey maps

1.2 The location of the Gubbio Valley

The Valley of Gubbio lies in the north-eastern corner of the modern administrative region of Umbria (Figs. 1.1 and 1.2), poised strategically on a watershed between the two coasts of Italy, even if geographically much closer to the Adriatic. It is a well defined tectonic valley (Chapter 2) virtually drowned in a complex sequence of sediments. Almost the whole region is defined as mountainous by scholars (Braudel 1972) and administrators (of the Comunità montana) alike. It is furthermore a former lake

basin that sits alongside a watershed. The valley itself drains into the Tiber, through various tributaries, most prominently the Chiascio. The northern side of the limestone escarpment, however, drains into the Sentino Valley which flows ultimately into the Adriatic. The flowing of these waters parallels the intermediate position of the Gubbio Basin within central Italy.

The Gubbio Basin is a rare self-contained geographical unit within north-eastern Umbria. To east and west are two major communication routes that flank but do not cross the valley itself. To the west there is the upper Tiber Valley which links the south to Etruria. To the east is the Gualdo Tadino Basin which in Roman times and later carried the Via Flaminia north from Rome through southern Umbria to the Adriatic via easy mountain passes and valleys. To the east and north lie the high Apennines, major barriers except through passes taken by the Flaminia and river systems such as the Sentino. To the south, lower hills prevent easy access from Perugia and the extensive former lake basins of central Umbria. Today, Gubbio is without a railway and only recently has been connected by better roads to the major communication routes to east and west.

1.3 Previous research in the Gubbio Valley

Until the start of the present project, the major professional archaeological interest in the area involved rescue work by the local Archaeological Superintendency in the town and its suburbs. This has expanded the knowledge of the Roman city from that recorded in early pages of *Notizie degli Scavi, Studi Etruschi* and elsewhere (Moschella 1939; Massaro 1941; Cecchelli 1942; Stefani 1942; Galli 1944–5). Some considerable antiquarian collections of lithic remains are housed in Perugia Museum, partly in the Bellucci collection, but principally from the work of a cleric, Pagliari, in the late nineteenth and early twentieth century (Pagliari 1885). Finds from the expanding agricultural lands were brought to him and revealed a wealth of Palaeolithic and Neolithic material from areas which, either because of vegetation or destruction of the landscape yield very little today. This same person also undertook some preliminary excavation work in the caves around the town of Gubbio and speculated about masonry structures on the flanks of Monte Foce (Pagliari 1890; 1920).

In more recent times research has been important but limited in scope. The University of Perugia has played the major part in archaeological research. Matteini Chiari (1979–80) undertook an interesting preliminary survey of the limestone peaks of the Gubbio Valley in conjunction with a wider survey of similar topographic positions in northern Umbria. This work not only emphasised the well-defined geography of the Gubbio Basin, but was the first to indicate the archaeological interest of areas such as Monte Ansciano and Monte Acuto. At the level of excavation, work has only been carried out in the neighbourhood of the town. Paola Guerzoni from the University of Perugia undertook excavations in the Vescovado on behalf of the Superintendency between 1981–2. This revealed a stratigraphy complementary to the other discoveries of the Bronze and Iron Age considered here (Chapter 4). For the birth of the current project, the work of Professors Meloni and Mezzanotte, in collaboration with David Whitehouse of the British School at Rome, must be given greatest importance. They undertook the excavation of the medieval Rocca Posteriore above Gubbio between 1975 and 1977, revealing Bronze Age levels that incidentally gave rise to the current project.

1.4 The development of the project

Most final reports on projects submerge their conclusions in *post hoc* justifications without reference to the pragmatic element in their research designs. The Gubbio Project (1983–7) was a fortunate convergence of the pragmatic and the theoretical.

The project was started in 1983, with the simple intention of completing the excavation started in the 1970s of the Rocca Posteriore, a strategic medieval fortification guarding the northern access to the city of Gubbio. This excavation had been focused on the medieval period, but had unexpectedly encountered Bronze Age material under the ramparts of the medieval fortification. For bureaucratic reasons, the renewal of this excavation proved not to be possible in 1983, and surface survey with a small team was undertaken in its place. The valley was easily defined as a regional unit. Within this unit the survey was targeted specifically at geomorphologically stable surfaces and well-defined topographical positions, including the immediate area of the modern city of Gubbio and the prominent limestone hills. Knowledge of these geomorphologically stable surfaces has improved through the work of the project and the survey was adapted accordingly. The range of material recovered in this preliminary season, emphasised the importance of the regional component and confirmed the Bronze Age as the key phase in the understanding of the processes behind the development of local settlement.

In 1984, the project was reformulated on a new footing, backed by extensive Italian (particularly local government), British and, in time, American support, that combined selective excavation, regional survey, environmental reconstruction and computerisation of the results. Three Bronze Age sites were selected for excavation (Monte Ingino, Monte Ansciano, and Monte Ansciano Basso (Sant' Agostino)) and the excavation of two of these was taken into a second season (1985). A phase of post-excavation and regional survey was undertaken in 1986, followed in 1987 by the completion of excavation on Monte Ansciano and the selective excavation of a Neolithic and Roman site, sampled from the sites found in surface survey.

The sites selected for excavation were investigated by a structured series of analyses moving from the general to the particular. Aerial photographic coverage, both wartime and modern, was examined for archaeological information. In the case of Monte Ansciano, infra-red photography was undertaken which enhanced some subsurface features and this was taken further by extensive resistivity and magnetometer survey of the limestone hilltop. In appropriate locations, augering was extensively employed to determine subsurface structures. In the case of Monte Ansciano Basso, colluvial slopes were extensively augered with little success and great difficulty, before trenching was undertaken with heavy machinery. In the case of the Neolithic site of San Marco, augering successfully followed detailed plotting of surface remains (Fig. 3.9) in detecting rich subsurface cultural deposits.

Once excavation was initiated, particular analyses were executed. In the case of Monte Ingino, a substantial midden deposit, an elaborate sampling scheme combining judgemental, random and structured elements within 1-metre square quadrats, was set up to recover microfauna, molluscs and carbonised seeds. In the case of the less substantial excavations, systematic sampling of individual contexts was undertaken.

These excavations provided well-dated firm points in the wider analysis of the landscape, undertaken by British, Dutch and Italian scientists (Fig. 1.3). The most elaborate case of this was perhaps the work at the Neolithic site of San Marco where the maximum amount of environmental information was extracted from an 18 x 3 m trench (Hunt *et al.* 1990; Malone and Stoddart 1992). The Dutch and Italian analyses commenced with the interpretation of aerial photographs. The Dutch analysis then concentrated on pedogenesis, established by an extensive augering programme first within the valley as a whole and then concentrated within the central portion of the valley (sections 2.2 and 4.1). The Italian analysis (section 2.1) concentrated on stratigraphic relationships. The British analysis focused on specific site studies, both from excavations and from important stratigraphic sequences.

The survey then developed in tandem with improved environmental information on the distribution of geomorphological and pedological units in the landscape. The original model was, somewhat ambitiously, the work of American scholars in the study of complex societies in Mesoamerica and the Middle East: the 100% study of a well-defined geographical region (Sanders *et al.* 1979; Blanton *et al.* 1982; Adams 1965). The advantage would have been a detailed understanding of the spatial development of a complex society without the difficulty in perceiving clustering of sites that arises from diffuse (however mathematically neat) sampling units. However, a critical study of these approaches recognised the qualified nature of 100% coverage, the lack of geomorphological control, dependence on highly favourable vegetational

cover and, in some cases, the recent antiquity of the processes of state formation. In the relatively temperate and upland Gubbio Valley, landuse was a major problem affecting visibility. It was, furthermore, soon perceived that the Gubbio Basin had been successively swathed in covers of sediment and affected by complementary zones of erosional instability on steep slopes. This geomorphological complexity made the 100% approach much more difficult to implement, particularly given the long timescales involved.

The survey was adapted to reflect these concerns. Surface survey in 1986–7 was concentrated in five transects selected to reflect balanced coverage of the length of the valley and to incorporate the maximum area of stable geomorphological/pedological zones and favourable modern landuse. Within these transect zones, relatively substantial percentages of field coverage were achieved and data collected to control for non-archaeological variability. Results are not presented here, but it should be remembered that substantial differences in visibility can arise in Mediterranean landscapes (Verhoeven 1991). Within these transects, an increasingly detailed strategy for the recovery of artefacts was adopted to measure continuous deposition of artefacts rather than discrete sites. This has allowed the contouring of artefact density across the landscape (Fig. 3.6).

After five years of fieldwork, it was decided, as originally planned, to draw the research results together and this volume is the result. This volume is not the final word, but a work of integration, leaving, for reasons of space, many implicit assumptions, details of methodology and catalogues of data to other reports. Each section of the project is, or will be, the subject of separate publications (Flavell *et al.* 1987; Stoddart and Whitehead 1991; Malone and Stoddart 1992 etc.). The present volume aims to be a coherent interplay of detailed excavation and regional analysis. Nevertheless, the very act of drawing together results has suggested avenues of future research (Chapter 8) for which this volume should act as a springboard.

1.5 Computing strategy

Notwithstanding a number of experiments and trials, when excavations commenced in 1984 the use of microcomputers on-site and for immediate off-site work was rare. The technology was still relatively primitive and expensive; and, with the exception of a small number of specially 'ruggedised' machines then appearing on the market, it was also ill-suited to the hazards of the on-site environment. Computer-based analysis during post-excavation work was, however, relatively common and

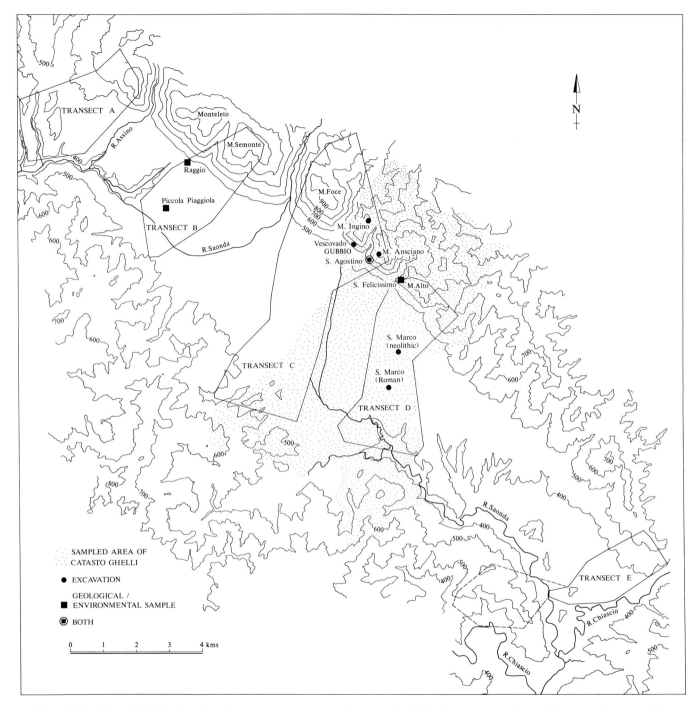

Fig. 1.3 The Valley of Gubbio. Location of survey transects, excavated sites, geological/environmental samples and the sampled section of the Catasto Ghelli

was often undertaken on office-based microcomputers and university mainframe machines.

At Gubbio, sponsorship by Olivetti made available a range of personal computers (IBM PC/XT compatibles) and hand-held microcomputers. At the outset, the intention was to collect data on-site using the hand-held microcomputers; to consolidate this onto the excavation database, and to carry out immediate validation and analysis on the personal computers held in the project office; and finally to transfer parts, or all, of the database to the mainframe computer facilities at the University of Cambridge for post-excavation analysis. This plan was soon modified in the light of doubts about the resilience and technical capabilities of the hand-held machines, and the appearance on the market in the mid 1980s of powerful statistical tools for use on personal computers. In the end, data was collected on-site using traditional manual recording methods. It was then entered into the excavation databases and all subsequent validation and analysis was carried out on the personal computers.

It was one of the research aims that the computers held in the site office should be used immediately to validate in-coming data, and to support a limited degree of statistical analysis which could then be used to guide the course of the excavations. To this end, a set of programs was developed to analyse artefactual and faunal diversity and fragmentation in the excavated matrix, and to validate the stratigraphic data by way of a Harris Matrix (Harris 1989). By accelerating the feedback of information to the excavators, it was hoped that work could be more accurately focused during the season; moreover, subjective conclusions about changing patterns in the strata could be tested objectively. On sites which were mostly composed of midden deposits, and in which it was extremely difficult to distinguish stratigraphic relationships during excavation, this was obviously of importance. Finally, it was felt that significant cost and time savings could be made in the post-excavation phase if much of the analytical work could be done during the excavation itself. As part of this goal, the site office was staffed throughout each season with a number of specialists who conserved, analysed and documented the artefacts which were recovered more or less as they were brought in from the sites.

In practice, not all the research aims were met. Some more traditional excavators found the adjustment to the immediate feedback of analytical results difficult to digest. However, in time the advantages became apparent. Slight stratigraphic anomalies were rapidly identified, although, in practice, this meant that more work was required of both excavators and computer staff in the whole recording process. It had been perhaps naïvely assumed that computers would enable the site data to be transferred to the computers in the site office with minimal alteration. This assumption had to be modified, although the computers in the project office enabled the gradual introduction of new management procedures and structures. Thus, major assets proved to be the logical resolution of stratigraphic relationships and the compilation of basic catalogues. A great success of the computer strategy was the support it gave to specialists based in the project office, many of whom made direct use of the database management facilities as part of this analytical work, allowing reports to be completed before the end of each season.

The personal computers proved themselves most useful in post-excavation work and in processing the survey data: all database manipulations and statistical analyses were carried out on them using dBase III and SPSS/PC programs, together with a series of commercially purchased or bespoke statistical programs. A very full and wide-reaching analysis was thus possible which allowed many different issues and theories to be explored through the range of data held on the databases.

1.6 Analytical methods

A broad range of statistical techniques were used during post-excavation work to assist in the summarisation and interpretation of the data collected. It must be emphasised that the combination of four principal excavations and extensive fieldwork over a number of seasons produced very large amounts of data, much more than could possibly be assimilated without the use of statistical analysis. Spatial analyses were undertaken at both the intra-site and inter-site scales. In addition to a variety of common mapping and association tests, the techniques employed included Trend Surface Analysis, Fragmentation Analysis, Type Diversity Analysis and contouring.

Trend Surface Analysis (Hodder and Orton 1976) was used to explore whether overall trends existed in the distribution of artefact types within the middens; it was also used to assess trends in the relative occurrence of different artefact types across the landscape. In both cases, deviations from surface trends (residuals) were subsequently contoured to look for patterning at the local scale.

Fragmentation Analysis aims to explore patterning in the degree of relative breakage suffered by artefacts, most commonly pottery. It was also used to examine bone fragmentation. Breakage is assessed by plotting numbers of items by type per unit area against their weight. A linear regression model is then fitted to the data to establish the overall trend in item breakage. The residuals to this model represent unit areas which have a degree of

Table 1.1. *Radiocarbon dates from Gubbio in chronological order of radiocarbon years (calibration based on computerised calculation (Robinson 1988) of the Stuiver and Reimer (1986) curve)*

Lab Number	Site Code	Material	Radiocarbon years bc	Radiocarbon years bp	Calibrated BC (1 sigma)	Calibrated BC (2 sigma)
Q-3228	R(aggio)	Peat	7700 ± 90	9650 ± 90	Beyond range	Beyond range
OxA-1853	S(an) M(arco) N(eolitico) 17 113-4E/215N	Charred *Triticum aestivum*	4480 ± 80	6430 ± 80	5457–5282	5518–5237
OxA-1851	S(an) M(arco) N(eolitico) 22 115E/214N	Charred *Triticum compactum*	4320 ± 70	6270 ± 70	5306–5209	5371–5082
OxA-1852	S(an) M(arco) N(eolitico) 22 116-7E/213N	Charred *Vitis* sp.	4295 ± 90	6245 ± 90	5301–5136	5384–4973
OxA-1854	S(an) M(arco) N(eolitico) 15 109-10E	Charred *Hordeum vulgare*	4170 ± 90	6120 ± 90	5222–4925	5294–4832
OxA-1855	S(an) M(arco) N(eolitico) 15 111-113E	Sheep/Goat bone	3800 ± 70	5750 ± 70	4731–4522	4790–4461
Q-	M(onte) I(ngino) 193	Charcoal	1160 ± 60	3110 ± 70	1453–1327	1515–1236
Q-	M(onte) I(ngino) 163B	Charcoal	1145 ± 60	3095 ± 60	1438–1312	1499–1201
Q-	M(onte) I(ngino) 163A	Cbarcoal	1090 ± 65	3040 ± 65	1405–1222	1453–1098
BM-2499	M(onte) I(ngino) 126	Charcoal	1140 ± 70	3090 ± 70	1442–1291	1515–1152
BM-2500	M(onte) I(ngino) 127	Charcoal	1010 ± 50	2960 ± 50	1296–1103	1371–1021
Q-3225	M(onte) A(nsciano) 365	Charcoal	1000 ± 50	2950 ± 50	1284–1087	1365–1010
BM-2502	M(onte) I(ngino) 50	Animal bone	980 ± 50	2930 ± 50	1249–1053	1344–983
BM-2501	M(onte) I(ngino) 50	Charcoal	970 ± 50	2920 ± 50	1234–1040	1316–962
Q-3224	M(onte) A(nsciano) 314	Animal bone	965 ± 45	2915 ± 45	1218–1039	1299–970
Q-3226	M(onte) A(nsciano) 402	Animal bone	950 ± 45	2900 ± 45	1196–1022	1281–948
BM-2592	M(onte) A(nsciano) 204	Charcoal	920 ± 90	2870 ± 90	1212–926	1354–834
Q-3223	M(onte) A(nsciano) 40	Animal bone	875 ± 50	2825 ± 50	1068–917	1191–847
Q-3227	M(onte) A(nsciano) 405	Animal bone	860 ± 50	2810 ± 50	1049–902	1176–841
BM-2591	M(onte) A(nsciano) 227/1	Animal bone	730 ± 50	2680 ± 50	891–803	962–781
BM-2594	M(onte) A(nsciano) 402/1	Animal bone	660 ± 50	2610 ± 50	820–769	891–612
BM-2593	M(onte) A(nsciano) 204/2	Animal bone	630 ± 50	2580 ± 50	809–670	839–562
BM-2504	Sant' Agostino	Charcoal	570 ± 80	2520 ± 80	795–513	837–407
BM-2503	M(onte) A(nsciano) 25	Charcoal	1670 ± 50 AD	280 ± 50	1530–1770 AD	1469–1955 AD
Q-3222	M(onte) A(nsciano) 16	Charcoal	1625 ± 35 AD	325 ± 35	1487–1637 AD	1456–1659 AD

fragmentation which is higher or lower than the overall trend. The residuals are standardised by dividing by the Standard Error and mapped to determine whether there is any patterning which may require further exploration. This technique proved to be important in understanding the formation of the Monte Ingino midden, and, in tandem with studies of ceramic type distribution, in detecting areas of medieval disturbance. It was also used in analysis of the survey results to detect anomalous artefact scatters. It should be noted that the use of this technique implied the weighing and counting of all recovered pottery.

Type Diversity Analysis has a similar purpose to Fragmentation Analysis, insofar as it aims to reveal the existence of unit areas which have a higher or lower than expected number of artefact (or other item) types. Diversity is assessed by plotting the number of a particular item recovered from a given unit area against the number of different types of the item which were recovered: for example, the number of rim sherds against the number of different types of rim. A linear model cannot be fitted to this as the number of possible types is clearly finite at any given period in time; instead, the overall distribution of types per unit area is used to generate a probabilistic linear model through simulation (Kintigh 1984). Residuals to this trend can then be standardised and mapped as in the case of Fragmentation Analysis.

The ceramic and bone assemblages recovered from the excavations were very substantial and required significant summarisation and statistical processing. In addition to simple tabulation and correlation analyses of ceramic data, tests for type groupings within the sites were undertaken using Principal Components Analysis on type occurrence matrices. This is not particularly sound practice in statistical terms but is, nevertheless, effective. Seriations of all major ceramic types were also carried out. Bone fusion and tooth wear states were cross-tabulated within species and phase. Measurements were then plotted and analysed for evidence of sexual dimorphism and outlying groups which might represent feral or wild animals.

1.7 The chronological framework: the basis for the rate of change

The chronological framework for the study of the valley has been established by a combination of geological, (material) cultural, radiocarbon and textual determinations. Dating of the early phases of the geomorphological evolution and human occupation of the valley is necessarily approximate since no direct dating has been possible within the valley, although direct dating of the lacustrine silts by TL dating might be possible at some future date.

The pollen studies of GEMINA and comparative Alpine chronologies can only be approximate (Chapter 2).

A much more accurate determination of dating has been achieved by the five radiocarbon determinations for the Neolithic site of San Marco. The four carbonised seed determinations by AMS dating (Hedges *et al.* 1990) cover a range of only three hundred years within the late sixth millennium BC (calibrated: Pearson *et al.* 1986). These dates agree with the dating by material culture for the generic Sasso Fiorano and Adriatic Impressed style of pottery (Table 1.1).

A similar convergence between material culture and radiocarbon determinations has been achieved for the Bronze Age and early Iron Age. A particularly detailed study of the pottery has been undertaken, set within the appropriate stratigraphic context and compared with the seventeen radiocarbon dates now available.

The construction of the later chronology of the Gubbio Basin ranges between a continuing dependence on ceramics (for instance in the rural Roman), stylistic comparison (for the Archaic bronze figurines) and textual documentation (for the medieval city and countryside).

1.8 A central issue: the chronology of the Bronze Age in Gubbio

The dating of the central Italian Bronze Age has become increasingly precise. *Core* areas have been dated by more refined typologies of metalwork and ceramics, keyed into other dating sequences by cross-dating and more recently dendro-chronology. Radiocarbon dating has been used very rarely except by the Swedes (Engstrand 1965, 1967), on waterlogged deposits (Alessio *et al.* 1975, 1978a) and in more *peripheral* areas. Gubbio is one such peripheral area where the chronological models established in core areas can be tested.

The sites of Monte Ingino and Monte Ansciano provide an interesting potential test for clarity of the now traditional distinctions made by Italian scholars between the full Apennine (*c.* 1400–1300 BC), the sub-Apennine (*c.* 1300–1200 BC) and the Protovillanovan (*c.* 1200–900 BC) phases of the Bronze Age (Fig. 1.4). Scholars working principally in Lazio have noted clear distinctions between these various phases (Peroni 1960; Fugazzola Delpino 1976). Stated simply, the full Apennine is denoted by incised rectilinear, curvilinear and point decoration, often infilled with white paste, principally on the body of vessels. The sub-Apennine is defined by the abandonment of this decoration, replaced by an emphasis on elaborate plastic, often zoomorphic handles. The Protovillanovan is denoted by new incised handle styles and the employment of incised and furrowed decoration on the body of vessels.

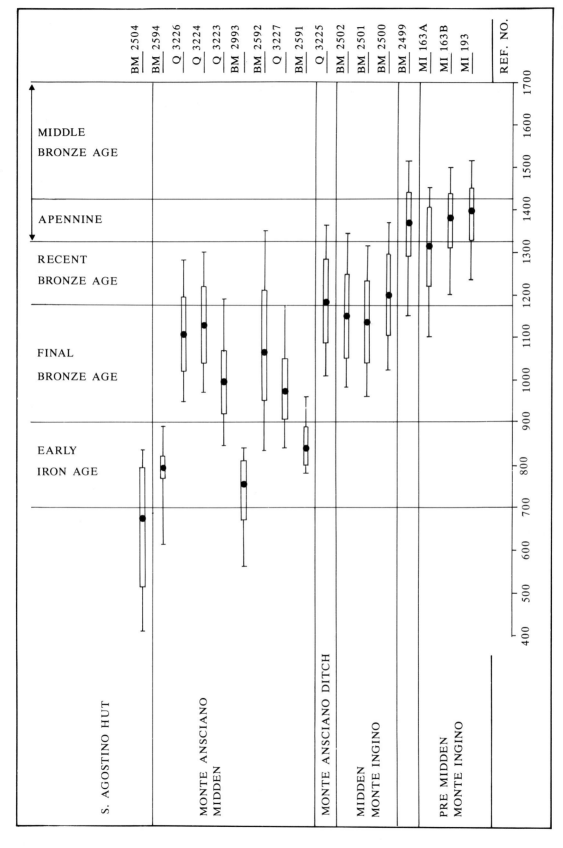

Fig. 1.4 Bronze and Iron Age chronology. Calibrated radiocarbon dates (centroid and 2σ) in stratigraphic order compared with the traditional chronology (in calendar years BC)

INTRODUCTION

This picture appears relatively clear, even if Swedish scholars have disagreed about aspects of the chronology (Berggren 1984).

The Marche area of central Italy (with which north-eastern Umbria seems to belong), however, appears to present a different chronological pattern. An attentive reading of Peroni reveals variations on the generally accepted results. Apennine decoration may be employed longer in the Marche than elsewhere (1960: 234), confusing the net distinction between Apennine and sub-Apennine. Furthermore a strong sub-Apennine tradition is noted in the Protovillanovan phase (1960: 235), confusing the clear distinction between sub-Apennine and Protovillanovan. This mixing of supposedly distinct chronological elements has continued in the most detailed reviews of the Bronze Age in the Marche (Lollini 1979). Most notably, material from the supposedly distinct chronological phases of Apennine and sub-Apennine, sub-Apennine and Protovillanovan are listed as from the same layer (layers 3 and 1 respectively) in the site of Bachero di Cingoli (Lollini 1979: 199, Fig. 6) and explained, in the latter case, together with the sites of Montefrancolo di Pollenza and Fontevecchia di Camerano as belonging to a transitional phase between the 'purity' of the preceding and succeeding phases (1979: 203).

It would be wrong to expect the site of Monte Ingino to provide a definitive solution of these issues, given the nature of the depositional and post-depositional conditions of the site. Nevertheless, the stratigraphic location of elements distinctive to these three phases suggests continuity rather than discontinuity. Unfortunately, as has been noted elsewhere (Barker 1981: 102), there is a lack of good stratified sites in the Marche area to clarify these issues further.

1.9 Ceramic typology

A local ceramic typology was an essential component in the resolution of chronological problems, given the very large number of sherds retrieved, particularly for the Bronze Age. Monte Ingino produced over 60,000 sherds, weighing more than 6,200 kg from excavation over an area of 130 m³. Monte Ansciano, with a thinner, more eroded stratigraphy over a much more extensive surface area produced more than 85,000 sherds weighing 5,200 kg. The San Agostino section site, which bridged the Late Bronze Age and early Iron Age, produced many fewer sherds from both survey and trial excavations. The total ceramic assemblage from these sites amounted to over 150,000 sherds, and it was decided to design a simple typological scheme (Fig. 1.5), independent of previous Italian schemes in order to record the feature sherds and

analyse the material on computer. There are arguments for and against creating a new typological scheme. In this case, it was felt that there was such intense debate that a strict adherence to a prior scheme would preclude the independent analysis of all the material found at Gubbio. The variation at Gubbio would have been simply clocked into a pre-existing system, sharing the same preconceptions. The typological scheme constructed was based on the analysis of rims, cordons, lugs, carinations, handles and bases. The fragmented nature of the pottery necessitated the primary analysis by these separate elements.

The rims were classified as eleven basic shapes, A–L. These shapes were then subsequently classified as: 1 – closed forms, 2 – vertical forms, and 3 – open forms. Further variants were then classed as 4 or 5 depending on the variations found in the assemblage. The A group had a square top, the B group a simple rounded top, the C group a rounded top emerging from a slightly curved neck, the D group a round, beaded rim, and the E group an angled rim-top emerging from a sharply angled neck. F forms were carinations, G rims were bowl forms with a sharply angled inverted rim, the 1 type with a rounded lip, the 2 type with a thick angled lip. The H rim type had a wide flat top and a sharply angled lip, 3 being a simple round-lipped bowl, and 4 having an outer ridge on a flat-topped inverted rim. I types were jars with rounded lip and narrow angled neck, opening to a shoulder. J forms had almond-shaped rim profiles, generally with everted or upright shapes. K forms were everted flat topped, round-lipped rims. L forms had double internal angles on the rim/neck. Carinations were classed under three types: 1 was sharply angled on both the inside and outside of the vessel; 2 was less sharply angled and had a similar curve above and below the carination; and 3 had a concave upper angle above the carination and convex angle below.

Employing the same 1, 2 and 3 classification for closed and open forms, bases were placed in four groups: A – flat-based, B – round-based, C – convex-based, and D – bases with a footring. Handles were classed as A, B, C, and D where A was rounded in section, B a flat strap handle and C the many variants of Apennine, sub-Apennine and Protovillanovan upstanding handles. D types had a triangular section. Lugs were all classified as A, with 1–12 to describe the variation between long horizontal lugs, upstanding rim lugs and lug-knobs on handles. Decoration was classified only as applied or incised.

Cordon decoration was classified according to decoration and repetition: A the straight undecorated cordons, B the twisted cordons, and C the cut, slashed or pinched variety; 1 for single, 2 for double, 3 for triple cordons, and 4 or higher for particularly ornate designs.

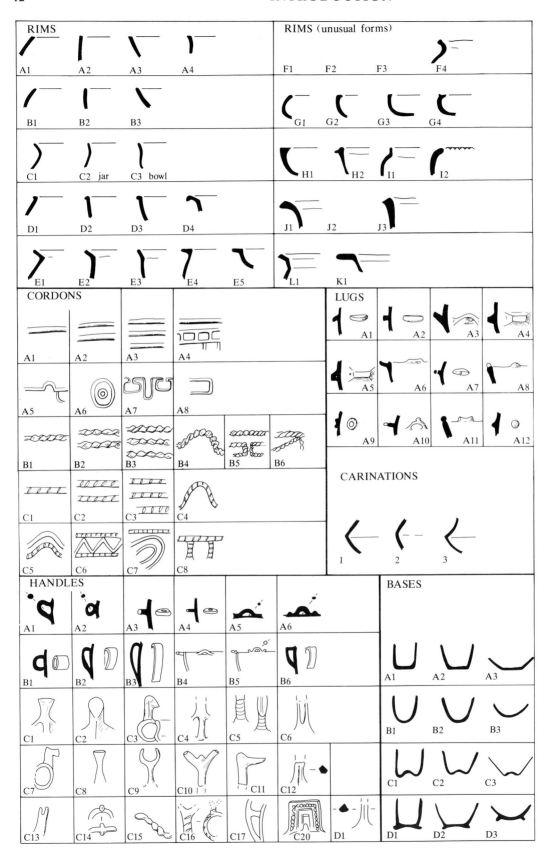

Fig. 1.5 The ceramic typology for the Bronze Age

SAN MARCO

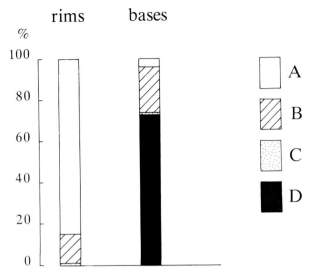

Fig. 1.6 Proportions of rims and bases at San Marco (Neolithic)

Most material could be classified under these forms from all pre-Roman material investigated by the project (Fig. 1.6). Each separate archaeological context was examined individually, and the number and combinations of characteristics were logged and then fed into a computerised database. This resulted in an immediate means of counting the total of different types of material, and because all the material was counted and weighed from each context, the fragmentation of each sample could be compared with others.

The results of the analysis are best described in the stacked histograms that the contextual/stylistic combinations produced (Fig. 1.7). This shows that at various stages through the chronological sequence, particular forms are more prevalent than others. Interestingly, many forms continue, even in small quantities long after they might normally have been considered abandoned. The two main sites, Monte Ingino and Monte Ansciano have an overlapping sequence, with Monte Ingino commencing in the Middle Bronze Age and being abandoned in the Final Bronze Age, and Monte Ansciano commencing in the Final Bronze Age and being abandoned quite some time after Monte Ingino, with several new types of pottery indicating a longer Late Bronze Age chronology.

1.10 The stratigraphy of Monte Ingino

The midden on Monte Ingino, whilst having areas of disturbance from the overlying medieval ramparts of the Rocca Posteriore, nevertheless preserved a clearly stratified deposit. The approximately 1.5 m thick deposit was excavated in contexts, many of which were divided into spits. The whole midden deposit was subdivided into metre squares, and all material was collected according to these, allowing control over spatial distribution.

The contexts were divided into eighteen phases of deposit. A–E were medieval, G and H were reworked Late Bronze Age midden, and I was less reworked midden. J and K represented the intact and thick deposits of the midden. Underlying the dark midden were Apennine/sub-Apennine levels, divided as follows: L pre-midden rubble, M pre-midden dumps, N daub surfaces, O pre-daub levels, and P a burnt soil level containing Apennine material from the first occupation of the site. Q represented a sterile land surface, with no cultural material. In all, some 308 contexts were recorded, although many of these proved to be equivalent to one another.

The pottery analysis which was undertaken concentrated on phases J–P, the intact levels of the pre-midden and midden. The illustrations of stacked histograms show these results which link Monte Ingino to Monte Ansciano. Through time, from the Apennine Middle Bronze Age, to the Final Bronze Age, general trends can be identified. For example, type A, B and E rims become less frequent, whereas C and D become more frequent. Round bases – type B – fall from about 25% in the early phases to none in the Final Bronze Age. Type D, the footring bases, occur only in phases L, M, N – the sub-Apennine pre-midden levels, and type C, the convex bases; first emerge in phase N, and continue to J.

In cordon decoration, clear patterns also emerge. Straight, untwisted or slashed types are always dominant, but especially so in the Apennine and sub-Apennine phases making up about 70%. Only in the final phase do twisted cordons (type B) become dominant. Slashed cordons (type C) are present as about 10–15% of the total until phase J when they too, increase to just over 20%.

Handles show distinct patterns. Round, rod handles increase from 20% in the sub-Apennine phases suddenly in the Final Bronze Age to 40% in phase K, and to almost 60% in phase L. Strap handles (type B) show a corresponding decrease from 60% in the Apennine levels and about 80% in the sub-Apennine levels, to 42% in K and about 26% in L. The rare D type, with a triangular section occurred only in phases M and J.

All three carinated forms were present in each phase, with the less sharply curved B form dominant in the early phases, particularly in the sub-Apennine, and decreasing markedly in the Late Bronze Age, when the more extreme convex/concave type C increased to over 70%.

INTRODUCTION

MONTE INGINO

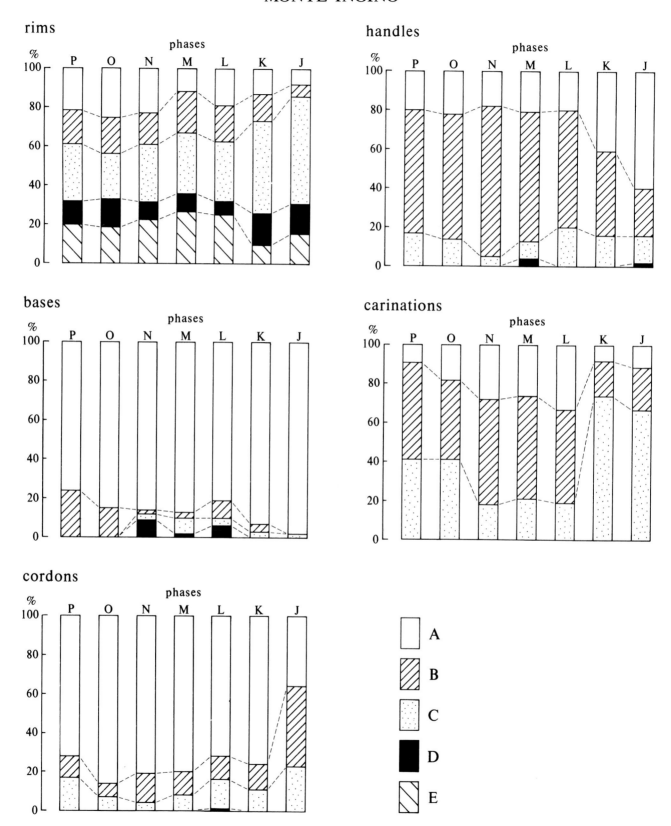

Fig. 1.7 Proportion of rims, handles, bases, carinations and cordons for pottery from Monte Ingino

MONTE ANSCIANO

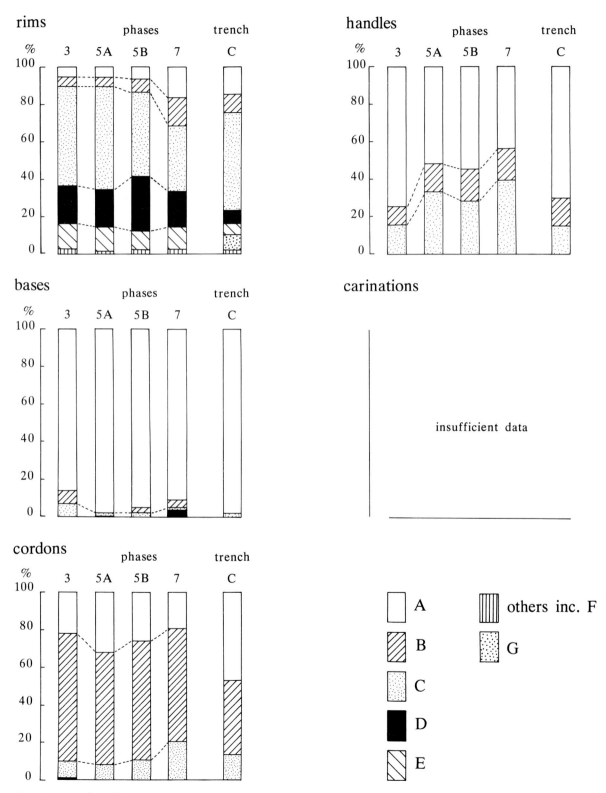

Fig. 1.8 Proportion of rims, handles, bases and cordons for pottery from Monte Ansciano

1.11 Monte Ansciano pottery analysis

The same typological scheme was used to analyse the four principal phases of the site and Trench C (Fig. 1.8). Here a number of new typological elements were distinguished, including the J-type rim, with its thickened proto-almond-shaped profile which becomes more frequent in the Iron Age of the Gubbio Basin. This is one indication of the later date of Monte Ansciano, confirmed by both proportions of pottery attributes and radiocarbon dates. Trench C appears to be placed within the earliest occupation.

1.12 Radiocarbon chronology

The seventeen radiocarbon dates fall into four distinct clusters with three dates lying outside these trends (Fig. 1.4).[1] The upper part of the pre-midden levels of Monte Ingino (phases L–M), containing a preponderance of Apennine and sub-Apennine elements, has three dates whose calibrations cluster around 1350 BC. The midden levels of Monte Ingino (phases J–K), containing a preponderance of Protovillanovan elements, have three dates whose calibrations cluster around 1150 BC. The one date from the ditch of Monte Ansciano appears to coincide with these dates, suggesting an overlap between part of the occupation of the two sites. Six dates from the midden phases (3, 5) of Monte Ansciano have a broader set of calibrated dates (with overlapping standard deviations) spread through 1100–900 BC. Finally, the single date from the early Iron Age levels of Sant' Agostino is centred on approximately 700 BC.

These general trends conform very well with standard dates for the various phases. The date 1350 BC is very close to the standard boundary between the Apennine and sub-Apennine. This date is close to other Apennine and sub-Apennine radiocarbon dates from Fonte Maggio (Gowlett et al. 1987), Grotta Misa (Ferrara et al. 1961) and more controversially the Luni and Tre Erici series (Engstrand 1965; 1967). The standard date for the early Protovillanovan is 1150 BC, while 1100–900 BC represents the standard range of dates for the later Protovillanovan. Similar radiocarbon dates for the Protovillanovan have been found from Tre Erici (Engestrand 1965) and Colle

dei Cappuccini (Ferrara et al. 1961). Finally 700 BC is quite acceptable for the early Iron Age. These results indicate a convincing confirmation of the accuracy of the standard dates for these phases in what might be classified as a remote upland area. In some ways this has already been known. The nearby cemetery of Pianello di Genga (Colini 1914a, 1914b, 1916) has long been a type site for the Protovillanovan, but its upland location does not appear to have strained its typological relevance for the whole peninsula. What is not so clear is the nature of the transition between these various phases. On Monte Ingino and in the Marche, the transition is not as sudden as in Lazio or other similarly well-researched areas of central Italy.

1.13 The structure of the volume

The introduction to this volume has served to outline the location, previous research, research aims, the major problems and the methodologies employed to bring about their solution. The following chapters synthesise this regional approach unburdened by the need to explain the background to the research now these have already been covered in this chapter. The analysis commences with the structure of the region and then proceeds, period by period, from the Palaeolithic to the medieval period. The final chapter synthesises the principal trends in terms of spatial organisation, demography, style and politics, and points to future avenues of research in the region.

[1] The three outliers (BM 2499, BM 2593 and BM 2594) can perhaps be explained by the site formation processes on Monte Ingino and Monte Ansciano. BM 2499 may represent an unnoted disturbance within the midden into earlier levels. BM 2593-4 may represent an unnoted disturbance of the Monte Ansciano midden before it was capped by a drystone platform in the sixth century BC. There is, though, no evidence from pottery or stratigraphy that this is the case. A further problem to be resolved is that animal bone samples (BM 2593 and BM 2594) taken from precisely the same context as other animal bone samples (BM 2592 and Q 3226 respectively) on Monte Ansciano have produced error limits of 2 standard deviations which fail to overlap. A last point to note is that the British Museum dates for Monte Ansciano are with one exception substantially later than the Cambridge dates. Bronze Age dates as late as the two Monte Ansciano dates have been found at S. Michele di Valestra (Alessio et al. 1973) and Grotta Misa (Alessio et al. 1964) and although stratigraphically problematic they do lie just on the extreme range of the standard dates for their phase of the Bronze Age.

2 THE ENVIRONMENTAL SETTING

The Pleistocene Basin of Gubbio (central Italy): geomorphology, genesis and evolution

2.1.1 Introduction

The Pleistocene Basin of Gubbio is one of the Apennine depressions that developed within the chains of folds and overthrusts that make up the Umbrian-Marche Apennines to the west of the Marche Ridge. Recently, study has been focused on the detailed structure of the surrounding area (Menichetti and Pialli 1986; De Feyter and Menichetti 1986) in the context of 'ramp and flat' models that envisage strong overthrusts for the central-north Apennine zone (Boccaletti et al. 1983; 1986; De Feyter et al. 1986; Calamita and Deiana 1988). However, no recent research has been carried out on the geomorphology, and specifically, on the Quaternary deposits. The Pleistocene sequence is somewhat complex and characterised in the lower part by considerable thickness (in places approaching 200 m) and frequent lignite layers (GEMINA 1963). The upper sediments consist of a number of alluvial terraces of limited thickness. The pollen analysis undertaken on the older sediments suggests an approximate Lower Pleistocene age for the onset of the infill.

The present section attempts to fill this gap in knowledge by illustrating the geomorphology and geology of the Quaternary of the Gubbio area, and the relationship between the different lithological and morphological units within the valley (Fig. 2.1). This allows some working hypotheses to be presented about the various phases of evolution of the landscape.

2.1.2 The geological and geomorphological context

The Valley of Gubbio is a narrow tectonic depression of about 22 km in length and more than 4 km in width trending NW–SE. Steep sides delimit the valley to the north-east, where altitude exceeds 900 m in many cases (Monteleto (945 m), Monte di Casamorcia (960 m), Monte Semonte (964 m), Monte Foce (983 m), Monte Ingino (908 m) (Plate 2.1)), and to the west, where altitude is rather less (Il Palazzaccio (753 m), Monte Salaiole (803 m)). From a geological point of view the valley is placed within the inner plain of the Umbrian Basin (Bally et al. 1986), separated from the Umbria-Marche ridge by an important fault situated a few kilometres east of the basin. This area, in common with much of the central Apennines, has a characteristic tectonic style of folds and overthrusts, complicated both by numerous backthrusts and by gravitational synsedimentary folds. The rootless anticline of Gubbio, composed of Mesozoic–Tertiary limestones and marly limestones, lies to the north-east of the basin (Barnaba 1958) delimited towards the east by the Piazza–Padule overthrust. These limestones contain many caves, some of which have proved to be of archaeological interest (Pagliari 1920; Viviani 1967; Sollevanti 1972). This structural element overlies the Monte Pollo syncline composed of Tertiary marly-arenaceous rocks which outcrop to the south-east and west of the basin.

The movements which created these structures date between the Langhian–Serravallian and the Lower Pliocene (10 MY–4 MY BP), while the first emersion of the area probably occurred during the Messinian (7 MY BP). The marine sedimentation in the Lower Pliocene moved to the east of the Umbria-Marche chain and to the west of the Tiber Lake (Ambrosetti et al. 1978; Cantalamessa et al. 1986a). The relief created after the emersion was in turn affected by erosion, which during a period of relatively low tectonic activity, led to the modelling of an extensive planation surface. This surface extended over a large part of peninsular Italy (Demangeot 1965) and is noted elsewhere in the Umbrian region (Desplanques 1969; Calamita et al. 1982) although some authors deny its existence (Raffy 1982). The folds and overthrusts mentioned above were in fact truncated by these processes. The erosion was fairly comprehensive affecting both the softer marly-arenaceous rocks and the more resistant limestone rocks from Jurassic to Miocene age.

At the end of the Lower Pleistocene (1 MY BP) the area began to be affected by a generalised uplift (Ambrosetti et al. 1982) associated with considerable tilting towards the east and west that favoured the deepening of the drainage network. This, in turn, broke up the continuity of the planation surface which only survived in areas of high relief and especially on more resistant rocks. The activation of normal faults is connected with these movements,

Plate 2.1 Gubbio from the south

producing the graben morphology that is characteristic of the Tyrrhenian side of the central Apennines (Demangeot 1965; Elter *et al.* 1975; Raffy 1982). The Gubbio Basin is one of these graben delimited to the east by a normal fault that is locally 1,000 m in depth, while minor faults delimit the western side.

In summary, the Gubbio Basin is a graben filled with fluvio-lacustrine sediments, set between a high escarpment to the north of its central portion, and marly-arenaceous formations on the hills encircling the remainder of the basin and is only broken by two principal directions of drainage to the north-west and the south-west.

2.1.3 The geomorphology of the area

The geomorphological map of the area has been made by employing Ortofotocarte of the Regione Umbria at a scale of 1:10,000 and reduced at the time of publication to 1:25,000. The method is that normally employed in Italy

(Gruppo Nazionale di Geografia Fisica e Geomorfologia 1982, 1986) with some modifications. These methods have been used also in areas adjacent to Gubbio (Ciccacci *et al.* 1985).

2.1.3.i Polygenetic landforms

The planation surface has been preserved on the limestone high relief of the anticline of Gubbio where the *Scaglia* layers dipping to the east are clearly truncated. Strong erosion has reduced this surface to a length of a few hundred metres, generally bordered by scarps with rounded edges. There has also been intense erosion along faults, trending in an Apennine and anti-Apennine direction, permitting the growth of an angular drainage pattern. In areas where the marly-arenaceous formation outcrops, the processes of erosion are still more intense and sometimes only 'summits of equal height' (Pecsi 1970) are preserved. It is difficult to establish if the high elevation which this older unit attains is a direct product of the Villafranchian modelling (3.2–1.0 MY BP) or caused by uplift of a later date. The indications gathered in the nearby Marche region (Cantalamessa *et al.* 1986b; Coltorti *et al.* 1991) or more to the south in Abruzzo, Umbria and Lazio (Demangeot 1965; Ambrosetti *et al.* 1978), where Middle Pleistocene marine sediments are also found at several hundred metres above sea level near the coast, appear to confirm the second hypothesis. At Monte Casamorcia, Monte Semonte and Monte Foce heights close to 1,000 m above sea level suggest Pleistocene uplift in the order of many hundreds of metres. Similar uplift is indicated by the 'summits of equal height' present where the marly-arenaceous formation outcrops to the east (Cima del Barco (810 m), Cima di Marzaccola (829 m), Cima Lanciacornacchia (860 m), Monte Petazzano (917 m)) and to the west of Gubbio (Monte Urbino (863 m), Monte Salasole (813 m)).

2.1.3.ii Structural and tectonic landforms

During the deepening of the hydrographic network, the different degrees of resistance of the rocks led to the modelling of structural escarpments. The steepest slopes correspond to the Calcare Massiccio (Lower Lias), to the *Maiolica* (Upper Titonian), to *Scaglia Bianca e Rosata* (Middle Eocene p.p.) and higher in the series, to the sandstone layers of the *Marnoso-Arenacea* (Serravallian–Tortonian). Elongated valleys and rock benches correspond to the *Marne a Fucoidi* (Aptian–Cenomanian), the Scaglia Cinerea (Upper Eocene–Oligocene) and the *Schlier* (Langhian–Tortonian). On the eastern side of the Gubbio anticline, following the lines of most easily eroded formations, asymmetrical valleys and flatirons were formed.

The influence of selective erosion had the maximum impact on the slopes delimiting the basin. In fact, it is difficult to establish the values of displacement due to Quaternary tectonics and the amount of differential erosion to the west of the main escarpment. At Gubbio, the displacement of the eastern fault is above 1,000 m, but this diminishes markedly to the north and south where it does not achieve more than 100 m, although, as has been noted on the western flank of the Umbria-Marche ridge (De Feyter *et al.* 1986) much of it can be masked by cutting planes within the *Scaglia Cinerea* and the *Schlier* formations. The fault scarp affecting the planation surface is not greater than one hundred metres to the north of the basin (near Madonna della Misericordia) and perhaps even less to the south of the Chiascio river. Similar displacements separate the planation surface of the limestone ridge from the eastern side of the basin as can be deduced from the height of the 'summit of equal height'.

The thickness of the Villafranchian sediments, sometimes more than a hundred metres (GEMINA 1963), indicates that faults became active at the beginning of the Quaternary which lowered the central part of the basin. In this sector, the limestone rocks of Jurassic–Eocene age are in contact with the basal part of the marly-arenaceous rocks in which the most easily erodible clay fraction predominates (Cattuto 1973). It is, therefore, probable that the dislevels created by tectonic action were accentuated by the effects of selective erosion.

The graben of the Assino is delimited to the north by a series of anti-Apennine faults located along the river itself and its right hand tributaries such as the Fosso Billi and the San Giorgio stream. These streams show clear capture of the earlier drainage network that ran from the north-west towards the south-east. Furthermore, the upper depositional surface of the earliest terraced unit in the area has evidence of slight anti-Apennine steps on the sides opposite these water courses.

At the southern border of the basin, a fault of similar orientation is placed in the valley bottom of the Chiascio and has allowed the capture toward the east of the nearby Gualdo Tadino Basin, that in the Lower Pleistocene probably drained toward the Topino (Cattuto 1973). The northern and southern limit of the basin are thus fault-line valleys. A similar origin can be hypothesised for the valleys that cut transversally the reliefs surrounding the basin. Menichetti and Pialli (1986) consider these anti-Apennine alignments primarily joints and secondarily normal faults, while Centamore *et al.* (1979) and Boccaletti *et al.* (1983) interpret them as side-slip faults.

It is probable that the displacement of these faults is modest, but it should not be forgotten that they were activated in the Quaternary and strongly influenced the modelling of the landscape. On the other hand, their thick network induces an underestimation of the total displacement which sometimes attain hundreds of metres, as shown in the karstic tunnels of the nearby Frasassi gorge (Coltorti and Galdenzi 1982).

2.1.3.iii Landforms, deposits and processes due to superficial running waters

Many gullies are active on the marly-arenaceous formation, while relatively few are found on limestone bedrock. On the other hand, the result of intense deforestation of the limestone bedrock led to slope-wash and rill-wash processes which have eliminated most of the soils.

Two important water courses, both tributaries of the Tiber, cross the north and south borders of the basin in an anti-Apennine direction: the Assino stream and the River Chiascio. Two streams, both named Saonda and tributaries of the previously mentioned rivers, run in opposite directions along the western side of the basin. The tributaries coming from the west are then immediately canalised towards the north and towards the south in contrast to those tributaries coming from the east that cross the entire basin more or less transversally. There is no well-defined rock-based watershed between the two Saonda streams, and the use of the same name for two streams running in opposed directions suggests long-standing difficulty in defining the limit of their drainage basin. The modern processes within the basin are limited to sporadic overfloods of the main water courses.

The principal geomorphological characteristics of the basin are derived from the action of these water courses, which, by alternating phases of incision and deposition in a period of uplift, have produced a typical terrace morphology similar to other parts of central Italy (Lipparini 1939; Villa 1942; Demangeout 1965; Raffy 1982). Six terraced lithostratigraphical units, placed at progressively higher levels above the thalweg have been identified. The four most recent units correspond to the 'alluvial complex', the fifth unit to the 'clayey-sandy unit with interbedded pebbles' (GEMINA 1963), and at the top, the depositional surfaces constitute morphostratigraphical units. The sixth unit, whose depositional surface is not preserved, corresponds to the 'clay lignite-bearing complex' (GEMINA 1963). These units have been defined as follows, proceeding from the more recent to most ancient:

(1) Gravels and sands of the River Chiascio (Unit 1)
     These sediments occur within the beds of modern rivers and their tributaries and floodplains. The water regime is seasonal with long periods of low discharge, generally in the summer months, alternating with high discharges on a ratio that can reach 1:70 (Cattuto 1973). In recent decades flooding has been rare, but was common in the past and could affect the whole alluvial plain. The seasonal character of rainfall created secondary water courses where rectilinear alternated with braided morphology and could occupy extensive areas. The majority of these water courses, including most of the Saonda streams and a section of the Assino, have been canalised since the seventeenth century (section 2.3), responding to increased agricultural occupation, so that today they are bordered by artificial levées. The Chiascio is, by contrast, a typical meandering river and traces of old meanders are visible in a large part of its alluvial plain. A meander course is also found in the upper part of the river in the nearby Gualdo Tadino Basin. This indicates the persistence of a water regime, established in equilibrium

with an undisturbed natural environment in the Early Holocene, which modern processes have not cancelled, as is the case in most of the mountain streams of the nearby Marche region (Coltorti 1991).

It is difficult to establish the extent of this unit in the plain adjacent to the streams that derive from the limestone escarpment of Gubbio. In most cases, on leaving the escarpment, they run in depressions between one Upper Pleistocene alluvial fan and another, but sometimes they occupy substantial parts of the same fans. The limits of these sediments are sometimes easily recognisable in aerial photographs, through colour variation. The Pleistocene materials have dark colours being weathered to brown, brown-calcium and brown-calcareous soils (Duchafour 1977). They correspond to cambisols and luvisols (section 2.2). Conversely, the Holocene sediments have A1C profiles, but of light colour as a result of the scarcity of organic matter (alluvial soils). The sediments of this unit, although fairly common in distribution due to the reduced thickness, are, in many cases, difficult to localise precisely.

The recent excavation of the Neolithic site of San Marco (Hunt *et al.* 1990; Malone and Stoddart 1992; section 3.2), on the slopes of the San Felicissimo fan, have demonstrated some of the Holocene modifications to the area. Below the ploughed horizon, fine sediments have been found containing open ground molluscs deposited by uncanalised streams. These are buried, pedogenised, colluvial sediments, preserved within and near Neolithic structures (Impressed and Sasso Fiorano culture of the late 6th millennium BC). The soil has a high organic content derived both from the natural environment and from the refuse of the settlement. This soil, although recarbonated, has undergone a decarbonation process with some clay migration. The pollens in it were derived from forest species with hornbeam, oak, hazel, pine and lime, mixed with herbs and cultivated elements.

The archaeological materials lie above a channel of approximately five metres in width, filled with evenly laminated travertine sands and interbedded with calcareous and travertine gravels and thin clay lenses. These sediments indicate that thick vegetation was present on the bank of the channels and the waters were enriched in CO_2 before the Neolithic. The pollen, molluscs and leaf imprints in the travertine indicate, in fact, a marshy forest (Hunt *et al.* 1990).

This channel lies above yellowish-brown silty clay loam, interbedded with fairly continuous gravel layers. No travertine elements are present. Similar sedimentary structures, in contrast to the overlying channel fill, are found in Upper Pleistocene fans and indicate sheet flooding events.

A marshy forest then colonised the area during the Early Holocene, associated with the deposition of travertine sediments, some kilometres from a spring, located most probably at the foot of the limestone slopes. The deposition of travertine ceased with the Neolithic, when there is also the first indication of degradation of the original forest cover, following the inception of agriculture. After this period the environment became progressively more open, probably following the placing of the area under cultivation. This is also the period when the deposition of travertine came to an end (Malone and Stoddart in 1992).

(2) Gravels, sands and clay of San Marco (Unit 2)
These sediments consist of fans with a well-preserved morphology that border the eastern flank of the basin and which are highly developed at the foot of the limestone escarpment between Padule and Raggio. The dating (*terminus ante quem*) of these sediments to the Upper Pleistocene (100,000–10,000 BP) is confirmed by the discovery of sporadic Upper Palaeolithic tools on the fan surface (section 3.1). The upper depositional surface of this unit has been slightly reworked by Holocene erosional and depositional processes of the previous unit 1. Locally, channels of some metres in width and depth, filled with gravel material have been noted at the surface which indicate the last phases of deposition. The channels can be identified by aerial photography as running radially from the fan head towards its distal part in a slightly sinuous direction. The rare sections that cut the fan deposits show a monotonous sequence of evenly stratified gravels to some depth, with rare interbedding of massive sands, sometimes separated by alluvial soils with a poorly developed profile, such as at Semonte. There is little stratigraphic evidence for the distal part of the fans or for the transitional zone into the alluvial plain. The only discovery of importance was peat deposits, dated 9650 ± 90 BP (Q–3228) in radiocarbon years brought to the surface by a drilling in the distal part of a fan not far from Mocaiana. The pollen content indicates an environment dominated by grasses with some pine, spruce and birch (section 2.3). The cold, dry, open steppe environment has similarities, allowing for local variation, with that suggested by Bonatti (1966) for the northern Mediterranean and confirmed by Alessio *et al.* (1986) and Cattani and Renault-Miskovsky (1989).

(3) Gravels, sands and silt of Querceto (Unit 3)
These are alluvial sediments occurring in a much more reduced area than the preceding unit. They have been affected by intense erosion following the general deepening of the drainage network, most probably during the last Interglacial (Calamita *et al.* 1982; Chiesa *et al.* 1988; Coltorti 1991). This erosion has been most intense at the foot of the eastern side of the basin, in particular in the central part of the basin now occupied by the Late Pleistocene alluvial fan and along the principal water courses. A partly preserved section of these sediments, which indicate the presence of an ancient alluvial fan, is found near Palazzo Dondana. Traces of similar sediments (too small to map) have been found near Casa San Bernardo (San Marco). More generally, they are found along the edges of the Late Pleistocene fans, delimited by scarps increasing in height towards the west and corresponding to the principal water courses. Their upper depositional surface is almost flat, or inclined slightly toward the west. Sections of considerable thickness have been observed infrequently in these sediments. At Querceto, near Mocaiana, the upper part of the deposit is made up of slightly cemented gravels. Alternating evenly stratified gravels and sands have been observed at Casa Colle and Casa le Capanne.

Slightly more developed soils than in the previous unit (brown, leached pseudogley soils) have been observed capping these deposits. Surface finds of the Middle Palaeolithic confirm the date of these deposits (*terminus ante quem*) to the final phase of the Middle Pleistocene.

(4) Gravels and sands of Casa Galvana di Sotto (Unit 4).
A strath terrace truncating Miocene sandstones has been observed in this area. A veneer of gravels and sands of a very shallow depth is present on this erosional terrace. Their altitude (a little over 364 m above sea level) is more elevated than the sediments of the previous unit. The erosion of the terrace and the deposition of these materials is therefore slightly older but always datable to the final part of the Middle Pleistocene. However it is difficult to establish whether the sediments were deposited during an incision phase, before the deposition of the Querceto unit, as its small thickness and extension would suggest.

(5) Gravels, sands and loams of Branca (Unit 5) (Plate 2.3)
These are alluvial sediments at a higher elevation within the basin, preserved both in the south-central part, between Ponte d'Assi and Casa Cerquattino, and in the north-central part between Palazzo Casacce and Massa (Plate 2.2). In the northern sector, the

Plate 2.2 The Valley of Gubbio from above Mocaiana

sediments are made up of large gravels up to blocks in size and, secondarily, by subangular, subrounded gravels and sands. The upper depositional surface is well preserved and varies from 530 m at Massa to 472 m at Palazzo Casacce, although this last occurrence appears to be slightly lowered by anti-Apennine faults. The sediments delimit a palaeovalley that approached the basin from the north-west with a high discharge at a moment when the Assino did not drain the basin. It is therefore evident that the Assino captured this part of the basin after the deposition of this unit. The thickness of these sediments, in this sector, is more than 20 m in places.

The Ponte d'Assi outcrops, placed at the confluence of the Rio Acquina, an important water course entirely excavated in the marly-arenaceous formation, with the Saonda, is made up principally of fine sands, silt and clay sediments, with rare and thin layers and lenses of pebbles. These layers are more frequent and even dominant towards the south, such as at Branca, where the deposit is slightly tilted against the slope, probably through gravitational movements associated with the faultline bordering the basin to the east.

Parallel layers of gravels alternating with clay and silt sediments, sometimes with slightly developed soil profiles, and containing freshwater molluscs (GEMINA 1963) at Casa Cerquattino and Casa Pianella, on the southern side of the basin, indicate a fluvio-lacustrine environment. The depositional surface varies slightly from 435 m at Ponte d'Assi to 400 m at Casa Cerquattino. At Casa Pianella the presence of these deposits up to 412 m in altitude suggests slight displacements in correspondence to the Chiascio valley along anti-Apennine faults joining Fossato di Vico and Corraduccio.

The thickness of this unit in the borehole drilled in the southern sector seems to be around 160 m (GEMINA 1963) but does not exceed 50–60 m at the

Plate 2.3 The main Pleistocene terraces from the south near Le Case

surface near Palazzo Galvana. Rock erosion surfaces, correlated with the upper depositional phase of these sediments, and corresponding to the distal part of a pediment morphology, have been observed in the valley slope at Castel d'Alfiolo, Villa Dondana, Casa Sassoia and Casa San Lorenzo.

GEMINA places this unit in stratigraphical continuity with the 'clay lignite-bearing complex' but, as is observable in the neighbourhood of Palazzo Galvana, where the lignite-bearing sediments occur in layers tilted 15–20 degrees to the north-east, there is an important unconformity between the two units.

The upper depositional surface has a well-developed soil profile (leached and fersiallitic soils). The discovery of sporadic Acheulean artefacts on the surface suggest a date (*terminus ante quem*) of the Middle Pleistocene.

It is probable that in the central and southern part of the basin the modern drainage network has been superimposed on that modelled after the incision of

this unit since both the Saonda streams run along the contact between this and the marly-arenaceous formation.

(6) Lignite bearing clays and sands of Palazzo Galvana (Unit 6)

These sediments are the principal fill of the basin and studied as such by GEMINA (1963) with a drilling programme in search of lignite. The most extensive occurrences are in the neighbourhood of Palazzo Galvana and exhibit massive and laminated clay layers 10 cm thick, interbedded with thin layers and lenses of sand and peat. This is a typical complex of sediments, whose lacustrine origin is shown by the fauna and flora preserved within it. This evidence consists of '*carietum* accompanied by an assemblage of *Tsuga, cedars, Pinus haploxylon, Picea orientalis, Liquidambar* etc.' attributed to the Gunz–Mindel Interglacial (GEMINA 1963: 74). Given the strong criticism of the Alpine chronology (Kukla 1975;

Nilsson 1989) this attribution has lost much of its significance. The fact that a proper cooling of the Mediterranean area only took place after the end of the Lower Pleistocene allows us to hypothesise that these sediments are older than this age.

The presence of 'green clays' some metres in thickness (up to 20 m in boreholes) have been noted between this unit and the bedrock. The boreholes of GEMINA (1963: 77) have also shown how 'the dipping of the lignite banks agrees with that of the underlying marly-arenaceous formation'. This evidence, if confirmed, other than revealing that the upper surface of the sequence has been severely truncated (the more recent units always present sub-horizontal layering), suggests the existence of movements of sindepositional folding. These were probably associated with fault activities, given that, as can be seen from a careful examination of the boreholes, the depth of the lignite layers varies considerably between boreholes very close to one another. On the other hand during the current work, greenish clays were discovered at 20 m depth near Casacce (411 m above sea level), east of Ponte d'Assi, in a recent borehole. Micropalaeontological examination[1] showed an assemblage attributable to the Upper Langhian (Potetti pers. comm.) with strong analogies to an occurrence on the western border of the nearby Basin of Gualdo Tadino. The borehole also seems to indicate the presence of the bedrock at 20 m from the surface in the central part of the basin, justifiable, if the GEMINA data are correct, only by the presence of a buried graben in the area (Fig. 2.1, sections). This strong tectonic activity appears to diminish progressively after this period, given that only a few faults displace the later units already described.

The total depth of this formation, based on the borehole data, varies between 50 and 200 m. In the northern part of the basin, it is very probable that these units are absent, given that bedrock has been observed below the 'gravels, sand and clays of Branca' without intervening lignite (Fig. 2.1).

The above sequence has strong similarities with that of the Tiber valley (Conti and Girotti 1977; Ambrosetti et al. 1988; Gregori 1988; Cencetti 1990). In this area the 'lower grey clay', contrary to that which occurs in Gubbio, is attributed to the Upper Pliocene while a 'sandy clay complex' separated by an erosional surface from the preceding sediments, is attributed to the Lower Pleistocene. However, at the present state of knowledge, it is not possible to exclude a similar attribution for the older Gubbio deposits.

2.1.4 Landforms, deposits and processes due to gravity

The slopes modelled on marly-arenaceous formation are strongly affected by gravitational processes. The movements of greatest dimensions are rock slump and rock block glide, although, in their lower parts, these can evolve to flows. Inside the valleys there are numerous earth flows of limited dimensions involving colluvial materials. Most of these mass movements are now inactive, although some of the superficial parts can be reactivated by solifluction and creep. The importance of these last processes are easily identifiable at the foot of the limestone slopes where they create the following litho- and morphostratigraphical unit.

2.1.4.i Colluvial deposits of 'I Cappuccini'

These are mostly composed of colluvial soils in which there is a highly variable relationship between debris and matrix, sometimes interrupted by quite thick (tens of centimetres) lenses of detritus. The upper depositional surface creates an inclined glacis with a progressive transition to the slope. These indicate periods when the slope was covered by wooded vegetation alternating with movements of creep, slope-wash and debris flow in less wooded phases. At the base of these sequences is frequently found, as at I Cappuccini or at Crocefisso, a soil that shows evidence of slight decarbonation probably associated with the vegetational cover of the Early Holocene. In the upper part, the plough zone occasionally covers archaeological deposits, ranging in date from pre-protohistoric to Roman. At the locations of San Domenico, close to the entrance of the Valle della Contessa and Casamorcia, the archaeological deposits can be even later in date. The sediments can be as much as 4 m in depth. Environmental analysis of these deposits has been undertaken at S. Felicissimo and S. Agostino (section 2.3).

2.1.5 Landforms and deposits due to crionival processes

Nivation hollows, some hundreds of metres in width, have been recognised near the summits of some slopes and occasionally at the head of gullies. Lower down they are sometimes filled with detritus which covers irregularities of the slope to produce rectified slopes. In locations where the thickness of this material is sufficiently great it has been possible to distinguish the following unit.

[1] The sample contained Praeorbulina transitoria, Globoquadrina altispira, Globogerinoides trilobus, Globogerinoides bisphericus, Globigerinoides subquadratus, Radiolari sp., Orbulina saturalis, Globorotalia praescitula, Hastigerina siphonifera, Globigerina praebulloides, Globigerina quinqueloba, Globigerina concinna, Sphaerodinellopsis, Globorotalia continuosa, Globorotalia siakensis, Globorotalia Archeomenardii.

2.1.5.i San Felicissimo/Crocefisso Debris

These are slope waste deposits which are extremely common in the Umbrian and Marche area, especially at the foot of rocks easily degraded by frost-shattering. They are made up of alternating layers of large angular clasts, between 1 and 10 cm in thickness, and layers of debris with variable percentages of sandy and silty sediments with, in some cases, limited evidence of weathering (Coltorti and Dramis 1987). These characterise the morphogenesis of the area during the cold Pleistocene phases although in the Gubbio Basin, these deposits can almost entirely be dated to the Upper Pleistocene. They represent one of the sediment sources of the extensive Late Pleistocene alluvial deposits already illustrated. At Crocefisso, where they cover the main east fault escarpment, their thickness is greater than 5 m.

2.1.6 Landforms due to human activities

The morphologies observed are those commonly encountered elsewhere. Quarries, reservoirs and river embankments are numerous. The road network has had a particular impact. When roads run parallel to the slope, scarps some metres in height have been created up slope. Although a large part of this road network was progressively abandoned at the end of the last century, the scarps have remained, sometimes smoothed by agricultural work to slight inclines.

2.1.7 The Pleistocene Basin of Gubbio: genesis and evolution

The Middle Pliocene was the peak of folding activity which led to the formation and accentuation of the principal fold structures at Gubbio. At the end of this period the relief previously created became subjected to intense subaerial erosion. These erosive processes continued until the Lower Pleistocene and led to the formation of an extensive planation surface whose modelling ended before 0.8 MY BP, when the area was affected by uplift that caused the deepening of the drainage network. The reactivation as a normal fault of the Apennine faults which delimit to the east the Gubbio Basin was probably linked to these movements; but it is difficult to establish how much the dislevel between the remnant of the planation surface and the bottom of the basin is attributed to tectonic effects or to selective erosion which certainly had an important role.

The lignite-bearing clays and sands of Palazzo Galvana were probably deposited in the Lower Pleistocene when a wide lake basin was in existence. The considerable thickness of this unit and the inclination sometimes above 15–20

degrees, conforming to the dip of the bedrock, suggests folding movements contemporary to the time of deposition. These movements are associated with the activities of faults that led to the formation of horst and graben structures at present buried under the plain.

It has been suggested that at this time the basin was self-contained in its drainage (Cattuto 1973), but this is difficult to establish with certainty, given that the summit of this unit is heavily truncated. Since this unit is preserved only in the southern part of the basin, tilting movements towards the south have probably taken place which have led to the formation of defended terraces (Dury 1970) in the northern sector and undefended terraces in the southern sector.

After these Middle Pleistocene events, phases of linear erosion during the principal Interglacials alternated with phases of accumulation during the cold periods. Within the erosion surfaces affecting the lignite-bearing layers, the gravels, sands and clays of Branca were deposited. These result from deposition in a fluvio-lacustrine environment with encroaching fans, derived mainly from the north-eastern sector of the basin.

The relative uniformity of surface height of this unit indicates that there was a change in tectonic regime within the area. Subsidence ceased and all the area was uplifted. Anti-Apennine faults were activated that helped the regressive erosion of the Assino in the northern sector while in the southern sector there was the capture of the nearby Basin of Gualdo Tadino which previously was a tributary of the Topino river. It is probable that these processes of fluvial capture followed climatic conditions favourable to linear erosion, that is during a very long Interglacial. This led also to the erosion of the Branca unit in a large part of the central sector of the basin.

Further depositional phases were connected to the cold periods at the end of the Middle and Upper Pleistocene that led to the deposition of the Querceto gravels, sands and clays and of the San Marco gravel, sands and clays, this last corresponding to the deposition of the San Felicissimo debris.

Finally, observations have been made of pedogenesis, linear erosion and local deposition of travertines dating to the early Holocene, which succeeded the deposition of the majority of the Chiascio river gravels and sands on the valley bottom and the colluvial deposits of the I Cappuccini at the foot of the slopes. The recent Holocene processes were characterised by intense processes of soil erosion, as a result of the progressive elimination of the vegetation following the human impact on the natural landscape (section 2.3).

2.2 Pedology

2.2.1 Introduction

The aims of the pedological research in the Gubbio basin were a reconstruction of the soil pattern and soil conditions in this basin during the Bronze Age to Roman period. Obviously, the present soil pattern and conditions are not identical to those during that period. Therefore, such a reconstruction requires a careful evaluation of the potential changes and an appropriate survey methodology. The methods employed during the survey are described below.

Soils represent the result of gradational (or landscape genetic) processes and of pedogenetic processes, which have been operating over a certain period of time (Bos and Sevink 1975). On stable land surfaces, that is in landscape units where erosional or accumulative processes are weak or insignificant, the soil properties are strongly controlled by pedogenetic processes, which may operate at different rates. Soil development under such conditions can be described in terms of chronosequences, of which the components represent successive stages in soil genesis. For the Mediterranean, such stages are relatively well established and the rate at which the various pedogenetic processes operate is fairly well known (Sevink et al. 1984; Cremaschi 1977). On unstable land surfaces, that is in landscape units where gradational processes (erosion or sedimentation) were highly active, soils tend to be weakly developed and to have properties which are strongly determined by the parent material.

The following example may serve to elucidate the foregoing theoretical considerations. Intermontane basins in the Mediterranean area are commonly filled with rather poorly sorted, primarily calcareous fluvial deposits. Soil formation in these deposits, during the initial stage, is largely limited to accumulation of organic material and slight leaching. In the calcareous parent materials the latter process is reflected in a gradual but commonly only slight decalcification of the top soil. Subsequently, if not subjected to erosion or covered by sediment, a partly decalcified soil with a cambic B-horizon will develop, followed by a soil in which clay translocation becomes a dominant process. However, if subjected to erosion or regularly receiving fresh sediment, the leaching will be ineffective and the soil will remain in an initial stage.

Within a landscape, stability and instability are closely connected with physiography. Moreover, patterns in landscape stability and instability, which can be translated in patterns of physiographic units, vary little over the period concerned. The floodplains in the Gubbio Basin for example, are highly unstable and can be assumed to have been unstable during the whole period concerned, and their geographical location is very unlikely to have

significantly changed. It is quite evident that the present-day soil pattern and conditions in these floodplains strongly resemble those during the Bronze Age. A survey in which physiography is used as a major criterion, thus allows for a distinction between units which have been unstable during the period concerned, and units which were more or less stable. The first units have soils which are and were in an initial stage of formation, while the latter soils may have changed since the Bronze Age. This approach has been used for the survey and explains the attention paid to the physiography as well as the nature of the soil map legend (Fig. 2.2).

With regard to the possible effects of the post Bronze Age pedogenesis the following remarks can be made. From the study of Cremaschi (1987) on the soils of the Po Plain, which has a climate comparable to that of the Gubbio Basin, it appears that decalcification in that area proceeded rather slowly, and that at least several millennia of soil formation were required to produce a decalcified top soil in calcareous and poorly sorted fluvial deposits. The subsequent stages, described above, required considerably longer periods of soil formation: post-Wurmian soil formation in calcareous, poorly sorted fluvial deposits led to the development of only superficially decalcified soils with a rather weakly developed agric B-horizon. In finer textured deposits soil formation was found to proceed more slowly, mainly because of the lower permeability of these deposits, which causes a less intense leaching.

For the Gubbio Basin the aforementioned results imply that over the period concerned (Bronze Age to recent), the properties of soils on stable surfaces probably only marginally changed as a result of pedogenesis. Such soils, if in an initial stage during the Bronze Age, may have acquired a decalcified top soil and a thicker Ah horizon. The latter tendency, however, may have been counteracted by the effects of deforestation and agriculture, which is known to cause a lowering of the organic matter content of the top soil. The effects of pedogenesis on soils, which were already in a more advanced stage of soil development, were most probably minimal, as the processes active during later stages require much longer time spans to produce measurable effects on the soil properties.

2.2.2 Execution

In the Gubbio Basin, two soil maps have been made: one reconnaissance survey in 1984 (Fig. 2.2) (Schomaker and Van Waveren 1984, Fig. 1), and one in 1987 (Finke and Sewuster 1987) (Fig. 2.7). This section however, only deals with the survey of 1987. Prior to the field work a preliminary aerial photo-interpretation was carried out.

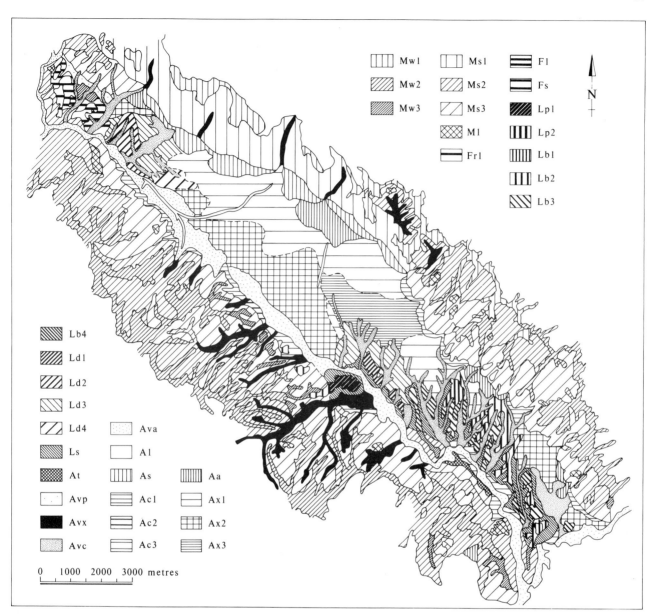

Fig. 2.2 Pedological map of the reconnaissance survey of 1984 in the Gubbio Basin, generalised after Schomaker and Van Waveren (1984). Simplified Key. Mw: Watersheds. (1. 1,000–700 m asl. 2. 700–500 m asl. 3. 500–400 m asl.); Ms: Denudational slopes (1. Very steep. 2. Steep. 3. Moderately steep); Ml: Palaeo slides; Fr1: Slightly convex terrace remnants; Fl: Palaeo slides; Fs: Steep denudational slopes; Lp: terrace remnants (Ponte d'Assi level) (1. Almost flat. 2. Slightly convex); Lb: Terrace remnants (Branca level) (1. Flat. 2. Almost flat. 3–4. Slightly convex); Ld: Terrace remnants (Padule/Mocaiana level) (1. Flat. Elevation *c*. 15 m. 2. Slightly convex. Elevation *c*. 15 m. 3–4. Almost flat. Elevation *c*. 10 m.); Ls: Steep straight denudational slopes; At: Alluvial terrace; Av: Alluvial valleys; Al: Artificial levées; As: scree slopes; Ac: colluvial slopes; Aa: alluvial fans; Ax: complexes of alluvial and colluvial slopes

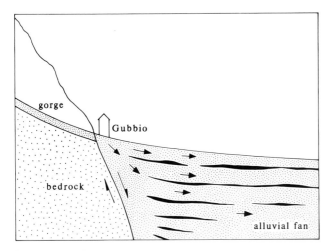

Fig. 2.3 Schematic cross section through the alluvial fan near Gubbio, indicating the interlayering of permeable and less permeable beds with subsurface water flow and geological faulting

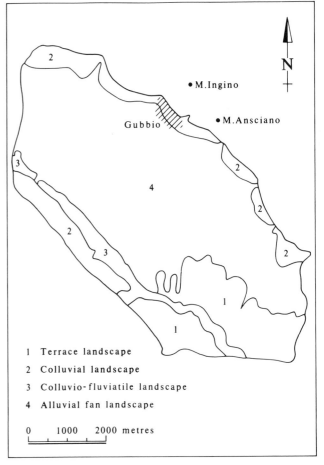

1 Terrace landscape

2 Colluvial landscape

3 Colluvio-fluviatile landscape

4 Alluvial fan landscape

0   1000   2000 metres

Fig. 2.4 Landscapes in the survey area of 1987. (Finke and Sewuster 1987)

Because of the scales of the final maps to be produced, two types of aerial photographs were used: black and white on a scale of 1:33,000 (Regione Umbria 1956); and full colour on a scale of 1:13,000 (Regione Umbria 1976).

During field work, 680 auger holes were made to an average depth of 1.20 m with a mean observation density of 19 auger holes per square kilometre. The position of the auger hole was determined in the field, depending on the morphology of the terrain and the result of the aerial photo interpretation. The cores were described following the terminology by the Food and Agriculture Organisation of the United Nations (FAO) *Guidelines for soil profile description* (FAO 1977). A field map at scale 1:10,000 was produced, which was generalised subsequently to a soil map with a scale of 1:50,000. Photo maps (*ortofotocarte*) (Regione Umbria 1983) served as field maps. Parts of the *Carta Topografica Regionale* (Regione Umbria 1977) served as the topographical base for the 1:25,000 maps.

2.2.3 Landscape units

Large scale tectonics in the Pleistocene caused the sinking of what is now a basin and probably, the uplifting of the surrounding mountainous area. Schematically, the faulting activity is indicated in Figure 2.3.

The tectonic activity strongly affected the sedimentation in the basin. GEMINA (1963), Schomaker and Van Waveren (1984) and Coltorti (section 2.1) distinguish several lacustrine phases in the Pleistocene. In these phases, fluvio-lacustrine clays accumulated which now form the terraces in the south-eastern and north-western parts of the basin.

In the early Holocene, lacustrine conditions disappeared and a fluvial system was formed (Schomaker and Van Waveren 1984). Accumulation processes became dominant in the central part of the valley, and erosion processes became dominant in the south-eastern and north-western parts. This resulted in a number of coalesced alluvial fans, possibly overlying terraces, in the central part of the basin. In the south-eastern and north-western parts of the valley, dissected terraces in fluvio-lacustrine sediments remain.

The surrounding mountains consist mainly of limestones and marls. Therefore the alluvial fan material is highly calcareous. All deposits encountered during survey had low sand contents. During the survey, several landscapes were distinguished in the basin floor on the basis of their genesis and the nature of the geomorphological processes active. In Figure 2.4, the location of the sub-landscapes in the survey area is indicated.

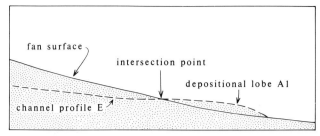

Fig. 2.5 Radial profile through the alluvial fan showing the position of the intersection point. Codes refer to the soil map codes (Reading 1978)

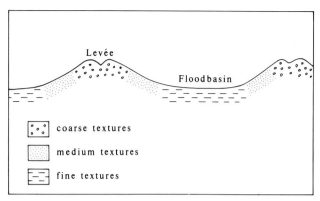

Fig. 2.6 Theoretical cross section through levées and flood basins

2.2.3.i Alluvial fan landscape

The morphology of an alluvial fan is the result of a number of erosional and depositional phases, both in time and in space. Looking at whole alluvial fans, factors like climate and tectonics are of importance when distinguishing erosional and depositional phases. For a certain location on an alluvial fan, site factors like local bedding gradient, permeability of the underlying sediment, sediment load and velocity of the stream determine whether erosion or deposition takes place.

Generally speaking, alluvial fans show a decrease in slope from the apex to the toe, giving a concave profile. However, this profile is commonly broken into a number of segments, each having a roughly even slope but decreasing rather abruptly into another straight slope of the bordering lower segment. Such a segmentation has been attributed to climatic changes or pulses of tectonic activity at the basin margin. The discontinuity in slope between two fan segments is caused when a stream channel cuts into the upper part of the alluvial fan and emerges onto the fan surface at the so-called 'Intersection Point' (Hooke 1967) (Fig. 2.5). Only below the intersection point does deposition take place. Others doubt the presence of such an intersection point.

The present intersection points on the alluvial fans of the Gubbio Basin are located near the most northern parts of the youngest levée and crevasse deposits. The alluvial fan above the imaginary line drawn through the intersection points of the present stream courses can therefore be considered to be presently stable in terms of deposition (and potentially unstable in terms of fluviatile erosion).

In the zone of deposition, natural levées are formed when flood waters of a stream overtop its banks. The stream velocity is then reduced, causing deposition of much of the suspended sediment near the channel. So the coarsest sediment is deposited near the channel, grain size decreasing with increasing distance from the stream course. This will cause a pattern of coarser textured levées

embanking a stream, gradually passing into finer textured depressions (flood basins) (Fig. 2.6). As the soils in this landscape are weakly developed, it is unlikely that the top of the alluvial fans are older than the Holocene.

This pattern of deposition becomes more complicated if a stream breaks its banks, leaving a tongue of coarser material over the finer flood basin material. The particle size of the material deposited also changes with distance to the apex of the fan (Reading 1978). Stream velocity decreases where the slope of the fan decreases. At the edges of the fan, where the slope is minimal, soil material is more clayey, whereas it is more gravelly towards the apex of the fan.

In alluvial fans, a large part of the discharge consists of water flowing in the subsurface. Since the levées have a better internal drainage than the basins because of their higher position and their coarser texture, ground water is closer to the surface in the flood basins. This may cause them to be swampy and unsuited for agriculture, unless artificially drained. When a terrain is sloping, and the soil is wet due to a high ground water level, colluviation may be a process of some importance.

Within the alluvial fan landscape in the Gubbio Basin, levées and flood basins of different age have been distinguished during the survey. Pedology was used as a tool in determining the relative age of a sub-landscape.

2.2.3.ii Terrace landscape (Fig. 2.8)

The terraces were most probably formed in the Middle and Late Pleistocene of fluvio-lacustrine, finely textured deposits (Schomaker and Van Waveren 1984). Most likely a part of the terraces was tilted due to tectonic activity, resulting in top levels dipping to the north-east. This may explain partly why the terraces were strongly dissected at their southern parts and eroded and/or buried

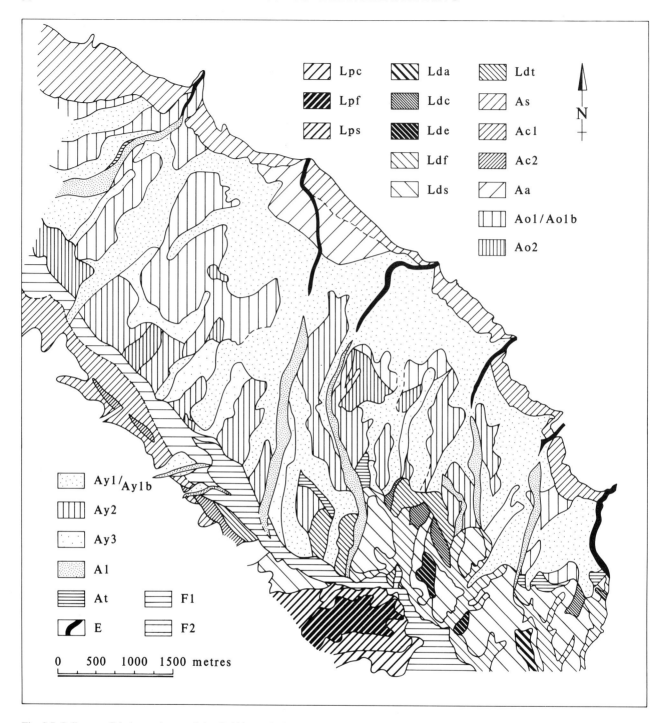

Fig. 2.7 Soil map of the central part of the Gubbio Basin from the survey of 1987 (generalised after Finke and Sewuster (1987))

KEY: To Figure 2.7

Soils in terraces

Unit	Height	Surface Age	Physiography	Slope form	Slope (degr)	Surface process	Soil depth	Drainage	Textures	Free CaCo3	Stoniness class	Soils
Lpc	400-420		P d' slopes o A	concave/ complex	2-10	colluviation	shallow	well	silty clay loam	+	0	Jc, Bk
Lpf	430-436	P	n s top t s levels e i	straight/ slightly convex	0-5	slight erosion	deep	moderately well	silty clay loam	0	0	Ao, Lg, Lo
Lps	405-430	L E							clay loam over silty clay loam	variable	0	Lo, Bk, Rc
Lda	417-423	I S	Padule/Branca level: top levels	flat	0-1	none	deep	well	silt loam over silty clay loam	0	0	La
Ldc	410-420	T O	slopes	complex	2-5	colluviation	shallow	moderately well	silty clay loam, (silt loam)	+ or + over 0	0	Jc, Bk, Be
Lde	403-418	C E	P top levels a l	flat	0-1	slight erosion	deep	well	(silt loam over) silty clay loam	0	0	Lo
Ldf	400-420	N E	d e top levels u v	flat	0-2	slight erosion	deep	moderately well	silty clay loam (silty clay)	over + +	0	Lv, Lo, Lg
Lds	400-425		l e slopes e l	convex	1-12	erosion truncated pofile	variable	(moderately) well	silty clay loam	variable	0	Bk, Be, Rc
Ldt	410-420		sub-horizontal tops	straight	0-4	severe erosion truncated profiles	shallow	(moderately) well	silty clay loam over silty clay	over 0 + +	0	Bv, Lo, Bk

Soils in alluvial deposits

Unit	Height	Surface Age	Physiography	Slope form	Slope (degr)	Surface process	Soil depth	Drainage	Textures	Free CaCo3	Stoniness class	Soils
As	435-570		scree cones /slopes	convex	10-55	colluviation mass movements	shallow	somewhat excessively	silt loam silty clay loam	+ +	1-3	Jc
Ac	425-480	H	footslopes	convex to concave	0-5	colluviation	variable	well	silt loam silty clay loam	+ +	0-1	Jc, Je, Bk
Aa	390-500	L	O upper	convex to straight	3-1 movements	mass movements	shallow	somewhat excessively	silt loam silty clay loam	+ +	0-3	Jc, Bk, Rc
Ao1	438-485	O	A o L l middle (lower)	complex to straight	0-3	alluviation colluviation	shallow/ moderately deep	well	silt loam loam, silty clay loam	topsoil: 0	0-3	Bk, Be, Jc
Ao2	433-457	C	L d U lower (middle)	straight	0-2	alluviation colluviation	moderately deep	moderately well	silty clay loam, silty clay, clay	topsoil: 0	0	Bk, Be, Jc
Ay1	405-490	E	V middle & lower I y	complex to straight	0-3	alluviation colluviation	shallow	well	silt loam loam, silty clay loam	+ +	0-3	Jc, Bk
Ay2	415-466	N E	A o lower (middle) L u	straight	0-2	alluviation colluviation	shallow	moderately well	silty clay loam, silty clay, clay	+ +	0	Jc, Bv, Bk
Ay3	410-441		n lower & middle F g	complex	0-2	colluviation/ alluviation	shallow	(moderately) well	silt loam silty clay loam	0 - + +	0	Jc, Bk, Je
Al	405-475		A e levée & N r crevasse bordering terrace	complex	0-2	alluviation	shallow	well	silt loam silt loam/ silty	+ + + +	0-2	Jc
At	415-435		landscape	straight	0-2	alluviation	shallow	(moderately) well	clay loam over silty clay loam	over	0-1	Jc, Bk

Soils in fluvial deposits

Unit	Height	Surface Age	Physiography	Slope form	Slope (degr)	Surface process	Soil depth	Drainage	Textures	Free CaCo3	Stoniness class	Soils
F1	392-426	Ho lo	valley bottom	straight	0-2	fluvial deposition/ erosion	shallow	moderately well	silt loam			
F2	420-434	ce ne	concave slopes grading to valley bottom	complex to concave	0-2	colluviation fluvia deposition			(silty clay loam)	+ +	0	Jc

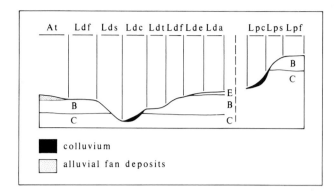

Fig. 2.8 Cross section through the terrace landscape. Codes refer to Fig. 2.7

at their northern parts. The northern part of the terraces gently rises up from the alluvial fan landscape. A terrain step is present in only a few places.

During the survey of the terrace landscape, terraces were subdivided on the basis of physiography and the degree of truncation of the soil profiles present, the latter indicating the magnitude of the erosion that took place mainly in the Holocene.

2.2.3.iii Colluvio-fluviatile landscape

At the valley bottom a zone of dominant fluviatile activity exists near the Torrente Saonda. Its waters are mainly supplied by lateral subsurface flows from the alluvial fans. Until recent times (Allegrucci pers. comm.) flooding occurred frequently, causing the deposition of layers of fresh, silty material near the stream channel. The fluviatile zone therefore, is somewhat coarser textured than some bordering lower parts of the alluvial fans.

During the survey, the fluviatile zone was subdivided into a transitional colluvio/fluviatile and a purely fluviatile zone.

2.2.3.iv Colluvial landscape

At the margins of the mountainous landscape and the basin, a zone exists where deposition of fine silty material takes place as result of mass movements. The mass movements may be the result of human activity in the past, for instance the clearance of forests and agricultural farming (Coltorti and Dal Ri 1985). In several places, cultural deposits containing sherds have been found buried under a layer of colluvial material.

2.2.4 The soils

The soils are classified according to the FAO system (FAO 1974). The units encountered in the area will be discussed briefly below.

2.2.4.i Fluvisols (J)

These soils are developed in very young alluvial and colluvial deposits. The soils have an AC profile. As the parent material of the soils originates from the calcareous rocks in the hinterland, almost all Fluvisols are calcareous too, and will be classified as Calcaric Fluvisols (Jc). If the young alluvial material is non-calcareous, the soil may be classified as a Eutric Fluvisol (Je). Fluvisols occur in all units of the fluviatile and alluvial fan landscapes. In the terrace landscape, Jc only occurs in colluvial deposits.

2.2.4.ii Regosols (R)

These soils only occur in severely eroded positions. The soils consist of weakly developed AC profiles. In the area surveyed, all Regosols are calcaric and occur in the erosion channels of the streams of the alluvial fans.

2.2.4.iii Cambisols (B)

Cambisols are relatively young immature soils. They have an ABC profile. The B-horizon however, is weakly developed: only some leaching and a very slight transport of iron may have occurred. Decalcification has been the criterion to distinguish these soils from Fluvisols. Decalcification was not prominent enough to meet the requirements of a Eutric Cambisol (Be) in all cases. So, partly decalcified soils were classified as Calcic Cambisols (Bk). Some Cambisols also have a fair content of swelling clays. These clays swell and shrink according to the moisture conditions in the soil. During the dry season, the soils can be identified by the presence of large cracks, and are subsequently classified as Vertic Cambisols (Bv). In the area surveyed, the soils nowhere met the more strict requirements for a Vertisol.

2.2.4.iv Luvisols (L)

Luvisols have a well developed A(E)BC profile. They occur in the terrace landscape. In these soils, clay and iron transport are clearly visible: the B-horizon is more reddish, has a higher clay content than the overlying and underlying horizons and has distinct illuviation cutans. Generally, the soils can be classified as Orthic Luvisols. The eluvial horizon need not be present since this horizon is highly erodible. Where the eluvial horizon is present and meets the colour requirements for the Albic horizon, the soil can be classified as Albic Luvisol (La). Where clay illuviation and (sub) horizontal position of the Luvisol impede the vertical drainage within 50 cm of the top of the profile, soils are classified as Gleyic Luvisols (Lg). In finely textured or eroded Luvisols with swelling clays, vertic features may be present. These soils are classified as Vertic Luvisols (Lv).

2.2.4.v Acrisols (A)

Acrisols differ from Luvisols by their low base saturation (Na^+, Ca^{2+}, Mg^{2+}, K^+ are low). This criterion requires laboratory analyses, which are beyond the scope of this survey. However, the soils of the Padule terrace level are supposed to meet this requirement.

2.2.5 The soil mapping units

The legend of the soil map (Fig. 2.7) has several levels of classification. On the highest level, physiography of the landscape is the differentiating criterion. In the terrace soils, the second level is based upon physiography too. In the soils of the fluviatile and alluvial deposits, various criteria have been used, like the texture and depth to which decalcification occurred.

In each soil mapping unit, soils have the same genesis and physiographic position. However, the stage of their development, together with other variations in soil characteristics can result in different soils within the same mapping unit. A more elaborate soil description can be found in Finke and Sewuster (1987).

L   The soils of the terrace landscape
This landscape is situated in the south-eastern part of the area surveyed. Remnants occur along the colluvial footslopes south of the Saonda stream. According to Schomaker and Van Waveren (1984) these terraces are of Late Pleistocene/early Holocene age, which is in agreement with the magnitude of the soil development found during the survey of 1987.

The boundary of the terrace landscape with the alluvial landscape is not clearly visible everywhere. In the northern part, the terraces are partly covered with deposits derived from alluvial fans. Generally, the flat top levels of the terraces are sloping one to two degrees in a north-eastern direction. This direction is contrary to the overall south-west direction of the slopes in the landscape. This may be due to tilting. In the terrace landscape, six major divisions have been made, which are based upon the physiography.

Each unit will be discussed briefly below (Fig. 2.7). All soils have a texture of silty clay loam. Mostly, the profiles are truncated, lacking the eluvial horizon. Some units reflect intensive reworking by Holocene colluviation. The area has been reclaimed for agriculture in historical times (Allegrucci pers. comm).

Lp The terrace remnants of the Ponte d'Assi level
This unit lies south of the Saonda stream near Ponte d'Assi, and comprises the highest terrace level in the area surveyed. Except in unit Lpc, the soils are well-developed Luvisols or Acrisols. In all units, the eluvial (E) horizon and a part of the illuvial (B) horizon have been eroded. Modern farming may even be accelerating this process. The existing truncated profiles consist of the lower parts of the B-horizon, and the C-horizon. They are silty clay loam textured.

The top levels consist of Ap–Bt–C profiles, are decalcified and moderately well drained. They may have hydromorphic properties. They are classified as Orthic Acrisols, and Gleyic or Orthic Luvisols. The soils on the slopes are calcareous B–C profiles. These can be classified according to their degree of truncation: Orthic Luvisol (Lo, slightly truncated), Eutric Cambisol (Be, decalcified, B-horizon weakly developed), Calcic Cambisol (Bk, weakly developed, partly calcareous soil with B-horizon), Calcaric Regosol (Rc, A–C profiles; strongly truncated).

Unit Lpc forms the colluviated lower terrace slopes. The soils are calcareous and well drained. The slope angle varies around three degrees and where the colluvial layer is thin, the underlying, original but truncated profile may be found. The soils have A–C profiles, or A–B–C profiles with a weakly developed B-horizon. They have been classified as Calcaric Fluvisols (Jc) or Calcic Cambisols (Bk).

Ld The soils in the Padule–Branca level
Lda Soils of the top levels
All soils are silt loam to silty clay loam textured. On unit Lda, the complete Ah–E–Bt–C profile is still discernible and consequently, there is either slight or no erosion. The soils are decalcified and well drained. Generally, hydromorphic properties occur within 1 m. depth: the B-horizon shows distinct reduction and oxidation mottles and accumulation of sesquioxides. The colour of the B ranges between 10 YR 5/8 and 10 YR 6/6. The colour of the E is 2.5 Y 7/3. Soils were classified as Albic Luvisols. Where the E-material has only partly been eroded, an Ap–Bt–C horizon sequence remains. This is unit Lde.

The E horizon has been disturbed by ploughing and is now part of the plough soil. Thus, the profiles are not severely truncated but merely disturbed. It was not very long ago that these soils were probably first reclaimed. They are decalcified and well drained but the mottles indicate water stagnation on the slowly permeable B horizon. Most soils were classified as Orthic Luvisols. On other worked terrace tops of the Padule level, the E-horizon has been truncated. An Ap–Bt–C profile remains. This is unit Ldf. Part of the Bt-horizon is now part of the plough soil. The topsoil is always decalcified. Lime may occur in the lower part of the profile. Normally, below 1.50 m, the profiles exhibit concentrations of ferro-manganese concretions. Generally the soils are moderately well drained, but some show gleyic properties below 50 cm. Most profiles show vertic features in the topsoil.

Soils were classified as Vertic, Orthic or Gleyic Luvisols. Unit Lds is found on terrace slopes ranging between two and fifteen degrees. Soils are moderately well to well drained. The topsoils may be decalcified. The textures range between silt loam and silty clay loam. Slope processes caused various stages of profile truncation. Where the C-horizon is exposed, soils are classified as Calcic or Eutric Cambisols or Calcaric Regosols. Layers containing large quantities of ferro-manganese nodules may be exposed. Unit Ldt comprises the severely truncated soils on sub-horizontal, flat or gently sloping levels. The Bt-horizon has generally disappeared. The soils are calcareous in the subsoil and moderately well drained. Many profiles show vertic features too poorly developed to be classified as Vertisols. Most soils are classified as Vertic or Calcic Cambisols or Orthic Luvisols.

A   The soils of the alluvial–colluvial landscape

Aa, Ao, Ay, Al, At Soils in the alluvial fan landscape
The alluvial fans investigated are the ones near Madonna del Ponte, Gubbio, Zappacenere, San Marco, Padule and Stazione di Padule. They occur adjacent to each other to form a broad sloping plain. These units cover the largest part of the area surveyed. The landscape built up by these fans consists of NNE–SSW orientated shallow ridges and depressions, hardly visible to the untrained eye. Most soils are shallow A–C profiles. As the material originates from the calcareous mountains north-east of Gubbio the content of sand is very low: less than 15%. All gravel and stones encountered in the area are (sub)angular limestone fragments.

Aa   Soils in higher alluvial fan deposits
This unit is found near Gubbio and consists of poorly sorted, coarse material having a stoniness percentage up to 15%. In this unit, auger holes have not been made because it is a built-up area. Soils were probably Calcaric Fluvisols or Calcic Cambisols.

Ao   Soils in older alluvial fan deposits.
This unit is found on the middle and lower alluvial fans. The deposits are decalcified at least in the topsoil. Textures range from silt loam to clay. The finest textures are in the lower part of the alluvial fan. Small inclusions of calcareous soils may occur having an area smaller than the basic mapping unit. In the upper middle part of the alluvial fan the unit may be overlain by younger deposits. In the lower part of the unit, erosion may have taken place. In this case too, unit Ao is bordered by calcareous deposits. Soils are dominantly Calcic or Eutric Cambisols with inclusions of Calcaric Fluvisols.

On the soil map this unit is divided into two sub units. Ao1 consists of coarser material, sometimes with a gravelly top layer. Unit Ao2 consists of fine material.

Ay   Soils in younger alluvial fan deposits
Moderately well- to well-drained soils developed in recent alluvial deposits. Textures range from clay to silt loam or loam. These usually very calcareous soils lack diagnostic properties other than (in a few cases) a calcic horizon. If present, this accumulation horizon is most probably caused by lateral subsurface transport of water rich in carbonates. Locally, buried profiles may be found. Hardly any soil development has taken place, therefore soils are classified as Calcaric Fluvisols with inclusions of Calcic Cambisols. Unit Ay1b can be correlated with positions on the middle alluvial fan and near stream channels on the lower part of the fan. It consists of the coarser material. Locally, small bands of gravelly material indicate former stream beddings. Unit Ay2 consists of finer textured soils. The unit can be correlated with positions on the lower alluvial fan between coarser textured levées and also with depressions between two fans. On the lower part of the alluvial fan they have relatively high water tables and may suffer from water logging. Unit Ay3 contains reworked alluvial fan deposits. Inclusions of partly decalcified soils occur. The unit can be found in the lower parts of the alluvial fans between coarser textured levées. Natural drainage has been or is imperfect due to high groundwater tables. Colluviation, strongly varying in magnitude over short distances, caused a complex pattern of relatively undisturbed soils together with soils containing buried profiles and soils with a high organic matter content. This is reflected by dark colours (2.5 Y 4/3)

extending over the whole profile. Part of the soils has a calcic horizon, probably caused by lateral accumulation.

Al Soils in levée and crevasse deposits
The crevasse deposits are found along the present stream courses and have a width of about 100 m. These are the youngest deposits on the alluvial fan. The texture is silt loam, occasionally silty clay loam. The soils are well drained, calcareous and may be gravelly. Locally, soils may suffer from high water tables because of the nearby presence of streams or less permeable layers in the subsoil. All soils were classified as Calcaric Fluvisols.

At Alluvial fan deposits overlying terraces
In the south-east and east of the survey area, alluvial deposits, covering terrace material, were found. Where the thickness of the cover exceeded 180 cm, soils were classified as Ao, Ay or Al. The boundaries between the At-unit and the terraces are not reflected in the relief. Textures are silt loam or silty clay loam over silty clay loam. Most alluvial material is calcareous and is classified as Calcaric Fluvisol or Calcic Cambisol. Slope angles were between zero and two degrees. Soils are often imperfectly drained because of the less permeable Pleistocene terrace material in the subsoil. Usually, this terrace material is decalcified.

As, Ac The soils of the colluvial landscape
As Soils in colluvial scree cones and slopes
Somewhat excessively drained soils in concave scree slopes. The soils are calcareous gravelly loams, silt loams and silty clay loams usually lacking any profile development. Buried profiles may occur. Mostly, soils are Calcaric Fluvisols.

Ac Soils in colluvium
Soils developed in medium textured colluvial deposits of varying age. Slopes seldom exceed seven degrees and are usually concave. Generally speaking, the colluvial layer is thicker down slope and contains less gravel. In the southern hill slopes, colluvium overlies truncated terrace soils. Most soils are well drained. In some soils several phases of colluviation can be distinguished, reflected by decalcified layers and layers containing sherds. Dominant soils are Calcaric Fluvisols with inclusions of Calcic Cambisols. If the colluvium is older, it is decalcified and the soils subsequently consist of Eutric Fluvisols or Eutric Cambisols.

F The soils in the colluvio-fluviatile landscape
This landscape covers the lowest parts of the survey area. The northern part of the valley drains towards the north, and the southern part drains towards the south. In the middle of the basin, near the farmhouses Torraccia I and II, no clear drainage pattern is present. This part is represented as a colluvio-fluviatile complex (F2). In the area where a distinct drainage pattern is present, a fluviatile unit (F1) was distinguished. The parent material of both units consists of recent deposits.

F1 River Saonda deposits
The soils in this unit are young and consist of calcareous AC-profiles. Textures vary between silt loam and silty clay loam. Drainage is moderately good. Water tables may be high, depending on the season. Gleyic features may occur. Soils are classified as Calcaric Fluvisols.

F2 Colluvio-fluviatile deposits
The soils in this unit are mainly AC-profiles. The textures are silt loam, occasionally silty clay loam. The soils are well drained and the groundwater table is deeper than in unit F1. Soils were classified as Calcaric Fluvisols with inclusions of Calcic Cambisols.

2.2.6 Conclusions

Within the various physiographic units distinction can be made according to the possible effects of post-Bronze Age soil formation, which was one of the major aims of the approach used. In the terrace landscape, boundaries between the various soil units may have shifted as a result of erosion and fluvial incision, but the soils on the stable surfaces show characteristics which evidently were acquired over a very long period of time. Since they represent soils in an advanced stage of development, the effects of post-Bronze Age pedogenesis are negligible. The soils, however, may have been slightly truncated as a result of man-induced degradation.

In the colluvial landscape, which comprises the units As and Ac, depositional processes determine the soil properties. It is not known whether such soil situations already existed during later periods, for example a massive deforestation during medieval times. This implies that a reconstruction of soils during the archaeologically relevant period is impossible. The colluvial–fluviatile landscape is marked by its high soil instability, implying that soil development is minimal and properties and patterns are governed by sediment properties and patterns. Although the patterns of this landscape may have shifted slightly, similar conditions will have existed during the Bronze Age.

Within the alluvial fan landscape, parent materials are marked by their high lime content. The extent to which the soils have been decalcified is indicative for their age, that is their stage of development. The survey shows that the soils mostly have a decalcified top soil (unit Ao). These units can be considered to represent the oldest surfaces in this landscape. Although the age of these surfaces cannot be established with certainty, the regular presence of Roman artefacts in the top soil of the units suggests that they are at least of Roman age, that is they remained stable from Roman times onwards. This conclusion is in accordance with the results of the study of Cremaschi (see above).

Archaeological remains from the Neolithic have been encountered in the upper strata of the alluvial fans and testify the relatively recent age of these strata. Within the upper strata palaeosols exhibiting a more advanced stage of soil development than that encountered on the oldest stable surfaces (see above) have not been encountered. This implies, that during the Bronze Age the soils must have strongly resembled the present soils, although they may vary in their lime content and organic matter. The patterns in soil texture, which are strongly related to the sedimentary facies, may also have differed from the actual patterns, but the overall distribution of fine, medium and coarse textures is not likely to have changed drastically, since these are geomorphologically controlled.

2.3 Vegetation, landuse and climate

2.3.1 Introduction: the sources

The reconstruction of the changing vegetation and climate of the Gubbio area is an intricate process. It requires the careful interweaving of modern botanical studies, the modelling of a theoretical climax vegetation and the measurement of human impact and climatic change, through studies of legal documents, samples of pollen and molluscs from geological and archaeological deposits.

Generalised studies of climatic records and modern vegetation and land use are abundant for the Regione of Umbria, particularly under the influence of the Comunità montana, and concentrated specifically in the adjoining Chiascio Basin (Cattuto and Cavanna 1971) because of its hydrological significance for the Perugia Basin (complicated by the construction of a dam in a geomorphologically unstable and seismic area). More recently, the University of Camerino has studied the modern vegetation of the valley. This work used the phytosociological method of the Zurich–Montpellier school. This employs a mapping technique which registers the presence, abundance and dominance of single species grouped by associations. These associations were then studied in relationship to local climate and geology allowing a predictive model for climax vegetation (Fig. 2.9). This idealised framework has

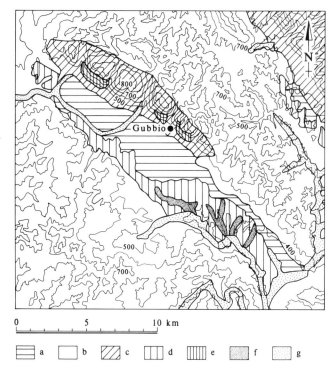

Fig. 2.9 Zones of potential vegetation: a Deciduous forest dominated by white oak; b Deciduous forest dominated by turkey oak; c Deciduous forest dominated by hop hornbeam; d Deciduous forest dominated by sessile oak; e Macchia of sclerophilous evergreen dominated by holm oak; f Deciduous oak dominated by white hornbeam; g Riverbank forest

provided a model which can be tested by environmental indicators.

The main environmental indicators for the prehistoric period are a combination of geomorphological information, pollen and molluscs. At one level this has taken the form of the generalised mapping of pedogenesis and stratigraphy over the whole region as reported in the previous two sections. At another level, attempts through site-specific studies have been made to quantify the unknown elements in the environmental equation. At the Neolithic site of San Marco (Hunt et al. 1990; Malone and Stoddart 1992; section 3.2), chronological control has been particularly effective. In the cases of San Agostino and San Felicissimo, chronological control has been effective for parts of the sequence, but must remain generalised, particularly for the Pleistocene phases. At the other excavated sites, while chronological control is good, environmental information has generally been less forthcoming, in spite of systematic attempts at its recovery.

Documents containing agrarian reports from the eleventh to the eighteenth century have been employed to reconstruct both the natural and agrarian environment of the territory of Gubbio. There are three sources of information: written records of land transactions which incidentally give information on land use, place names and the first *catasto* of the Gubbio area. The first two must clearly be approached with great caution. The third (reproduced for the first time in this volume in readable form for its agrarian information) is much more reliable. The agrarian contracts, conserved in the various local archives, dating to the period before this first *catasto*, are about 500 in number and cover about five centuries. Of this mass of documents, about 150 have been chosen from amongst the *protocolli* in the *Fondo Notarile* of the state archive of Gubbio as the most interesting for our work, by selecting some notaries (about twenty) who had particularly specialised in agrarian contract work. This group of Gubbio notaries almost certainly drew their specialisation from their social position as part of the landowning *borghesia*. Research was also undertaken in the Bishop's Archive at Gubbio, working on the *Fondo Moretti* which collected together almost all the agrarian documentation of lands belonging to the bishop. Thus, information was available on both lay and ecclesiastical ownership. The whole procedure of land registration was placed on a much more formal footing under Napoleonic influence and it is from this period that we have the systematic coverage of the first *catasto*.

2.3.2 The modern climate and vegetation

The difference in altitude (*c.* 350–900 m above sea level) between the limits of the basin have produced a marked local variation in climate, best appreciated in the winter months when snowfall can affect only the uplands. Within a short horizontal distance, considerable differences in micro-climate can be readily distinguished which must have had a major seasonal impact on human populations.

Unfortunately, local meteorological records are based on only two stations, one located at Gubbio (529 m above sea level), and the other at Padule (445 m above sea level) (rainfall only) to the south-east. The chief information to note from these modern records (1952–82) is a highly arid period in July when temperatures rise to their peak (average 22°C) and rainfall reaches its lowest point (an average 43 mm out of a total 1,089 mm for the year) (Cattuto and Cavanna 1971; Biondi *et al.* 1990). Otherwise, with the exception of a peak of 145 mm in November and a subsidiary peak in March (97 mm), rainfall is relatively evenly spread throughout the year. This rainfall profile is typical of locations under the shelter of limestone escarpments placed to the north-east, such as at Assisi. The annual cycle of temperature follows a regular pattern with its lowest average in January (4.5°C). In spite of these

seasonal variations, there have never been any serious water problems in the Gubbio area, given the presence of springlines in the local limestone geology which remain active throughout the summer months.

The recent vegetational studies (Biondi *et al.* 1990) have distinguished three principal vegetational zones associated with three types of landscape: the limestone escarpments, the marl-sandstone hills and the Pleistocene terraces (Fig. 2.10). A fourth and even a fifth landscape probably existed on the colluvial footslopes of the limestone escarpments and on the alluvial fans above the flood plain, but human interference has been too severe to preserve a modern trace of the climax associations.

The limestone escarpments have a potential climax vegetation of mixed deciduous woodland, dominated by black hornbeam and, in a few exposed areas, by evergreen macchia dominated by holm oak. Some of the more exposed flanks of the escarpment have a greater presence of pubescent oak. Once clearance has taken place, pastureland is dominated by *Bromus erectus*. Recolonising species are dominated by broom and juniper. The modern cover is drastically different as a result of massive deforestation. The artificial appearance of this sector of the landscape is compounded by the reforestation with foreign species.

The marl-sandstone terrain, which occupies a much greater surface area locally, is dominated by turkey oak. In areas of recolonisation, *Juniperus communis* is the most active species.

The heavier soils of the valley bottom, the Pleistocene terraces, preserve an unusual, relict vegetation with its high proportion (75%) of euro-mediterranean, euro-asiatic and boreal, as opposed to local species. For example, this vegetation comprises the southern limit of *Calluna vulgaris* and *Hypericum humifusum* and the easterly limit of *Cicendia filiformis* within the Italian peninsula. The vegetation as a whole is dominated by common oak (*Quercus petraea*) as well as *Quercus robur* and *Quercus cerris*. Less dense forest cover consists of *Malus florentina*, *Rosa arvensis* and *Fragula alnus* in most zones and *Populus tremula* in areas of accumulated water. At the edges of woodland, *Calluna vulgaris*, *Erica scoparia* and *Genista germanica* are prevalent.

The banks of the smaller streams of the valley bottom are today deforested, but the larger river courses may give a better indication of more developed vegetation. The River Chiascio and parts of the Saonda are bordered by willow (*Salix alba*) and black poplar (*Populus nigra*). Some small valleys have concentrations of white hornbeam (*Carpinus betulus*) while other river courses have viburnum (*Viburnum opalus*) and elm (*Ulmus minor*)

The potential vegetation of the lower calcareous

formations of the valley bottom is much more difficult to reconstruct for the reasons given above. Colonising species appear to be very similar to those of the limestone escarpment. A deciduous woodland is considered the most probable climax vegetation perhaps dominated by pubescent oak.

2.3.3 *The development of climate and vegetation (Fig. 2.19)*

The reconstruction of the vegetation and climate of the Plio-Pleistocene phases of the valley's development is afflicted by the chronological imprecision inherent in biostratigraphic studies in the Neogene. A substantial pollen study was undertaken during the search for lignite deposits in the valley during the 1960s, indicating a forest landscape of *Pinus haploxylon, Tsuga, Cedrus, Picea, Carya, Pterocarya, Zelkova* and *Liquidambar* dated to the Gunz–Mindel interglacial (Lona and Ricciardi 1961; GEMINA 1963). A consideration of the known extinction datums for taxa such as *Liquidambar, Tsuga* and *Carya* in northern Italy (for example Bertolani Marchetti *et al.* 1979) suggests that a late Lower Pleistocene age, possibly as young as 0.95 MY is probable for these beds.

Slope waste deposits, formed against the northern edge of the basin, provide a long, if discontinuous, sequence of environmental change from the cessation of major tectonic activity during the middle (Coltorti pers. comm.) or near the end of the Middle Pleistocene, until virtually the present day. The nature of the formation and lithology of these deposits unfortunately militates against either the use of environmental indicators such as pollen, or against the construction of a complete, uninterrupted sequence. For example, a pollen sample taken from one of these deposits near Raggio produced very low concentrations of pollen (3,000–6,000 pollen grains per cubic cm) with a high percentage of crumpled and broken grains. The most important characteristic of the deposit was an 80–95% count of Compositae Liguliflorae. As discussed elsewhere by Bottema (1975), this is simply indicative of the high resistance of Compositae to the highly corrosive conditions of colluvial deposition and can give little guide to local vegetative cover. Insubstantial soil profiles that formed during temperate periods are also unlikely to survive. Weathering of the lower part of the sequence is likely to have destroyed the warm-climate molluscs, that in the upper part of the sequence seem to have been recycled from soil profiles into debris-flow or mudflow deposits during succeeding cold stages. There is thus a real possibility that some temperate episodes may be missed in the research. There is also a significant possibility that

during some cold episodes, conditions were unsuitable for the initiation of debris flows or mudflows. Lastly, some layers may have been removed by erosion.

In spite of these very real complications, the study of molluscan assemblages and the sedimentary sequences of these deposits has been fairly successful in adumbrating the general pattern of climate and vegetation. Two principal sites, San Agostino (Fig. 2.12) and San Felicissimo (Fig. 2.11), have been studied where the later part of the sedimentary sequence can be at least approximately dated by archaeology. With this combined evidence, complex vegetational cycles can be hypothesised, dominated by climatic change in the Pleistocene and early Holocene and by human impact in the later Holocene (Fig. 2.13).

For the slope deposits to form, an abundant supply of debris must have been present which in turn must have been largely unconsolidated to have been available for erosion and transport. Binding vegetation must therefore have been absent as a precondition for the debris and mudflow events which laid down the majority of the slope deposits. This hypothesis can be supported by the sparse open-ground mollusc assemblages from unit D at San Felicissimo and unit F at San Agostino. Molluscs seem largely to have been weathered out of the lower horizons. In the Pleistocene, the most likely limiting factor for vegetation was some combination of drought and cold. Occasional intense precipitation events would have been necessary to mobilise the sediment, but at San Felicissimo the stratification might imply no more than a few dozen such events during the hundred thousand or so years of the Late Pleistocene and thus a recurrence interval of over 2,000 years. Mauro Coltorti (pers. comm.; Coltorti and Dramis 1987, 1988; Calderoni *et al.* 1989) suggests that laminar erosion may be responsible for these effects and that, in any case, frost shattering became effective from about 50,000 BP indicating that a shorter interval of 1,000 years between events may be more appropriate.

As discussed above, in the Holocene the natural climax vegetation of the Gubbio area is forest in various forms which would have adequately bound sediments together and which would have supplied the humic matter for brown forest soils to develop. Such a forest soil seems to have survived at San Felicissimo, where the lower levels of unit C contain only woodland taxa. Forest vegetation in the Holocene could have been destroyed by naturally occurring fires started, for instance by lightning strikes, but, in the later Holocene, forest is probably more likely to have been cleared by human populations. The presence of potsherds in unit A at San Felicissimo and in unit D at San Agostino and the archaeological sites at both localities (Roman and Bronze to Iron Age respectively) provides

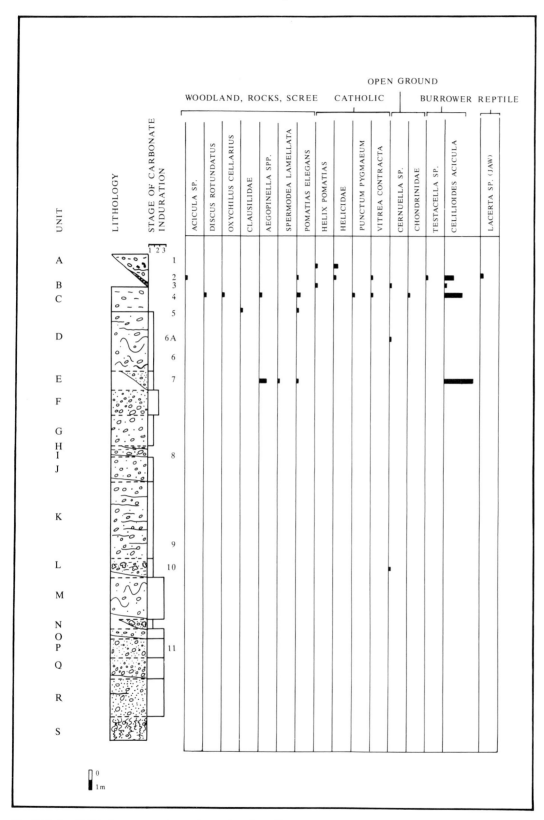

Fig. 2.11 San Felicissimo: composite section and mollusc diagram

40   THE ENVIRONMENTAL SETTING

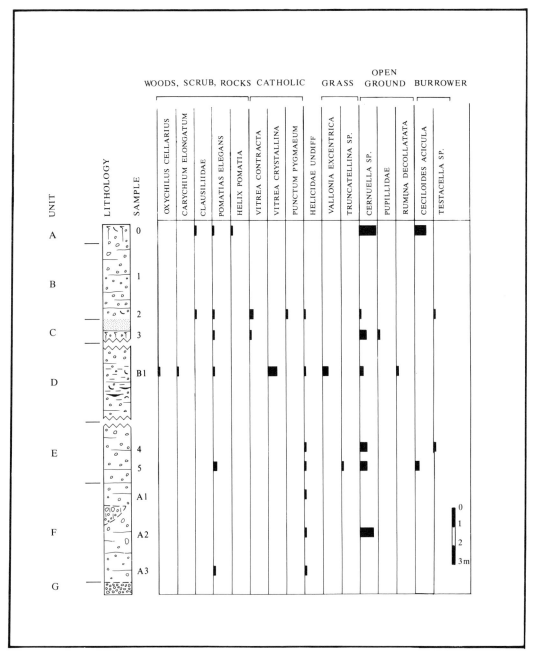

Fig. 2.12 Sant' Agostino: composite section and mollusc diagram

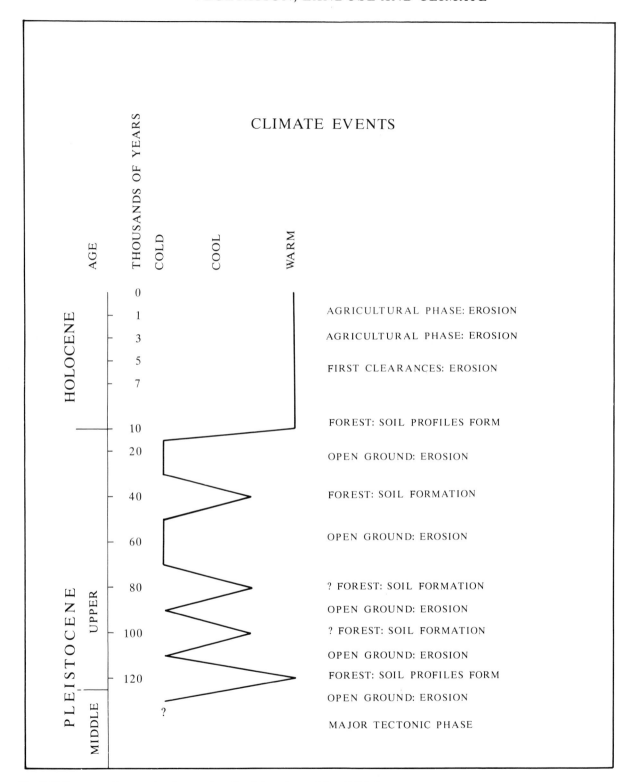

Fig. 2.13 Summary diagram showing events at Sant' Agostino and San Felicissimo

firm evidence of human activity on the slopes during the Late Holocene.

Forest would also have been the typical vegetation during temperate stages in the Pleistocene, as is suggested from the molluscan evidence in unit E at San Felicissimo and perhaps from the base of unit F at San Agostino. Such forest soils would have been very vulnerable to erosion once the forest retreated at the start of following cold stages, but the molluscs of the forest phase(s) seem to have been recycled into the mudflow deposits of the following cold stage(s) and thus preserved.

In the absence of molluscs, calcrete induration may give some indication of palaeoclimate. Calcretes have previously been reported from slope deposits in Tuscany by Coles *et al.* (1984) and Gilbertson and Hunt (1987). These authors suggested that calcrete formation took place during fairly dry temperate phases, with stage 1 calcretes forming during the Holocene and stage 3 calcretes forming only during the last and previous interglacials. The stage 2 calcrete in unit F at San Felicissimo can be taken, therefore, as evidence supporting the suggestion on molluscan grounds, of a temperate episode prior to the deposition of unit E. Similarly, the stage 3 calcretes in units M, O, P, Q and R at San Felicissimo may be taken as evidence for one, or probably more, major temperate phases of interglacial or near-interglacial status.

There is no dating evidence for the lower parts of the sections at San Agostino and San Felicissimo. The ages are suggested by analogy with environmental records elsewhere in Europe, notably the long cores at Castiglione (Follieri *et al.* 1988); Grande Pile (Woillard 1978) and Ioannina (Wijmstra 1978). Temperate and cold episodes at Gubbio (Fig. 2.13), interpreted from molluscan and sedimentary evidence, have been approximately matched with these sequences on a 'count from the top' basis. It is acknowledged that this procedure is extremely uncertain, since many climatic events may have left no trace in the sampled localities. Nevertheless this procedure can, in spite of all the difficulties mentioned above, provide an approximate minimum estimate of age for a horizon. Basin margin sequences in the Italian Apennines certainly merit more study to add refinement and accuracy to the current picture.

A more refined estimate of a fixed point in the vegetational sequence has been provided by the analysis of a peat deposit found in the bottom of the basin near Piccola Piaggola. This deposit dated to the early Holocene (9650 ± 90 BP in radiocarbon years (Q–3228)) contains an assemblage of open, mainly herbaceous, but also woodland species (Table 2.1). The composite evidence suggests the formation of a peat deposit in locally boggy conditions, dominated by the growth of sedge, set within a wider

Table 2.1. *Pollen assemblage from near Piccola Piaggola, Gubbio (in per cent)*

Trees	*Betula* (Birch)	3%
	Pinus (Pine)	27%
	Picea (Spruce)	7%
Shrubs	*Salix* (Willow)	3%
Herbs	Gramineae (Grasses)	15%
	Cyperaceae (Sedges)	35%
	Artemesia (Sage-brush)	3%
	Chenopodiaceae	1%
	Filipendula	1%
	Ranunculaceae	1%
	Rubiaceae	1%
	Thalictrum	1%
	Umbelliferae	2%

more upland landscape occupied by shrubs (for example willow) and trees (pine, spruce and birch). Willow is likely to have been on the margins of the boggy ground. The absence of thermophilous species is similar to the situation in relict vegetation found today in the lower parts of the valley, reflecting the relatively high altitude (380–400 m above sea level). The pollen sample shows some evidence of the first colonising species promoted by the warming conditions of the Holocene.

Other local details are provided by the environmental information from the excavated sites. The most valuable information is provided by the Neolithic site San Marco (Hunt *et al.* 1990; Malone and Stoddart 1992) of the late sixth millennium cal. BC. The site was established in an area of rather damp mixed oak forest, where there had previously been pools of standing water and marsh, presumably growing in a disused distributary channel of the alluvial fan. Some clearance took place at the time of the construction of the site, and this later greatly increased, with locally arid, exposed grassland, by the time of abandonment.

Other significant evidence of at least locally important clearance around sites is found in the Bronze Age. The presence of *Bromus* amongst the floral remains collected from Monte Ingino suggests the local presence of scrubland. Charcoal samples, which have been examined, all derive from slow immature growth (Taylor pers. comm.) which, allowing for selective collection for kindling, also suggests the local presence of scrub growth. Pollen has not survived in these open mountain-top sites, but molluscan evidence, where available, confirms the presence of a locally open landscape.

These individual site-orientated foci, providing insights into local environments, suggest an increasingly active human intervention in the environment that must have reached its climax in the Roman period. It was only at this stage that the vast majority of the landscape was systematically cleared for human settlement and agriculture. The consequences must have been severe for soil retention, particularly on the steeper slopes, as the slope waste deposits discussed above demonstrate. It is possible that the first agricultural impact of the Neolithic or Bronze Age removed a thin covering of fertile aeolian soil that could never be recovered.

The full intricacies of these cycles of landuse can only be recovered when documentary information becomes available, although a geomorphological contribution is becoming available for the Marche (Coltorti 1991). The documents reveal shorter-term cycles that cannot easily be detected in the *longue durée* of prehistory. The Iron Age and Roman periods must be included, for these purposes, within prehistory. Evidence for vegetational change is necessarily indirect. For the Iron Age the evidence from Sant' Agostino (section 4.2) suggests a sophisticated cereal agriculture which in turn implies substantial clearance most probably of the footslopes of the limestone escarpments. The Roman period represents a further period of extensive use of landscape, which must have been accompanied by more widespread clearance for agriculture. By this stage, we can probably envisage a substantially more open landscape with regular spacing of farmsteads (section 6.2). The limited molluscan evidence from San Felicissimo and San Marco (Roman) appears to substantiate this by the presence of open ground species, although it is difficult to generalise from this evidence since clearance would be expected in the immediate neighbourhood of a farmstead. One aspect is clear, that by the Roman period the vegetation of the Gubbio valley had become, definitively, not a response to climatic change, but a response to socio-economic conditions. The fluctuations involved can be detected in the medieval documents.

2.3.3.i Eleventh to thirteenth centuries AD

We are, at present, unavoidably, faced with a large gap in evidence until the early medieval period. In the eleventh century, the territory was cultivated only in the immediate area of the city of Gubbio and in the *Curtis* of the individual feudal castles. At the beginning of the eleventh century AD, the combination of demographic growth and the declining control by feudal lords over their land, allowed more liberal forms of peasant contract (*chiamate di livello – enfiteusi*) and led to important economic changes. These included the cutting of woodland and the transfer of pasture and uncultivated areas to more intensive

arable practices. This process was more marked in the neighbourhood of the city, as the documents confirm, by citing localities such as Pozzogemolo, San Secondo, San Agostino or close to the mouth of the Camignano River (Cenci 1915: 70, 71, 93). It also occurred around castles, particularly on the hills overlooking the city and close to watercourses with watermills. This last fact is also confirmation of the importance of the mill as an economic resource by the eleventh century (Cenci 1915: 55).

The cultivation involved in these changes, replacing woodland, was not only cereals, but also vines, olives and fruit trees. This particularly involved the introduction of mixed cultivation (such as wheat with rows of vines) which was suitable for hill farming (Allegrucci 1980: 14). One should not forget that woodland continued to be present, as indeed today, in the valley bottom (Corrado 1984: 38). These damp woodlands were much less affected by the expansion of cultivation. In fact, there is evidence that many of them continued into the first half of the sixteenth century, the period of major drainage and land reclamation. Place names such as Padule and Il Laghetto hint at the existence of poor water control and marshy areas that limited the expansion of agricultural cultivation (Corrado 1984: 41). Corrado claims that these woodlands were not cleared until the first half of the eighteenth century. We consider it more probable that, already at the end of the sixteenth century, much land was placed under cultivation and that this included former woodland. This pattern has some documentary confirmation in the fifteenth to sixteenth century. There are protestations, by peasants holding land in the hunting reserves of the Montefeltro and the della Rovere, of damage to crops and vines, during hunting (Allegrucci 1982: 96).

The further economic expansion at the beginning of the thirteenth century, led to a new demographic growth when Gubbio was forced to enlarge its city walls and construct new buildings. Accompanying this was the need to open up more ground for cultivation, particularly in the hill and even upper hill areas. There is further corroboration of this process in that documents referring to place names suggesting wooded terrain (Cerqueto, Monte Acera, Colle Cerrone, Cerquattino, Sterpeto) record cultivation in this period.

2.3.3.ii Fourteenth century AD

The fourteenth century is a period of major importance for Gubbio both commercially and economically (Chapter 7). This century was accompanied by a further major demographic increase which profoundly affected the surface area under cultivation. The lower hill areas that surrounded the Gubbio Basin (Monteleto, Monteluiano,

Semonte, San Alfiolo, Branca) were placed under the cultivation of vines, olives, fruit trees and the new crops of flax and hemp. This allowed the peasants to be definitively established on their land, now that the landowner, based in the city, had ceded control into their hands (Allegrucci 1980: 99).

This demographic growth forced the peasantry to cultivate additionally those lands of poor return located in mountain areas such as Piazza, Villa Magna, Castiglione and so on. This in turn allowed sufficient surplus to support the growing urban population (Allegrucci 1980: 103). The process continued, as discussed above, until the 1348 plague which killed almost half the population, and led to the return of woodland and uncultivated areas, subsequently favouring the more extensive practices of animal husbandry (Archivio Vescovile Gubbio, M. 2, C. 30 v., 31r.).

This was the position for the entire fourteenth century, continuing even into the first half of the fifteenth, when there was a new phase of economic expansion.

2.3.3.iii Fifteenth century AD

In the first years of the fifteenth century the hill areas close to the city which had been previously cultivated returned to woodland, and the major emphasis was on animal husbandry. This continued through the first half of the century. Many documents of the second half of the century indicate an economic revival dependent on the development of the city. The peasantry were encouraged to clear the ground, to clear woodland and once more to cultivate wheat, vines, olives and fruit trees. The necessity to place the hill areas under cultivation was so pressing that the peasant was ceded the ownership of the harvest and of the ground itself if he had cleared more than three *mine* each year, during the five years prescribed in the contract (Archivio Statale Gubbio, Fondo notarile, vol. 94, C. 165r). This very favourable clause is not found in later contracts and suggests a great demand for grain production. The Comune of Gubbio made an edict in 1422 that obliged all landowners to sow or have their lands sown with good grain as prescribed in the decree of the Comune or face a large fine in the Camera Comunale (Menichetti 1980: 266). Therefore, from the middle of the fifteenth century the Gubbio area entered a new phase of cultivation and vegetational history.

The hill and upper hill areas such as Serra Brunamonti, Santa Maria di Burano, Piazza and Petazzano were again cultivated with grain, apples, pears and olives. Flax and hemp were also cultivated as an important subsidiary income for the peasant family, confirming the commercial demand from the city of Gubbio.

By the end of the fifteenth century, agricultural expansion had affected a considerable part of the territory of Gubbio, including all the hills and that part of the valley bottom not covered by unreclaimed woodland and waterlogged ground. This intensive agricultural expansion can also be noted from the protestations of shepherds who were no longer able to find suitable pastures and had to take their flocks into the Marche (Allegrucci 1980: 222).

2.3.3.iv Sixteenth to seventeenth century AD

The sixteenth century is the century of land reclamation and drainage of a large part of the Gubbio Valley. Many documents report drainage and cultivation of localities (Cipolleto, Canne Grecole, Padule, Il Laghetto and so on) in the plain, to provide an agricultural surplus for the urban population (Archivio Statale Gubbio, Fondo Notarile, vol. 355, C. 145r; Menichetti 1980: 267). Rows of vines were important in the plain. Some documents required the planting of a certain number of willows, poplars and *venchi* along the streams (for example Saonda) for the defence of their banks and the excavation of ditches to guarantee the easy flow of water (Archivio Statale Gubbio, Fondo Notarile, vol. 580, C. 389v).

Continual agricultural expansion took place in the sixteenth century, only slightly arrested by the plague of 1527 and various famines that struck the population from 1590 to 1593. A major halt to this economic and demographic expansion arrived with the plague of 1623, which coincided with war and famine, creating a shortage of manpower for agricultural production. The landowners, instead of investing in the agricultural sector and alleviating the situation, worsened the problem by obliging the peasant to cultivate the farm in the same way with no help in the form of finance or additional manpower, at a time when the attrition of war had its effect on harvests and livestock (Archivio Statale Gubbio, Fondo Notarile, vol. 1188, C. 42r). Consequently, the cultivated areas were not abandoned as in previous centuries, although the peasantry were placed under considerable pressure. The whole seventeenth century saw a number of economic cycles, the result of famine and war which are reflected in the contemporary agricultural contracts (Archivio Statale Gubbio, Fondo Notarile, vol. 1189, C. 146r). The patterns of cultivation did not change until the end of the eighteenth century, because of the technological stagnation of landowners unwilling to invest in agriculture and of the inadequate economic means of the peasantry. There was no investment in the new types of production required by the national markets.

It is fortunate that the 1760–9 *Catasto Ghelliano* give a detailed picture of the layout of vegetation and landuse at this stage before further radical changes in the landscape.[1] This record has been transcribed for a transect across a central portion of the valley to the south east of Gubbio (Fig. 1.3) to show the distribution of worked land (Fig. 2.14), meadow (Fig. 2.15), pasture/unworked land (Fig. 2.16), coarse pasture (Fig. 2.17) and woodland (Fig. 2.18). The patterns are clear. Arable land was concentrated in the valley bottoms, but considerable clearance had taken place over the whole width of the valley. Meadow (*prato*) was relatively rare and concentrated down along the river courses in the bottom of the valley. A low proportion was, however, distributed throughout the landscape, although with some tendency to avoid the major routeways. Abandoned land and low value pasture (*pascolo a sodo*) were located on the unstable slopes of the edge of the valley, even though many of these were easily accessible to the city. These slopes would have been relatively rocky, unfertile and subject to rapid run-off of water. Abandoned land was also to be found in the remoter areas of the lower part of the valley which would have been subject to flooding. Coarse pasture (*macchia*) was exclusively located on the marl-sandstone slopes of the southern edge of the valley. Finally woodland had been considerably reduced to small pockets on the edges of the Pleistocene terraces in the bottom of the valley and larger stretches on the limestone escarpment to the north.

The technological stagnation at the end of the eighteenth and beginning of the nineteenth century is reflected in the *mezzadria* contract which prevented the marked increase in agricultural production that took place in some other parts of Italy. Only towards the beginning of the 1800s, with the introduction of new agricultural techniques and new agricultural tools, was there a real, if weak, agrarian transformation in common with the whole of Italy. One side effect was the collection of prehistoric artefacts from these newly ploughed lands (Pagliari 1885). A new pressure was the construction of the railways through the Apennines which contemporary records from the Marche estimate consumed a third of the remaining oak forests (Biondi 1982). The destruction of the forests has continued up to the present day as shown by a comparison of the 1893 and 1952 editions of the IGM map of the Padule area within the Gubbio Valley. A 47% reduction occurred in the intervening years (Biondi *et al.* 1990: 214).

2.3.4 Comparisons with records elsewhere in central Italy

Recent years have seen the emergence of a strong body of research on Late Pleistocene and Holocene climate and vegetational change in Lazio with the publication of detailed pollen cores from Castiglione (Alessio *et al.* 1986; Follieri *et al.* 1988), Martignano (Kelly and Huntley

1991) and the Agro Pontino (Hunt and Eisner 1991; Hunt 1992). With the exception of the Agro Pontino study, from a coastal graben in limestone country, all of this research is from volcanic crater lakes. There is some evidence that the well-drained volcanic country in Lazio had a distinctly unusual floral development at times, when compared with records from limestone areas (Hunt and Eisner 1991). It is also probable that the steep sides of some volcanic crater lakes were not exploited agriculturally until as late as the medieval period and thus the course of early farming is not clear at all these sites. There are also problems with the dating of some sites (Kelly and Huntley 1991) and with the continuity of some of the sequences. Hunt (1992) has suggested that the coldest phases of the last glacial period are represented by non-sequences in most sites in central Italy. Alternative sources of information on the palaeoenvironment of the last glacial period include studies of slope-waste deposits (for instance Coltorti *et al.* 1983), alluvial deposits (Gilbertson and Hunt 1987) and loess sequences (Cremaschi 1979).

In the central Apennines, Holocene pollen diagrams are still rare, but are known from the Colfiorito Plateau (Bonomi Ponzi 1985; Marchesoni 1959; Paganelli 1956, 1958). There is also recent work in the Ligurian Apennines (Cruise 1991; Lowe and Watson 1992). In southern Italy, the work of Watts (1985) provides a detailed environmental sequence. In the Molise, Holocene landscape changes ascribed to human activity have been described by Hunt (in preparation).

There are clear indications from the palaeoenvironmental research carried out by the Gubbio project that the general climatic pattern registered elsewhere in central Italy also applied to the Gubbio Basin. Steppe-like vegetation is widely registered during the last glacial period (Bonatti 1966, 1970; Frank 1969; Follieri *et al.* 1988; Hunt and Eisner 1991). Slope-waste deposits in the Apennines point to intermittent periglacial conditions at this time (Coltorti *et al.* 1983) and these are widespread around the Gubbio Basin.

Major climatic ameliorations with forest development are known from the early part of the last glacial period (Follieri *et al.* 1988) and are probably reflected by

[1] The following catastal regions from the centre of the Valley of Gubbio were transcribed by Rachel Fulton: La Villa d'Anciano (Bastardello 5, surveyed in 1761), Villa Monticelli (Bastardello 23, surveyed in 1763), Villa di S. Erasmo (Bastardello 4, surveyed in 1760–1), Parocchia di S. Agostino (Bastardello 4), S. Viturino (Bastardello 32, surveyed in 1765), S. Giustino (Bastardello 32), S. Margherita del Condoto (Bastardello 5), Barco (Bastardello 3, surveyed in 1760). The catastal survey was closed in 1768 or 1769 and the archival maps were produced in 1770.

Worked land

0   500   1000 metre

Town of Gubbio

Fig. 2.14 Landuse taken from early registration records. The
distribution of worked land. White = <25%; Light stipple = 25–50%;
Heavy stipple = 50–75%; Black = >75%

Meadow

0   500   1000 metre

Town of Gubbio

Fig. 2.15 Landuse taken from early registration records. The distribution of meadow. White = <25%; Light stipple = 25–50%; Heavy stipple = 50–75%; Black = >75%

Pasture and unworked land

0   500   1000 metre

Town of Gubbio

Fig. 2.16 Landuse taken from early registration records. The
distribution of Pasture and unworked land. White = <25%; Light
stipple = 25–50%; Heavy stipple = 50–75%; Black = >75%

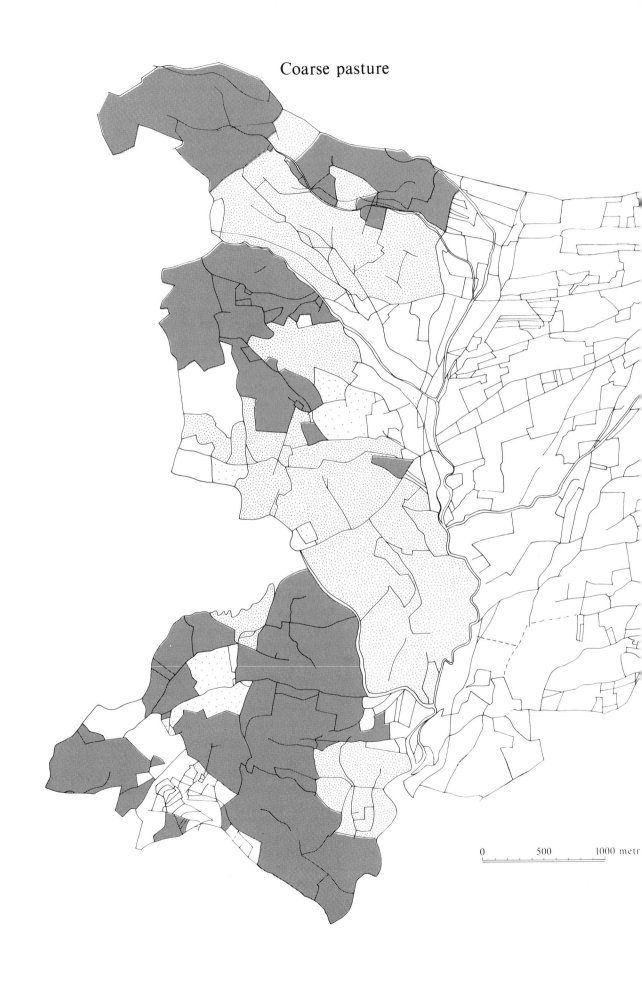

Coarse pasture

0   500   1000 metr

Fig. 2.17 Landuse taken from early registration records. The distribution of coarse pasture (*macchia*). White = <25%; Light stipple = 25–50%; Heavy stipple = 50–75%; Black = >75%

Woodland

0   500   1000 metr

Town of Gubbio

Fig. 2.18 Landuse taken from early registration records. The distribution of woodland. White = <25%; Light stipple = 25–50%; Heavy stipple = 50–75%; Black = >75%

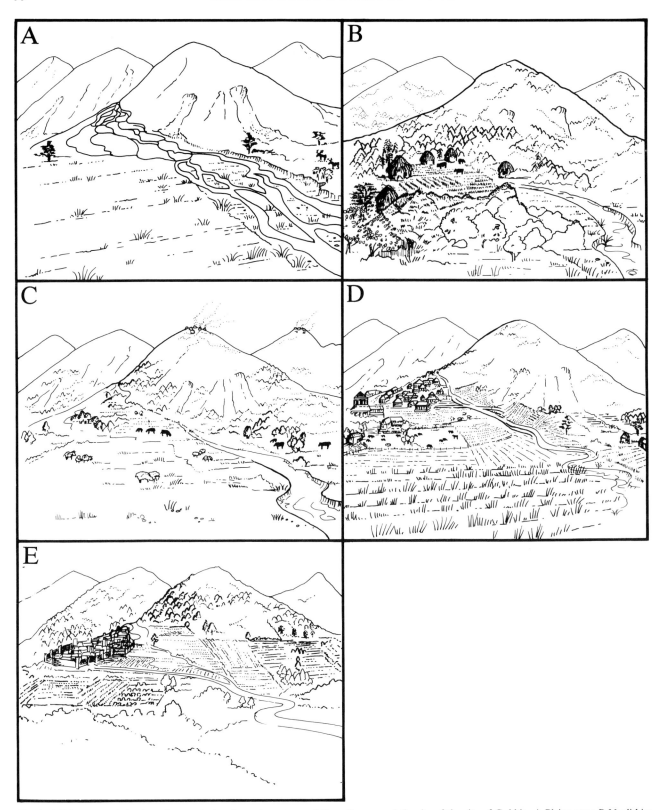

Fig. 2.19 Diagrammatic landuse changes during the various stages of the valley around the site of the city of Gubbio. A Pleistocene; B Neolithic; C Bronze Age; D Roman; E Medieval

palaeosols at San Felicissimo and Sant' Agostino in the Gubbio Basin. A series of weak ameliorations have been postulated from the middle part of the glacial period (Watts 1985; Follieri et al. 1988) but correlation between sites is uncertain. At Gubbio, one certain cool forest phase and possibly others in this period are known from San Felicissimo.

During the latest part of the last glaciation the climate was very cool and dry until approximately 14,000 BP (Hunt and Eisner 1991). Around this time, temperatures rose significantly, but continuing drought prevented the wide spread of forest vegetation. The late Glacial Stadial is very poorly known in Italy, but Hunt and Eisner (1991) suggest that around 12,000 BP the climate deteriorated sharply. There was a short, cold–humid phase, then a minor amelioration followed by a further phase of intense cold and aridity. The environmental record in the Gubbio Basin is not detailed enough to show all these events clearly.

The early Holocene was warm and dry enough to prevent the spread of forest vegetation at low altitude for more than 2,000 years (Hunt and Eisner 1991; Hunt 1992). In the Gubbio Basin near Raggio, a peat deposit of early Holocene age has yielded pollen evidence for park woodland with stands of pine, spruce, willow and birch, which is compatible, once altitudinal effects have been considered, with the evidence for oak-dominated park woodland from low altitude (Hunt and Eisner 1991).

Eventually the climate became sufficiently moist for closed woodland to develop. In the lowlands, this forest was dominated by oak although pine was important in the first phase of forest development and other broad-leaved trees rapidly became significant (Alessio et al. 1986; Hunt and Eisner 1991; Kelly and Huntley 1991). The precise pattern of forest development at this time is site dependent, so few generalisations can be made. At higher altitude, the early forests, for instance on the nearby Colfiorito plateau, were often rich in pine. These woods were invaded by chestnut, then oak, hazel, ash and small hornbeam (Bonomi Ponzi 1985; Paganelli, 1956, 1958; Marchesoni 1959). Little trace of these forests has been found in the Gubbio Basin, though a Holocene forest soil with woodland molluscs was found at San Felicissimo and tufas with broad-leaved tree leaf casts, forest molluscs and a little pollen indicative of broad-leaved forest were found stratified below the Neolithic site at San Marco.

The pattern of Neolithic invasion and exploitation of the inland forests is very variable. Early Neolithic phases are rarely clear in pollen diagrams (Kelly and Huntley 1991; Hunt and Eisner 1991) and it is probable that large-scale (semi-) permanent vegetation disturbance only occurred in most areas during the Bronze Age (Hunt in

press). From that time onward, the landscape was probably largely vegetationally 'modern' during settlement expansion phases, though significant forest regeneration took place rapidly and repeatedly during episodes of diminished human activity (Gilbertson and Hunt 1987; Hunt et al. 1992). The pattern of floral development after the early Neolithic is intensely localised across central Italy, reflecting different types, levels and chronologies of landscape exploitation no doubt determined by local cultural and economic factors. Although various authors have postulated periods of more or less humid climate and consequent rising and falling lake levels in central Italy during the Holocene (for example Segre 1990: 181–2), a recent review (Hunt 1992) demonstrates that lake-level variation is not consistent even within Lazio, nor is lake-level change unequivocally linked with climate change.

In the Gubbio Basin, although remarkably early Neolithic farming took place at San Marco and probably on other similar sites, its effects seem to have been very localised. Only in the Bronze Age do we see the consequences of large-scale agricultural clearance on the slopes around the basin, notably at San Agostino where a slope-waste unit of Bronze Age date extends over a kilometre around the mountainside. As has been noted elsewhere in Italy and around the Mediterranean (Gilbertson and Hunt 1987; Hunt et al. 1992; Hunt in press; Bell 1982), the disruption of soils and vegetation by agriculture led to massive soil erosion and colluviation, not only on the steep margins of the basin, but also on the low-angle slopes of the basin floor, as for instance at San Marco, where the Neolithic site is buried by up to a metre of silty colluvium. From evidence elsewhere in Italy (Hunt in press b), the early Roman period was a time of agricultural expansion and intensification in localities suitable for large-scale farming. This was probably the case in the Gubbio Basin, but there is no unequivocal environmental evidence for its effects.

Local comparisons become much easier, once study of vegetation proceeds into the medieval and modern periods. Comparable studies of documentary sources have been made for the nearby Apennine valley of Fabriano (Biondi 1982). A similar pattern of cyclic expansion and retraction of cultivated areas can be detected, confirming the general pattern of the Gubbio area. The rich monastic and other documents of the Casentino Valley of the upper Arno, some 80 km to the north-west, have provided an even more detailed tapestry of historical ecology from, at first sight, a similar landscape (Cherubini 1984; Wickham 1988). A closer examination, however, shows this valley to be both much more mountainous and lacking an important city as its major focus, unless one includes

Arezzo which lies outside the valley itself. The eleventh century documents, although giving indications of a varied landscape, make considerable reference to woodland. The emphasis on forestry increased into the late Medieval period, and was combined with pastoralism as the major landuse of the area. The probable late development of pastoralism is an important point, given the immemorial status often accorded to it (Wickham 1988: 164). By contrast, the Gubbio Basin appears to have had a much more mixed and varied vegetational cover.

3 THE FIRST HUMAN OCCUPATION AND THE TRANSITION TO AGRICULTURE

3.1 The evidence of lithics

3.1.1 The nature of the evidence

The surface survey undertaken between 1983 and 1987 recovered a total of 5,241 pieces of worked stone of which 870 were tools and 431 cores. The collection is, therefore, quite small by comparison with most excavations and each location consists of a small number of finds or even of a single piece. The largest single collection of tools from one area was 154 from the later excavated site of San Marco (area 325), but since this site was surveyed over two years (1985 and 1986), care has to be taken when comparing the location directly with other distributions in the valley. None of these other distributions are comparable since the next richest locality (area 301) produced 134 artefacts (of which only 27 were tools). This number of finds may also be approached if closely related localities are lumped together. This approach gives 120 pieces of worked stone for area 174 and 93 pieces for area 53. The poverty of each location (once the effects of previous research, sampling by the current project, vegetational cover and geomorphology have been considered) might suggest that few, if any long-term settlement sites have been discovered and that, prior to the Neolithic, occupation of the Gubbio Valley was sporadic. This record contrasts with other valleys in Umbria where thousands of pieces may be collected in a single day (Coltorti pers. comm.; Calzoni 1928; Galiberti 1982), but is not unusual on other surface surveys in central Italy, including the Agro Pontino survey in coastal Lazio (Loving and Kammermans 1991).

Given the nature of the lithic collections, therefore, the most appropriate means of describing the material is by generalised typo-chronology. The collections can be divided into four main groups: the Middle Palaeolithic, the Upper and Epi-Palaeolithic, the Neolithic and the Later Prehistoric. The divisions between these typological groups is not always clear, particularly when dealing with such small collections but these are broad enough to permit a generalised discussion of the prehistory of the valley.

Table 3.1 presents the richest sites, the number of tools recovered from them and the features used to assign them a typological date.

3.1.2 The Middle Palaeolithic (Figs 3.1–3.2; Tables 3.1–3.2)

This period dates between 210,000–35,000 years ago and typologically similar industries can occur at extreme ends of this range. It is, therefore, difficult to date the initial occupation of the valley, but the following points may be helpful in suggesting a date between 120,000–80,000 years for this.

Firstly, this is the time range during which climatic conditions would be most favourable to an upland occupation. Although the Gubbio area was never glaciated, the glacial periods would have been marked by harsh periglacial conditions which have left their morphological effect in the valley (section 2.1). Visits to the valley are likely to have been of short duration and probably seasonal if they occurred during cooler times. The record of the valley probably represents the summer visits of small foraging and hunting parties which began in the interglacial.

Secondly, an argument for dating this phase to 105,000–80,000 years ago could be made on the basis of the wind gloss on some of the stone tools of this period. This gloss is produced by wind-blown particles abrading the exposed surfaces of discarded implements. Several Middle Palaeolithic pieces show this, including the larger biface, where the glossing is restricted to certain parts of the artefact surface. This could support the argument that vegetation cover was poor at the time of tool discard, permitting the sand-blasting and strong winds may have been associated with the onset of the Last Glacial at about 105,000 BP. The initial stadial of the Last Glacial was relatively mild until 80,000 BP and so little change in the patterns of hominid movement and occupation would have been necessary at this time. Visits to the Gubbio Valley in summer would probably become more sporadic during

Table 3.1. *List of areas with more than five characteristic pieces*

Area number	Number of tools and cores	Characteristic types
Middle Palaeolithic		
52	10	Levallois core, side and end scrapers, denticulate
53	25	Biface, Levallois cores, side scrapers, burins, Tayac point
56	9	Side scraper, denticulates, notches
62	5	Levallois flake, side scraper, burin, denticulate
66	9	Levallois core, side and end scrapers, denticulate
92	5	Levallois core, side scrapers, burin
93	6	Levallois point, side scrapers, burin, notch
111	7	Side and end scrapers, notches
174	34	Disc and Levallois cores, Levallois flakes, Mousterian points, side scrapers, burins, pseudo-Levallois points, backed knife
210	11	Disc cores, Levallois flake, side scrapers, notches and denticulates
232.01	5	Levallois core and flakes, Mousterian point, denticulate
236	12	Disc cores, side and end scrapers, truncations
240	6	Side and end scrapers
241	5	Mousterian point, side scrapers, denticulate
301	34	Levallois core, point and flake, side scrapers
309	5	Backed knife, notch, denticulate, end scraper
312	6	Side and end scraper
313	11	Levallois core, limace, side and endscapers
614	7	Side scrapers, denticulates, notches.
690	5	Levallois flake, side scrapers, burin, denticulate
703	7	Side scrapers, burins, notches
704	8	Side scrapers, denticulates, notches, truncation
755	6	Side scrapers, truncations
776	5	Disc core, side scrapers, notches
Upper and Epi-Palaeolithic areas		
53	6	Blades, end scrapers
694	7	Blades, end scrapers, burins, core scraper
703	8	Blades, end scrapers
704	8	Blade core, blades, carinate scraper
773	28	Blades, end scrapers, side scrapers, blade core
776	16	Blades, end scrapers, side scrapers, blade core
Neolithic (bladelet) areas		
7	8	Truncated and backed bladelets, bladelets and blades
63	5	Microblade core, bladelets, blade
325	290	Microblade cores, retouched blades, bladelets, blades
773	22	Microblade cores, bladelets, retouched bladelets, blades
776	13	bladelets

this time and cease with the onset of full glacial conditions after 80,000 BP.

Thirdly, study of soils by Dutch soil scientists working with the project has suggested that "woodland surfaces represent Pleistocene surfaces" (Schomaker and Van Waveren 1984, 20) in the Branca region. The Middle Palaeolithic collections come principally from just below these surfaces. Provided this stratigraphic interpretation of surface material is correct, the artefacts are, therefore, older than the terrace formation. Such terrace formation is probably associated with either a glacial or stadial and so the Middle Palaeolithic at Branca would pre-date 120,000 years BP or post-date 105,000 years BP. This does not take account of tectonics, however, which probably means the situation is more complex. Furthermore, it does not allow for the possibility that the artefacts may be younger than the deposits in which they are now found, which might be the case if processes such as deflation had taken place.

A final comment on the dating of the Middle Palaeolithic material is that it is almost entirely produced on flint from the R4 member of the Scaglia Rossa – a unit found in the surrounding limestone hills. The artefacts are mostly made on river cobbles and so a gravel source is suggested. Later material includes much more material from the *Majolica* unit which underlies the *Scaglia Rossa*. The R4 flint that does occur in the later collections appears to be generally smaller than the preceding Middle Palaeolithic material. It is possible, therefore, that this use of flint shows selection according to availability and that the Middle Palaeolithic precedes the phase of downcutting that incorporated the Majolica flint into river gravel. Study of the river gravels extant in the southern part of the valley may be informative in this respect.

In summary, arguments can be made for the Middle Palaeolithic of the Gubbio Valley to date between 210,000–25,000 years BP, with a probable increase in the frequency of sporadic visits by people in the range between 120,000–80,000 years BP.

The raw materials used during the Middle Palaeolithic were almost exclusively local river gravels, although

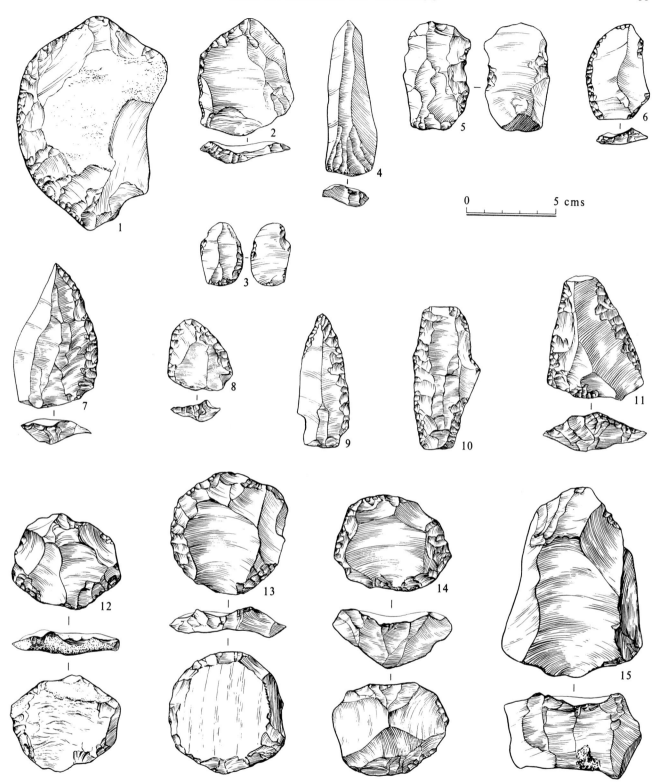

Fig. 3.1 Middle Palaeolithic tools and cores. (Drawn by John Wymer on the basis of originals by Tim Reynolds.) 1 Side scraper (Site 301); 2 Side scraper (Site 301); 3 Side scraper (Site 235.02); 4 Levallois blade (Site 301) 5 Denticulate (Site 210); 6 Backed knife (Site 54.02); 7 Side scraper (Site 174); 8 Side scraper (Site 66.01); 9 Side scraper (Site 53); 10 Side scraper (Site 53); 11 Broken Mousterian point (Site 174); 12 Disc core (Site 173); 13 Levallois core (Site 211); 14 Levallois core (Site 192); 15 Levallois core (Site 301)

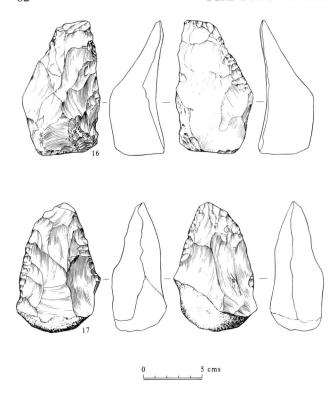

0   5 cms

Fig. 3.2 Middle Palaeolithic bifaces. (Drawn by John Wymer on the basis of originals by Tim Reynolds.) 16 Middle Palaeolithic biface (Site 52.02); 17 Middle Palaeolithic biface (Site 53.02)

occasional pieces of quartzite and silicified shale occur. These may also occur in the river gravels but their source is otherwise exotic. One interesting aspect of the Middle Palaeolithic technology is that there is no evidence for *in situ* manufacture of handaxes in the valley. No handaxe trimming flakes were recovered at either the handaxe bearing localities or elsewhere in the valley. Since these trimmers are produced in some numbers anywhere where regular handaxe production is taking place, it is suggested that the handaxes were imports from outside the study areas. The Branca terraces were a known collection point of handaxes to collectors from early times (see the museum collections in Perugia museum) and collecting activity may have had a particularly profound effect on this class of artefact. Only two broken examples were found from this prime area.

Despite the lack of evidence for biface production, the Middle Palaeolithic finds between them do show all the stages of lithic reduction: primary (cortical) flakes, flake blanks, éclats débordants, cores, flake tools and platform edge rejuvenation flakes have all been recovered. Of the more patterned forms of core reduction both disc and Levallois cores are represented but most of the cores are smaller than the flake tools collected. Reduction of cores

is, therefore, taken to very economic limits. It is possible that the disc and Levallois strategies are related with the Levallois core being the product of a single major removal off the surface of an otherwise disc core. Once a piece falls below a certain size such single removals are more useful in producing the largest possible flake. These two strategies may perhaps be better viewed as variants of the same approach to core treatment. A number of Kombewa flakes were recovered and also a number of cores on flakes, both of which would suggest reduction techniques aimed at the maximum use of the flint available. Additionally, the proportion of double side scrapers to single side scrapers is also high, perhaps suggesting refreshing of tool edges to conserve a piece within the tool kit and also a maximum use of the edges of the blanks produced. A number of tools have been made on broken flake fragments and shatterpieces. This economy in the use of flint would be appropriate if visits to the Gubbio Valley were short and involved small numbers of people because it would permit increased mobility and requires less time investment in the extraction of basic raw materials.

The finds of Middle Palaeolithic material from the Gubbio Valley match those of earlier collections held at the Perugia museum and those from elsewhere in Umbria (Coltorti pers. comm.) where Levallois-rich industries with well-made scrapers and points are common, and assemblages lacking such fine pieces using thicker blanks and Quina retouch also occur. The relationship between these two assemblage forms is not clear. In Gubbio, both types of industry are represented, but as collections are so small it is not certain whether they existed synchronously in different parts of the valley, as two aspects of a single occupation or whether they are chronologically isolated. In terms of technology, the latter assemblage grouping would appear to represent a later stage of reduction and a more economic use of flint.

The collections are too small to discuss the material in terms of Bordes' assemblage variants (Bordes 1961). However, type fossils of an Acheulean tradition are present, while side scrapers clearly dominate the flake tool assemblage.

The distribution of Middle Palaeolithic findspots is pre-eminently geomorphological (Fig. 3.5). The main concentrations of artefacts were found on the three major Pleistocene terrace formations of the valley: the Branca area in the south-east, the Ponte d'Assi terrace in the centre and the uplifted Massa terrace in the north of the valley. The relatively rare finds outside these well circumscribed locations probably represent penetration of the late Pleistocene and Holocene alluvial fans by various forms of agricultural disturbance (including irrigation works). The relative density of material from the Branca

Table 3.2. *Middle Palaeolithic assemblage composition for selected areas*

Area	Number of pieces	Cores		Tools		Blank character	
53	93	Levallois	3	Side scrapers	9	Prepared platform	4
		Disc	1	Notches	3	Flakes	70
		Informal	13	End scrapers	3	Blades	7
				Burins	1	Bladelets	0
				Piercers	1		
				Tayac points	1		
				Bifaces	1		
		Total	17	Total	19		
174	120	Levallois	1	Side scrapers	17	Prepared platform	19
		Disc	2	Mousterian points	3	Flakes	70
		Informal	2	Notches	1	Blades	6
				Backed knives	1	Bladelets	3
				Levallois flakes	5		
				End scrapers	1		
				Burins	2		
				Pseudo-Levallois point	1		
		Total	5	Total	31		
301	134	Levallois	4	Side scrapers	15	Prepared platform	11
		Disc	3	Notches	3	Flakes	106
		Informal	10	Denticulates	1	Blades	4
		Blade	1	Backed knives	2	Bladelets	0
				Levallois point	1		
				Levallois flake	1		
				End scrapers	1		
				Pseudo-Levallois point	1		
		Total	18	Total	25		

area (about 60% of the tools/cores) does, though, tentatively suggest a behavioural pattern that surfaces from the prominent post-depositional distortions of the evidence. It is no accident that this location is the major point of access to the valley and a major intersection point with the Gualdo Tadino Valley to the south.

3.1.3 The Upper Palaeolithic – Epi-Palaeolithic (Fig. 3.3; Tables 3.1 and 3.3)

The identification of smaller-scale traditions within this phase is problematic as the earliest Upper Palaeolithic industries in Italy, the Ulluzian and the Aurignacian, both include microlithic elements which could be mistaken for the products of the final Upper Palaeolithic and Epi-Palaeolithic industries. This problem compounds that of small collections to make the attribution of localities to cultures worthless. The richest Upper Palaeolithic collections are from areas 773 and 776 with 74 and

70 pieces respectively. No other Upper Palaeolithic collection comprises more than 35 pieces. The material from areas 773 and 776 is presented in Table 3.3, while the evidence for the Upper Palaeolithic phase in the Gubbio Valley can be evaluated from Table 3.1.

The evidence of this phase indicates no greater exploitation of the valley than in the previous Middle Palaeolithic. Indeed the evidence suggests the reverse. This may, however, be a product of the greater length of time occupied by the Middle Palaeolithic and a matter of exposure, since the Pleistocene terraces, the major relict landscape in a stratigraphic position to produce Middle Palaeolithic material, were almost completely covered by the survey. Generally, the Upper Palaeolithic is marked by an increase in site numbers and density of material when compared with the preceding phase, but this does not happen in the case of the Gubbio Valley. Allowing for the potential over-representation of the Middle Palaeolithic, it would appear that the Gubbio Valley was at best still

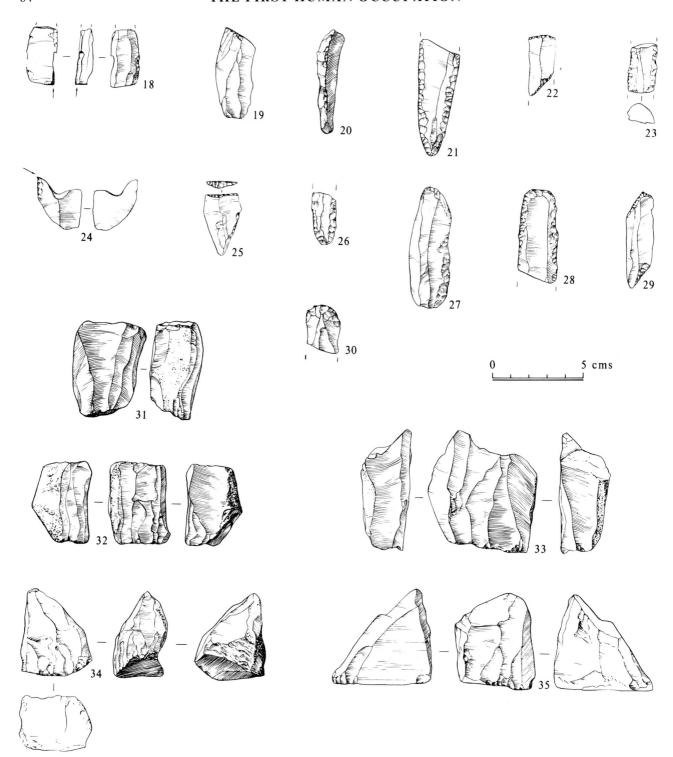

Fig. 3.3 Upper and Epi-Palaeolithic tools and cores. (Drawn by John Wymer on the basis of originals by Tim Reynolds.) 18 Burin (Site 239); 19 Blade from an opposed platform core (Site 253.03); 20 Partially vested blade (Site 978.01); 21 Retouched point on a blade (Site 1271); 22 End scraper on truncated blade (Site 911); 23 Double end scraper on a blade (Site 116); 24 End scraper on a retouched blade (Site 95.01); 25 End scraper on a retouched blade (Site 26.04); 26 Double end scraper on a blade (Site 310); 27 End scraper on a retouched blade (Site 95.01); 28 End scraper on a retouched blade (Site 94); 29 Double obliquely truncated blade (Site 1279); 30 End scraper (Site 1271.02); 31 Blade core on cobble (Site 1023); 32 Blade core on cobble (Site 210); 33 Blade core on cobble (Site 94); 34 Pyramidal blade core (Site 111); 35 Pyramidal blade core (Site 254.02)

Table 3.3. *Upper and Epi-Palaeolithic assemblage composition for selected areas*

Area	Number of pieces	Cores		Tools		Blank character	
773	74	Blade	1	End scrapers	2	Blades	8
		Bladelet	1	Side scrapers	4	Bladelets	20
		Informal	1	Notches	1	Flakes	39
		Scraper	1	Denticulates	2		
				Burins	3		
				Piercers	2		
				Retouched blades	2		
				Microliths	1		
				Blade elements	1		
				Points	1		
				Truncated blades	2		
				Retouched blades	3		
		Total	4	Total	24		
776	70	Blade	1	End scrapers	1	Blade	3
		Informal	1	Side scrapers	2	Bladelets	14
		Micro-	1	Notches	4	Flakes	25
				Burins	2		
				Retouched blades	1		
				Retouched bladelets	1		
				Backed bladelets	1		
		Total	3	Total	13		

only subject to occasional short-term, low-intensity visits and there is no clear evidence that this occurred prior to the maximum of the last Glacial at 18,000 years BP. So it may be that the improving conditions of the late Pleistocene and the early Holocene saw use of the valley by Epi-Palaeolithic and Mesolithic bands of hunter-gatherers. Areas 773 and 776 are characterised by a mixture of blade and bladelet production. Retouched tools are rare, but amongst these scrapers, burins and notched pieces are typical. Blade cores were prepared by the cresting technique. Intensive use of raw materials may be suggested by the presence of core tablets produced during the rejuvenation of blade and bladelet cores. The pieces in this collection are smaller in all dimensions than the Middle Palaeolithic material and a greater variety of flint types has been used. No selection of a particular type of flint for tool support or blank production can be detected. Most stages of reduction are present, suggesting *in situ* knapping. All materials used are of local origin.

The distribution of Upper Palaeolithic and Epi-Palaeolithic findspots is more extensive than the preceding Middle Palaeolithic. At the Branca end of the valley, the upper surface of the main Pleistocene terrace continues to be an important location, but the alluvial fans at the end of the valley are equally favoured. The preference for

occupation of alluvial fans is particularly emphasised by the finds in the mid part of the Monte Semonte transect which represent a major increase compared with the preceding phase. Unfortunately the main factor behind the distribution of these finds is geomorphological and of greater assistance in dating the morphology of the terrain than inferring cultural behaviour.

3.1.4 Neolithic (Fig. 3.4; Table 3.4)

Neolithic industries were identified by collections of bladelets and specialised bladelet cores such as those associated with the Neolithic site of San Marco. The site is more fully discussed elsewhere (Malone and Stoddart 1992), but as the site provides the only sizeable assemblage, it will be used to discuss the other areas. In addition, the San Marco area provided the largest single surface collection of the survey. The surface material comprised a total of 1,638 pieces including 154 tools and 136 cores.

The Neolithic industry is a predominantly microblade assemblage with the majority of cores showing single platforms, small-size and fine fluted facets. These features occur on the very smallest pieces and chest punches and devices for holding the cores would have been required. Whether the industry represents the work of a few

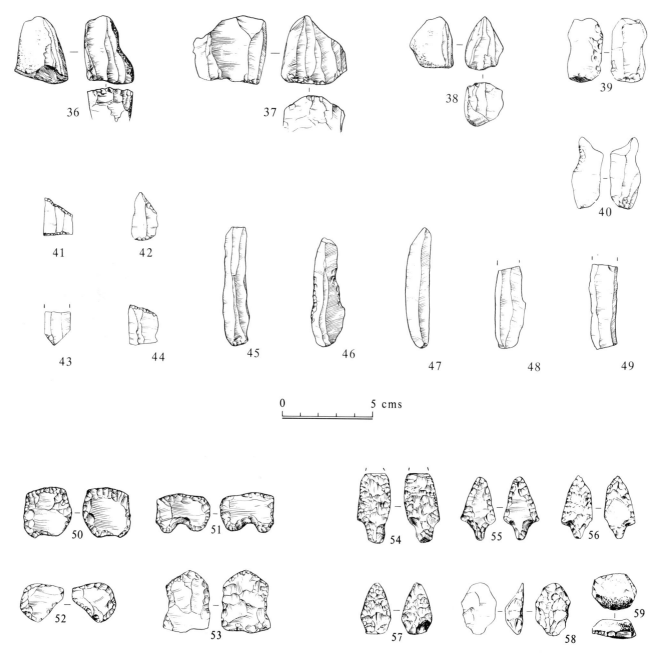

0   5 cms

Fig. 3.4 Post-Palaeolithic cores, blades, arrowheads and tools. (Drawn by John Wymer on the basis of originals by Tim Reynolds.) 36 Bladelet core (San Marco Neolitico (325)); 37 Bladelet core (San Marco Neolitico (325)); 38 Bladelet core (San Marco Neolitico (325)); 39 Flake scraper (San Marco Neolitico (325)); 40 Retouched notch (San Marco Neolitico (325)); 41 Bitruncated blade (San Marco Neolitico (325)); 42 Bitruncated blade (San Marco Neolitico (325)); 43 Truncated and snapped blade (San Marco Neolitico (325)); 44 Truncated and snapped blade (San Marco Neolitico (325)); 45 Blade (San Marco Neolitico (325)); 46 Retouched blade (San Marco Neolitico (325)); 47 Blade (San Marco Neolitico (325)); 48 Blade (San Marco Neolitico (325)); 49 Blade (San Marco Neolitico (325)); 50 Gunflint (Site 1168); 51 Strike-a-light (Site 925); 52 Strike-a-light (Site 924); 53 Strike-a-light (Site 242.05); 54 Arrowhead (Site 235.02); 55 Arrowhead (Site 236); 56 Arrowhead (Site 109.01); 57 Arrowhead (Site 241); 58 Button scraper (Site 66); 59 Button scraper (Site 259.01)

specialist flint workers is difficult to determine; since the excavation only yielded secondary deposits in ditches, it was not possible to map knapping floors. In addition to the microblade industry, there is a series of well-made flake tools. Retouch is more commonly applied to the flake component than to the microblade component when the relative frequency is considered. The details of the San Marco assemblage are given in Table 3.4. The other Neolithic areas in the valley had similar material to the San Marco area, but never in the same quantity. The richest areas other than San Marco are 773 and 776 with 22 and 13 characteristic pieces respectively. Such pieces are bladelets and bladelet cores and overlap with earlier industries is possible; indeed there appears to have been both an Upper/Epi-Palaeolithic and Neolithic occupation at this location.

In general the Neolithic industries are refined with well-made and delicate bladelets and cores suggesting considerable investment of time in the preparation of materials. All pieces are small and raw material could have been obtained from the hills in thin slabs rather than from the river gravels. Materials do, however, resemble those found in the preceding Epi-Palaeolithic in terms of types and sources. The delicate microblades were probably used in composite tools and a series of backed and/or truncated microblades bearing sickle gloss implies that at least some were mounted in hafts for cutting cereals. A large part of the Neolithic flint is burnt. All stages of reduction are represented. As with other phases, the material is in keeping with other industries recovered from Umbria (Coltorti pers. comm.)

3.1.5 Later prehistoric

This phase is represented by a series of single finds comprising mostly bifacially retouched arrowheads. These are usually tanged but not barbed and at least two display clear signs of impact damage. They do not associate with any knapping debris and probably are the result of discard of broken pieces while hunting. A final series of pieces to note is that of four strike-a-lights/gunflints showing a continuing use of flint by man in the Gubbio valley until only a century ago.

3.1.6 The distribution of flint in the landscape

Contouring of the distribution of all types of struck flint within the transects across the valley summarises the trends described above at a more general level (Fig. 3.6). Almost all flint has been found on the alluvial formations of the valley and correspondingly very little flint has been

Table 3.4. *San Marco Neolithic site assemblages*

Type	A. Field survey material		B. Excavated material	
	Number	(%)	Number	(%)
All pieces	1638	100.00	4132	100.00
Tools	154	9.40	193	4.67
Cores	136	8.30	136	1.50
Flakes	625	38.15	1405	34.00
Blades	146	8.91	203	4.91
Bladelets	483	29.48	2230	53.96
Chips	108	6.59	232	5.61

Note:
Many burnt and shattered fragments are excluded from this summary. The overlap between types means that the sum of frequencies does not equal the total of pieces.

found on the largely eroded upper slopes of soils formed on limestone or marl-sandstone origin.

In the southerly Branca transect, most finds are Palaeolithic in date and thus found on the relict Palaeolithic terraces. Lesser quantities of material are found on the main alluvial fans and even smaller quantities on the heights above Branca itself. In the central transects, there are concentrations on the Ponte d'Assi Pleistocene terrace and very dense Neolithic concentrations on the later alluvial fans at their midpoint. In the case of the Neolithic period, it is much more difficult to determine whether the effect is geomorphological or behavioural (Fig. 3.7). The Semonte transect is subject to a very similar effect; a few major concentrations dominate the distributions on the alluvial fans. In this case, the dating is, however, broader since there appears to have been re-occupation of late Palaeolithic locations in the Neolithic. The northern (Loreto) transect is dominated by the presence of an elevated Pleistocene terrace with a corresponding major concentration of lithic material. These composite lithic distributions demonstrate clearly the complexity of the post-depositional effects. Only parts of the the alluvial fans can be claimed as broadly contemporary landscapes for the study of lithic distributions, almost exclusively of Neolithic or later date.

3.2 The transition to agriculture

Human settlement and landuse in the Gubbio Basin changed markedly during the sixth to fifth millennia BC. Agriculture was introduced in the form of cereal production and animal husbandry. For the first time, the subsistence economy began to have a profound effect on the landscape of the valley. Woodland clearance made way for cultivation,

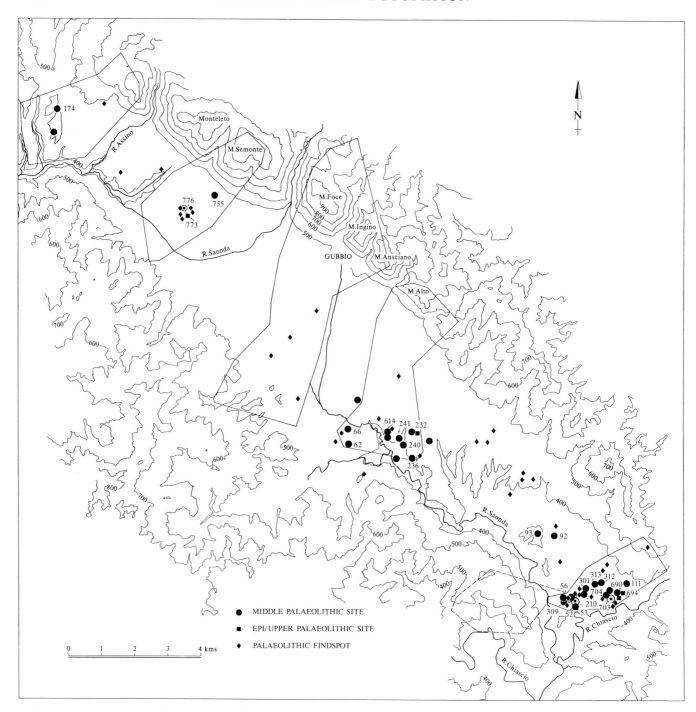

Fig. 3.5 Distribution of Palaeolithic locations in the valley

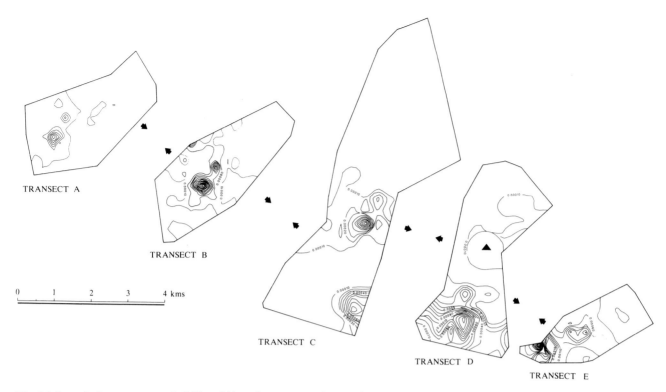

Fig. 3.6 Smoothed contour map of all flint within valley transects. Contour interval of 0.0001/m². Triangle represents peak of density on the surface of the excavated Neolithic site

and open-air settlements were constructed in the lower parts of the basin.

The survey of the basin produced clear evidence of Neolithic sites, with some two dozen concentrations of lithic and ceramic material (Fig. 3.7), and depending on the local geomorphological conditions, dark patches of soil associated with these clusters.

Three major clusters of Neolithic settlement focused on the lower ends of the alluvial fans which form the lower slopes between the steep limestone escarpment on the north side of the basin and the two Saonda rivers to the south. The northern cluster of sites below Monte Semonte consists of nine artefact concentrations over an area of about a square kilometre, situated on raised, light alluvial soils, drained on all sides by minor seasonal streams. Around the fringes of the sites numerous arrowheads were picked up, suggesting off-site hunting activities away from the settlements. South of the city of Gubbio, a second cluster of another nine sites focused on the southern tip of the extensive alluvial fan. Covering an area of about 1.3 km square, this cluster is as concentrated as the northern group. However, the sites are further from the Saonda rivers and their tributaries, and off-site hunting does not appear to have been important around the settlements. The southern cluster of sites is located on a much more elongated alluvial fan, extending south from Monte Alto towards the southern Saonda river. The sites are spread over a larger, more linear area, with the eleven sites situated on narrow alluvial ridges cut either side by small streams that flow from north to south across the fan. The present streams and their predecessors have left significant geomorphological features, which provide effective drainage in an otherwise low-lying area. The sites are often large scatters, almost merging into each other. The large site of San Marco is situated in the northern part of the cluster. Off-site hunting activities appear to have focused on the lowest part of the fan, overlooking the Saonda river and its banks. Numerous arrowheads were located in this zone. Another area of major off-site hunting took place at the south-east end of the valley, immediately above the Chiascio river, around the 400 m contour. Here in an area empty of all other evidence of Neolithic activity, numerous arrowheads indicate the importance of the area for hunting, and perhaps fowling and fishing. The antiquarian collections of Bellucci and Pagliari (1885), where provenances are known, confirm this impression: considerable logistical, off-site activity, represented by more than one hundred arrowheads, on the upland margins of the basin in places such as Serrabrunamonti.

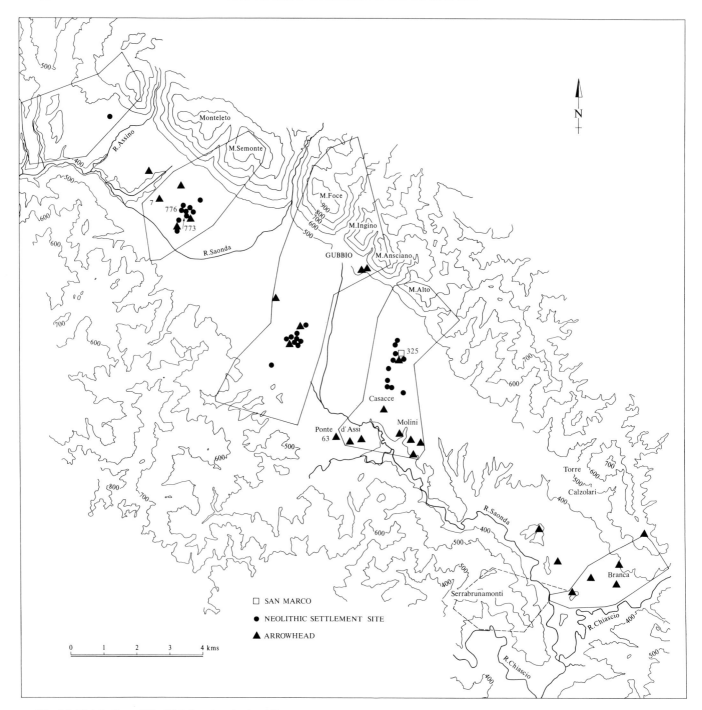

Fig. 3.7 Distribution of Neolithic locations in the valley

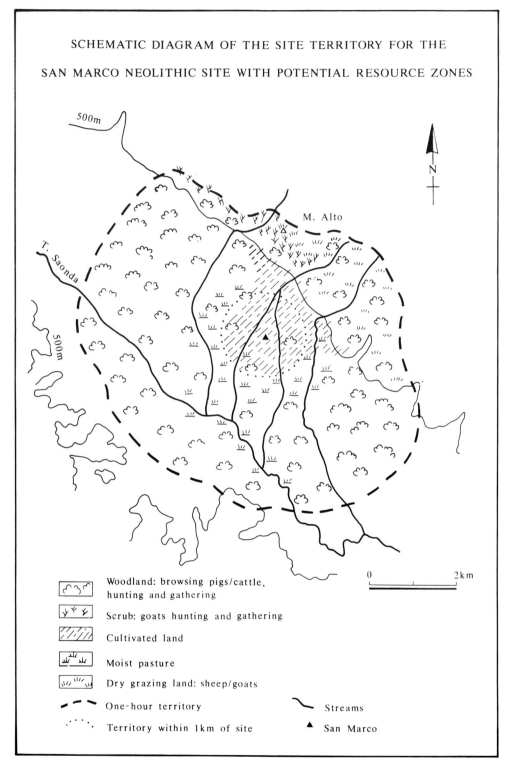

SCHEMATIC DIAGRAM OF THE SITE TERRITORY FOR THE
SAN MARCO NEOLITHIC SITE WITH POTENTIAL RESOURCE ZONES

Woodland: browsing pigs/cattle, hunting and gathering

Scrub: goats hunting and gathering

Cultivated land

Moist pasture

Dry grazing land: sheep/goats

One-hour territory

Territory within 1km of site

Streams

San Marco

Fig. 3.8 Catchment of the Neolithic site

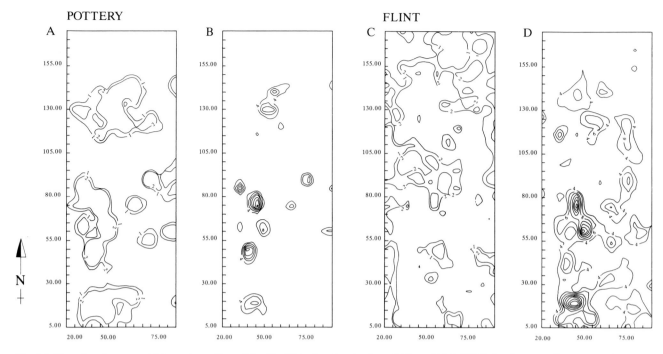

Fig. 3.9 Plot of surface material from the surface of the Neolithic site, showing low (A/B) and high (C/D) density areas. Fragments of pottery and flint per 25 m². A/C: contour interval of 1. B/D: Contour interval of 2

The largest and densest scatter of superficial Neolithic material was at the site of San Marco. Identified first through geomorphological work by M. Coltorti, who noted distinctive black soil stains in the ploughed field, the site was then subjected to intensive surface survey over two seasons in 1985–6 (Fig. 3.9). Pickups of material were plotted on a 5m grid across the field, together with plots of the dark soil patches, which were sampled by augering. This work suggested a close relationship between the dark soils and the artefacts.

Thirteen years before the excavation, the field had been deep trenched for a vineyard, with metre-deep parallel trenches scored across the subsoil of the field. Since that time, the vineyard had been abandoned, and annual ploughing for cereals disturbed only the top 45cm of the ploughsoil. The consequence of this disturbance was to make the underlying Neolithic deposits very visible on the surface of the field, more so than less disturbed, but other apparently comparable sites in the valley.

Geomorphological work on the site showed that prior to the Neolithic settlement of the area, the location had originally been a silted river channel. Environmental evidence showed that the understorey of the local broadleaf woodlands was wet, supporting ferns and orchids, but that nearby there were drier areas supporting plants such as juniper and grasses. The formation of travertine in the stream bed indicated slow-moving water with little surface

run-off due to the thick vegetation. Once the Neolithic community moved into the area, the landscape changed quite drastically. Pollen analysis shows that clearance took place, although substantial areas of woodland remained, with bracken and ferns covering open areas. Cereals were being grown nearby, as well as the weeds and grasses of cultivation. Molluscan evidence supports this picture, indicating wooded and open areas around the site. In the late stages of the settlement, clearance appears to have continued, and the molluscan evidence suggests that the area immediately around the site was almost treeless.

The excavation was of modest size (Malone and Stoddart 1992), an 18m long by 3m wide trench with small extensions. Located over a particularly rich dark soil patch at the south end of the field, the excavation located a Neolithic ditch and a pit, both severely truncated by ploughing to within about 15–20 cm of the base (Fig. 3.10; Plate 3.1). Smaller and apparently later gullies crossed the ditch and pit. The upper 75–95 cm of deposit had been badly churned up through ploughing, clipping and rotating the underlying black ditch and pit fills into the ploughsoil (Fig. 3.12). No living floors or structures were found, as would be expected from the degree of disturbance to the site. Even the most substantial timber buildings would leave little trace a metre below ground level. However, the ditch and pit fills indicate that these features were closely

San Marco Neolitico

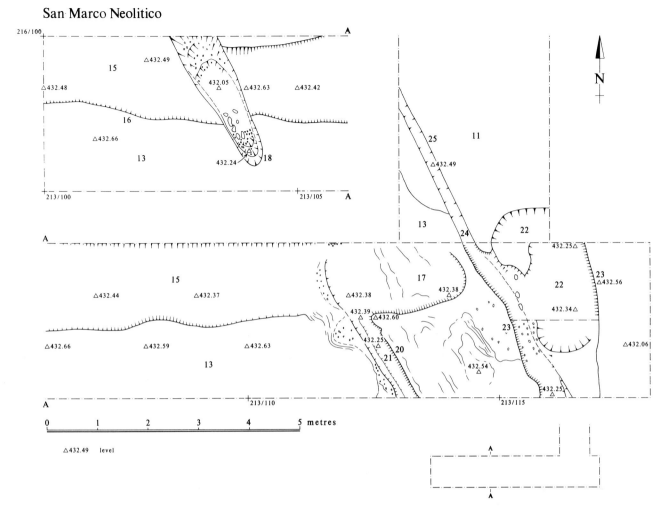

Fig. 3.10 Plan of the excavated Neolithic site showing ditch and location of contexts

connected to a settlement. Food debris including burnt refuse and animal carcasses, pottery, daub and lithic waste were thrown into the ditch and pit, which suggests that these features were certainly utilised at some stage of their life for rubbish disposal.

The pottery retrieved from the deposit was typical of the earlier Neolithic of north-east and central Italy, relating to Sasso Furbara and Fiorano ceramic styles. [14]C dates obtained from carbonised seeds and bone provide a secure chronology of the last years of the sixth and early fifth millennia BC (Table 1.1).

Several almost intact vessels were found in the ditch and restored (Fig. 3.11, 3.14–3.15). A typological study was made of the individual sherds, and 1,058 sherds were studied (excluding the whole pots), rims, bases, handles, lugs, fabric and decoration were all classified in a simple typological scheme which is reported more fully elsewhere

(Malone and Stoddart 1992). From the 500 rims found, vessels appear to have been small, with diameters of 25–30 cm, and tending towards a closed form, which may have been better for food storage. Bases were either rounded and connected to carinated shapes, or had heavy, footed, flat bases. Handles were generally of the flat strap type, and often large (45%). They were attached on or just below the rim. Of the 176 lugs, a wide range of types was found and examples from small protuberances on the body of the vessel to upstanding rim lugs were recorded. Often on larger sherds, both handles and lugs were found together, each having a separate function for lifting or stabilising the vessel. Decoration was relatively rare, and took the form of incised and impressed patterns scratched into the fabric when wet. Some impressions were crude fingertip and fingernail marks, typical of material from the Marche and Abruzzo. Other patterns were more

Plate 3.1 San Marco Neolitico under excavation

geometric and carefully executed, in the style of the Sasso–Fiorano styles. Fabric analysis indicated that decorated pottery was made of softer fabrics, and was more prone to disintegrating in the ploughsoil, so the 14% of decorated sherds found are no doubt under-represented in the assemblage. Many sherds were finished by smoothing the surface, others were burnished, and in one or two cases, may have had painted surfaces. Fabric analysis was initially done at a crude level, distinguishing 5 types, from coarse to fine. Subsequent macroscopic and thin section work by Skeates then divided the sample into 35 overlapping fabric groups. Survival of the different fabrics was very dependent on the hardness and porosity of the sherd and the type of temper used in its manufacture. Only one sherd appeared to be of material obtained from outside the valley, having volcanic sand as temper.

Other finds consisted of two examples of grindstones of local sandstone. A small square hammerstone was also found. Two soft sandstone objects may have formed tool tips, perhaps digging stick points. A finely pressure-flaked

arrowhead represents an example of the finer lithic technology. Personal ornament was simple, with a broken drilled pebble bead. Two flat fossil shell beads and a bone or tusk polished necklace spacer, a fossil cockle shell with a drilled hole and a clam shell formed the full extent of decorative objects. Bone tools made from sheep/goat bone were used as points and needles (Fig 3.13).

The lithic industry is predominantly microblade based, with single platform cores, small in size with delicately fluted facets. Knapping techniques would have employed chest punches and devices for holding the core. Apart from the microblades, a number of tools were made from retouch flakes. The whole industry would have required much care and preparation in selecting the raw material and making the delicate cores. Raw material is local chert and flint, obtained in slabs from the surrounding hills or from river gravels. The tool kit included awls, scrapers, notched blades, denticulates, burins, knives, microliths and backed blades. There is much resemblance between the preceding Epi-Palaeolithic industry and the Neolithic,

San Marco Neolitico

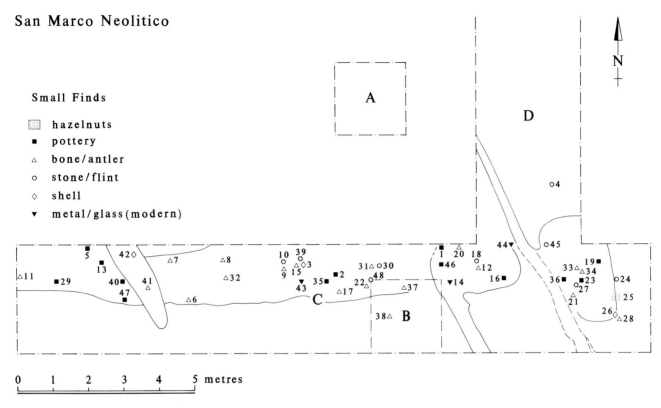

Fig. 3.11 Plot of small finds from the excavated Neolithic site

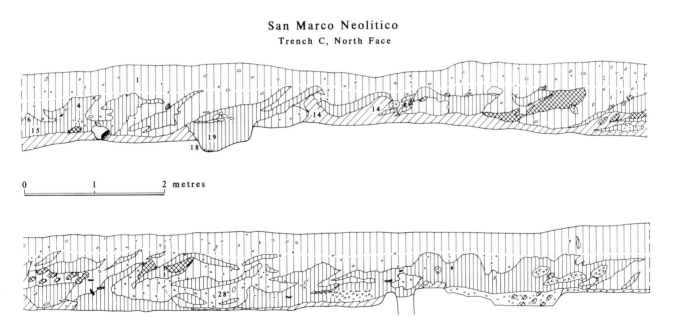

Fig. 3.12 Section of excavated Neolithic site, showing deposits overturned by plough (dense vertical lines)

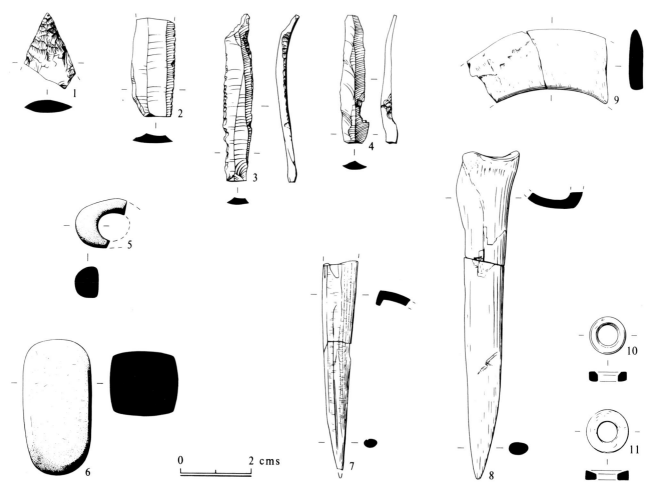

Fig. 3.13 Selection of small finds: 1-4 Flint; 5 Stone bead; 6 Polishing stone; 7-9 Bone; 10-11 Shell

with similar material and knapping techniques used. The microblades were probably used in composite tools, and a series of backed or truncated blades show evidence of sickle gloss, implying that the Neolithic farmers used the blades hafted in handles for cutting cereals or reeds. No polished stone was recorded, and neither was imported crystalline rock, suitable for polishing. Of the 5,770 lithic fragments retrieved from survey and excavation, 28% were from the surface of the field, and 72% from the excavation trench. Very small pieces indeed were found in sieving and hand excavation, chips and bladelets making up 59% of all the excavated lithics, in contrast to the 36% of all the survey lithics.

The excavation strategy was, in part, directed towards the retrieval of plant and animal remains, using a systematic programme of sampling.

Animal remains, whilst forming only a modest sample of 2,000 fragments, of which only 31.6% could be assigned to species, nevertheless provided an interesting record of the hunted and husbanded subsistence economy (Table 3.5).

Sheep and goat were the dominant species (38.1%) with both animals present. Mortality data suggest that there were at least two culling stages, with the animals slaughtered before the age of 24–36 months and after 48 months. Such a pattern might suggest that animals were kept for milk, meat and wool products.

Cattle, whilst less numerous than sheep/goat (30.6 %), probably represented the principal meat source. Many animals were kept beyond the age of 18 months, although some were culled at that stage and others at 28–36 months. Some cattle reached maturity, probably to provide secondary products and for breeding.

Pigs were much less important (18.7%) but, nevertheless, played a role in the subsistence economy. Some pigs were slaughtered before they reached a year old, others at

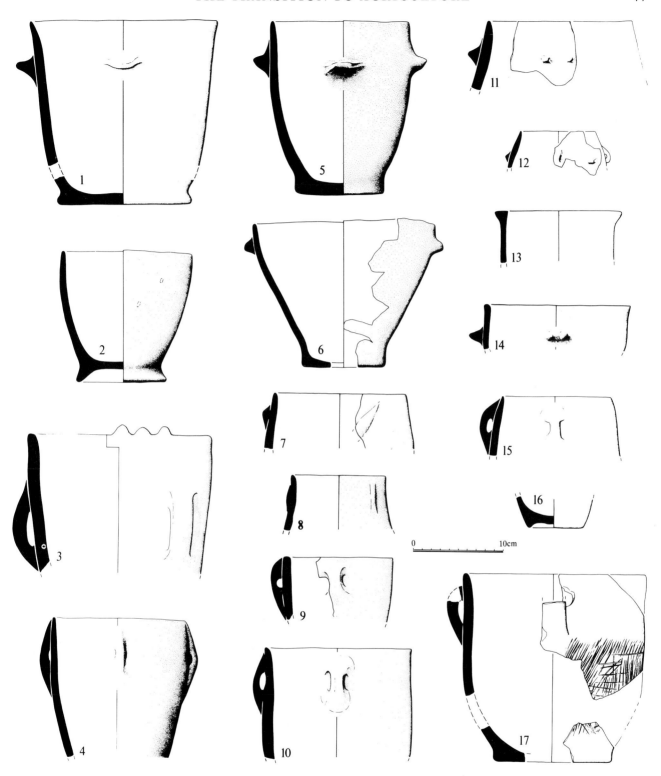

Fig. 3.14 Range of pottery forms from the Neolithic site

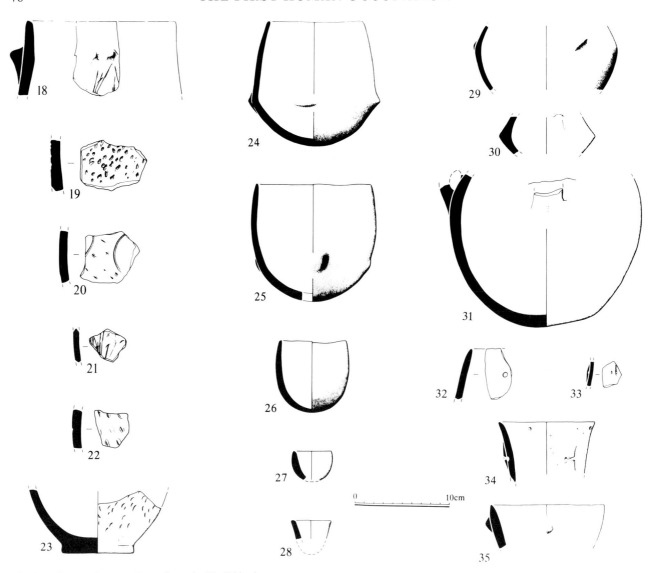

Fig. 3.15 Range of pottery forms from the Neolithic site

about 2 years, whilst the rest were kept until they were mature around 30 months of age. Such a calculated kill pattern for all the main domestic species indicates that the San Marco community operated an intensive regime, producing the maximum from their animals at the various stages of their lives, including meat, milk and other secondary products.

Domestic dogs were present on the site (6.5%), and the discovery of a near complete skeleton suggests these animals were pets/working animals, with this example buried whole in the ditch with the refuse.

Wild animals provided variety in the diet, and may have been an important supplement at times. Wild boar may have been hunted in the woods, together with red and

roe deer (5.3%), hares or rabbits (0.2%), and birds (0.6%). Whilst no fish bones or water fowl were found, these might also have been obtained from the countryside nearby.

The dogs may have been kept to assist with herding the animals in the local fields and on the high pastures of the limestone hills and scrubby slopes. Sheep and goats would have been particularly well adapted to dry grazing offered by the hills, whereas cattle would have been better adapted to the damp lowland pastures of the Gubbio Basin. Pigs would have flourished in the damp oak woodlands of the basin, feeding on roots, acorns and other woodland products.

Subsistence crops and collected foods were recovered

Table 3.5. *Animal bone fragment sample*

Species	Approximate number of fragments	Percentage of the species identified in sample
Cattle	155	30.6
Sheep/goat	193	38.1
Pig	95	18.7
Canid	33 + 150[a]	6.5
Roe deer	20	3.9
Red deer	2	0.4
Deer	5	1.0
Hare/rabbit	1	0.2
Bird	3	0.6
Total	507 + 150[a]	100.0
Unidentifiable	1421	
Total	2078	

Note:
[a] 150 fragments belong to a partial skeleton.

through a programme of soil sampling and wet sieving. Pollen data suggested that cereals had had an impact on the local environment of the site. Carbonised evidence provided detailed information of the types of cereal crops from the site. A total of 1,592 charred plant items were recovered, consisting of 822 seeds, 72 chaff fragments and 694 nut fragments.

Of the cereals, only 40% could be classified. Only *Triticum* (wheat) and *Hordeum* (barley) were present, but within these, several types were identified including hexaploid naked wheats (Triticum sphaerococcum, *Triticum compactum, and Triticum aestivum*). Club wheat was identified (Costantini pers. ident.) as well as *Triticum aestivum S. L.* A single dense-eared rachis of free-threshing wheat was also recovered. Two hulled wheat species, the tetraploid Emmer (*Triticum dicoccum*) and a diploid wheat, Einkorn (*Triticum monococcum*), were identified from seeds, spikelet forks and glumes. The barley sample was much smaller, half that of the wheat sample, which may be a preservation bias rather than reflect the actual proportions of cereals grown. Half the barley sample was *Hordeum vulgare*, including 6-rowed hulled and naked types.

Legumes were, like samples from most Neolithic sites in Italy, poorly represented. Only 14 seeds were recovered. These included pea (*Pisum sp.*) and *Vicia/Lathyrus sp.* A single flax seed (*Linum sp.*) might represent the use of the plant for oil or fibres. Fruits and nuts were collected from the countryside around the site and included fig (*Ficus carica*), blackberry or raspberry (*Rubus idaeus* or *fruticosus*), elder (*Sambucus sp.*), grape (*Vitis sp.*), hazel nuts (*Corylus sp.*) and wild bullace plum (*Prunus institia*). Other seeds

belong to grasses and weeds of cultivation which would have flourished on wasteland and around the settlement, including *Galium, Papaver, Polygonum* and *Rumex*.

The presence of threshing debris (rachis and glumes) indicate that on-site food processing took place, and that waste material and over-roasted cereal grains were dumped in the ditch and pit. The pit produced the highest amounts of all classes of carbonised plant remains and chaff, and this suggests that it may have functioned in the roasting/drying process required to process some types of grain.

The wheat and barley grown at Gubbio would have been well adapted to the local environment, with the wheat flourishing on the damper and heavier soils of the basin floor, and the barley thriving on the lighter, well drained soils on the upper alluvial slopes. The soil study made of the Gubbio Basin shows that some of the most highly suitable modern soils for low-input cereal production occur within a short distance of the site, although soil conditions have changed radically since the Neolithic (Hunt *et al.* 1990).

A study of the one-hour territory surrounding the San Marco Neolithic site by Jenny Harding attempted to assess the resources available to the Neolithic community (Fig. 3.8). A one-hour radius was established through a number of walks out from the site, noting soils, streams, vegetation and slope in each direction. The territory lay for the most part (66%) within the basin, with 18% in the limestone mountains to the north, and 16% in the low, undulating hills to the south. A perennial stream lay within five minutes walk to the north of the site, and the main River Saonda, thirty minutes to the south. The width of the river effectively meant that the southern side of the basin was beyond the habitual exploitation territory of the neolithic settlement. Agricultural activities could have taken place over much of the territory, with different soils exploited for various crops. However, since the level of technology was probably that of digging sticks in small garden-sized plots, lighter soils were doubtless selected for ease of tillage. The distribution of polished stone axes from the Bellucci antiquarian collections confirms this impression. Eleven stone axes are known from the immediate Gubbio area, whereas smaller numbers have been found on the heavy soils of the valley: Branca (3), Ponte d'Assi (2), between Branca and Torre Calzolari (2), Molini (1), Casacce (1).

The site of San Marco itself must have been seasonally boggy, with slow moving streams and marshy conditions very close by confirmed by the presence of ochreous mottled gleys underlying the site. The woodland soils would have maintained a constantly damp environment. The construction of the ditch may indicate that efforts were made to ease the flow water away from the living area of the settlement, in an attempt to keep it dry. The removal of trees in the late phases of the site could have meant that drainage became more rapid, and instead of providing a drier environment around the settlement, flooding took place instead. This could be one reason why the site was abandoned.

Local resources included plentiful wood for burning and house building, clay for pottery and daub, chert pebbles from the river and chert slabs from the hills for lithic tools, and local stone for grinding tools. Food was obtained from husbanded and hunted animals for meat and other products and from local gathered and grown plants, fruits and nuts. Few, if any items had to be obtained outside the valley, once the initial introduction of agricultural products had taken place. Judging by the density of other contemporary/near contemporary settlements within a few kilometres of the San Marco settlement, we may presume that there was a thriving community of simple farmers settled in the valley, and that over the period of two or three millennia, they transformed the valley from a wooded wilderness to a partly cleared agricultural human landscape.

The detailed information from San Marco and its environs remains a relatively unique insight into the early stages of agricultural substitution of hunter-gathering in central Italy, if recent reviews are accurate (Grifoni Cremonesi 1987). However, there are indications from the southern edge of the Po Valley (Barker *et al.* 1987) and the northern edge of the Florence Basin (Martini and Sarti 1991) that early agricultural communities made similar choices of alluvial fan environments. For instance, the Late Neolithic site of Neto di Bolasse near Sesto Fiorentino also appears to have been located close to water courses on an alluvial fan in a wooded environment. These similarities, however, disguise major differences in chronology and subsistence organisation; more interdisciplinary studies are required to model the subtleties of agricultural development.

4   THE DISSECTION OF A BRONZE AND EARLY IRON AGE LANDSCAPE

4.1 Site territories and landuse

4.1.1 General introduction

This chapter provides an integrated approach to the potential landuse of the principal known Bronze Age sites of the Gubbio Basin. A generalised environmental survey is combined with a detailed examination of the immediate environment of the sites to elucidate the opportunities and difficulties facing the prehistoric inhabitants in subsistence production and logistics (such as access). Since the majority of these sites have been excavated, it is also possible to combine external evidence with the internal evidence of the sites themselves.

A general assumption is made in the following analysis, namely that *subsistence* production during the Bronze Age was largely autonomous. Thus it is reasonable to assume that a 'territory' around each site will have been habitually exploited for day-to-day economic requirements. This assumption is particularly valid for the Bronze Age of the Gubbio Valley, as the effects of a more complex economic system of landuse probably had little impact in central Italy until the middle of the first millennium BC (Spivey and Stoddart 1990), and in Gubbio until the latter part of the same millennium (Chapter 5).

A second important assumption is that the landscape has not changed appreciably in terms of topography, water resources or soils, since the Bronze Age. This assumption does not hold for the Neolithic (Hunt *et al.* 1990), since soils in the Gubbio Valley have changed considerably since that time. The geomorphological and palaeoecological information summarised in Chapter 2 suggests, however, that the Bronze Age landscape was essentially similar to that of the present day, in terms of soils and even to a considerable extent, vegetation outside cultivated areas.

The technique of site catchment analysis employed here (Higgs and Vita Finzi 1970) was developed precisely with these aims in mind, to explore the nature of a site's territory and its potential for various subsistence practices. In this context, it is important to distinguish between the terms 'territory', described above, and 'catchment' which

(in agreement with Flannery 1976), denotes a more extensive area from which both occasional and daily needs were supplied. The nature of the catchment as opposed to the territory will be dealt with more fully later in the chapter (4.1.3).

Site exploitation territories have been defined (Fig. 4.1) for the excavated sites of Monte Ingino, Monte Ansciano and San Agostino and for the unexcavated sites of possible Bronze Age date at Monte Alto and Catignano. Within these territories, potential resource zones and sources of raw materials have been identified and evaluated in terms of Bronze Age economic landuse. Specialised attention is given later in this section, to the evaluation of soils in the Gubbio Valley for the Bronze Age arable landscape.

4.1.1.i The methodology for exploring site exploitation territories

For a mixed agricultural economy in a pre-state society, Higgs and Vita Finzi (1970) have suggested that the site exploitation territory may be usefully approximated by making walks of one hours' duration outwards from the site along various radii. This is based on the principle that travel time is a major limiting factor for the economic usefulness of land for cultivation. In spite of the critiques of this principle of site catchment analysis, particularly when employed in more complex societies (Gaffney *et al.* 1985; Reynolds 1979: 48–9) it remains true that ethnographic accounts show, within general trends, the diminished economic returns for cultivation beyond 1 km from the site (Chisholm 1962). It has to be emphasised that in the present study of the landuse patterns of late second and early first millennium populations, we are dealing with a novel agricultural system where it is assumed that complexity of land holding and elaborate logistical locations for agricultural production had not yet developed. The settlement system and more particularly the subsistence evidence suggest a co-operating economic unit to allow equitable access to pastoral and arable resources (sections 4.2 and 4.3). Complexity of landholding did not become

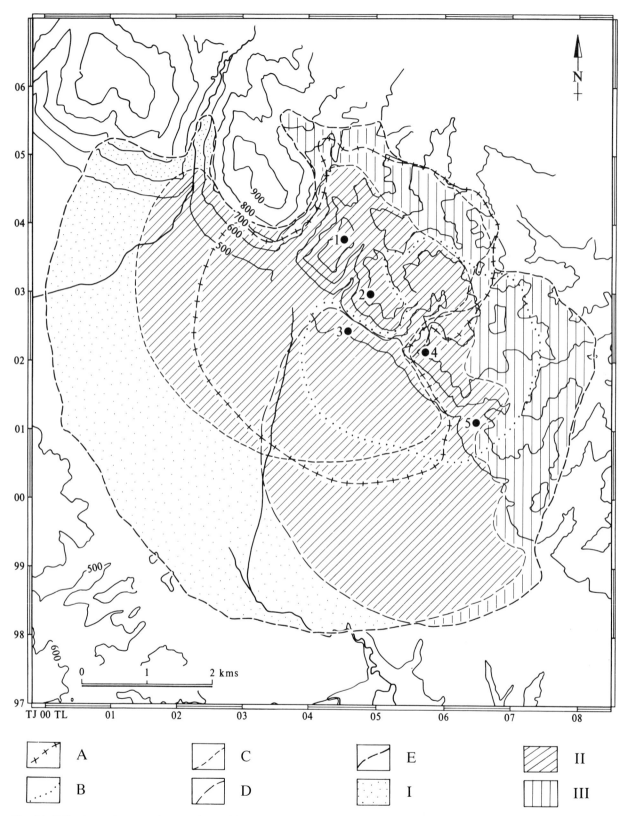

Fig. 4.1 Collective territory one-hour territory of the Bronze Age sites: 1 Monte Ingino; 2 Monte Ansciano; 3 S. Agostino; 4 Monte Alto; 5 Catignano; A Territory of Monte Ansciano; B Territory of Monte Alto; C Territory of Monte Ingino; D Territory of S. Agostino; E Territory of Catignano; I Territory only accessible to (lowland) San Agostino; II Territory accessible to upland and lowland sites; III Territory only accessible to upland sites

apparent in the Gubbio Valley until the late first millennium (Chapter 6).

Travel time is very much conditioned by the terrain. A site's habitually exploited territory will usually reflect the influence of topography on access; non topographic impediments to travel such as vegetation are more difficult to assess. Ideally the walks should follow radii from the site, so that in conditions of flat terrain a site would have a circular territory. These conditions do not however apply to the Gubbio circumstances, even within the plain. In practice, it is probable that individuals would have travelled along established routes offering least resistance and employing logistical stops for the storage of tools and produce. This would apply particularly to the upland area where better progress can be made by following contoured routes, avoiding steeper gradients and steep drops. Such routes were followed to establish a set of points at the limit of each site's one-hour territory. Between these points, the territory limits were deduced from 1:10,000 photographic/topographic maps *(ortofotocarte)*. The distorting influence of topography is evident. During the walks observations were made of the topography, geomorphology, Quaternary deposits (especially where revealed in sections), drainage and landcover in addition to the other observations made by others in this volume. From the observations of present-day physical attributes within these territories and with due consideration to environmental change since the Bronze Age, broad resource zones may be proposed and suggestions made about viable economic practice for the Bronze Age population. Possible sources for resources employed in site activities may also be identified.

One clear result of the construction of the individual territories of these sites is that they overlap to some considerable degree. Assuming the contemporary occupation of these sites (confirmed for the Late Bronze Age by excavation evidence), this could suggest a highly competitive division of terrain between the respective sites. However, a more probable explanation is the presence of an integrated system of sites with a collective territory represented by the merger of the individual territories (Fig. 4.1). A more complex landownership remains a possibility, but we lack the land boundaries of northern Europe (Bradley 1984: 115–18) that might provide evidence of this. An integrated system of sites would have provided the ready and equitable distribution of arable and pastoral resources in this vertical landscape.

An important resource within the collective territory is arable land. Since soils (and associated resources) are a major factor limiting lowlevel agricultural technology, a specialist soil study and land evaluation was undertaken, using the two principal cereals identified as important in the palaeobotanical work on the excavated sites. The area sampled in this work was determined by the collective site territories (Fig. 4.1).

4.1.2 Land evaluation

4.1.2.i Main principles and definitions

Decisions determining traditional settlement and subsistence cultivation are governed by factors that generally suit a particular community's needs. For instance, a safe shelter, suitable agricultural conditions and raw materials were all factors that influenced the way land was exploited. The main characteristics of each landunit would consequently determine how it was exploited under a given technology. Modern landuse, however, is far more complex, with conflicting, and often obscure demands made upon the landunit which may be independent of the landunit's natural characteristics. The Food and Agriculture Organisation of the United Nations (FAO) has consequently developed a standardised procedure for evaluating a landunit, whether traditional or modern and complex. It is this procedure which has been adopted here, as a means of attempting an assessment of prehistoric landuse.

Land evaluation 'involves the execution and interpretation of basic surveys of climate, soils, vegetation and other aspects of land in terms of the requirement of alternative forms of land use' (FAO 1976: 1). Land evaluation implies the matching of Land Utilisation Types (LUTs) with Land Qualities (LQs). Therefore, the Land Utilisation Types have to be defined first. An LUT is a kind of landuse, often defined for a specific crop, 'described in a degree of detail greater than that of a major kind of land use' (FAO 1976: 10). It consists of a set of technical specifications in a given physical, economic and social setting. Secondly, the LUTs have to be matched with the LQs in order to obtain suitability ratings for a landunit. A Land Quality 'is a complex attribute of land which acts in a distinct manner in its influence on the suitability of land for a specific kind of use' (FAO 1976: 12). Four classes are used to rate each landunit for the Land Qualities: s1 (highly suitable); s2 (moderately suitable); s3 (marginally suitable) and n (not suitable). Land evaluation however, is not only involved with the physical qualities of the land. The economic and social context has to be considered too.

The concept of land evaluation is applicable to prehistoric landuse and Land Qualities. However, several aspects to be considered are not easily reconstructible or, worse, not known. For instance, detailed information on crop requirements is absent, as well as our knowledge of socio-economic factors influencing decisions upon the kinds of crops to be produced. Also, it is difficult to define the suitability classes mentioned above for each Land Quality, for it is unknown what a Bronze Age Land Utilisation Type requires of a certain Land Quality. Inaccurate boundaries between the suitability classes of a Land Quality may result in an inaccurate rating. This inaccuracy may over- or underestimate the Land Quality as a limiting factor. Thus, for a Bronze Age land evaluation, the ratings for each Land Quality must be considered carefully. If necessary, the LUT and the LQ have to be matched several times with different ratings. At this stage, feedback with archaeologists is necessary.

The level on which a land evaluation is carried out can vary considerably. For instance, Boerma (1986) describes a three-step palaeo-land evaluation of an area located near the Euphrates in Syria. This evaluation took the following factors into consideration:

(1) Site location.
(2) Resources for hunting, fishing and gathering.
(3) Resources for cultivation.

In the current research, a slightly different approach was used. An evaluation was carried out only for a specific crop type. The reasons for this are twofold:

(1) Evaluation of site location was not a principal aim of the soil survey. Furthermore, political and religious factors may influence the choice of settlement, and environmental determinism would result from an evaluation based only on environmental factors.
(2) In the Bronze Age, agriculture was the main source of food. Collecting systems like hunting and gathering were most probably practised principally in the areas less suited for agriculture.

In this research Bronze Age farming for cereals will be considered. First, we present a definition of the Bronze Age Land Utilisation Type. Secondly, the Land Qualities considered to be the most important are discussed. Finally, LUTs and LQs were matched. The results are also mapped. For the LUTs, the LQs and the crop requirements, various publications were consulted. The most important are: Purseglove (1972), Renfrew (1973), Phillips (1975), Vink (1975, 148–149), Doorenbos and Kassam (1979) and Batterink *et al.* (1982).

4.1.2.ii The Bronze Age Land Utilisation Type

McVicar *et al.* (section 4.2) report that the dominant seeds recovered from the sediments of Monte Ansciano and Monte Ingino are *Triticum dicoccum* (emmer wheat), *Triticum spelta* (spelt wheat), *Setaria Italica* (italian millet) and *Hordeum vulgare* (barley). The following

evaluation is based on a mixed barley and emmer wheat cultivation since carbonised grains of this type were amongst the most dominant found by flotation of the sediments from the Bronze Age levels of the excavated sites. These crops also have comparable demands on soil texture, soil moisture and other conditions, although it is reported that in Roman times, wheat was grown under more humid conditions than barley (Ampolo 1980). Ampolo reports that these crops were often grown as a mixed crop in Roman times. This was probably done to assure a reasonable yield in both dry and wet summers. He also gives estimates of yields in Roman times under varying conditions. In this evaluation, it is assumed that barley and wheat were grown as a mixed crop. Tillage is assumed to have been done with oxen and ard, with the ard providing the most limiting factor in determining the workability of a field.

From about 800 BC (Ampolo 1980) a new cropping system appears to have been introduced into central Italy by the Greeks. By about 600 BC, an integrated polyculture of grain, vine and olive was also introduced, initially within Etruscan Italy, that is along the west coast of central Italy (Spivey and Stoddart 1990; Barker 1988). This agricultural system may also have comprised a two-year rotation of hay and cereals. The cropping systems which are supposed to have preceded this scheme are the *a campi ed erba* and the *debbio* systems (Ampolo 1980). The first system indicates that land was abandoned for some time after harvesting to regain its fertility. The second system is the same as the well known slash and burn system. In this evaluation, a cropping system like the *a campi ed erba* is assumed, comprising one year fallow and one year cereal farming in rotation on a field.

The Land Utilisation Type is, therefore, defined as follows: rainfed mixed cereal farming of barley and wheat in a two year rotation of fallow and arable. Ploughing was performed by oxen (although with restricted input (section 4.2)) and further tillage with hand tools. It is assumed that there was no, or very primitive, drainage/irrigation and minimal manuring. The land utilisation type was of very low input.

4.1.2.iii Land Qualities

Land Qualities are descriptive properties which often cannot be assessed directly. Mostly, a combination of Land Characteristics serves as an approximation of a Land Quality. Land Characteristics, such as texture, consistence, mottling and so on can be surveyed directly in the field. In the FAO's *A framework for land evaluation* (FAO 1976) a number of Land Qualities are given. We considered some of them inapplicable to the Land

Table 4.1. *Land Qualities not taken into consideration for the Bronze Age land evaluation for cereal farming*

| Land Quality | Depending upon/ characterised by | Not significant for Bronze Age (B.A.) Land Evaluation | | Other/remarks |
		no applicability	data deficiency	
Radiation regime	Total radiation; day length	–	–	Can be assumed to be uniform within the area; not limiting
Temperature regime extremes and averages	Temperature	–	–	Can be assumed to be uniform within the area; not limiting
Nutrient retention	Degree of leaching of added nutrients	*	–	Little or no manuring assumed in LUT
Air humidity affecting growth	Extremely high or low air humidities	–	*	Can be assumed to be uniform within area; probably not limiting
Conditions for ripening	Soil and climatic factors	–	*	Assumed to be uniform within the area; probably not limiting
Climatic hazards	Frequencies of thunderstorms, hail	–	*	Can be assumed to be uniform within the area
Excess of salts	High ECe-values	*	–	No high salinity within the area
Pests and diseases		–	*	Not reconstructible
Potential for mechanisation	Trafficability etc.	*	–	(Bronze Age LUT)
Conditions of land preparation and clearance	Type of vegetation, humidity etc.	*	*	Not easily reconstructible
Conditions affecting storage and processing	Moisture affecting the harvested crop	–	*	No data on method of storage; possibly uniform within the area
Conditions affecting timing of production	Commercial gain by out-of-season farming	*	*	B. A. agriculture was probably subsistence agriculture
Access within the production unit	Accessibility of individual fields	–	*	Location of B. A. production units not known
Size of potential management units	LUT, machinery etc.	*	*	
Location	Existing & potential accessibility	–	*	B. A. infrastructure unknown

Utilisation Type defined above (Table 4.1). The Land Qualities considered to be of importance for the Bronze Age LUT are described below. Of these, moisture availability, oxygen availability and workability were considered to be the most important.

Moisture availability
Crops are affected by moisture availability through the effects of moisture stress on growth. The severity of the effects of moisture stress varies according to the development stage of the crop. Wheat, for instance, is most sensitive to drought in the flowering stage.

The initial determinant of moisture availability is the ratio between the rainfall and the potential evapotranspiration. Moisture deficiency is modified by soil moisture storage, which is dependent on the texture of the soil and local factors such as the depth of groundwater.

Moisture availability was assessed by calculating the

relative evapo-transpiration deficit for every period of the growing season. The effects of the relative evapo-transpiration upon yield decrease are known for every period (Doorenbos and Kassam 1979). Rainfall and temperature data from Perugia and Gubbio were used (Riccardi 1966) and the calculation of the relative evapo-transpiration deficit was carried out for a number of different soil moisture storage values, each representing a texture class.

Oxygen availability
Most plants need to take in oxygen through their rooting systems and may suffer restricted growth or ultimately death if they are deprived of it. Oxygen is available above the water table and limited or absent below it. Occurrence of stress due to oxygen shortage therefore depends on:

– the occurrence of excess rainfall compared with the crop requirements;
– the ability of the site to shed excess water, either as runoff or by infiltration and percolation;
– the aeration porosity of the soil;
– the presence of a groundwater table.

Oxygen availability was assessed by soil drainage class data.

Nutrient availability
The availability of nutrients strongly influences the yield of a crop where the least available nutrient is the most limiting factor. Unfortunately substantial chemical analysis is necessary to obtain accurate data.

Nutrient availability was assessed in a qualitative way by using the soil map legend units as an indicator. Holocene soils were supposed to be rich in all nutrients since no significant leaching has taken place. The Pleistocene terraces were supposed to be poorer, especially those on the Ponte d'Assi level and those having an eluvial horizon.

Rooting conditions
Rooting conditions are controlled by the effective soil depth and the ease of root penetration. The effective depth is the depth to a limiting horizon, such as rock, gravel, hardpan or a toxic layer.

The rooting conditions were assessed by considering the consistency of the upper metre (maximum rooting depth of the soil).

Conditions affecting germination or establishment
Germination and establishment are the critical periods in the development cycle of a crop. The condition of the seedbed is therefore a determinant. This condition depends mainly on the susceptibility to surface sealing, the consistency of the topsoil and the content of gravel. This Land Quality was assessed with these three variables. The susceptibility to surface sealing is reflected by the texture of the upper 15 cm of the soil.

Flood hazard
Flood hazard refers to damage to crops by water above the ground surface, caused by standing or flowing water. The sensitivity to flood hazard was assessed by looking at the location: a location near a stream channel showing evidence of overtopping its banks frequently was considered sensitive. This corresponded to the young levée and crevasse deposits and the colluvio-fluviatile landscape.

Soil toxicities
The presence of large amounts of aluminium, calcium carbonate, gypsum, manganese, acid sulphate and other elements may cause toxification of a sensitive crop. Since both barley and wheat are not very sensitive to calcium carbonate, and since acid sulphate and gypsum most probably are not present in the soils of the Gubbio Basin, only aluminium and manganese may cause toxicity. Both may be present in slightly toxic amounts in the most acid parts (being the top levels) of the Ponte d'Assi and the Padule–Branca terraces.

Soil workability
Workability is the ease with which the soil can be cultivated or tilled. The soil characteristics that determine the workability as well as the assessment of it, are described in section 2.2. The soil workability map is added to this report (Fig. 4.3).

Erosion hazard
The negative effects of soil erosion in agricultural farming are well known and need not be explained here. In this land evaluation, the erosion hazard was assessed by combining observed soil erosion data with terrain slopes.

Soil degradation hazard
The physical, chemical and biological degradation of soil properties can have a pronounced effect on crop yields, oxygen availability, rooting conditions, nutrient availability and so on of a soil.

Physical degradation comprises various processes, deteriorating the structure and bulk density of the soil. Crust formation at the soil surface is an indication of physical degradation. Soils with a high silt or fine sand content may be particularly prone to physical degradation. A high content of free $CaCO_3$ decreases the tendency towards degradation. Both texture and presence of free $CaCO_3$ were used for the assessment of the physical degradation hazard.

The chemical degradation hazard refers to short term

changes in the chemical properties of the soil. Particularly acidification brought about by incorrect application of fertilisers may affect nutrient availability and thus be harmful. The chemical degradation hazard was most probably about the same magnitude in the whole survey area. It was coped with to some extent by the rotating cropping system. Biological degradation refers to decline in the organic matter content of the soil. It affects factors such as nutrient availability and erosion hazard. Organic matter content was not measured, so direct assessment was not possible, although it is likely to have changed substantially since the Bronze Age.

The Land Qualities were matched with the landuse requirements of the LUT defined above. This matching was done for every mapping unit of the soil map separately, to make local relevance optimal. Every mapping unit was given suitability values for each of the Land Qualities, considering the demands of the Land Utilisation Type. Possible suitability values were: s1, highly suitable; s2, moderately suitable; s3, marginally suitable and n, not suitable. From the ten suitabilities an overall Suitability was derived. The overall Suitability classes are indicated with S1, S2, S3 and N. If any of the ten Land Qualities was classified as not suitable, the overall Suitability was also given this classification. Otherwise, the overall Suitability was obtained in a two-step process. Firstly, the three most important Land Qualities were considered: moisture availability, oxygen availability and workability. The most limiting value of these three was taken as an interim value. Secondly, the other seven Land Qualities were considered. If more than three of these were more limiting than the interim Suitability derived from step one, this Suitability was downgraded. Upgrading could not take place, since high Suitabilities cannot compensate a limiting one. Finally, the Suitability ratings of the mapping units were used to produce a suitability map (Fig. 4.2).

4.1.2.iv Results

When looking at the suitability map, it appears that all highly suitable fields are located on the younger alluvial fan deposits. Moderately suitable fields can be found in the colluvial landscape, the alluvial fan landscape and near the margins of the terrace landscape. Most of the marginally suitable fields are located on the alluvial fans which are mainly restricted by difficult workability (Fig. 4.3).

Non-suitable fields tend to be concentrated in the southern part of the survey area, namely the terrace and the colluvio- fluviatile landscapes. The soils of the colluvio-fluviatile landscape were considered to have been unsuitable for Bronze Age cereal farming mainly because of the flooding hazard. The suitability of most soils in the terrace landscape was severely limited by a very difficult workability, a high erosion hazard, a high soil degradation hazard, a low nutrient availability or a combination of these. Since workability, erosion hazard and soil degradation hazard are crop independent Land Qualities, the Terrace Landscape would most probably also have been unsuitable for other kinds of Bronze Age arable farming.

A number of fields on the alluvial fans were considered unsuitable for the Bronze Age LUT. The reason for this was the very difficult workability or the flooding hazard. These fields were probably also unsuitable for other kinds of crop farming in the Bronze Age.

For a more complete picture of Bronze Age farming, other LUTs would have to be defined. These must comprise minimally an LUT for extensive grazing, an LUT for hunting and gathering, and one for cultivation systems other than cereal farming.

4.1.2.v Conclusions

During the Holocene, the surface layers of the alluvial fans of Madonna del Ponte, Gubbio, Zappacenere, San Marco, Padule and Stazione del Padule were formed. On these coalescing fans, zones of low and high recent activity (in terms of erosion and/or deposition) could be distinguished.

Decalcified topsoils indicate zones of low recent activity. No potsherds were found in soil material deeper than one metre below the present surface. Therefore these deposits are probably older than the periods in which most pottery was produced.

Calcareous soils are present in zones of high recent activity. Sherds were found at depths ranging from one to more than two metres indicating that accumulation processes have been active. Some calcareous soils are of uncertain age because of high groundwater levels preventing soil development, or of lateral transport of calcium carbonates preventing decalcification. Because of the risk of flooding in the winter on the alluvial fans and on the valley bottom, settlement most likely took place on higher, better drained positions in the landscape. Therefore, sites may be found at or near the surface on the coarser textured older alluvial fan deposits, on colluvial footslopes and on the edges of the terraces. As no deposition took place on the older coarser alluvial fan deposits, sites may have been disturbed by recent agricultural activity. In the coarser textured younger deposits however, they are more likely to be found buried if on the middle and lower alluvial fans. Risk of flooding will have impeded Bronze Age cereal farming on soil units F1, F2 and Al (see Fig. 2.7). Terrace

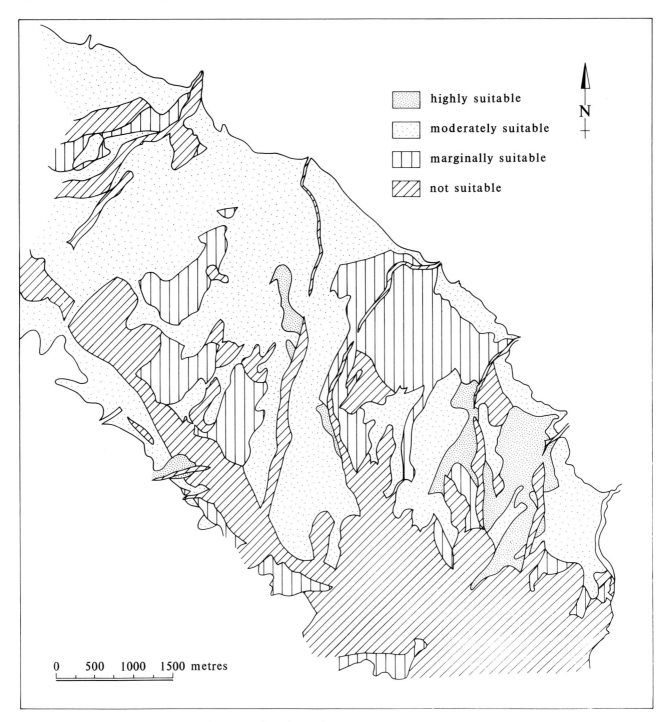

Fig. 4.2 Soil suitability map for *Triticum dicoccum* and *Hordeum vulgare*

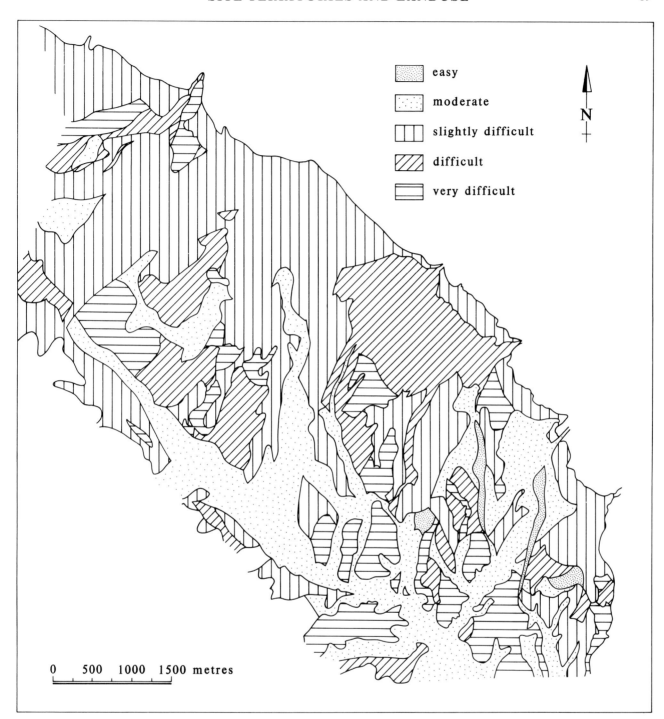

Fig. 4.3 Soil workability map

soils are severely limited for crop farming; workability, erosion hazard, degradation hazard and a low nutrient availability are the main limiting factors. These factors, as they are crop independent, will also impede crop farming other than cereal farming. Highly suitable fields for cereal farming are found on the younger alluvial fan deposits. Moderately suitable fields are found on the middle alluvial fan and in the colluvial landscape. Land evaluation for Land Utilisation Types comprising other crops or extensive grazing is recommended.

4.1.3 Site exploitation territories

As illustrated earlier, all five exploitation territories encompass both an upland area and an area of the Gubbio Valley. The sites Monte Ingino, Monte Ansciano and Monte Alto are situated on distinct hilltops beside the valley, whilst Catignano is situated on a lesser hill that is still over 100 m above the nearby valley. The Late Bronze Age and early Iron Age sites of Vescovado and Sant' Agostino are located on the footslopes of Monte Ingino and Monte Ansciano respectively, bordering the valley. An essential preliminary to the consideration of the territories of these sites is the control for environmental change in the light of earlier chapters.

4.1.3.i Environmental change

The genesis of the topography in which these territories lie has been described in the earlier chapters and had for the most part taken place by late Pleistocene – early Holocene times. Pleistocene climatic changes may be largely responsible for the deeply incised valleys of the limestone uplands and consequently for much of the valley alluviation. In fact today's topography in this area probably differs very little from that of the Bronze Age or indeed Neolithic times. The change was more probably a matter of degree with the geomorphological processes active then continuing up until the present day.

In broad terms, the steep hill slopes have been progressively denuded of loose stone materials and limestone regolith largely by fluvial erosion, especially gullying by meltwaters and storm run-off. Material thus removed has largely been deposited within the upland valleys and at the junction with the Gubbio Valley as alluvial fan deposits and footslope accumulations. Most of the sections in the uplands exposed bedded deposits of limestone scree with finer deposits in varying densities. Such deposits both underlie and overlie the Sant' Agostino *in situ* Iron Age hut floor, indicating mass movement and other geomorphological processes in pre- and post-Iron Age

times. These deposits contribute greatly to the footslopes between the Gubbio Valley and the limestone uplands.

The transport of material from the upper slopes to aggrade the valley bottoms was probably greatly accelerated since the Bronze Age by clearance of natural vegetation in the uplands. In some places palaeosols have been identified within the sediments (Schomaker and Van Waveren 1984), indicating that stable land surfaces have existed locally between phases of deposition.

The study of soil development in the Gubbio Valley (section 2.2) identifies stable and unstable landsurfaces within the valley landscape, but as similar conditions of soil development, erosion and deposition will have existed in Bronze Age times, it is concluded that today's soils strongly resemble those of the Bronze Age.

Drainage conditions in the valley are known to have changed considerably since the Pleistocene with evidence for several lacustrine phases (Schomaker and Van Waveren 1984). Since the early Holocene, drainage of the valley has been fluvial. Today a number of small streams flow into the Gubbio Valley, through the deeply incised valleys of the limestone uplands. These streams then flow generally south-south-eastwards across the valley joined by tributaries issuing from the valley deposits, eventually to join the Torrente Saonda on the southern side of the valley. This is the principal drainage channel of the Gubbio Valley.

Many of the tributary streams from the uplands are ephemeral, resulting from meltwater and storm-runoff within their small catchments; their channels are often dry in summer months. At times of peak flow, however, such streams could have caused flooding over much of the alluvial fan landscape, thereby contributing to fan formation and perhaps causing seasonal water-logged conditions in parts of the valley. Also, a high watertable in parts of the valley may have caused marshy conditions in certain areas which are possibly reflected in local place names (section 2.3). Travertine found at San Marco Neolitico possibly provides evidence of a high watertable giving rise to springs, as it requires flowing water rich in calcium carbonate for its formation.

Naturally drainage channels will have shifted in position throughout their existence, and possible old stream channels have been identified on the geomorphological map by Coltorti (section 2.1). Besides natural changes to the drainage pattern in time, present drainage patterns in the uplands and in the Gubbio Valley have been modified by people, especially since the sixteenth century (section 2.3) to facilitate agriculture, communications and urban development and to reduce flooding risks. Particularly in the valley, much surface drainage is controlled by ditches and some streams have artificial levées.

Patterns of vegetation are intimately related to topography, soils and drainage, though changes to the vegetation of this area since Neolithic times must in most part be attributed to the effects of human exploitation of the landscape in response to increasing population and economic pressures. Woodland was far more extensive in both upland and lowland landscapes prior to the sixteenth century (section 2.3). The map of vegetation potential (Fig. 2.9) therefore has some considerable relevance for the Neolithic and Bronze Age landscapes. Steep slopes in the uplands which today have limited scrub and woodland cover, may once have supported denser woodland on thicker soils which have now been greatly eroded following vegetation clearance.

4.1.3.ii Resource zonation and potential landuse

In order to make suggestions on economic practice, it is important to look at the spatial distribution and accessibility of potential resources within the territories.

Arable land
It is assumed that Bronze Age populations employed simple hand tools such as 'digging sticks' and light wooden ards combined with animal traction for cultivation in a manner that was not radically different from that suggested for Iron Age populations in northern Europe (Reynolds 1979: 61–3), and that they required light, well drained soils for most successful crop production. The report of the soil scientists above, focusing on soil quality within the site territories has identified areal extents of soils according to their suitability for low technology, low input cereal farming in the Bronze Age.

Only the one-hour territory of Sant' Agostino (and by implication Vescovado although uncalculated) encompasses sizeable areas of highly suitable soils for this landuse type though each territory has large areas of moderately suitable soils. The latter occur within the territories mainly on alluvial fan landscapes where groundwater can be close to the surface and may cause wet ground conditions in places. Emmer wheat could be more tolerant of such conditions than barley which is better suited to light, well-drained soils. Barley is shallow rooted and could have been cultivated on the upland footslopes or perhaps on thin soils within the uplands. Bronze age populations may then have been able to cultivate barley in close proximity to the sites of Monte Ingino and Monte Ansciano, perhaps on the gentler slopes just to the north and north-east of the sites, whereas it was necessary to descend approximately 300–400 m of steep slopes to reach the valley bottom soils.

Animal husbandry
It seems reasonable to believe that as recently as the fifteenth century AD (section 2.3) large areas in and around the defined territories were more heavily wooded than today. Leaf impressions in travertine and the presence of woodland mollusc species from the excavated Neolithic site give some support to the belief (section 2.3) that more substantial areas would have been wooded in prehistory perhaps approximating the estimates of the characteristics of a climax woodland by botanical research (section 2.3). The distribution of settlement and development of the economy suggests that significant clearance of this woodland was probably only undertaken for the first time during the Bronze Age. During much of the period, the valley would, therefore, most probably have been covered by a moist woodland environment which remained relatively cool and moist during the summer months. Such conditions would have been favourable for the browsing of cattle and pigs. Pigs, a significant component in the bone samples (section 4.2), are versatile eaters of household refuse and woodland produce and could thus have been kept both close to the settlement and taken to local woodlands. Cattle, a relatively minor component of the bone samples (section 4.2), may have exploited the moister pastures available in areas of natural sparse tree cover or in man-made clearings in the valleys, providing good grazing land, although seasonal waterlogging could have limited their use.

Poor water retention by the thin soils overlying limestone bedrock would have produced dry rough grazing areas in the uplands, especially once any protective cover had been cleared. These grazing areas may too have suffered from seasonal limitations, possibly becoming desiccated in late summer months and so restricting the number of grazing animals per unit area of land. Sheep, a significant component of the bone samples (section 4.2) are grazing animals well suited to uplands such as those in which the sites are located. Although they are selective grazers sheep are more successful than cows in coping with the heat, sparse water and poor summer pastures of the Mediterranean region (Barker 1985). Goats are also dairy animals suited to the upland part of the territories. As versatile browsers they could have been kept on the steeper, scrub covered slopes around the sites. Sheep and goats would probably have grazed the areas around the upland sites and perhaps beyond to the north and north-east, although it has often been noted that taking stock further than one hour's walk from the site necessitates a different system of stock management to offset the greater costs involved (Gamble 1982, 164).

Hunting and gathering

The red deer, present in small quantities from Monte Ingino, are both a potential source of meat and antlers for tool manufacture (Barker 1985). Tolerant of varied environmental conditions, they could have existed in both valley and upland landscapes of the site exploitation territories; today feral deer graze over a substantial proportion of Monte Ansciano's less precipitous slopes in a *parco naturale*. Roe deer, present in small quantities on both the excavated Bronze Age sites, is much more a woodland species and would, therefore be expected to be concentrated in forested areas, both the remnants on the upland areas and in the lowland areas. Smaller game, less prominent in the archaeological record, would have been available seasonally in similar ecological zones. The same zones would have provided other gathered resources ranging from nuts to berries, perhaps principally eaten off site, and firewood and more substantial construction materials that were brought back to the occupation areas. Woodland resources would have been readily available in the Bronze Age since there had been no preceding human pressure on the landscape.

Freshwater fish, present in small quantities from Monte Ingino, were most probably caught in the one perennial stream located between Monte Ingino and Monte Foce or alternatively the major streams within the valley, the Saonda and the Assino, although these were only within the 'territory' of the hillslope sites of Sant' Agostino and Vescovado.

Water supplies were most probably derived from the natural springline down the hillside from the upland sites, in spite of the effort involved, or from the ephemeral streams passing the hillslope sites.

Flint was the other major resource available within the collective territories of the contemporary sites. Although some chert deposits were available in the limestone bedrock, most flint was derived from cobbles in the local streams.

4.1.3.iii Summary of the attributes of individual sites and their exploitation territories

Monte Ingino

This site, with extremely limited space, surrounded on three sides by very steep slopes, is well situated for defensive purposes. Its position is very good for viewing the surrounding hills and valleys far beyond the one-hour territory. Equally, the distinctive form of the bipartite Monte Ingino peak can be readily made out from points on the horizon. Although located some 400 m above the Gubbio Valley, the valley bottom can be quickly reached

today by walking down the north-east slopes and then along the south-east slopes of Monte Ingino. A relatively large area of the Gubbio Valley is therefore encompassed by Monte Ingino's one-hour territory. The diagrams of the site exploitation territories shows the degree to which the upland topography has distorted them, particularly that of Monte Ingino. Monte Foce and the ravine between it and Monte Ingino severely restricts access to and from the site in a westerly and northerly direction.

Today ephemeral and perennial water sources can be reached after approximately twenty minutes' walk from the site. Most land in the immediate vicinity of the site is potentially dry grazing land suitable for sheep and goats. Pockets of suitable soils on some gentler slopes are today used for cereal production, so production of barley, for example may have been possible close to the site. As can be seen from the site territories diagram (Fig. 4.1), this site's one-hour exploitation territory embraces almost equal proportions of upland and valley resource zones by virtue of its location.

Monte Ansciano

This site can be reached by a thirty minute walk from Monte Ingino, and it too is favourable for defence and communications. Access to the Gubbio Valley is more difficult from this site, and today it is easier to use the path on Monte Ingino's slopes. Travel in a south-easterly direction is greatly restricted by the deeply incised valley between Monte Ansciano and Monte Alto. To reach a present-day perennial water source requires a thirty minute walk.

Monte Ansciano has a broad hilltop, more suitable for extensive domestic occupation, with gentler north-east facing slopes at present grazed by deer. Today these hillslopes are extensively denuded with only a thin soil layer over the limestone bedrock. It is possible that deeper soil deposits suitable for some crop cultivation existed on these slopes in the Bronze Age and until the denudational consequences of vegetation clearance rendered arable practices not viable. This would apply to all hillslopes in this area. As in the case of Monte Ingino, the exploitation territory for Monte Ansciano is made up of almost equal proportions of upland and valley resource zones.

Sant' Agostino

Situated on the footslopes of Monte Ansciano, this site has the largest one-hour territory. The Torrente Saonda across the valley can be reached within one hour. It should be noted that at the time the site was occupied the valley may not have been as well-drained as at present. Seasonal waterlogging may have existed in places but there is no evidence within the soils to suggest permanent waterlogging (Schomaker and Van Waveren 1984; Finke and Sewuster 1987). Perennial streams flow close to the site today which is located on the edge of moderately suitable arable land. The slopes around the site have a south-west aspect favouring cultivation. Steep gradients considerably hamper access to the upland area, although both Monte Ingino and Monte Ansciano are well within the one-hour territory. The excavated site of the Vescovado is in a similar topographical position, but the territory has not been estimated.

This site location is therefore also suitable for the exploitation of both the woodland moister pastures and arable land of the valley, and the drier grazing and scrubland of the uplands. Its position on the lower south-west facing slopes of Monte Ansciano could suggest that crop production activities became a more important part of the early Iron Age economy when settlements were concentrated on these slopes.

Monte Alto (unexcavated site)
This site location is again favourable for defence purposes as it has steep slopes to the north-west and south-west of the hilltop and good visibility of the Gubbio Valley and neighbouring hills. A quite deeply incised stream on the north-east side of the hill combined with steep wooded slopes also hinders movement to and from the hilltop so that the easiest approach to the hill is from the east. Hence, Monte Alto's one-hour territory is highly restricted to the north-west, west and south, but spreads to the north-east and east to include substantial areas of woodland, grassland and some arable land. Steep slopes between Monte Alto and Monte Ansciano prevent access between the two sites within one hour and topography has greatly restricted the extent of potential arable lands in the valley accessible from the site within one hour.

Catignano (unexcavated site)
Although this site is located on a relatively low hill, deep stream valleys to the immediate north-west and south give it a defensive element. Soils at the site are very thin and overlie limestone regolith, but nevertheless manage to support a crop today. Access to the potential arable land of the Gubbio Valley is good, and the site's one-hour territory encompasses much of the potential dry grazing land of Monte Alto's territory together with much land to the east and south-east. Today, a perennial stream runs a short distance from the site.

4.1.3.iv Discussion and conclusions

Based upon the technique of Site Catchment Analysis, the use of the one-hour time contour to delimit site exploitation territories helps focus attention on the potential and the problems of particular site locations. It provides an environmental context for the site allowing possible resource zones to be identified and their significance evaluated in terms of site economy. Excavated organic and inorganic materials may then be related to the immediate environment, offering more information on resource availability and the ways in which they were used. In this way, land in the Gubbio Valley has been evaluated in detail by Finke and Sewuster above for arable land use, concentrating on the principal crops recovered in a carbonised state from the sites themselves.

Each site examined here benefits from an intermediate ecotonal location around which its exploitation territory encompasses large proportions of both upland and lowland resource zones. Such site locations which optimise local resource exploitation opportunities have been noted elsewhere in Italy for prehistoric sites, for example Monte Covolo at the junction between the Po Plain and the northern Apennines (Barker 1981a).

Patterns of landuse and the concept of the exploitation territory are complicated when the territories of contemporary neighbouring sites overlap. As can be seen in Figure 4.1, each of the one-hour site territories has a considerable area of overlap with neighbouring sites. From the excavated archaeological evidence, it is believed that the sites of Monte Ingino, Monte Ansciano and Sant' Agostino were contemporary for at least part of their occupation. Use of land within the habitually exploited areas may then have been restricted by some degree of co-ordination in order to avoid the problems of overlapping territory. As an alternative hypothesis, each site may have specialised in certain economic functions suited to its most accessible resource zone and shared in each other's products. For example, the sites of Monte Ingino and Monte Ansciano are well situated for pastoral activities in the drier grazing lands of the uplands, perhaps supplemented by some barley production, hunting and gathering. Sant' Agostino, on the other hand, was in a better position to take advantage of the more extensive workable soils along the north-eastern side of the Gubbio Valley and to exploit the animal and plant resources of the valley environment.

This study has examined the sites from an environmental perspective in an attempt to reconstruct potential landuse and economy in the Bronze Age around Gubbio. Together with certain excavated materials from the sites themselves, the examination of the sites' one-hour territories does favour the practice of a mixed cereal and stock-keeping economy.

4.2 Agriculture

The agricultural evidence for the Late Bronze Age and early Iron Age in the Gubbio Valley is principally drawn from the excavation of two hilltop sites: Monte Ingino and Monte Ansciano. This poses particular problems of interpretation. Although there is supporting material available from topographical and pedological studies of the region, it remains true that any reconstruction of contemporary agricultural practice, and of the contemporary subsistence economy, is likely to be biased by the nature and location of these two sites. As a result, while it is possible to make inferences from the available evidence and to establish an interpretation of these sites which places them within a broader regional context, it would be wrong to extrapolate from them in order to reconstruct the regional economy. Monte Ingino and Monte Ansciano afford, at best, an insight into one particular aspect of the region's agriculture.

4.2.1 Monte Ingino

The bone assemblage recovered from Monte Ingino is very large, well in excess of that recovered from any other published central Italian Bronze Age site (Table 4.2). In total over 500 kg of skeletal material was removed from the matrix, representing more than 25,000 individual bone fragments. All strata were exhaustively dry-sieved using 0.25″, or metric equivalent, meshes and recovery of small elements (metatarsals, metacarpals and phalanges) was unusually high. Selective wet-sieving was also carried out, resulting in the recovery of small rodent and fish bones.

The identified sample runs to over 12,000 elements, 88% of which can be attributed to the Late Bronze Age midden which formed most of the excavated strata. Identification did not seek to distinguish sheep and goat, nor was sexing carried out. The skeletal material, especially that from the midden, was highly fragmented with jaws showing notably high levels of damage. About 77% of the teeth recovered were found loose in the matrix with an overall ratio of loose teeth to empty sockets of 7:1. There was, however, very little evidence of scavenging by dogs in terms of gnawing and chewing of recovered elements.

Domesticates (caprines, pig and cattle) dominate the assemblage (Table 4.3): in total, other species present (roe and red deer; dog; badger; vole; pine marten; hare; mouse; weasel; mole; crow; pigeon) constitute no more than 10% assessed on Minimum Number of Individuals (MNI), or 8% assessed on Number of Individual Specimens (NISP).[1] In the midden, the ratio between caprines, pigs and cattle, based on averaged MNIs for bones and teeth, is roughly 7:4:1. For pre-midden strata the ratios are similar within the tolerance implied by the much smaller sample size.

The age structures of the domestic species were jointly assessed on bone fusion and tooth wear, neither approach being felt to be sufficiently reliable in its own right to allow clear inferences to be made on the kill pattern. In particular, there are often problems with taking bone fusion ratios at face value because of the impact of castration on fusion rates. The percentage of fused to non-fused elements was assessed for a range of elements[2] and graphed by species (Fig. 4.4; Tables 4.10 and 4.11); the median age of fusion, and normal range, are taken from Silver (1969). For tooth wear, a simple five-grade scale was used, calibrated to Grant's published tooth wear states (Grant 1982) as follows:

Unworn:	(a)
Very early wear:	(b)–(c)
Early wear:	(d)–(e)
Middle wear:	(f)–(j)
Late wear:	(k)–(p)

No attempt was made to link this scale formally to age. The purpose of the tooth wear data was to provide additional information for comparison with that supplied by bone fusion. This being the case, it was felt to be sufficient to observe the general trend of tooth wear taking into account normal eruption ages; the latter were also taken from Silver's 1969 paper.

In the case of caprines (ovicaprids), most of the animals in the assemblage seem to have died either in the first year or towards the end of the second year of life. This is supported by the high ratio of dP4 to P4 (Table 4.4), which suggests that many of the animals in the assemblage were killed before the loss of dP4 at around 21–24 months. This interpretation is given further weight by observations on the molars. Some 67% of M1s are in a moderately advanced state of wear (Table 4.5) while the later erupting M2 (9–12 months) shows much less pronounced wear, with a spread of values across early and very early wear states. The relatively low number of M3s recovered by comparison with M1 and M2 (179 M1; 118 M2; 52 M3) further supports the idea that many of the animals represented in the assemblage were killed before this tooth erupts towards the end of the second year of life.

The kill pattern for pig, as suggested by bone fusion ratios other than that for the scapula (Fig. 4.4), indicates that perhaps as many as two thirds of the animals represented were less than one year old at death. Some of the elements examined were clearly very immature; this may explain the disparity between MNIs as calculated on

---

[1] Both measures were constructed using computer programs published by Klein and Cruz-Uribe (1984).
[2] In the case of unfused elements, the higher of the counts for shafts and epiphyses was used.

Table 4.2a. *Percentages of Late Bronze Age faunal assemblages accounted for by major species on sites in central Italy; based on Numbers of Individual Specimens (based on Stoddart 1987)*

	Monte Ingino Midden	Monte Ansciano LBA	Grotta a Male[a]	Luni Tre Erici[b]	Luni Acropolis[c]	Narce 13th/12th century[d]	Narce 12th century[d]	Narce 11th century[d]	Narce 10th century[d]
Pig	33	16	18	20	3	20	15	21	23
Cow	11	15	34	43	16	33	29	29	23
Caprine	48	68	37	35	44	44	53	47	48
Dog	7	1	1	–	3	2	2	1	2
Deer	+[e]	+[e]	1	–	10	2	–	+[e]	+[e]
Wild boar	–	–	–	–	+[e]	–	–	–	–
Sample size (NISP)	9097	1870	260	68	523	61	331	513	539

Note:
[a] Pannuti 1969 [b] Gejvall 1967 [c] Lepiksaar 1975 [d] Barker 1976 [e] Present at <1% of total assemblage

Table 4.2b. *Percentages of Late Bronze Age faunal assemblages accounted for by major species on sites in Central Italy; based on Numbers of Individual Specimens (based on Stoddart 1987)*

	Torrionaccio[a]	S Giovenale Middle Protovillanovan[b]	S Giovenale Late Protovillanovan[b]	Sorgenti della Nova[c]	Monte Rovello LBA	Ancona Colle dei Cappuccini Protovillanovan[d]
Pig	6	22	36	60	13	16
Cow	19	18	13	9	50	23
Caprine	69	55	50	13	31	19
Dog	5	1	–	1	1	4
Deer	–	4	1	–	3	20
Wild boar	–	–	–	11	–	17
Sample size (NISP)	236	82	72	159	231	1830

Notes:
[a] Placidi 1978 [b] Sorrentino 1981 [c] Caloi and Polombo 1981 [d] Wilkens 1990

dental and non-dental elements denoting under-representation of pig bone in the assemblage. The dentition itself is clearly consistent with a young population. The ratio of dP4 to M3 is 164:52 indicating that most of the animals represented in the assemblage were under 17 months at death (Table 4.4). This is backed up by wear state data (Table 4.5). Here 45% of M1s show no appreciable wear and 40% light or very light wear; this suggests that for most of the animals this tooth had only recently erupted, which is consistent with the idea that the majority of the pigs represented were dead before reaching the age of 1 year.

The data for cattle are much more difficult to interpret because of the relatively small sample size and the fact that many bones fuse during the same broad age ranges. It is, however, evident that there is no sharp fall-off with increasing age, as is the case of caprines and pigs (Fig. 4.4). There appears, on the contrary, to be a gradual decrease, with around one third of the animals represented having been killed sometime between 1.5 and 2 years after birth, and a further third being killed between 2 and 3.5 years. The wear state evidence tends to support this interpretation, with a strong bias towards middle and late wear stages in M1 and M2 (Table 4.5).

In addition to these major species, a small number of fish, rodent and bird bones were also recovered. The former fall into two groups: eels and cyprinids. Detailed identification of the cyprinids has not been possible, although barbel and chub may be present. The bones come from large individuals: the eels are estimated to have been in the region of 75 cm in length while the

Table 4.3. *NISP and MNI for Monte Ansciano and Monte Ingino on bones and teeth*

	Monte Ansciano Phase: LBA		Monte Ansciano Phase: Archaic		Monte Ingino Phase: Midden		Monte Ingino Phase: Pre-midden	
	NISP	MNI	NISP	MNI	NISP	MNI	NISP	MNI
Bones								
caprines	1055	36	151	7	4368	102	159	10
pig	243	12	46	3	3011	49	126	8
cattle	235	8	52	3	1012	15	74	6
dog	12	2	3	1	680	14	14	2
roe deer	1	1	–	–	17	2	–	–
red deer	1	1	–	–	6	1	11	1
badger	–	–	–	–	3	1	2	1
Totals	1547		263		9097		386	
Teeth								
caprines	925	73	141	15	1419	95	106	12
pig	230	14	24	3	931	68	85	7
cattle	258	21	53	6	256	13	30	4
dog	2	1	–	–	194	18	9	2
roe deer	2	1	–	–	–	–	–	–
red deer	–	–	–	–	18	1	3	1
badger	–	–	–	–	1	1	1	1
Totals	1417		218		2819		234	

cyprinids vary from 25 to 40 cm. Assuming that the eels were caught in fresh water, this suggests that both were taken from rivers or lakes rather than from one of the local mountain streams (A. Jones, pers. comm.). The birds include woodpigeon, crow and raven and the rodents a number of species of vole and mice.

The floral evidence from Monte Ingino is much less abundant than might have been expected given the nature of the deposits: processing of approximately 440 kg of matrix yielded only 1,380 carbonised fragments, excluding wood charcoal. In total 155 samples were taken from the strata using a mixture of random and directed sampling. These were initially broken down using a solution of hydrogen peroxide and the flot removed into a 300 micron sieve for washing. The residue was then wet-sieved through 2mm and 1mm gauzes. Carbonised seeds were identified from the flot and residues using a low power (x10/x40) microscope and removed by hand for further identification.

Although most of the excavated matrix at Monte Ingino can be attributed to the Late Bronze Age midden (sections 1.10 and 4.33), and many samples were taken from these contexts, most of the plant material was actually recovered from pre-midden contexts. This is in striking contrast to the faunal remains, of which the vast majority come from the midden. Such a contrast cannot easily be explained by poor preservation conditions: the

presence of large quantities of carbonised wood in the midden would argue that carbonised seeds should have survived. It is likely, therefore, that during the phase represented by the midden deposits, most crop processing was either carried out on a part of the site remote from that which was excavated, or that the majority of plant material arrived on the site pre-processed.

Most of the plant remains recovered consisted of charred cereals, with spikelet forks, glume bases and grains being preserved (Table 4.6). Hulled wheats are represented by the presence of grains which fall into a number of morphological categories but may represent spelt wheat (*Triticum spelta*) and emmer (*Triticum dicoccum*). The free-threshing wheats were represented by a group of small-seeded, squat grains which can probably be attributed to bread or hard wheat (*Triticum aestivum/durum*). In addition, there were other caryopses which resembled bread/club wheat (*Triticum aestivo-compactum*). Only two rachis fragments were recovered from the free-threshing wheats and in both cases they can probably be attributed to *Triticum durum* or *Triticum turigidum*. The presence of the diploid wheat einkorn (*Triticum monococcum*), and of Rye (*Secale cereale*) is only tentatively suggested, being based on the recovery of two grains for which firm attribution is not possible.

The grains of barley (*Hordeum*) are almost exclusively

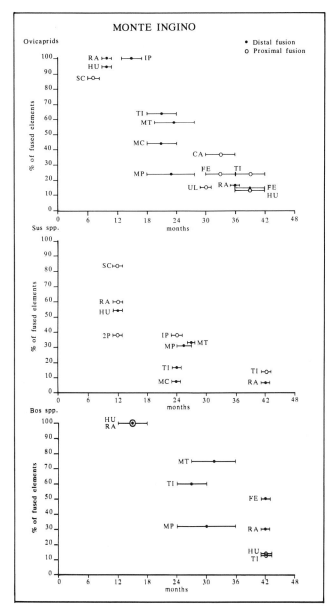

Fig. 4.4 Fusion rates of bones: Monte Ingino

Table 4.4. *Numbers of teeth recovered for the three dominant species in the midden (Phases J and K), Monte Ingino*

Tooth	Sus spp.	Caprines	Bos spp.
DI	8	4	–
I	240	106	38
C	61	3	–
dP	14	7	–
dP1	–	–	–
dP2	25	19	2
dP3	81	83	4
dP4	164	184	12
P	8	1	6
P1	2	–	–
P2	20	24	2
P3	51	106	26
P4	52	124	45
M	2	44	41
M1	179	325	37
M2	118	318	29
M3	52	126	12

Table 4.5. *Wear states for Sus spp., Caprines and Bos spp. from the Late Bronze Age midden, Monte Ingino*

Sus spp.	dP4	M1	M2	M3
Unworn	21	21	9	7
Very early wear	24	11	4	8
Early wear	19	8	8	3
Middle wear	14	4	2	0
Late wear	6	2	1	0
Caprines				
Unworn	1	1	7	9
Very early wear	1	9	41	10
Early wear	2	22	38	9
Middle wear	47	93	36	14
Late wear	15	10	0	4
Bos spp.				
Unworn	0	1	0	0
Very early wear	0	0	3	2
Early wear	3	3	2	0
Middle wear	1	8	11	2
Late wear	2	10	2	1

of the hulled variety; only one seed appeared to be naked and it is possible that this represents a hulled grain which had lost its lemma. No fragments of ear were recovered and so it is impossible to determine whether the barley was lax- or dense-eared. Both straight and twisted barley grains were recovered suggesting that six-rowed hulled barley (*Hordeum vulgare*) was being cultivated. Broomcorn millet (*Panicum miliareum*) occurred in very many of the samples. By contrast, oats (*Avena sp.*) was rarely present.

As far as pulses are concerned, the only cultivated species definitely identified was the field pea (*Pisum*

sativum), which was represented by a few carbonised grains. The other legume fragments were so poorly preserved as to prevent adequate identification.

A range of other plant species was recovered, although the quantity of non-cultivars was generally low. Many of the species, such as *Polygonum aviculare*, represent weeds

Table 4.6. *Monte Ingino plant remains: summary for major horizons*

Phases:	Middle Bronze Age		BA/sub-Appenine	LBA midden	Medieval		Total
	pre-daub	daub			A	B	
soil in kg.:	8	58	153	104	42	34	399
Species No. of samples:	4	17	54	34	15	15	139
Wheat							
Triticum monococcum							
?grains (1 sd. spklts)	–	–	1	–	–	–	1
Triticum dicoccum							
grains (1 sd. spklts)	–	–	2	–	2	–	4
grains (2 sd. spklts)	–	1	20	7	16	–	44
spklt forks	1	3	27	6	9	4	50
glume bases	1	–	14	3	11	1	30
Triticum spelta							
grains	–	2	14	3	9	2	30
spklt forks	–	1	5	–	2	1	9
glume bases	–	–	6	3	1	–	10
Triticum aestivum/durum							
grains	–	–	6	–	13	1	20
Triticum cf. *durum/turigidum*							
rachis frag.	–	–	2	–	–	–	2
Triticum aestivo-compactum							
grains	–	1	4	–	3	1	9
Triticum indet.							
grains	1	2	28	5	18	2	56
glume bases/basal nodes	–	–	12	–	1	2	15
Barley							
Hordeum vulgare							
straight grains	–	–	9	–	4	–	13
twisted grains	1	1	6	–	1	–	9
indet. grains	–	–	1	6	4	–	11
?naked grains	–	–	1	–	–	–	1
Other cereals							
Avena sp.							
grains	–	1	1	–	2	–	4
Panicum miliareum							
grains	3	37	148	38	57	53	336
Cerealea indet.							
grain frags.	5	35	267	66	142	34	549
cf. *Secale cereale*							
grains	–	–	–	1	–	–	1
Pulses							
cf. *Pisum sativum*	–	–	4	3	–	–	7
Pisum/Vicia sp. frag.	–	–	1	1	–	10	12
Other plants							
Bromus cf. *secalinus/mollis*	–	1	7	–	13	–	21
Other Gramineae	1	2	12	2	11	2	30
Caryophyllaceae	–	–	1	–	1	–	2
Chenopodium sp.	–	–	3	–	–	1	4
Cornus mas	–	–	–	4	–	2	6
cf. *Cladium mariscus*	–	–	–	–	1	–	1
Galium sp.	–	3	9	2	2	–	16

Table 4.6. (*continued*)

	Phases:	Middle Bronze Age		BA/sub-Appenine	LBA midden	Medieval		Total
		pre-daub	daub			A	B	
	soil in kg.:	8	58	153	104	42	34	399
Species	No. of samples:	4	17	54	34	15	15	139
cf. *Stachys* sp.		–	–	–	1	–	–	1
Labiatae		–	1	4	–	–	–	5
Vicia sp. (small)		–	1	3	–	1	3	8
Leguminosae indet.		–	–	5	1	3	–	9
cf. *Malva* sp.		–	–	1	1	1	–	3
Polygonum cf. *aviculare*		–	–	2	–	1	–	3
Polygonum/Rumex ssp.		1	2	–	–	1	–	4
Sambucus sp.		–	12	9	–	2	–	23
cf. *Viola* sp.		2	–	–	–	–	–	2
Indeterminate		1	4	7	3	3	1	19
Total cultivated seeds		6	55	334	86	173	80	734
Total non-cultivated plants		4	23	57	12	39	8	143
Total plants		11	82	398	101	215	89	896
Total carbonised fragments		17	110	642	156	335	120	1380
Concentrated fragments/kg soil								3.172

of cultivation whereas other species may have been gathered, for example the cornelian cherry (*Cornus mas*). One plant which may have been cultivated, although it is more frequently interpreted as a weed, is *Bromus*. The recovery of a single fruit resembling that of the saw-toothed sedge (*Cladium mariscus*) may indicate the gathering of sedges and their transportation to the site.

4.2.2 Monte Ansciano

The faunal sample recovered from Monte Ansciano, while smaller than that from Monte Ingino, is still comparatively large in relation to that from other Late Bronze Age and early Iron Age sites in central Italy. Around 3,500 identifiable elements were recovered from a total sample of over 12,000 bone and tooth fragments. About 86% of the identified fraction can be attributed to the Late Bronze Age, represented by Phases 3 to 5; most of the material comes from the midden deposits which constitute Phase 5. The remaining material is associated with Archaic period activity, much of which probably represents redeposited Late Bronze Age matrix. The recovery strategy used was essentially the same as that employed on Monte Ingino, and the number of small elements present in the identified sample was similarly high.

The assemblage is, yet again, dominated by domesticates (Table 4.3); other species (dog, roe and red deer) account

for only 6% assessed on MNI and less than 1% assessed on NISP. The ratio between caprines, pigs and cattle in the Late Bronze Age assemblage, based on averaged MNIs for bones and teeth, is roughly 4:1:1. There are, however, very significant disparities between MNI as calculated on bones and on teeth for caprines and cattle, with bones consistently underestimating MNI by around 50%.

This disparity is difficult to explain in terms of the recovery strategy or differential preservation. It is true that the bone from the Late Bronze Age midden deposits was highly fragmented; but this is also true of that from the Monte Ingino midden, for which teeth and bone MNIs are in general agreement for these animals. The fact that the disparity is less marked in the case of pig MNIs for teeth and bones tends to imply that this pattern is not a product of differential preservation or scavenging. Neither is there any evidence from ageing that the caprines and cattle were particularly young at death, the likely cause of MNIs disparity for pig in the Monte Ingino midden. Analysis by skeletal element (Table 4.7) shows that the number of long bones and other body elements is depressed by comparison with both mandibles and loose teeth; the incidence of caprine distal tibia, calcaneum and astragalus is also unusually high by comparison with other elements. The reason for these patterns remains unclear.

For the Archaic assemblage, bone and teeth MNIs are also inconsistent, and have an average ratio caprines:pig:

Table 4.7. *MNI and NISP by bone for dominant species in the LBA phases of Monte Ansciano*

Element	Caprines MNI	Caprines NISP	Sus spp. MNI	Sus spp. NISP	Bos spp. MNI	Bos spp. NISP
Maxilla	73	454	8	88	20	115
Mandible	73	471	14	142	21	143
Mandibular condyle	34	34	12	19	6	10
Hyoid	0	0	0	0	0	0
Atlas	0	0	0	0	0	0
Axis	0	0	0	0	0	0
Scapula	5	13	3	4	4	14
P. humerus	5	14	3	10	2	6
D. humerus	14	39	9	11	2	8
P. radius	8	18	3	4	3	12
D. radius	18	55	8	19	5	13
P. ulna	8	10	3	9	1	2
D. ulna	0	0	2	4	0	0
Carpals	4	24	2	8	4	10
P. metacarpal	21	56	3	16	1	2
D. metacarpal	16	64	3	19	7	17
1st phalange	9	77	3	13	3	13
2nd phalange	7	35	2	6	1	8
3rd phalange	3	17	1	5	1	6
Innominate	12	70	4	12	4	19
P. femur	11	39	1	2	2	11
D. femur	8	39	3	10	2	6
Patella	0	0	3	4	1	1
P. tibia	4	21	3	7	2	9
D. tibia	36	87	4	7	3	4
P. fibula	0	0	0	0	0	0
D. fibula	2	3	1	2	0	0
Calcaneum	33	67	4	8	2	4
Astragalus	33	79	4	7	2	4
Navicular	12	23	1	2	5	8
Cuboid	0	0	3	3	0	0
Cuneiform tarsals	1	1	1	1	6	9
P. metatarsal	11	48	4	24	6	16
D. metatarsal	14	68	4	24	8	22
Lateral metapodial	0	0	0	0	0	0
P. sesamoids	0	0	1	1	0	0
D. sesamoids	0	0	1	3	0	0

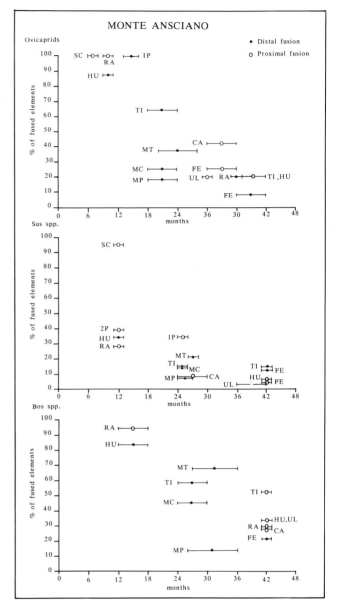

Fig. 4.5 Fusion rates of bones: Monte Ansciano

cattle of 10:3:4. These figures suggest a relative fall in the dominance of caprines and a rise in cattle in the Archaic assemblage; however, it is difficult to establish the significance of this given the smaller size of the later assemblage (and its probable residuality).

As at Monte Ingino, the age structure of the assemblage was jointly assessed on bone fusion and tooth wear. The size of the Monte Ansciano assemblages, however, means that the data show much more variability thereby making detailed interpretation difficult. This is particularly true of the Archaic Phase material which is really too incomplete in the case of cattle and pigs to permit firm conclusions to be drawn.

The caprine kill pattern for the Late Bronze Age phase, assessed on fusion ratios (Fig. 4.5), suggests that many of the animals present in the assemblage were killed at between 18 and 24 months. This finds support in the tooth wear data (Table 4.8) which show that around 76% of M1s are in moderately advanced states of wear whereas

Table 4.8. *Tooth wear for Sus spp., Caprines and Bos spp., Monte Ansciano*

	Late Bronze Age			Archaic		
	M1	M2	M3	M1	M2	M3
Sus spp.						
Unworn	2	4	1	1	2	0
Very early wear	8	11	1	1	0	0
Early wear	4	6	0	3	2	0
Middle wear	7	0	2	0	1	0
Late wear	3	0	3	3	1	0
Caprines						
Unworn	1	1	3	0	0	0
Very early wear	8	38	39	1	5	3
Early wear	14	77	23	3	12	3
Middle wear	162	78	21	26	15	5
Late wear	28	14	8	10	6	3
Bos spp.						
Unworn	0	2	0	0	0	0
Very early wear	2	4	1	0	0	0
Early wear	8	2	0	0	0	0
Middle wear	6	4	1	0	0	1
Late wear	30	15	7	7	0	0

Table 4.9. *Monte Ansciano plant remains*

	Context					
Species	27	31	121	172	201	207
Triticum indet. grains	–	–	–	1	–	–
Hordeum vulgare indet. grains	1	1	–	–	–	–
Panicum miliareum grains	–	–	–	1	–	2
Cerealea indet. grain frags.	–	–	–	–	1	3
Vicia faba	–	–	1	–	–	–
Cornus mas frags.	2	–	–	–	1	–

only 38% of M2s (eruption at 9–12 months) and 22% of M3s (eruption at 18–24 months) are in middle wear states. Unfortunately, the incidence of dP4 and P4 was not recorded at Monte Ansciano. For the Archaic phase, the pattern appears to be very similar notwithstanding much greater variation in the tooth wear states. The incidence of individuals over two years of age is probably no more than 20%.

Perhaps as many as 70% of the pigs represented in the Late Bronze Age assemblage were killed before the end of their second year of life (Fig. 4.5). A small number of individuals also appear to have been culled sometime during their fourth or subsequent years. The dental evidence supports the idea of a predominantly young kill, with the majority of M2s being unworn or in early wear (Table 4.8): this tooth erupts at between 7 and 13 months after birth. The pig kill pattern for the Archaic Phase appears to be similar to that for the Late Bronze Age phase. It is possible that the individuals at Monte Ansciano may have been slightly older on average than those present in the Late Bronze Age midden on Monte Ingino. The tooth wear pattern for both M1 and M2 contains a noticeably higher incidence of early and middle wear states than that observed at Monte Ingino. This could be an artefact of differences in foraging patterns rather than the age of culling; however, it is also true that MNI

calculated on teeth and bone are in close agreement here, something which would be less likely to be true if the assemblage contains a high proportion of very young animals. The fusion ratios can be taken to support the idea that fewer animals were killed before reaching 12 months than at Monte Ingino, although the much smaller sample size makes rigorous comparison difficult.

The pattern for cattle for both the Late Bronze Age and Archaic phases is difficult to establish with any confidence given the size of the assemblage. The fusion ratios (Fig. 4.5) give no clear trend and suggest kills of animals from upwards of 2 years, with a significant number of mature individuals being present. This is supported by the dental evidence (Table 4.8), which shows that the majority of M1, M2 and M3 are in advanced states of wear, with a scattering of earlier wear states also being present.

Two rodent bones and three bird bones were recovered from Late Bronze Age contexts but have not yet been identified.

The floral evidence from Monte Ansciano is extremely scant (Table 4.9). Some 32 samples were taken from 22 contexts. From the total of 92 kg of matrix which was floated and sieved, 14 identifiable carbonised fragments were recovered of which only 9 come from phased contexts. The Late Bronze Age material comprises 4 unidentified grain fragments attributable to the Cerealea, 2 grains from Broomcorn millet (*Panicum miliareum*), and a cornelian cherry stone (*Cornus mas*). Broomcorn millet was also recovered from the Archaic Phase, as was a single grain of one of the wheats (*Triticum* indet.).

4.2.3 Sant' Agostino

The evidence from Iron Age Sant' Agostino is strikingly different. No animal bones were found in the very small

Table 4.10. *Fusion ratios for Caprines, Sus spp. and Bos spp. from the midden (Phases J and K), Monte Ingino*

Element	Fusion point	NF:F	%F	Approximate age of fusion
Caprines				
SC	PF	0:180	100	6–8 months
RA	PF	0:143	100	10 months
HU	DF	31:199	87	10 months
1P	DF	0:362	100	13–16 months
TI	DF	78:140	64	18–24 months
MC	DF	55:18	25	18–24 months
MT	DF	31:18	37	20–28 months
MP	DF	207:45	18	18–28 months
UL	PF	78:20	20	30 months
CA	PF	69:49	42	30–36 months
FE	PF	152:52	25	30–36 months
RA	DF	160:40	20	36 months
FE	DF	156:14	8	36–42 months
TI	PF	39:10	20	36–42 months
HU	PF	33:8	20	36–42 months
Sus spp.				
2P	PF	128:83	39	12 months
RA	PF	48:19	28	12 months
U	DF	52:27	34	12 months
SC	PF	3:62	95	12 months
1P	PF	22:127	34	24 months
TI	DF	40:7	15	24 months
MC	DF	175:28	14	24 months
MP	DF	189:15	7	24–27 months
MT	DF	84:22	21	27 months
CA	PF	75:6	8	24–30 months
UL	PF	76:2	3	36–42 months
HU	PF	29:2	6	42 months
FE	PF	87:4	4	42 months
FE	DF	45:6	12	42 months
RA	DF	89:0	–	42 months
TI	PF	19:3	14	42 months
Bos spp.				
HU	DF	2:10	83	12–18 months
RA	PF	1:17	94	12–18 months
TI	DF	10:14	58	24–30 months
MC	DF	11:9	45	24–30 months
MP	DF	45:7	13	24–36 months
MT	DF	6:12	67	27–36 months
RA	DF	10:4	29	42 + months
FE	DF	26:7	21	42 + months
HU	PF	2:1	33	42 + months
TI	PF	10:11	52	42 + months
UL	PF	4:2	33	42 + months
CA	PF	8:3	27	42 + months

Table 4.11. *Fusion ratios for Caprines, Sus spp. and Bos spp. from the Late Bronze Age (Phases BA1 and BA2), Monte Ansciano*

Element	Fusion point	NF:F	%F	Approximate age of fusion
Caprines				
SC	PF	2:13	87	6–8 months
RA	PF	0:20	100	10 months
HU	DF	2:42	95	10 months
1P	DF	0:94	100	13–16 months
TI	DF	35:63	64	18–24 months
MC	DF	9:7	44	18–24 months
MT	DF	9:12	57	20–28 months
MP	DF	69:22	24	18–28 months
UL	PF	11:2	15	30 months
CA	PF	56:33	37	30–36 months
FE	PF	26:8	24	30–36 months
RA	DF	31:7	18	36 months
FE	DF	32:5	14	36–42 months
TI	PF	13:4	24	36–42 months
HU	PF	13:2	13	36–42 months
Sus spp.				
2P	PF	5:3	38	12 months
RA	PF	2:3	60	12 months
HU	DF	6:7	54	12 months
SC	PF	1:5	83	12 months
1P	PF	8:5	38	24 months
TI	DF	5:1	17	24 months
MC	DF	11:1	8	24 months
MP	DF	11:5	31	24–27 months
MT	DF	14:7	33	27 months
CA	PF	7:0	0	24–30 months
UL	PF	7:0	0	36–42 months
HU	PF	8:0	0	42 months
FE	PF	2:0	0	42 months
FE	DF	6:0	0	42 months
RA	DF	15:1	6	42 months
TI	PF	6:1	14	42 months
Bos spp.				
HU	DF	0:11	100	12–18 months
RA	PF	0:17	100	12–18 months
TI	DF	2:3	60	24–30 months
MC	DF	2:0	0	24–30 months
MP	DF	17:8	32	24–36 months
MT	DF	2:6	75	27–36 months
RA	DF	7:3	30	42 + months
FE	DF	3:3	50	42 + months
HU	PF	7:1	13	42 + months
TI	PF	6:1	14	42 + months

Table 4.12. *Sant' Agostino plant remains: summary*

Triticum dicoccum	
grains (1 sd. spklts)	1
grains (2 sd. spklts)	7
tear drop grains	5
Triticum aestivum s.l.	
grains (2–4 sd. spklts)	30
aestivo compactum grains	18
grains (1 sd. spklts)	2
indet. grains	17
Triticum indet. grains	8
Hordeum vulgare	
straight grains	22
twisted grains	18
indet. grains	38
Cerealea indet.	
grain frags	229
Bromus cf. *secalinus/mollis*	3
Gramineae indet. grains	4
Polygonum aviculare agg.	2

excavated area and the cereal remains were limited to *Triticum aestivo-compactum* (club/bread wheat), *Hordeum vulgare* and, in much smaller quantities, *Triticum dicoccum* (Table 4.12). If taken at face value, this may represent both specialisation and intensification once agriculture was concentrated on the lowland areas to the south of Monte Ingino and Monte Ansciano.

4.2.4 Interpretation

In terms of the relative proportions of animal species as measured on numbers of individual specimens, Monte Ingino and Monte Ansciano are fairly atypical when compared to other published Late Bronze Age sites in central Italy, the principal differences being the high proportion of pig and the low proportion of cattle (Table 4.2). Unfortunately, the manner in which other sites have been published makes it impossible to compare them on the more secure basis of minimum numbers of individuals. The only comparable site is San Giovenale (Sorrentino 1981), where pig outnumber cattle throughout the Late Bronze Age and into the Archaic period, although the small sample size must cast doubt on the statistical significance of this pattern. Also exceptional is the high percentage of canids present at Monte Ingino: only Torrionaccio produced a comparable figure. Insofar as the assemblage shows approximately equal percentage representation of pig and cattle, Monte Ansciano is more similar to other published sites, most notable the Late

Bronze Age and Archaic phases of Narce and the Middle Protovillanovan phase at San Giovenale. Even so, the ratios between caprines, and pig and cattle lie at the limits of those from published sites.

The liminal position of Monte Ingino and Monte Ansciano is not, perhaps, unexpected. Overall, the published faunal assemblages from the Late Bronze Age of central Italy do not show a coherent pattern other than a general dominance of caprines. Nor does there appear to be much direct correlation with environmental factors: comparable lowland sites such as Torrionaccio and Sorgenti della Nova present markedly different faunal assemblages, whereas San Giovenale and Monte Ingino are very similar despite the fact that they would have been subject to radically different environmental conditions (Stoddart 1987; Spivey and Stoddart 1990). Whilst the cause of this diversity is, as yet, uncertain it is clear that no simple economic model will accommodate the available data in any detail. Barker's thesis of a semi-pastoralist society operating a transhumant system between the coastal littoral and the Apennine uplands (Barker 1972) does not contradict the evidence but equally it does not account for the observed diversity.

At Monte Ingino and Monte Ansciano, the overall kill pattern for pig is not remarkable by comparison with medieval and early modern European practice, and is consistent with exploitation of this animal as a fresh meat staple. One might expect most animals to be culled towards the end of their first year when they would have attained a reasonable carcass weight under typical foraging regimes. The possibility that many of the animals were juvenile may suggest, however, that a significant number were killed for fresh pork before reaching their peak carcass weight. This would represent under-utilisation of this resource from a purely economic perspective and may imply a regime which supported a certain degree of self-indulgence. Young pig and suckling pig are typically feasting delicacies.

Comparison with other published sites is difficult owing to their small sample sizes but suggests that this culling pattern is not typical of the Late Bronze Age in central Italy. At Narce, which affords the best comparative sample, Barker (1976) concluded that most pigs were killed in their second and third years. This practice is perhaps consistent with the rearing of mature bacon-weight pigs for preservation as hams and sausage and for the rendering of animal fats. At Sorgenti della Nova (Caloi and Palombo 1981), there was a broader spread of ages than at Narce but no marked concentration on young animals as found at Monte Ingino. The pattern may be closer to that observed at Monte Ansciano, where there appears to have been a tendency towards culling of older animals than at Monte Ingino; however, it is impossible to make a more direct comparison in the absence of qualifying age ranges. Patterns similar to that of Sorgenti della Nova occur in the *Bronzo finale* levels of Monte Rovello (Caloi and Palombo 1985) and at Luni (Lepiksaar 1975), whilst those from San Giovenale (Sorrentino 1981) echo Narce.

By comparison, the kill pattern for cattle is fairly typical of that observed at other Late Bronze Age sites in central Italy, and indeed on most Italian sites until well into the early modern period. Cattle were probably kept principally to provide traction rather than for their meat or dairy products. Kills would have been more or less opportunistic, representing the culling of excess calves and those animals whose useful working life was over, hence the spread of values across the bone fusion and tooth wear states. The relatively low presence of cattle by comparison with other domesticated species suggests that the economy represented by the Late Bronze Age middens on Monte Ingino and Ansciano had only limited require-ments for traction. This is consistent with the low incidence of cultivars and the virtual absence of any evidence of crop preparation; it is possible that much if not all cereal grain was imported onto the site from elsewhere.

The caprine kill pattern is not dissimilar to that recorded for other published sites, although there are discrepancies of detail. At Narce a significant proportion of caprines appear to have been killed before the end of their second year, and the majority were dead before entering their fourth year (Barker 1976). Other sites are published in ways which make detailed comparison difficult but it is clear that this pattern is not unique. At Sorgenti della Nova (Caloi and Palombo 1981), the majority of animals were adult at death, but not old; and at Monte Rovello (*Bronzo finale* levels) there is almost equal representation of young, sub-adult and adult animals but few more mature or old individuals. At Luni (Lepiksaar 1975), the majority of caprines are said to have been in excess of three years at death; however, the wear state evidence upon which the assertion is based would equally support the idea that the animals were killed sometime during their third year of life. The middle Protovillanovan assemblage from San Giovenale (Sorrentino 1981) con-tained a predominance of adults, although the age range implied by this classification is unqualified. At both Monte Ingino and Ansciano, it appears that around one third of animals were killed sometime towards the end of their first year of life or shortly after the beginning of their second; and that two-thirds or more were dead by the beginning of their third year. This suggests slightly younger culling than that observed at the above sites but the herd management regime does not appear to be different in its essentials.

Such a culling pattern has generally been associated with farming of caprines for secondary products, principally wool and milk. However, the assumptions upon which such an interpretation is based need to be questioned. A wool herd would normally be composed of a mixture of ewes and castrated rams since the latter often produce superior fleeces; milk herds rely on their breeding ewes. Assuming that the caprine herds of Late Bronze Age central Italy consisted largely of sheep, something which is difficult to establish from the published evidence but which is widely held to be true (Barker 1976: 300–1), it seems likely that the flocks would have been composed primarily of breeding ewes with a secondary component of castrates. Together with a small number of goats, such a herd structure would provide a basis for wool and milk production.

Maintenance of this herd structure requires a particular culling strategy which should be reflected in the recovered faunal assemblages. A cull of between 20% and 40% towards the end of the first year or the beginning of the second is explicable in terms of removal of the majority of castrates after their first shearing and attainment of a reasonable carcass weight. However, reduction of the herd by a further 30% to 50% at around two years is difficult to understand. Ewes reach their reproductive peak at 4 years, after which point they tend to decline on rough hill pasture because of the effects of dental attrition. It makes little sense to cull a large proportion of them at around 2 years if the primary aim is to maintain the herd for milk and wool. By this age only two or at most three shearings will have been possible. Further, the ewes will only have come into milk once, if at all: Varro recommended in the first century BC that ewes should not be put to the ram until they had reached 2 years of age. If at Monte Ingino and Ansciano only around 30% of the herd survived into their third and subsequent years, this would appear to be much more consistent with a herd structure aimed towards production of meat and possibly wool rather than milk and wool.

On the other hand, it is possible that the Late Bronze Age assemblages from Monte Ingino and Ansciano represent only a partial view of the culling pattern and that they cannot be taken at face value in the determination of overall herd management regimes. Certainly, the midden deposits from which they are drawn present anomalies in terms of their faunal and material culture components (sections 4.3 and 4.4) which, taken together, make it difficult to accept that they represent typical domestic refuse from permanent settlements. Monte Ingino has yielded a quantity and range of bronzes which is unparalleled on other Late Bronze Age domestic sites and appears out of place if the midden simply constitutes ordinary settlement refuse. There is good circumstantial evidence for secondary products in terms of material culture such as loom weights and milk boilers; however, as has been pointed out the culling pattern for caprines based on the recovered faunal remains is not very consistent with an economy based on secondary products; nor does the pattern for cattle suggest maintenance of a dairy herd. The culling pattern for pigs is unusual by comparison with other published domestic sites of this period and cannot be considered typical of a permanent settlement where one would anticipate rearing of many animals to their full carcass weight for production of bacon, hams and sausage.[1] In addition, while there is evidence for cereal consumption, the low recovery rates obtained despite intensive sampling and good preservation conditions for carbonised material would seem to suggest that such staples were not present in any great quantity and may have been imported, already processed, onto the site. At Monte Ansciano, the low incidence of cattle and caprine long bones by comparison with cranial elements might possibly be explained if carcass joints were either being disposed of elsewhere on the site or being exported from it.

By contrast, many of the patterns observed in these Late Bronze Age assemblages start to make sense if one regards both sites as essentially seasonal camps which formed part of an extensive settlement system based on transhumant semi-pastoralism (Barker 1975). If this were the case then only part of the overall herd management regime would be represented in the faunal assemblages, namely that associated with summer subsistence and autumn aggregation prior to return to the Adriatic coastal lowlands. Faunal evidence from the coastal site of Colle dei Cappuccini at Ancona suggests a much more balanced, and arguably complete, subsistence economy spread evenly between cow (23%), pig (16%) and caprines (19%), as well as heavy reliance on wild animals such as pig (17%) and deer (20%) (Wilkens 1990).

This interpretation of the sites would explain the apparently profligate culling pattern observed for pigs. If the herds were driven back to the coast with the sheep then the mature animals selected for fattening would not be present in the assemblages. Even if pigs were kept throughout the year on the high pastures, there would be no requirement to manage the litters for long-term subsistence beyond fattening a few pigs for those who remained behind to tend them. For the purposes of these upland sites, pigs could be managed largely for fresh meat production as suggested by the culling pattern. Indeed,

there would be a positive advantage in reducing the herds to selected breeding sows and a few boars before the winter to conserve feed. Thus, the autumn aggregation of flocks before the return to the coastal plains might well have been accompanied by pig kills and the associated feasting which accompanied such events well into the early modern period in Mediterranean Europe.

The pattern observed for caprines also makes more sense if the faunal assemblages are seen as refuse from seasonal camps. The yearling rams and ewes will probably have been shorn together with the adult castrates and ewes shortly after reaching the upland pastures in the late spring. This would be the first shearing of their adult fleeces and would allow the shepherds to assess its quality and determine which animals to mark for culling (Varro II, II.2–5). The animals might then be killed during the season for fresh meat or, in the case of ewes, held over until autumn when their viability and milk yield would be known. Assuming that breeding practice followed that in use in classical times (Varro II, II.9), lambing would be complete by mid October. At this point the shepherds would be in the best position to further cull the herd on the basis of gender balance, observed viability, and milk yield before driving the flocks back to the coastlands (Varro II, I.24).

Overall, this regime is likely to result in a predominance of sub-adults in the faunal assemblage representing yearling castrates and ewes as well as a smaller proportion of older animals culled after lambing was completed. This is the pattern observed at Monte Ingino and Ansciano. As is the case with pigs, this culling would have made available appreciable quantities of fresh meat late in the season which could have been consumed in feasting before the journey back to the coastlands or preserved for later consumption. The relative proportions of long bones to other elements in the Monte Ansciano midden might possibly support arguments for the latter practice on that site. Presumably culling of older ewes and castrates took place at the littoral settlements, the animals being removed from the herd before its annual journey to the high pastures on the basis of their strength and viability for breeding.

If one accepts that both of the Late Bronze Age middens originate from seasonal camps then it is not, perhaps, surprising that the relative proportion of cattle is low. Even if the camps were semi-permanent, with a small

[1] Early culling of domestic pigs might also be a reflection of a high status site, or one where the economy was sufficiently prosperous to permit relative profligacy in meat consumption. The point to be made is that Monte Ingino does not exhibit a pattern which is typical of known permanent settlement in central Italy at this period.

number of inhabitants remaining through the winter, it is unlikely that crop production would have been a major activity and thus the need for traction would have been small. Cereals could have been brought up from the coastal plains in the spring which would explain their low incidence and the absence of evidence for crop processing. One should also not be surprised by the relatively high incidence of canids in the bone assemblage from Monte Ingino given the nature of the site.

The purity and relative richness of the cereal sample from San Agostino suggests a greater specialisation and intensification of cereal production on lowland sites by the eighth century BC. Interpretation of the sixth century BC phases of Monte Ansciano, immediately above San Agostino, as a seasonal ritual site provides an interesting contrast. It is probably significant that the proportion of caprines in the assemblages falls in relation to both pig and cattle and this may mark changes in the transhumant pattern towards more extended or semi-permanent occupation. Unfortunately, the size of the Archaic sample is too small to explore this idea further.

4.2.5 Conclusion

During the Late Bronze Age, the uplands of Gubbio probably served as summer and autumn pastures for transhumant pastoralists from permanent settlements on the Adriatic coastal plains. They established seasonal camps in the hills at sites such as Monte Ingino and Monte Ansciano. These were not, however, simply summer shielings: the size of the midden at Monte Ingino, for example, and its contents suggest that these seasonal sites were of a significant size and duration. It is possible that they functioned as aggregation centres in the autumn before the flocks were driven back to the coastlands and were the site of autumn culls after lambing had finished, perhaps associated with feasting.

There is little evidence from the sites that they had economies which would support permanent settlement, either in terms of herd management regimes as represented by culling patterns or arable farming as represented by cereals and other crops recovered during excavation. They must be understood as part of a more extensive agricultural economy involving the seasonal movement of animals, supplies and various primary and secondary products between upland and lowland settlements of varying degrees of permanence.

4.3 The settlement system of Gubbio in the Late Bronze Age and early Iron Age

4.3.1 The developing settlement system

The early Bronze Age in the Gubbio Basin appears to be represented by only one site [51: see Fig. 4.6] which has produced ceramic material and small quantities of flint. This was located on marginal Pleistocene clays in the centre of the southern part of the valley. Antiquarian finds from the Bellucci collection of Perugia museum, however, show a much more widespread distribution ranging from Branca (bronze dagger: Bellucci Bianco 271) and Gubbio/Valfabbrica (copper axe: Bellucci Giallo 2839) to Molini (bronze dagger: Bellucci Bianco 271) on the fringes and Gubbio in the centre (two bronze daggers: Bellucci Giallo 3826 and 2004). A few other isolated findspots of late prehistoric arrowheads in the basin point to activity of similar date. The location of the one known settlement, and the limited range of material culture, suggest that few technical or economic changes had occurred between the Neolithic and the early second millennium BC, except the introduction of metallurgy on a limited scale.

Within half a millennium, a very different settlement pattern was emerging in the Gubbio area (Fig. 4.6), and indeed across most of central Italy (section 4.4). Lowland sites were supplemented by prominent hilltop settlements often commanding views over mountain routes and grazing areas. Within the Gubbio valley, one site [163] in a lowland position can be tentatively identified as dating to the Middle or Recent Bronze Age, although further research and perhaps excavation would be required to clarify its chronology. It is placed in an area long exploited by earlier Neolithic settlement on a well-drained alluvial fan in the northern section of the basin. Pottery, querns, daub and black silty settlement residues were recovered.

At a higher altitude (c. 900 m) one site appears to have become prominent, Monte Ingino (Fig. 4.7; Plate 4.1), midway along the edge of the basin, commanding views over the valley and also the strategic passes through the mountains to the north including the Sentino valley where other contemporary settlements have been located (section 4.4). The site was only excavated on the northern flank of the northerly of the twin peaks of Monte Ingino just below the medieval Rocca Posteriore (Fig. 4.10). This northerly flank commands a particularly spectacular view along the approaches to the Sentino Valley from the Gubbio Basin. It is highly probable that a more extensive settlement (on admittedly a very limited site) may have occupied the long spine of the hilltop and in particular the

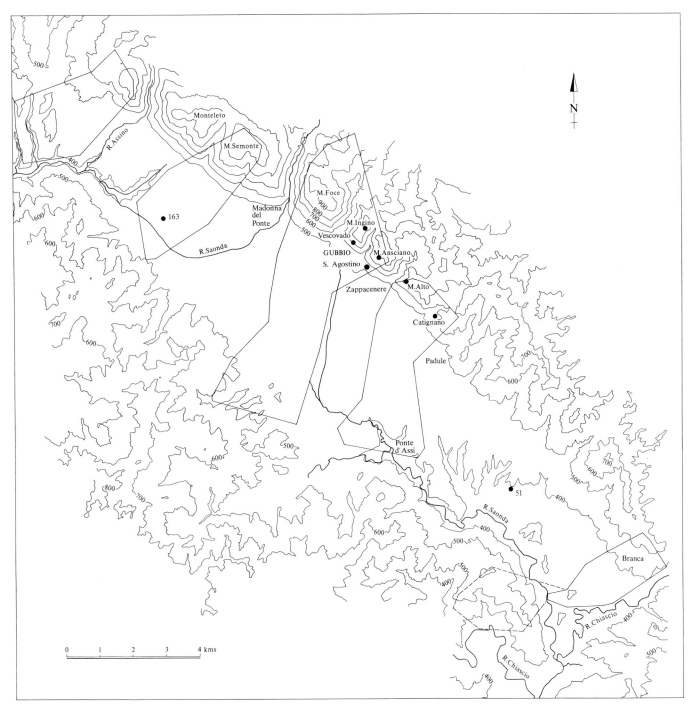

Fig. 4.6 Distribution of Bronze Age sites in the Valley of Gubbio

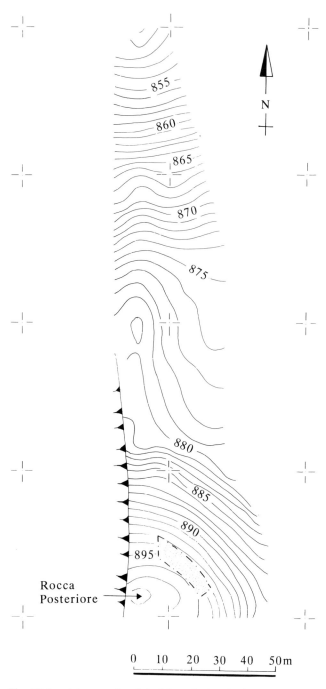

Fig. 4.7 Local topography of the Monte Ingino site (excavation area shown by stipple)

two peaks, one at the southerly as well as the northerly end. Prehistoric occupation of the northerly of these two peaks is almost certain since the excavation lay immediately below. Other areas were excavated, on the northerly peak, by the University of Perugia and the British School at Rome (Meloni 1987), and by the current project, lower down the hill to the north and on the spine between the

two peaks. Only medieval structures and very residual prehistoric remains were discovered.

The surviving evidence suggests that occupation of the northern peak was a new foundation in about 1400 BC since the soils beneath this level were sterile. This evidence may represent an extension to an earlier occupation on the peaks themselves. It is clear that the excavated area is on the edge of the settlement on a partly artificial rubble platform below the summit, on which between about 1400 and 1200 BC a series of daub dumps and daub surfaces were laid down perhaps to provide a level living space on an otherwise very precipitous limestone surface (Fig. 4.8). It is probable that this was either an area of temporary encampment outside the peak area or a processing area on the edge of the settlement that involved combustion and dumping of clay.

In the period between 1200 and 1100 BC or slightly later, both the internal organisation of the settlement and the relationship to local sites changed once more. On the site of Monte Ingino, the intensity of activity increased, but there was no substantial attempt to extend the settlement onto the lower reaches of the hillside. The excavated area is still clearly peripheral to the main settlement above, but collected the very domestic refuse that is so rare in almost every other excavated domestic area in central Italy (Figs. 4.9 and 4.11). The black sediments which were dumped in discrete mounds rich in pottery, bone and other refuse, dramatically indicate the increase in productive potential of the period (section 4.2 and below).

At the same time the relationship to contemporary sites also changed. There is no evidence for continuing occupation of the wide expanse of the valley floor, an area occupied at least since the Neolithic by substantial settlement. Local populations were instead drawn towards the colluvial footslopes at the foot of Monte Ingino and the neighbouring Monte Ansciano, setting up the co-operative system of sites discussed as a potential catchment in section 4.1. The excavated evidence from the Vescovado and San Agostino excavations is unfortunately derived from colluvial deposits where natural rather than cultural processes have become dominant. These contained pottery, daub, metal and carbonised remains moved from their primary position. It is, therefore, difficult to be precise about their function beyond what can be hypothesised from their topographical position.

From about 1100 BC or slightly later, occupation shifted, or at least expanded, from the restricted summit of Monte Ingino to the more extensive summit of Monte Ansciano (Fig. 4.12; Plate 4.2). Here structural remains have been uncovered that give a clearer indication of the nature of the occupation. A small ditch with an internal

Plate 4.1 Monte Ingino under excavation

drystone wall was constructed around the summit within which a midden collected (Fig. 4.13), again rich in pottery and bone, but much less rich in metalwork or other domestic utensils. Beyond the summit area, evidence for a large, oval, post hole structure was detected next to an interrupted ditch (Fig. 4.14). Eroding pottery and preliminary interpretation of geophysical results showed that the settlement continued over the whole summit of the hill, but excavation in other locations found only very limited evidence which might indicate a larger settlement. It is, though, possible that terracing which has been discovered in other contemporary upland sites in Liguria (Maggi and Nisbet 1990) simply did not survive on these eroded hilltops, unless protected by particular conditions such as a later sanctuary or localised soil cover. On the current evidence, it seems that in the two, probably successive, cases of Monte Ingino and Monte Ansciano, an outpost was maintained as a seasonal upland focus while the majority of the population were located (for reasons of space, access to resources and climate) on the colluvial slopes below.

It is difficult to address the density of off-site activity with the effectiveness possible for the Neolithic period, given the curation of bronzework (Stoddart and Whitehead 1991). However, the antiquarian Bellucci collection from the museum in Perugia gives some idea of surrounding landuse. Two bronze sickles (Bellucci Bianco 7847 and Giallo 1715), one broken, have the provenance of Gubbio, suggesting cultivation activities in the central part of the valley, confirming our tentative division of the landscape into upland grazing and lowland arable. In addition, three complete bronze axes (Bellucci Bianco 4634, Giallo 6636 and Giallo 5233) and the blade of a bronze axe (Bellucci Giallo 6016) also have the provenance of Gubbio. Two of these are described as *ad alette* and one is almost certainly the same as that illustrated by Bietti Sestieri (1973: Fig. 14, 2). These finds give a further indication of a concentration of activity, in this case felling activities, in the central part of the valley. A further blade of a bronze axe with a provenance peripheral to Gubbio (Toppello) suggests that there was some activity beyond this central area and also, most importantly, that at least some of the

Monte Ingino

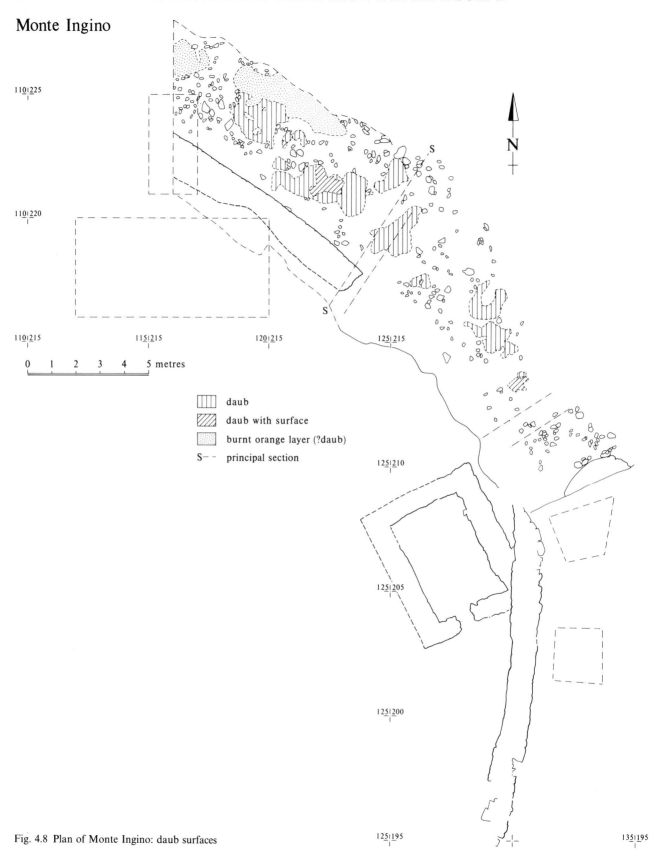

Fig. 4.8 Plan of Monte Ingino: daub surfaces

Monte Ingino

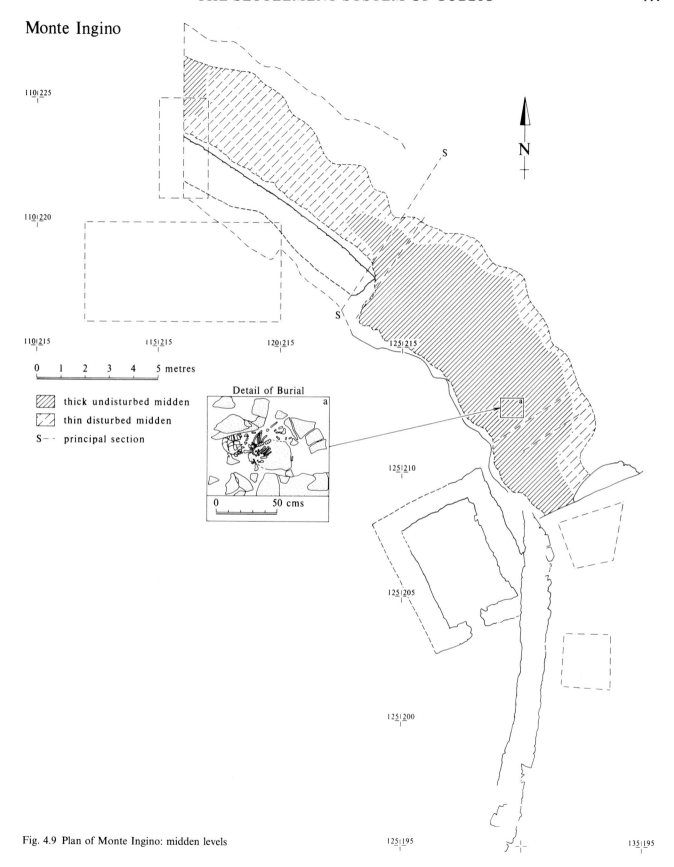

0   1   2   3   4   5 metres

▨ thick undisturbed midden

▧ thin disturbed midden

S─ ┄ principal section

Detail of Burial

0   50 cms

Fig. 4.9 Plan of Monte Ingino: midden levels

Monte Ingino

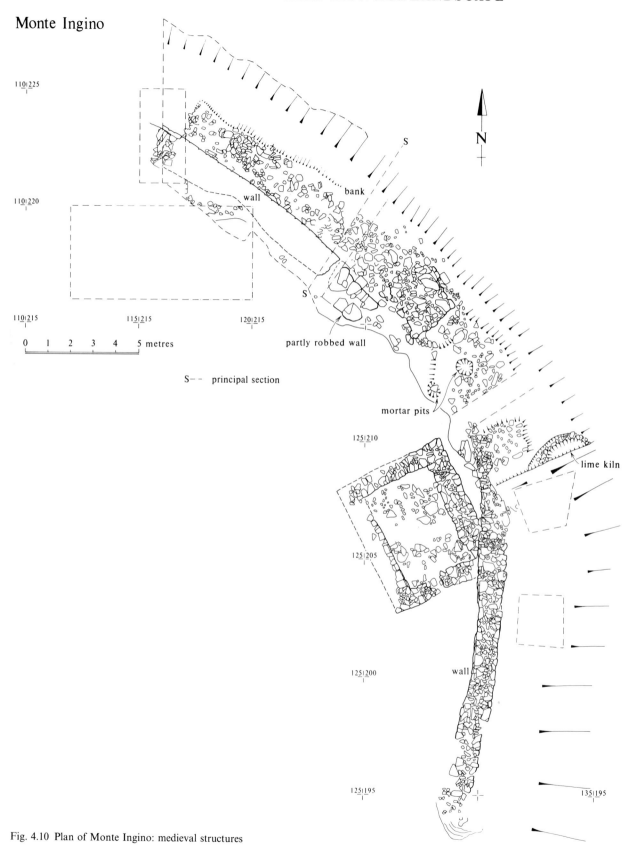

110|225

110|220

110|215

0   1   2   3   4   5 metres

S-- principal section

wall

bank

S

S

partly robbed wall

mortar pits

N

125|210

125|205

125|200

125|195

lime kiln

wall

135|195

Fig. 4.10 Plan of Monte Ingino: medieval structures

Monte Ingino

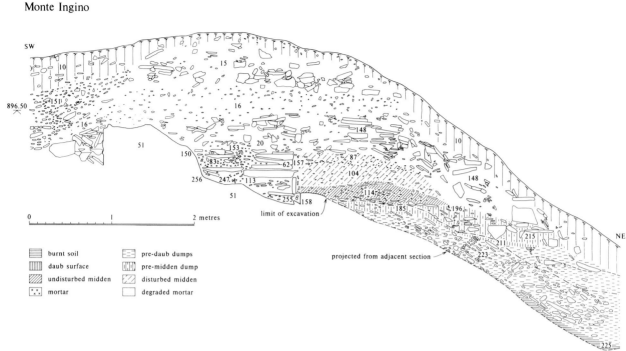

Fig. 4.11 Monte Ingino: section through the stratigraphy

provenances are accurate to more than to the nearest comune. The low intensity of the finds gives credence to these functional interpretations; there is no evidence locally for the depositional landscapes created by other Bronze Age societies (Bradley 1990).

It is clear that after about 950 BC these upland outposts of society were abandoned and the whole population collected on the slopes below the mountains of Monte Ingino and Monte Ansciano. These sediments are highly unstable colluvial slopes subject to sheet wash (Chapter 2) and unfortunately have not preserved many intact remains. However, the surface survey uncovered eroded fragments of protohistoric pottery across the whole southern edge of Monte Ansciano, suggesting that the concentration of settlement is not simply a product of subsurface excavation preceding modern urban development around Gubbio (although some possible protohistoric pottery has been found in a similar position on Monte Semonte). In road cuttings through the sediments on the slopes of Monte Ansciano (loc. San Agostino) a vertical pattern of eroding pottery was discovered. The only *in situ* remains were excavated by the Soprintendenza Archeologica per l'Umbria (under the direction of Maria Cristina De Angelis) in a precarious location several metres above the base of a road cutting. The road had just failed to destroy the last 50 cm of a hut platform in which carbonised seeds and a small quantity of Iron Age pottery was discovered.

A second excavation in the area of the Bishop's Palace by the University of Perugia (directed by Paola Guerzoni) on the slopes at the top of the town of Gubbio uncovered colluvial deposits in which there were residual remains of Iron Age pottery. It is unfortunate that the very nature of the terrain militates against understanding the organisation of what we hypothesise to be the first clustering of settlement, where six centuries later the city of Iguvium was to develop. Provided we accept the current evidence, it appears that the central location of modern Gubbio within the valley had an attraction for societies before the onset of urbanisation or state formation. The slopes of these limestone mountains afford good control of and easy access to the whole valley, including the vertical dimensions of the landscape immediately behind. To this must be added the advantages of the good drainage of the limestone colluvial slopes and easy access to the fertile alluvial fans and small watercourses immediately below (section 4.1).

4.3.2 Changing technology and production

There are obvious problems in making a simplistic interpretation of the midden deposit on Monte Ingino (see below) stratigraphically placed above what may be a peripheral working area of a settlement. Furthermore, there are probably very different practices of curation and

Monte Ansciano

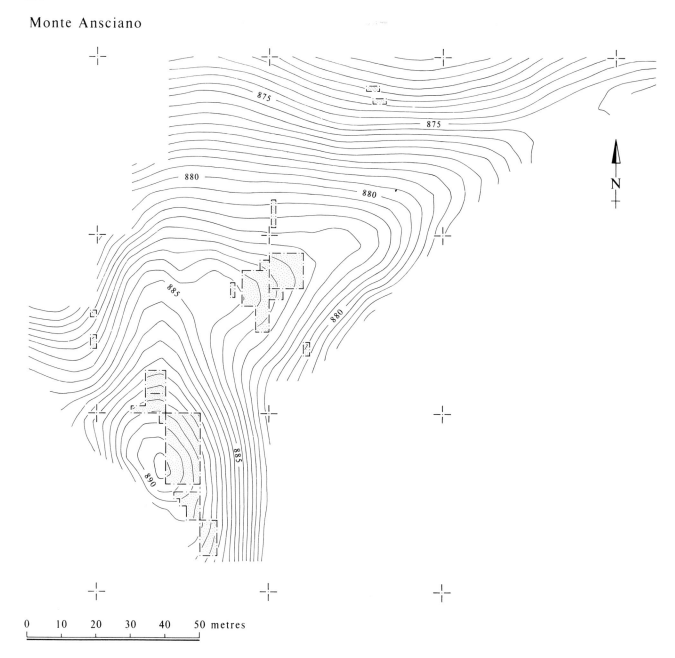

Fig. 4.12 Local topography of the Monte Ansciano site (excavation area shown by stipple)

waste disposal during the three hundred years or so of occupation. However a few simple observations on the type of deposition do form a consistent picture.

Some types of deposition are fairly consistent throughout the sequence, especially if observed against the great increase in waste disposal from about 1200 BC onwards. Disposal of horn, bone, spindle whorls, rubbing stones and flintwork took place throughout the sequence except for some of the earlier more sterile levels (Fig. 4.15).

Flintwork, although locally of poor quality, was still employed even in the developed bronze-using economies of the Final Bronze Age. Some of the flintwork, such as the arrowheads, is of a higher quality, but identifiable as second millennium in date by their broad thick-flaked surface. One bronze arrowhead is also known from the antiquarian Bellucci collection in Perugia museum (Bellucci Giallo 1327) These sectors of the productive economy seem to have continued virtually unchanged over the

Plate 4.2 Monte Ansciano under excavation

whole later Bronze Age. Both Santa Paolina (Filottrano) (Rellini 1931: Figs. 9 and 11) and Casa Carletti (Monte Cetona) (Calzoni 1936) show similar continuity.

Other types of disposal changed radically: principally, food refuse (section 4.2), pottery and metalwork (Figs. 4.17–4.27). From the pre-midden phases, there were just over 12,000 sherds weighing less than 1,500 kg. From the undisturbed midden phases there were nearly 30,000 sherds of pottery recoverd (of which less than 2,500 were fineware), weighing more than 3,000 kg. This demonstrates a greatly increased rate of deposition which involved an increased proportion of storage vessels and other types of coarseware. Specialised coarsewares remained a very small proportion of the whole. Nevertheless the one fragment of cooking stand (fornello) (Fig. 4.21, 6) and the two fragments of milk boilers (with internal rims) (Fig. 4.21, 4, 5) as well as sieves (Fig. 4.19, 28, 30) and spouts (Fig. 4.19, 32, 33) are probable indicators of the use of secondary products from the pastoral economy (section 4.2), in the form of cheese and fermented milk products.

The quality of ceramic production also improved over time. Limited micro-analysis of the fabrics of samples from Monte Ingino and Monte Ansciano (Skeates pers. comm.) was undertaken selectively on the chronological extremes of the Bronze Age sequence: the Apennine/ sub-Apennine phases of Monte Ingino (1400–1300 BC) and the final phase of the Protovillanovan represented by Monte Ansciano (c. 1100–900 BC). The comparison of these two blocks of samples shows improvement in the control of firing, greater standardisation in thickness and a decrease in coarse inclusions. There is also a decrease in the level of burnishing and a greater degree of surface porosity. It is possible that by the later period, pottery was being produced by a more limited group of craftsmen with less interest in the appearance of the final product, but more in its efficient production. This may in turn indicate a stage towards the specialisation of production, although almost certainly still at the community level. Similar trends have been noted in the *Bronzo Finale* of upland Liguria (Wagner 1990: 248). The material from

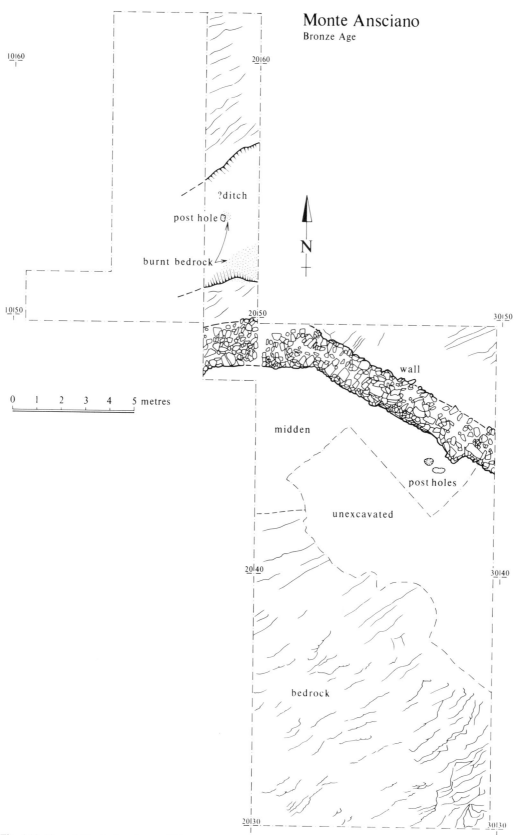

Fig. 4.13 Plan of Monte Ansciano: midden area

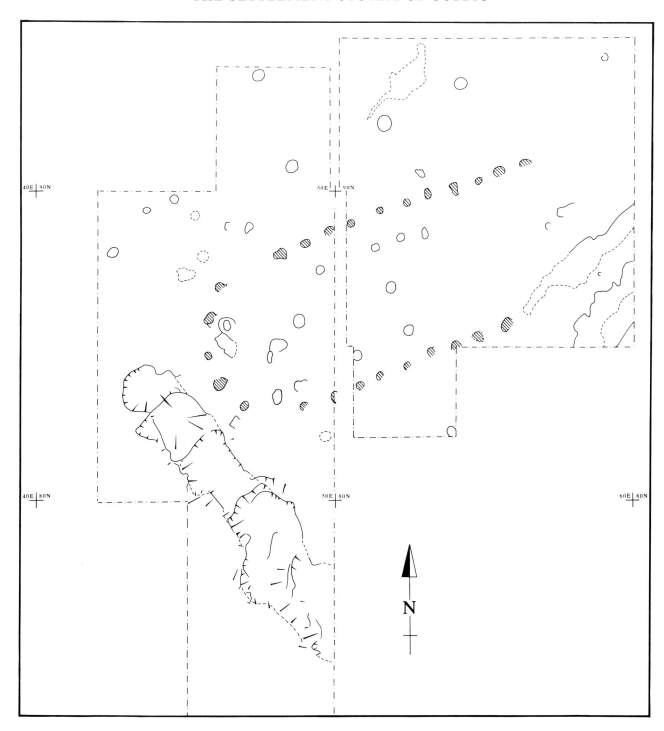

Fig. 4.14 Plan of Monte Ansciano: post hole area

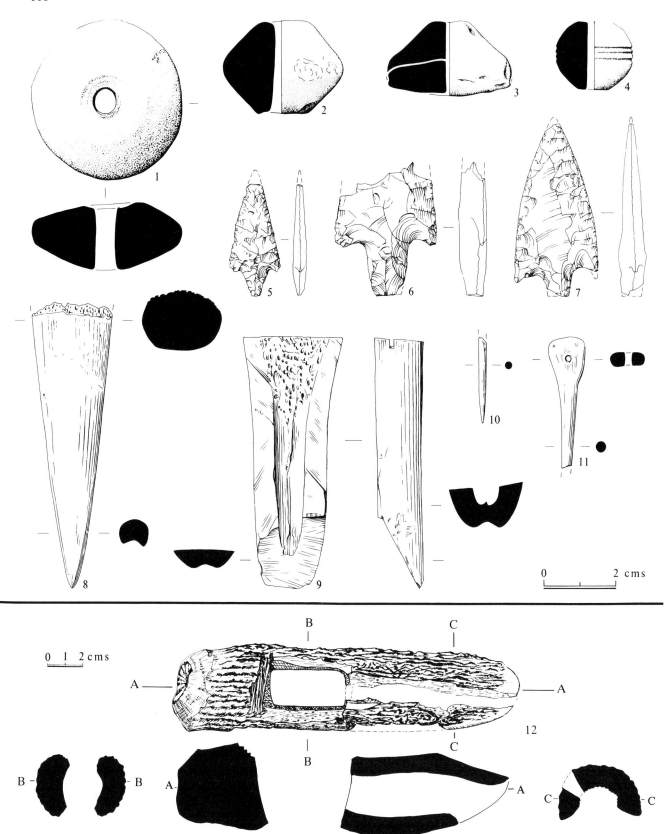

Fig. 4.15 Functional items from Monte Ansciano and Monte Ingino. Above line: 1–4 Spindle whorls; 5–7 Flint arrowheads; 8–11 bone tools. Below line: Bronze Age (?) antler haft

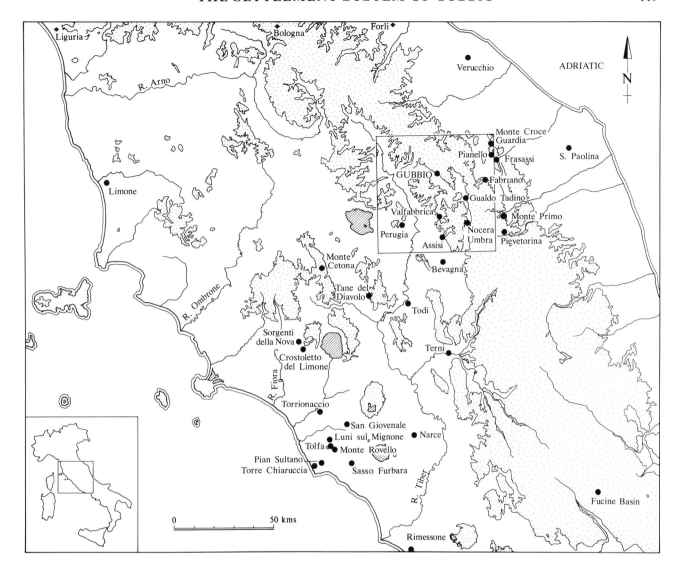

Fig. 4.16 Sites discussed in Chapter 4

the Iron Age site of Sant' Agostino was not included in this analysis, but the one piece of ribbed fineware shows an even higher standard of production whereas the coarsewares are fairly crude (Fig. 4.20: 27).

The increased deposition of metalwork fits into the pattern that has been convincingly argued by other scholars: namely that there was a general change in bronze production in the later Bronze Age of Italy. The use of bronze was low and curated until about 1300–1200 BC, but thereafter there was a notable increase in production, in terms of both range and quantity of metalwork (Peroni 1969). Even making allowances for the differing nature of the lower and upper levels of Monte Ingino (Chapter 1 and above), the site appears to conform to this general pattern of changing production,

with only ten pieces of metalwork (6%) from the lower levels (Apennine and sub-Apennine), and 108 (63%) from the upper levels, the middens of the Final Bronze Age. The remaining 31% were found in parts of the midden reworked during the medieval period (Fig. 4.10). It is also at this time of intensive metallurgy that glass beads were imported into the site. All the blue glass beads were found in the midden levels.

4.3.3 The meaning and function of the middens on Monte Ingino and Monte Ansciano

Assessing the meaning and function of large accumulations of rubbish is not a problem unique to the Bronze Age on Monte Ingino, but has been considered in the context of

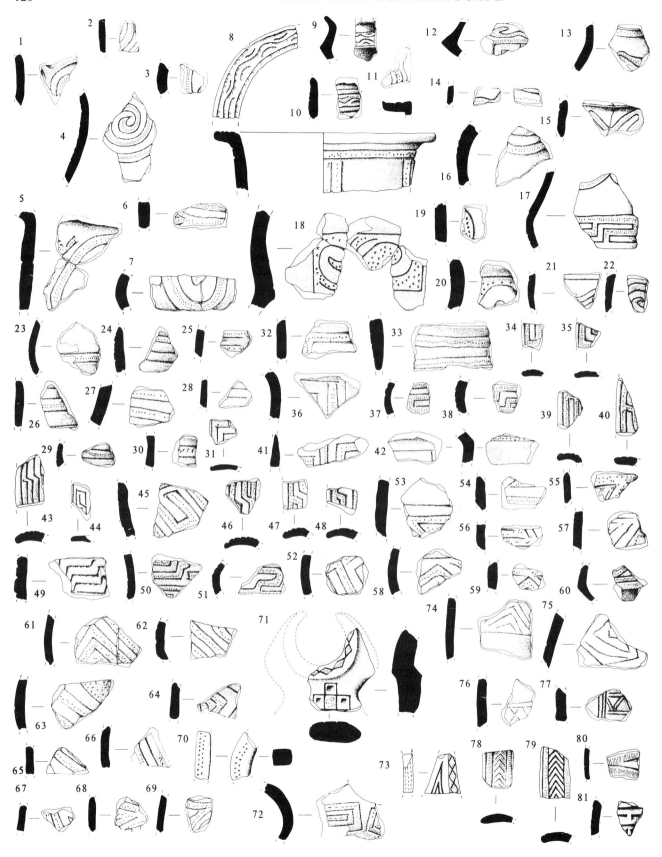

Fig. 4.17 Pottery. Apennine styles from Monte Ingino. Scale 1:3

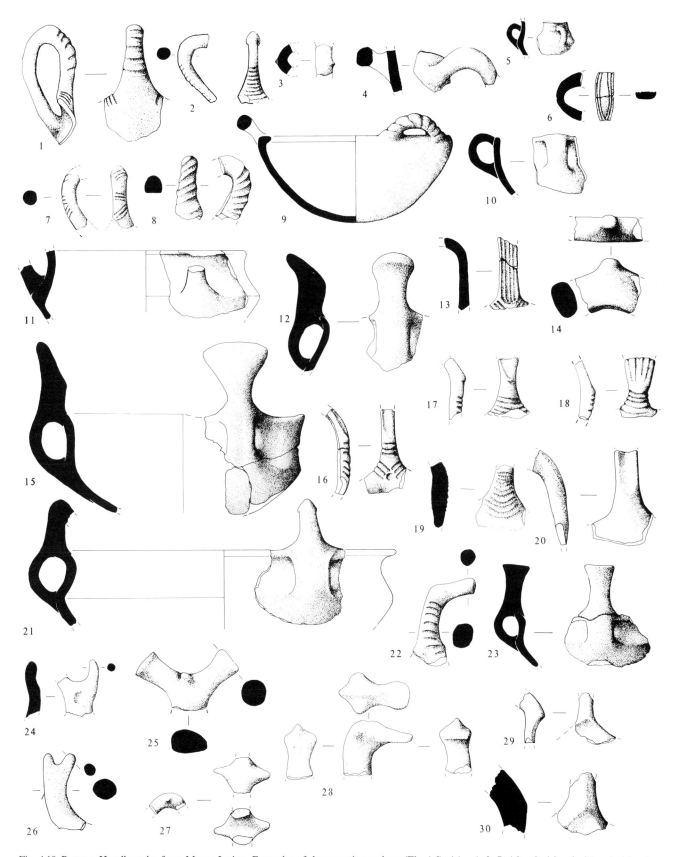

Fig. 4.18 Pottery. Handle styles from Monte Ingino. Examples of the ceramic typology (Fig. 1.5): A1 = 1, 2, 7; A2 = 8; A3 = 3; A4 = 4; A5 = 9; B1 = 5, 6; B2 = 10–11; B3 = 13; B4 + A10 lug = 14; C1 = 15; C3 = 16–21; C5 = 17–19; C6 = 20; C7 = 22; C8 = 23; C9 = 24; C10 = 25; C11 = 28; C12 = 29; C13 = 26; C14 = 30; D1 = 30. Scale 1:3

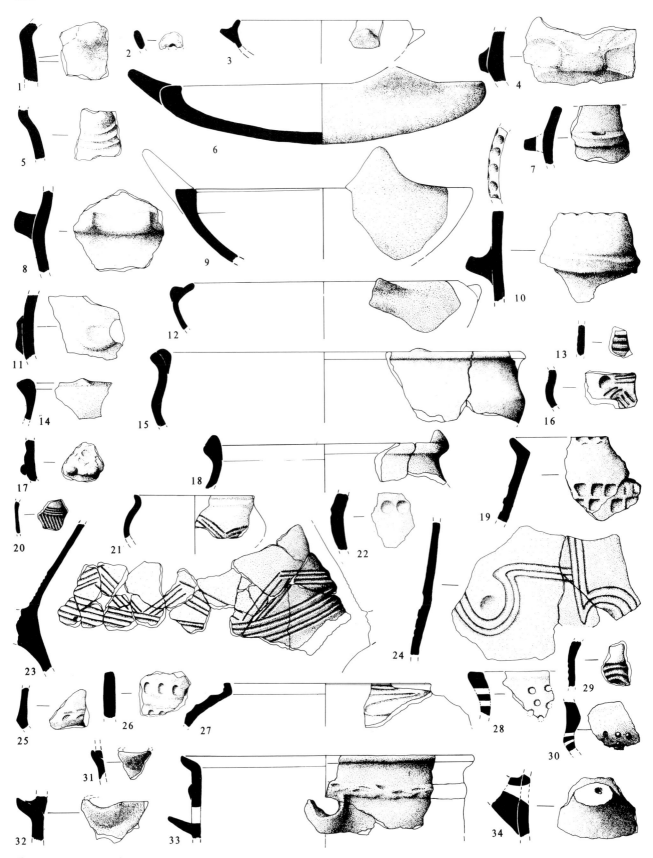

Fig. 4.19 Pottery. Lug forms, decoration and miscellaneous forms from Monte Ingino. Examples of the ceramic typology. Lugs: A1 = 1,3; A2 = 10; A3 = 8; A4 = 4; A5 = 7; A6 = 9; A7 = 2; A8 = 14–15, 18; A9 = 11; A12 = 17. Rims: C1 = 21; F3 = 15; F4 = 27; G1 = 12; G2 = 6; H1 = 9; I1 = 10. Grooved decoration = 13, 16, 20, 24, 29. Roulette decoration = 21, 25; Stamped decoration = 29; Dimpled decoration = 26; Spouts and strainers = 28, 30–32, 34. Scale 1:3

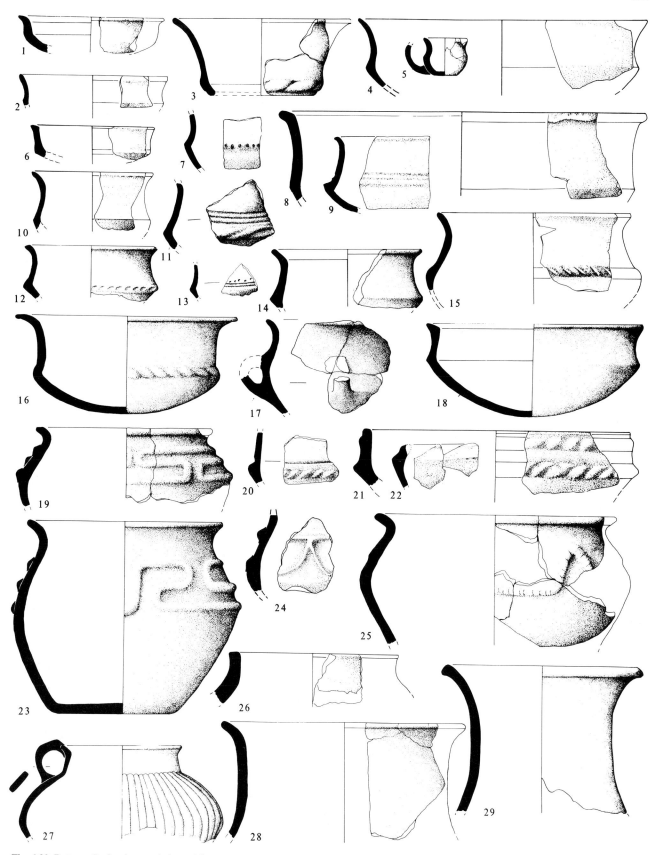

Fig. 4.20 Pottery. Carinations and rims of finewares and finer coarsewares from Monte Ingino, Monte Ansciano and Sant' Agostino. Carinations: Type 1 = 5–6, 12, 25; Type 2 = 8; Type 3 = 1, 4, 7, 9–11, 13–18. Rims: A1 = 21–22; A3 = 6; A4 = 26; C2 = 1, 16–17, 28–29; E5 = 18; F2 = 8; F3 = 2; F4 = 19; L1 = 27. Cordons: A5 = 24; A7 = 19, 23; B2 = 21; C4 = 25. Grooved Decoration = 13. From Monte Ansciano: 5, 9, 22 (?), 23; from Sant' Agostino (Iron Age): 27, 29. Scale 1:3

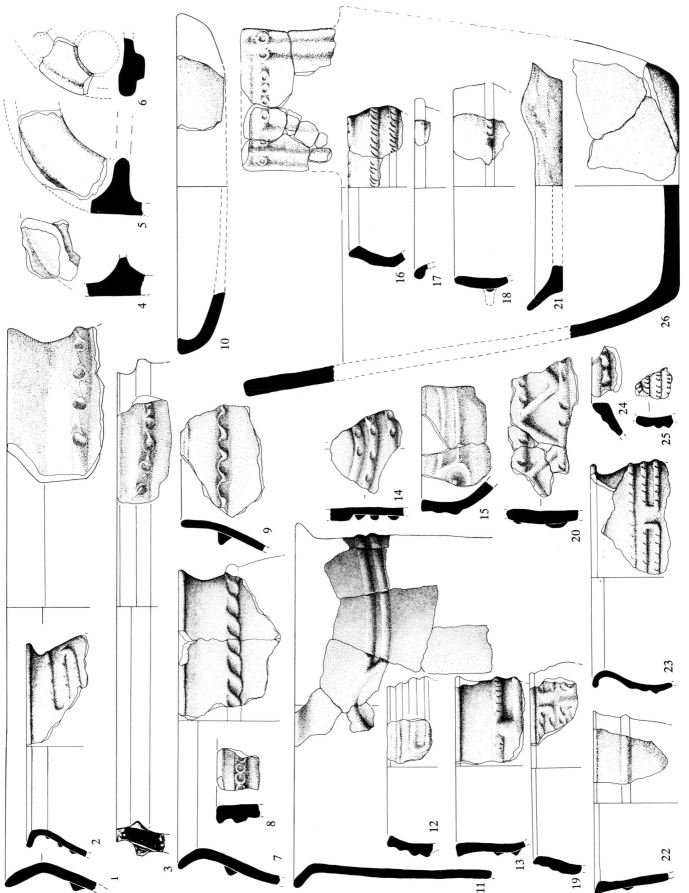

Fig. 4.21 Pottery. Milk-boilers/fornelli and coarsewares from Monte Ingino. Cordons: A1 = 22; A2 = 15; A4 = 2, 12; A5 = 11, 13; B1 = 1, 3, 7, 8, 9; B5 = 19; C1 = 24; C2 = 16; C3 = 14, 23; C3 and C4 = 25; C6 = 20; C20 = 26. Lugs: A8 = 21; A9 = 15. Milk boiler/fornello fragments: 4, 6. Rims: A1 = 18; B1 = 9; C1 = 7; C2 = 11; D1 = 3, 13, 19, 22; D2 = 8; E1 = 1; E4 = 1; H1 = 22; H1 = 10.

other exceptional accumulations of refuse, for example in the British Bronze Age (Needham and Sørensen 1988) and is important in the interpretation of humic deposits closer at hand in the Terramare Bronze Age of northern Italy (Säflund 1939). In the Gubbio case, are we principally dealing with a chance survival on a mountain top or a cultural phenomenon of significance? The fact that there are two middens, located in unusual positions on mountain tops, if otherwise somewhat different in character, suggests the strong possibility that we may be able to characterise a cultural phenomenon which would be simplistically described as domestic. However both the Gubbio deposits were fortuitously protected (and to a certain extent disturbed) by later structures, although in the case of Monte Ingino this took place as many as two thousand years later.

It is difficult to find an assemblage of artefacts with which to compare the middens of Monte Ingino. An important constraint is that few other sites have had similar collection strategies (involving both sieving and systematic metal detection of the deposits) of similar classes of deposit. One potential comparison is with Frattesina which has also been systematically sampled (Bietti Sestieri 1975–80: 227). The order of scale of Frattesina is, however, completely different; this can be expressed simply through the character, quantity and range of metalwork finds (Bellintani 1984). Monte Ingino was not a major production centre, but at the receiving end of the exchange networks (section 4.4).

An alternative source of comparison for the Gubbio middens is also north of the Apennines in the Po Valley. One famous class of sites is that of the *terramare* settlements, of rather earlier date, which have been famous since the last century as black mounds with large accumulations of organic and cultural debris (Säflund 1939; Ammerman and Butler 1978). The antiquarian collections contain, if it is assumed that smaller fragments were simply not recovered, similar numbers of bronze pins and similarly sized objects. However larger more precious objects, such as axes, daggers and spearheads occur in much greater numbers suggesting much less attention to the curation of metal supplies. Later sites in the Po Valley appear to have less deposition of metalwork (Catarsi Dall'Aglio 1976: 261; Salzani 1984), except in the form of occasional hoards (De Min and Bietti Sestieri 1984: 403–5) and with the important exception of the production centre of Frattesina (Bietti Sestieri 1975–80, 1981).

Comparisons with more characteristic settlement sites from central Italy to the south of the Apennines provide more immediate contrasts. The same quantity of domestic rubbish and particularly of metalwork has been retrieved and recorded from no other published site in this part of central Italy. Other domestic sites have typically produced relatively low quantities of material from Final Bronze Age levels: Torrionaccio (9), Casa Carletti (*c.* 45), Narce (45), Sorgenti della Nova (all bronzes found between 1973–9) (15). It is particularly significant that the most extensive excavation of a Final Bronze Age site in central Italy, at Sorgenti della Nova, has produced a mere fraction of the quantity of material from Monte Ingino (173) and Monte Ansciano (67). One similarity is the small size of the material recovered. Only the pins (up to 14 cm in length) and the one axe can be considered relatively large objects. A simple explanation of these contrasts is that few other Bronze Age middens have been discovered. Most settlement excavations have investigated those parts of the site deliberately kept clean by their occupants. Calzoni claimed to have found midden deposits at Casa Carletti (De Angelis 1990: 88) and it is significant that he found, in common with Narce, relatively large quantities of bronzework.

The interpretation of the Monte Ingino and Monte Ansciano middens as domestic rubbish deposits is supported by many constituent elements. Firstly there is the high quantity of material that cannot be easily attributed to any certain function: Monte Ingino (24 (14%)) and Monte Ansciano (24 (36 %)). Many of the scraps of metal recovered are waste products from bronzeworking. Secondly, other items in the assemblage fit well into a domestic assemblage. Knives and fragments of sheet bronze are the most common items. A number of further finds suggested bronzeworking: droplets of copper alloy, offcuts and fragments of larger objects deliberately broken by bending or chiselling (Winsor pers. comm.) (MA84/6 SF24; MI84/50 SF 204; MI85/127 SF 265; MI 85/999 SF 424–6). On Monte Ansciano there appears to be a particular collection of scrap metal fragments that are either residual Bronze Age within the Archaic levels or Archaic in date (SF 289, 400, 127, 249). Almost exclusively missing are precious metals and larger bronze items that form prominent components of hoards of the period: spearheads, swordblades and axes. The one exception to this distinguishes Monte Ansciano from Monte Ingino. The former produced not only a virtually pristine axe, but also bronze fragments (blade and horns from the butt) from the weakest parts of the axe (the cutting edge and the hafting area) that suggest the use of axes was a more frequent activity on Monte Ansciano. Whereas heavy woodcutting appears to have been restricted to Monte Ansciano, finer working of materials such as wood, bone and leather, suggested by the small awls and chisels, appears to have occurred on both sites.

An analysis of the relatively high number and unusual ratios of dress pins and fibulae in the Gubbio sites illustrates some of the problems with the analysis of the midden phenomenon. The cause could be chronological, stylistic or functional. Alternatively and less culturally interesting, the numbers could be the result of a natural loss ratio or the product of statistical vagaries with relatively small samples. There are 28 definite pins from Monte Ingino and 7 definite pins from Monte Ansciano. Collectively, probable/possible pins and fibulae approach 30% of the Monte Ingino and over 20% of the Monte Ansciano assemblage. A conservative estimate of the ratios of pins:fibulae places them in the order of 3.5–2.5 to 1 for both Monte Ingino and Monte Ansciano. On contemporary settlement sites from central Italy there is generally parity between recovery of pins and fibulae (for example Casa Carletti) or larger quantities of fibulae (Torrionaccio and Sorgenti della Nova). Cemeteries give an even more emphatic pattern of the predominance of fibulae (for example Pianello di Genga (Peroni 1963a) and Frattesina (De Min 1986)), including cases where pins are completely absent (Sasso di Furbara) (Brusadin Laplace 1984–7). A third class of sites – hoards – present a similar range to settlements and cemeteries from relative dominance of fibulae (Gualdo Tadino) (Peroni 1963c) to complete absence of pins (Monte Primo and Contigliano) (Peroni 1963b; Bonomi Ponzi 1970).

One explanation of these patterns could be chronological since this ratio would be perfectly allowable, indeed exceeded by earlier sites. Earlier sites include those of the *terramare* where pins dominate the domestic assemblages (Säflund 1939). The ratio could be a reflection of the early Protovillanovan date of the material on Monte Ingino but fails to explain a similar phenomenon on Monte Ansciano.

A second possible explanation is stylistic or cultural. The Gubbio sites are so placed as to have contacts with both central and northern Italy. It is highly probable that the Gubbio sites are following a cultural preference towards the use of dress pins that continues in the Iron Age of northern Italy. The excavation of the Late Bronze Age sites of Borgo-Panigale near Bologna (on a very small sample) (Catarsi dall'Aglio 1976: 261–2) and Mariconda (Salzani 1984) suggests that this may be the case. Pin fragments are much more frequent.

A third possible explanation is functional. The dress pin not only involved a simpler manufacturing technology but was most probably associated with a different form of dress. A dress pin can perhaps be associated with a heavier over-garment appropriate for the upland sites of Gubbio. The complementary expectation of this explanation would be to find a preponderance of fibulae worn by the contemporary communities in the valley below. The closest support that we have locally is from the nearby cemetery of Pianello where the ratio is 3:1 in favour of fibulae.

The interpretation of the middens is complicated by the fact that there are some differences as well as similarities between the two sites of Monte Ingino and Monte Ansciano. Both are located within a very short distance of the summit of their respective mountains. The principal components of the middens are pottery and bone in both cases. However, the midden on Monte Ansciano consists almost entirely of pottery and bone and only contains two metal objects. A subtle difference in the placing of the middens may explain this difference. The source of the Monte Ingino midden material may have been a settlement located immediately up slope and therefore the midden might be in a secondary position where material was dumped in discrete mounds from above. The Monte Ansciano midden material may have collected almost *in situ*, since the midden and its retaining wall forms the primary structure on the summit, and thus have been part of the original area for the activities that formed the midden. The overall degree of fragmentation of the pottery was slightly greater in the case of Monte Ansciano (an average of 8 g as opposed to almost 11 g per sherd) which could be caused by *in situ* trampling. The explanation for these middens must, therefore, encompass both refuse clearance (Monte Ingino) and *in situ* formation in a clearly defined enclosure.

It would be wrong, however, to interpret these assemblages as purely domestic, even though at first glance they represent normality on a rather more detailed scale. Final Bronze Age societies probably did not have the clear distinctions between the ritual and domestic spheres that appear with supposed clarity in modern societies. In fact the ritual was very probably embedded within social and domestic activities. The one hint of this is the discovery of two broken fibula catchplates with embedded broken blades on Monte Ingino. This evidence of an apparently ritualised action has great similarity to a similar find from the hoard of Rimessone (Delpino and Fugazzola Delpino 1979). No simple technological cause can explain this wrapping of a broken blade in a broken catchplate.

The clearest evidence for the partly ritual character of these deposits rests in their location (on mountain summits) and the periodicity of their accumulation. The exposed position of the sites and the faunal evidence suggests that we are in fact dealing with seasonal bursts of activity, representing peaks of consumption and production. The liminal nature of these sites would have encouraged ritual activities centred around consumption and production as an extension of the regular domestic routine. These mountain peaks were most probably seasonal meeting points of segments of communities from as far afield as the Adriatic coast, as well as those more locally based in the valley below. Given the social organisation of these communities, rituals were not highly structured, except in the case of death. It is these rituals which have left a more visible trace in the midst of the Apennine valleys.

4.3.4 Social foundations: social analysis of the cemetery of Pianello di Genga

The cemeteries of the Late Bronze Age in central Italy are generally small in size (up to fifty individuals) and consist of cremations in small urns with a restricted range of grave goods (razor, fibula, pin and so on) (Bietti Sestieri 1984a). At present there is no clear evidence for Bronze Age burial at Gubbio except for the poorly preserved remains of a child and two loose molars. The complete child was aged between 5 and 6 years old (Higgins pers. comm) and fairly conclusively dated to the Final Bronze Age from its position, without a well-defined grave cut, within the Bronze Age midden. The discovery of an infant treated informally in this manner, suggests the working of principles of age in the allocation of formal burial. An alternative reason is that some stigma was attached to a sickly child that had suffered from chronic anaemia at some stage in infancy.

The well-known cemetery of Pianello di Genga may be representative of the formal burial practices undertaken by populations resident at Gubbio. It is located within 35 km of Gubbio, set within the Apennine mountain passes. This cemetery has graves typical in central Italy in terms of burial rite (inurned cremation) and limited range of gravegoods (fibulae, pins and so on). There is also no evidence of differential treatment of the dead. In another respect, however, the cemetery is somewhat exceptional: its size of more than 500 cremations. A small contributing population could have been sufficient to provide bodies for the cemetery over the at least one hundred years of occupation, but the cemetery still represents a different attitude to death when compared with contemporary tombs on the Tyrrhenian coast. The simplest explanation of this cemetery is as one exploited seasonally by aggregated groups in the uplands. This fits very neatly within the pattern suggested already for the midden phenomenon on Monte Ingino.

4.3.5 Summary of the model

The excavated sites on Monte Ingino, Monte Ansciano and the linked lowland sites of Vescovado and San Agostino, encapsulate the local settlement history. Monte Ingino was first occupied in isolation as a seasonal settlement, during the period 1400–1200 BC. In the period 1200 to about 1100 BC, occupation of Monte Ingino continued, but in a much more intensive form, perhaps in relationship to lowland settlements at the foot of the

colluvial slopes in the basin and coastal settlements which could have been located on the Adriatic coast. Towards the end of this period, upland occupation shifted from Monte Ingino to Monte Ansciano which was probably occupied until about 950, even 900 BC, the period immediately before the Iron Age. Monte Ansciano offered greater occupation space as well as similar potential for visibility of the surrounding countryside, but not the narrow mountain pass. By the eighth century BC, the mountain tops had been abandoned and occupation had shifted entirely to the colluvial slopes of the basin lying beneath, and more specifically, to the locations of San Agostino and Vescovado.

These sites thus represent points in a dynamically developing system, at times linked one to another, at times in succession to each other. There is strong evidence that the upland sites never contained the whole social community on a permanent basis. The upland areas were rather, areas of aggregation, that verged on the ritualistic, in association with seasonal activities. These upland posts became strategic but peripheral locations, occupied periodically by a subset of both local and related communities. In such middle range societies, the separation of the domestic from the ritual, was not the dramatic distinction applicable in societies which had crossed the threshold of state formation. Ritual was almost certainly deeply embedded in the social and domestic, in ways in which the modern mind finds difficult to envisage.

The final stage, the abandonment of the peak positions, provided a potential for urbanisation that was much delayed in its implementation (Chapter 5). The location of settlement on the lower parts of the colluvial slopes offered all the advantages of space and control required by a complex society. However, the pressure and competition required to move society in that direction did not arise until the arrival of the Romans and then it was too late to be more than fleetingly part of an independent polity.

4.4 The regional setting of Gubbio in the Later Bronze Age and the early Iron Age

4.4.1 The socio-economic context

Middle Bronze Age settlement organisation is still best understood in terms of the model of transhumant patterns that have been gradually refined over time (Puglisi 1959a; Östenberg 1967; Barker 1981b; Barker and Stoddart in press). Permanent settlements on the coast (such as Luni sul Mignone) were linked to ritual locations (for example Belverde on Monte Cetona), and staging posts for summer grazing in the Apennines, both in valley bottoms at Nocera Umbra (Bonomi Ponzi 1985b, 31), in caves along river valleys (Frasassi gorges) and on peaks and ridges such as Monte Ingino and Santa Paolina (Filottrano) (Rellini 1931).

The Later Bronze Age, represented at Gubbio, is socially a phase of middle range societies, that is neither strictly egalitarian in character nor exhibiting any material steps towards wealth differentiation or central organisation. This has been established locally for Gubbio through the study of the Pianello di Genga cemetery (Peroni 1963a) and is the conclusion reached in the study of the Po Valley settlement and cemetery of Frattesina (Bietti Sestieri 1981; De Min 1986). The only visible differentiation is along lines of sex and perhaps age (section 4.3). Other aspects of this pattern have been given in more detail elsewhere (Bietti Sestieri 1984a; Barker and Stoddart in press), but can be summarised here. Settlements are generally of small dimensions (less than 15 hectares in size), and show little evidence of internal differentiation; although claims have been made on relatively scanty evidence for some sites like Luni sul Mignone and Sorgenti della Nova. Cemeteries, similarly, have little investment, with the exception of Crostoletto di Lamone in Lazio where mounds were constructed above the graves (Poggiani Keller and Figura 1979). The numbers of graves are also generally small, comprising tens rather than hundreds of graves. The major exceptions to this rule are Pianello (500 cremations), already discussed in the previous section, and Timmari (250 cremations), located in a similar co-ordinating zone on the Apennine Murge plateau area of modern Basilicata, in the south of Italy (Barra Incardona 1976) where the high Apennines, the Murge, and the Bradano river valley system cross. In spite of the exceptions for the size of cemeteries, there is no evidence that any individual or social group in this society had managed to maintain differential access to power. The increased use of metal did, however, produce a potential for the accumulation of wealth. The only evidence that this was achieved could be interpreted from the increase in number of metal hoards. These have been found close to Gubbio at Gualdo Tadino (this may alternatively be a grave), in the lake basins to the south at Monte Primo di Piediluco and Piediluco Contigliano, and also to the north at Poggio Berni and the Casalecchio hoard in Romagna.

Various implications arise out of this socio-economic background. Three lines of evidence will be explored that allow a more detailed understanding of the inter-regional, spatial patterns for the period: the social (measured principally by settlement organisation), the stylistic (measured in terms of the distribution of material culture) and the economic (measured through the assessment of exchange).

4.4.2 Settlement organisation

A variety of types of settlement system had developed by the end of the Bronze Age in central Italy, but without any selective advantage of any particular region or group. Economic development had reached a stage where specialisation was possible beyond a level that simply reflected the local environment. However, economic advantage had not yet been made of the varied possibilities of that environment.

In the lowland areas of modern Lazio about 150 km to the south-west of Gubbio, stable permanent settlements had developed, sometimes with the original foundation dating as far back as 1400 or 1300 BC. Claims have been made for differential social ranking within some of the larger, more intensively researched settlements (Luni sul Mignone, Monte Rovello, Sorgenti della Nova) (Bietti Sestieri 1984a; Biancofiore and Toti 1973; Negroni Catacchio 1981). However, the evidence is currently inconclusive, and differently sized buildings may simply have had different functions. The overall settlement system presents an unhierarchical character where spacing is relatively regular, each settlement controlling its own immediate territory, and where the range in site size (between 1 and 15 hectares) does not suggest any strong processes of centralisation. Much of the Lazio terrain is volcanic in origin, where processes of river erosion have created settlement positions on naturally defended spurs or 'islands', isolated by local streams. The placing of settlements on *alture*, slightly remote positions above lower terrain, has dominated concepts of Late Bronze Age settlement organisation in central Italy (Carancini *et al.* 1990).

Reassessment of this certainly biased picture has been forced by recent rich discoveries in very specific lowland sectors of otherwise upland areas. The implications of these discoveries have in turn, perhaps, been drawn too far (Carancini *et al.* 1990: 140ff.), even though alluvial areas (as in Britain) may well provide many of the future discoveries, once more obvious areas have been searched. In the specific context of the upland lake basins of southern Umbria and the Abruzzo, fertile lacustrine soils appear to have been very attractive most notably for late Bronze Age settlement. Dense lowland settlement is not, though, a pattern that can be definitely extended to all the tectonic valleys in central Italy.

In the Fucine Basin, there was a long tradition of settlement at this high altitude (*c.* 660 m above sea level), which continued into the Bronze Age (Radmilli 1977; Irti 1981). There were considerable fluctuations in the density and distribution of sites that are only now being established (D'Ercole 1986; Radi 1986). In the Piediluco Basin

(South-east of Terni), the attraction to these perilacustrine soils appears to have been almost exclusively Bronze Age in date (Carancini *et al.* 1986, 1990), placed approximately on the contour 370 m above sea level. This process appears to have had a much greater degree of continuity of occupation from the early Bronze Age into the early Iron Age than in many other areas of central Italy. The number of sites occupied appears to have increased from two in the early Bronze Age, to about twelve in the Final Bronze Age, before declining slightly and then sharply in the two phases of the Iron Age. Tentative evidence has recently appeared that Final Bronze Age settlement may have been in association with perilacustrine conditions at Perugia (Cenciaioli 1990). The same situation does not apply to the Gubbio Valley since the process of drainage of the lake basin took place much earlier as shown by the last dated peat formation of the early Holocene (section 2.3). It is more probable that some Neolithic sites in the Gubbio Basin were placed in similar environments, with plentiful supplies of nutrient-rich sediment in close proximity to water, if not necessarily open water. The phase of intensive use of this resource, therefore, took place at a considerably earlier date and only one Bronze Age site has been found in a lowland position within the valley.

To the east of Gubbio, a further pattern seems to have prevailed in the upper reaches of the Apennines. Here, upland and valley settlements guarded the routes through the mountains, granting access to seasonal pasture and lowland agricultural lands. These are the sites recorded by Rellini (1931), more recently researched by Lollini (1979) and synthesised by Barker (1981b) into an elegant, developed model of transhumance between permanent lowland settlements such as Colle dei Cappuccini at Ancona on the coast (Lollini 1956), and upland ridge sites such as Santa Paolina (Filottrano) (Rellini 1931). The lowland coastal sites of the Marche probably parallel the situation in coastal Lazio to the west. One particular eastern concentration of upland sites is on the Sentino river valley that is directly accessible from the Chiascio Valley immediately to the east of Gubbio. These sites, most specifically Pianello, Monte Santa Croce and Caverna di Frasassi, will be encountered again in the discussion of stylistic networks.

Recent research also allows comparison to be made with the high Apennines of eastern Liguria (Maggi and Nisbet 1990; Maggi 1990a). In this area, some developments are the reverse of that at Gubbio. For instance, there was a decline in the number of sites occupied in the Late Bronze Age. However, these same sites became more permanent and substantial investment was made in drystone features, including terraces, in a manner followed on a much more restricted scale on Monte Ansciano. The

choice of rocky hilltop sites also shows some similarities to that encountered at Gubbio: rocky hilltop sites suitable for control of pasture, as well as crossing points on watersheds. Typical sites are the Castellaro di Zignago, located at 960 m above sea level (Mannoni and Tizzoni 1980) and the Castellaro di Uscio at 721 m above sea level (Maggi 1990a). Although abandonment was commonplace in the early Iron Age, as at Gubbio, settlement re-occupation took place on many sites in the pre-Roman period, in complete contrast to the Gubbio sequence. These settlements of the Ligurian Apennines give the appearance of greater isolation and hence economic independence than their counterparts at Gubbio. Upland settlement at Gubbio was always part of a broader settlement system that included the communities in the valley below (section 4.1).

To the north of Gubbio through the mountain passes on the Po Plain there appears to be a type of settlement organisation very broadly similar to that of Lazio, although not as densely packed (Bietti Sestieri 1981). Nucleated settlements are between ten and twenty kilometres apart and up to 9 hectares in size. The most notable site is that of Frattesina which was an important production centre in the eleventh and tenth centuries BC (below). Gubbio was thus located in the high mountains between two vibrant economic areas in the Late Bronze Age: the communities of the Po Valley to the north and the Tyrrhenian communities to the south-west.

The settlement organisation represented at Gubbio in the Late Bronze Age is, however, best paralleled by the situation on Monte Cetona (Calzoni 1954; Cipolloni 1971), also located between these two vibrant economic regions. Monte Cetona is a high limestone peak (1,148 m) which dominates the tectonic basin of the Val di Chiana. The sides, summit and caves on this mountain appear to have been relatively densely occupied with Bronze Age sites. The caves of Belverde have a sequence, partly ritual in nature, which goes back to the Neolithic. Recent excavations have shown that occupation was not restricted to the caves themselves, but extended into the open ground outside (Martini and Sarti 1990a). In the Final Bronze Age, settlement appears to have been increasingly concentrated higher up the mountain, although this was also a time when the nearby site of the later Etruscan city of Chiusi was first occupied. The new site of Casa Carletti was founded in an open position at about 700 m on the eastern flank of the mountain. At the same time, the very summit was also occupied (Cipolloni 1971; Martini and Sarti 1990b) and there is fairly conclusive evidence that the drystone wall which follows the 1,100 m contour dates to the same period of the Final Bronze Age as the pottery, animal bone and hearths which it enclosed. If this is the case, the nature of the deposit appears very similar to that of Monte Ansciano.

The overall pattern of the interregional settlement structure in central Italy is skewed asymmetrically towards the east, following the major structural constraints of peninsular Italy. The Apennines and the foothills of the Apennines (with a predominance of tectonic valleys aligned approximately north–south) swing east, leaving extensive volcanic plains and lowlands to the west, and rather more restricted Plio-Pleistocene clay foothills to the east. By the Final Bronze Age, in the lowlands both to the east and west, permanent stable settlement developed that retained important contacts with the increasingly permanent settlements of the upland areas located in between (section 4.2). The western approaches to the upland Apennines contained both dense lacustrine settlement clusters and hilltop clusters of the type found at Monte Cetona and Gubbio. Gubbio appears to have combined both a seasonal and permanent component of settlement, made possible by the verticality of the terrain and economic contacts with the east coast. Temporary seasonal aggregation, drawing on local and east coast populations, combined with limited domestic rituals, was part of this pattern. In the Apennine passes, ritualised aggregation was an even more important component, indicated principally by the size of a cemetery such as Pianello.

The transformation of the Bronze Age landscape at the beginning of the Iron Age is a pattern shared by north-eastern Umbria, the Marche and even to the north of the Apennines in Romagna (Bonomi Ponzi 1991a). There are, though, regional differences. At Gubbio, there is continuity in part of the landscape, namely the colluvial footslopes on the northern side of the valley where Iron Age occupation continues. It is very probable that the local settlement organisation around Assisi followed a similar trajectory, even into later times (section 5.1). Protohistoric material has been found on Monte Subasio whereas the evidence for later occupation is on the southern colluvial slopes. In the upland lake basin of Piediluco, there was a marked decline in the number of sites but not a complete abandonment. Some Umbrian sites appear to show greater discontinuity, in some cases not even occupied into the later Bronze Age (Nocera Umbra). This discontinuity appears to be shared by many sites in the Marche (Pievetorina). In areas that were precocious in socio-political development in the coming centuries (such as Bologna and Etruria), the change took the form of increasing nucleation associated with the distinctive Villanovan cultural style. In the upland areas related to Gubbio, such rapid socio-economic processes did not develop. Nevertheless, these upland areas were not completely shielded from these wider developments. Within the new socio-economic framework, substantial upland sites no longer had such a significant role. One approach was to control lowland access to the uplands from strategic positions within valleys. Iron Age occupation therefore did not usually take place in the same positions as in the Bronze Age, but in areas where socio-political control was possible (Terni, Todi, Bevagna, Nocera, Gualdo Tadino), strengthened in some mountainous areas by upland forts.

4.4.3 Stylistic networks

The distribution of style zones during the period adds a dynamic element to the regional interactions discussed above. The distribution of stylistic elements of material culture, during the period 1400–1000 BC, can be best described as clinal, with zones of higher variability, including the Marche in which the Gubbio Basin of north-east Umbria lies. The stylistic repertoire of this period is highly developed, offering great, and yet rarely realised, potential for forming boundaries in preserved material culture. The expectation of many scholars has been to find groupings, but in spite of many attempts, the styles (*fogge*) created do not come sharply into focus (Peroni 1980). This is not the fault of the analysis but arises through the very nature of the social context which is being considered.

The period 1400–1200 BC is normally subdivided into pure Apennine and sub-Apennine phases. As already discussed in Chapter 1, these are not easily distinguished on Monte Ingino. However, for the purposes of the analysis of stylistic attributes, comparison can be most easily undertaken within the parameters already determined by Italian and German research (Peroni 1960; Müller Karpe 1959). The nature of the depositional processes of the midden mean that whole vessels do not survive, but the fragmentary components do, and some of these – decoration and handles – provide distinctive attributes for comparison across space and time.

The elements involved do appear to have been part of a deliberate display, principally on drinking vessels. It is highly conceivable that the decorative attention paid to these vessels in prehistory reflects the importance of domestic rituals within a society which, whilst sedentary, was still involved in sending age sets and other subgroups out some distance to control sheep and other livestock. With the Apennine style, bands of decoration covered the sides of small, often carinated, bowls and cups, and more rarely decorated the rims and handles. The sub-Apennine style developed a profusion of handles, with decoration focused on the area just above the handhold. The

Protovillanovan style combined a more restricted repertoire of handle styles, together with a new style of channelled decoration. All these styles have the domestic drinking vessel in common, although it must be kept in perspective that finewares form a very small percentage of the ceramic repertoire (section 4.3).

The Apennine decorative style is highly distinctive. Many parts of the vessels were covered with incised and point decoration, drawn in elaborate curvilinear and geometric forms. At this level, the general Apennine style is instantly recognisable and indeed one of the most recognisable styles of prehistoric Italy. At another level, local variants within this common language of shapes quite naturally developed by quite simple transformations of more general stylistic rules. The Apennine material has been illustrated in its full range (accounting for 90% of the fragments) in this volume to demonstrate the range of variability from one site, that of Monte Ingino.

Geometric forms provide the vast majority of the motifs from Monte Ingino (Fig. 4.17). Some components of motifs are readily recognised in neighbouring sites in the Marche, although care has to be taken when only fragments of a complete design have survived. For instance, stepped parallel lines (Fig. 4.17, 49) can be matched fairly exactly at Grotta Moniche (Frasassi) (Rellini 1931: Tav. X, 16). Other motifs, for example the chevron design (Fig. 4.17, 61), are broadly similar in conception to Pievetorina (Rellini 1931: Fig. 28). One distinctive location, much employed in the Marche for the placing of these designs is on the rim of the vessel. The closest parallels to Gubbio examples (Fig. 4.17, 34–40, 43, 46–48) are found at Spineto (Frasassi) (Rellini 1931: Tav. IX) and Grotta Moniche (Rellini 1931: Tav. X, 15). Rim decoration is not the exclusive preserve of geometric decoration, however. One highly distinctive curvilinear rim design from Monte Ingino (Fig. 4.17, 8) has the closest combination of rim form and decoration at Santa Paolina (Filottrano) (Rellini 1931: Tav. III, 7), whereas further afield, but still within the Apennines, there are close parallels both for rim and decoration but not within the same precise combination at Grotta a Male (Pannuti 1969: Fig. 11), in the Abruzzo.

Geometric decoration also takes a much more microscopic form. One example is triangular impressed decoration on a fragment of a semicircular handle (Fig. 4.17, 70). This has a broad resemblance to an example from the site of Pian Sultano in the relatively lowland area of Lazio (Fugazzola Delpino 1976: 40, Fig. 10, 9). The decorative style is, though, more similar to examples from Marche sites such as Santa Paolina (Filottrano) (Rellini 1931: Tav. II, 13).

Curvilinear designs are less common, although perhaps with a rather higher prevalence in the Marche area than elsewhere in central Italy. One prominent example, which is relatively well preserved on Monte Ingino, the simple ribbon spiral (Fig. 4.17, 4, 7) is a long recognised Marche trait (Peroni 1960: 120, Mot. 6C) with close parallels at Santa Paolina (Filottrano) (Rellini 1931: Tav. II, 17) and Monte Santa Croce (Sentino Valley) (Puglisi 1959b: Fig. 14) as well as further afield at Belverde (Monte Cetona) (Calzoni 1962: Tav. IX, a, d), Santa Maria in Belverde (Sarti 1990: 51) and Pian Sultano in Lazio (Fugazzola Delpino 1976: Fig. 11, 15). However, more generalised versions of this stylistic trait occur throughout peninsular Italy (Cuda 1990).

In some cases, the geometric and curvilinear are combined, either in the form of superimposed bands (Fig. 4.17, 17), or in the form of curvilinear elements placed within a geometric structure. The possible permutations within a grammar that is not strongly prescribed, militate against finding exact parallels. However, similar stylistic solutions have been found in locations as far afield as Torre Chiaruccia (Fugazzola Delpino 1976: Fig. 6, 6) in Lazio.

The most striking feature of the Marche style is only recorded in one example from Monte Ingino: a highly decorated upstanding handle. This highly decorative feature of the Marche was made famous by the discoveries at Santa Paolina (Filottrano) in the Marche (Rellini 1931: Tav. IV–VI). These represent a distinctive exuberance of this phase in the upland Apennine region, yet still linked explicitly to drinking and small eating vessels.

The prominence of Santa Paolina (Filottrano) in almost every stylistic similarity of Apennine elements within the Monte Ingino stratigraphy is fairly conclusive. One significant factor is their physical proximity to one another. Another may well be their social proximity, since both occupy ridge-type positions serving similar roles within the Apennine communities. Recent work (Cocchi Genick et al. 1991–2) has identified typical motifs of the central Adriatic area. Many of these are shared by the Gubbio pottery. On a more general level, the styles of the Apennine communities clearly followed with little impediment the far-flung contacts maintained by the transhumant economies, and attempts to find discrete stylistic groups tend to mirror the density of research.

Links within the sub-Apennine stylistic networks can be best attested through handles, as first systematically established for chronological purposes by Peroni (1960). Many of the handle styles are very widely distributed. A good example represented on Monte Ingino (Fig 4.18, 23) is the upright cylindrical extension to a strap handle (Peroni 1960: Tav. IX, b1), shown by Peroni to have been distributed from Scoglio del Tonno, Coppa Nevigata (Puglia) and Lipari in the south to Filottrano in the

Marche. Many further examples derive from sites such as Luni sul Mignone (Östenberg 1967: Fig. 23, 28) in Lazio and Cortine di Fabriano (Lollini 1979: Fig. 1, 13) and Pianello di Genga (sub-Apennine settlement underlying the cemetery) (Lollini 1979: Fig. 1, 25) in the Marche. A similarly wide distribution can be noted for the distinctive duck-head handle (Fig. 4.18, 28) which has close similarities, not only with examples in the Marche (the recurring Santa Paolina (Filottrano) (Rellini 1931: Tav. VIII, 6)), but also less exactly at San Giovenale (Fugazzola Delpino 1976: Fig. 35, 9), and Luni sul Mignone (Fugazzola Delpino 1976: Fig. 43, 11). It is difficult to find many handle types of a more restricted range. The most probable candidate is a variant of the axe handle (Fig. 4.18, 15) which was recognised by Peroni to be largely restricted to the Marche region (1960: 97–8). Recent work has shown the very great variety of axe-type forms, emphasising the length of the tradition (deriving from the Early Bronze Age) and its prominence in the Marche region, particularly by reference to northern Italy (Ceccanti 1979).

The period 1200–1000 BC is much more easily distinguished on Monte Ingino as a coherent phase. This is a more clearly defined chronological phase represented by stylistic networks that continue to be far-flung in terms of their connections. Some signs of regionalisation, or some form of differentiation, can now be noted, most notably in *Latium vetus* (Bietti Sestieri 1984a) and elsewhere (Barfield in press). This trend has been sometimes exaggerated by the wish of scholars to foresee later trends of state formation and ethnic differentiation in earlier societies, which, whilst undergoing major changes, have not undergone changes sufficiently drastic to have a boundary–forming effect on material culture. The detection of this relative regionalisation is considerably aided by the large increase in the quantity and range of material culture (most especially metalwork) in which stylistic traits can be measured. The economic changes registered above (sections 4.2 and 4.3) had their concomitant effect on the elaboration of material culture.

Pottery continues to play an important role in the recognition of the stylistic range of material culture. The variants present at Gubbio (Monte Ingino and now also Monte Ansciano) tend to be less elaborate than those found in some other locations. The large stout handles which are so prominent in locations such as Monte Croce Guardia di Arcevia (Lollini 1979: Fig. 4) and Colle dei Cappuccini di Ancona (Lollini 1979: Fig. 5B, 4) to the east in the Marche, and which take a tubular form in locations such as Sorgenti della Nova (Rossi 1980) and Casa Carletti (De Angelis 1979: Fig. 3, 4), are completely absent from either Monte Ingino (*c.* 1200–1100 BC) or Monte Ansciano (*c.* 1100–1000 BC). Elaborate antler-

type handles recovered from Casa Carletti (De Angelis 1979: Fig. 1, 4) to the west, and Santa Paolina (Filottrano) (Rellini 1931: Tav. VIII, 4) and Caverna di Frasassi (Rellini 1931: Tav. XIV, 4) to the east in the Marche, are also missing. The typical handles (Fig. 4.18, 16–20) are more delicate, even refined, often with typical furrowed and sometimes dimpled decoration that has its closest parallels at Perugia (Cenciaioli 1990: 90, 1.18) and in the complex of sites on Monte Cetona, including principally the peak (or Vetta) (Cipolloni 1971: Fig. 8, 12, 13, 15) and Casa Carletti (De Angelis 1979: Fig. 3, 7) on the eastern side of the same mountain.

Whilst finewares provide the most elaborate decorative features, coarsewares are not without stylistic information. This is less surprising if one considers the size of some of these containers which must have towered over a seated individual. These same vessels, in some cases, contained the liquids, be they milk or alcohol based – dispensed in the smaller, more highly decorated, vessels discussed above. In most cases, though, they would have been more suitable for dry storage of grain and other foodstuffs as dramatically recovered intact in the excavations of Belverde of Monte Cetona (Calzoni 1954). The main decoration represents an elaboration of the cordon, principally placed on the vessel to grant greater strength proportional to its greater size. On the smaller vessels (Fig. 4.20, 19, 23) meander designs are quite common. On the larger vessels a regional variant peculiar to the Marche (Peroni 1960: Tav. XIII, Presa 3) is the handle interlinked with the paired cordon which has also been found at Grotta Moniche (Rellini 1931: Tav. X, 13) and Grotta del Mezzogiorno (Puglisi 1956: 163, Fig. 41, 3), in the Sentino Valley.

By the time of the *Bronzo Finale* period (1200–900 BC), a wealth of comparisons can be made with other materials. However, whereas it can be probably assumed that the majority of pottery was made locally and that we are perceiving style, rather than physical exchange of objects, decorative items in other materials – bone, glass and especially metal and amber could easily have been imported, given their probable higher value, greater potential for display and relative ease of transport (see also below).

The bronzework from Monte Ingino and Monte Ansciano fits the general pattern of Protovillanovan bronze production, consisting of a general peninsular-wide stylistic network, combined with some distinctive local variations and developments (Peroni 1969; Bietti Sestieri 1973, 1976). The best fit to the regional groups detected by recent work is to the Gruppo Marecchia–Chienti group (Peroni *et al.* 1980: 71, Tav. XL), but it is difficult to establish a means for adequately testing the validity of these groups or understanding their social meaning.

The pins are not only, as already pointed out in the previous section, the most numerous items, but, as visible elements of dress (together with brooches), a consciously distinctive indicator of style following the criteria established by Wobst (1977). Worn at eye level, they were more likely to engage recognition by socially related observers than many of the more commonplace elements from the midden deposit. Their stylistic similarities fit the general spatial patterning of the Protovillanovan style.

The most numerous group of pins in the Gubbio collection have nail or raised nailheads grading into conical heads, combined very often with horizontal and herring-bone decoration on a neck that is often swollen. Part of this broad category, the examples with nailheads or slightly raised nailheads, has its closest parallel with the Casa Carletti group of Carancini (1975: 211). With the present state of knowledge, it is impossible to overcome the sampling problems brought about by a more than eightfold increase (from 4 to c. 35, with the addition of the Gubbio material) in knowledge of this particular pin form. Inevitably the definition of the type changes when the variation is better understood. In this case the site that gives its name to the type, now appears to be a minority variant. The type is still known from only three find spots, two settlements and one cemetery (Casa Carletti, Gubbio and Pianello di Genga) in a manner relating more to the lack of discoveries in Umbria than to a real distribution.

In spite of these problems, individual pins from Gubbio have close similarities to individual pins from the upland settlement of Casa Carletti (near Chiusi) to the south-west and the cemetery of Pianello to the east in the Apennines. The plain raised nailhead, undecorated, swollen neck pin of Casa Carletti (Carancini 1975: Tafel 48, 1499) has close parallels in two pins, one from Monte Ansciano (the most similar) (Fig. 4.22, 7) and the other from Monte Ingino (less stubby) (Fig. 4.23, 13). The more graceful, nailhead pins with herring-bone and horizontal decoration on the swollen neck from Pianello (Carancini 1975: Tafel 48, 1501–3) have many close parallels (allowing for bending) from Monte Ingino (Fig. 4.23, 1, 11, 16, 20).

Other pins have stylistic similarities over an even wider region. The globular-headed pin above three ribs (Fig. 4.22, 19) has closest similarities to examples from the north of the Apennines. The examples with more conical heads (Figs. 4.23, 14 and 4.22, 9) have a wide distribution from the Limone (Livorno) hoard on the Tyrrhenian coast (Carancini 1975: 1647, 1649, 1650; Peroni et al. 1980: 45–6) to Fontanella Graziola and Bergamo to the north of the Apennines (Carancini 1975: Peroni et al. 1980: 25–7) and to Castellace in Calabria. Other examples are found at Belverde (Monte Cetona, Tuscany) and the hoard of Poggio Berni (Forlì, Emilia), slightly closer to

Gubbio. One spherical-headed pin (Fig. 4.22, 3) has similarities with examples in the Po valley at Cremona (Müller Karpe 1959: Tafel 88, 20) and Peschiera (Müller Karpe 1959: Tafel 104, 76), at Narce (Macnamara 1976: 134, n.30) from closer at hand at Casa Carletti (Calzoni 1936: 334) and on the summit of the same mountain of Monte Cetona (Cipolloni 1971: 168). One pin (Fig. 4.22, 17), short and squat, decorated in herring-bone and horizontal incisions over almost its entire length with a head composed of three ribs separated by three swellings, appears unique.

The style of the a rotella pin-head, because of its generic nature, is very widely distributed and it is probably wrong to make too many typological distinctions. The Narce type (Carancini 1975: 326–9) is broadly the same form with the closest parallels from locations such as the Coste del Marano (Tolfa) hoard (Carancini 1975: Tafel 83, 2685), although other examples are known from the settlement of Colle dei Cappuccini at Ancona (Carancini 1975: Tafel 83, 2688) and the cemetery at Verucchio (Carancini 1975: Tafel 83, 2674). The rarer type of plain pin (Fig. 4.22, 1) might have provided the pin for pin-heads of this type (Macnamara 1976: 136, 31). Rolltop pins (Fig. 4.22, 15) have parallels that are broadly spread chronologically and geographically; the closest examples have been found at Pianello (Müller Karpe 1959: Tafel 56, A10) and Gualdo Tadino (Peroni 1963c).

The fibulae generally have very wide parallels in similarly dated contexts. The complexity and combination of elements within the only complete fibula (Fig. 4.26, 4) is perhaps unique and a published parallel has not been traced. However the combination of elements suggests a date in the ninth century BC. Many of the other fibulae are fragmentary and precise parallels are, therefore, difficult to establish. One broken piece (Fig. 4.24, 9) appears to be part of a bow of a violin bow fibula with similarities to finds from northern Italy at Frattesina (Von Eles Masi 1986: 5, n.29; 7, nn.39–40) and Mariconda (Von Eles Masi 1986: 7, n.43). A broken piece of an arch bow with twisted segments (Fig. 4.24, 2) has parallels in a number of hoards from southern Umbria such as Contigliano, Piediluco and Monte Primo. The simple twisted arch bow type (Fig. 4.24, 10) is particularly widespread over a much broader area, with similar examples from south central Europe (Betzler 1974: 65–6, nn.135–8) as well as closer to hand in northern Italy (Von Eles Masi 1986: 16ff.). Large symmetrical catchplates, often with embossed decoration have a very wide distribution throughout central Italy and into the Balkans.

Explicitly decorative items manufactured in other materials follow a very similar pattern. The most notable of these items is a bone comb (Fig. 4.28, 8) with circular

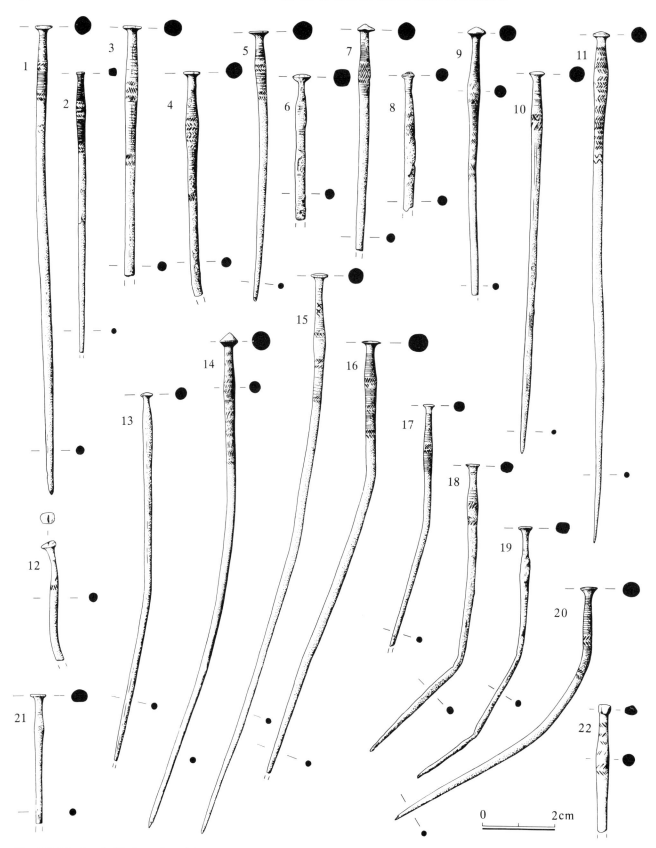

Fig. 4.22 Metalwork. Pin forms from Monte Ingino and Monte Ansciano. From Monte Ansciano: 9, 12, 14, 22

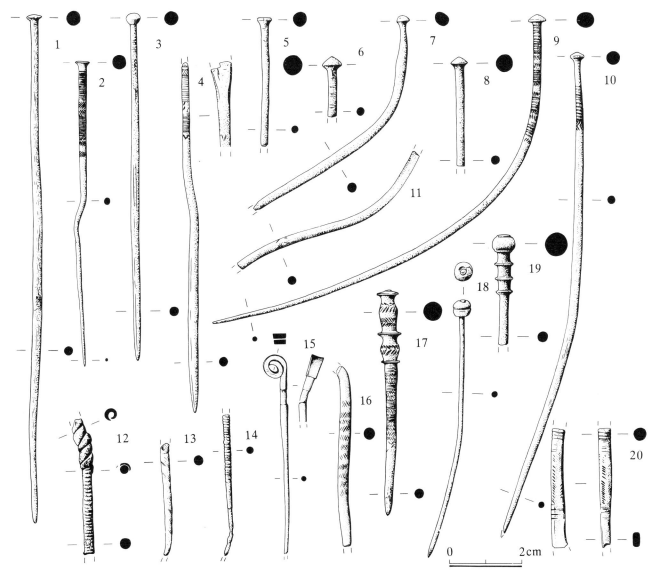

Fig. 4.23 Metalwork. Pin and miscellaneous (fibula ?) forms from Monte Ingino and Monte Ansciano. From Monte Ansciano: 7, 11, 14, 15, 16, 18

decoration that has close parallels from Pianello (Tomb 143) and Frattesina (Bietti Sestieri 1981: 147, Fig. 10.8, 4). A bone button with similar stylistic details of incised circles, has similarities with one found at Pianello. Clay animal figurines (Fig. 4.28, 1–3) are also commonly found in contemporary settlements, both close at hand (Santa Paolina (Filottrano), Colle dei Cappuccini (Ancona)) and further afield (Luni sul Mignone) and the tradition itself goes back into the *terramare* of northern Italy (Säflund 1939: Tav. 40, 1–18). The fragmentary bone head of a pin (Fig. 4.28, 7) has broad parallels over a much wider area: at San Giovenale, Torrionaccio (Cassano and Manfredini 1978: Fig. 65, 6), Luni sul Mignone, on Monte Cetona (Calzoni 1933: 97, Fig. 78), in the cave of Tane del

Diavolo near Orvieto (Calzoni 1939: Tav. XXXVIII, 3), in the cemetery of Pianello di Genga (Tomb 131) and at Monte Croce Guardia di Arcevia. The spoked wheel-head in bronze, serving a similar role to the bone pin-head, is a very long-lived type of wide distribution (Macnamara 1976: 136–7) described for historical reasons as Narce type (Carancini 1975). Fairly close parallels emanate from both close at hand in the Marche at Santa Paolina (Filottrano) (Rellini 1931: Fig. 27) and Colle dei Cappuccini at Ancona (Lollini 1979: Fig. 5, B1), and from a well-known hoard in central Italy, Coste del Marano (Bietti Sestieri 1973, Fig. 7, 9). Detachable pin-heads, both in bone and bronze, belong to a tradition that goes back at least to the *terramare* of northern Italy (Säflund 1939: Tav. 65, 1–18).

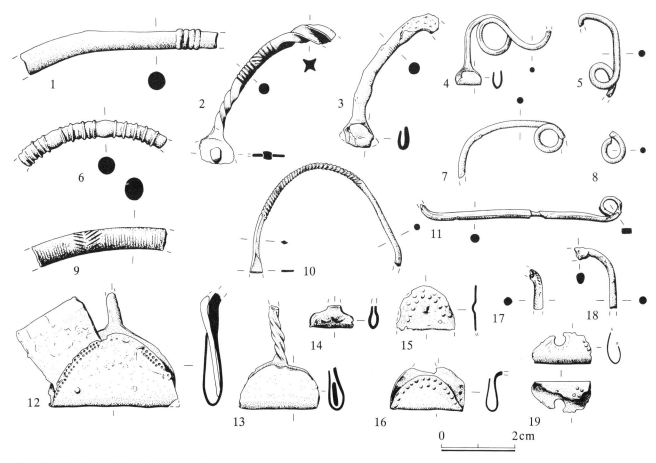

Fig. 4.24 Metalwork. Fibula forms from Monte Ingino and Monte Ansciano. From Monte Ansciano: 2, 11, 19

Within these complex, repetitive, even confusing, networks of style, some general patterns can be perceived. The Apennine and sub-Apennine styles show major contacts with similarly placed sites like Santa Paolina (Filottrano) in the Marche Apennines. In the *Bronzo Finale*, the contacts are still principally with Pianello and its satellite sites in the Sentino Valley, but some of the stylistic attributes are shared also with the contemporary sites on Monte Cetona. Beyond these contacts of greatest similarity, the sites at Gubbio are recognisably part of the wide networks of style that pervade peninsular Italy from at least 1400 BC and only show slight trends towards regionalisation towards 1000 BC. At another level, although requiring statistical proof and further research, the Apennine and pre-Apennine geographical area appears to have started as an area of high variability of styles (within the Apennine and sub-Apennine stylistic zone) and moved towards slight regionalisation and lower variability during the Protovillanovan stylistic phase. Interestingly, ceramic styles, although almost certainly

locally made, do not show consistently more local attributes than items such as decorated bone and metal which might be more subject to exchange processes.

The stylistic evidence for the early Iron Age of Gubbio is limited by the scarce finds that have so far been made. In general Umbria is notable (Bonomi Ponzi 1991a: 55) for similarities in ceramics with both the Etruscan and Latial cultural areas. The available evidence from San Agostino (Fig. 4.20, 27) suggests that the major contacts were with the Latial area. Some of the out-turned rim styles (Fig. 4.20, 29) also re-surface in the early Roman coarseware pottery of the Gubbio area. However, some almond rims of Etruscan tradition are also present in the very late Roman period (section 5.1).

4.4.4 Exchange processes

From the outset of settled agricultural communities it is evident that exchange in both basic raw materials and luxuries took place. By the second millennium BC,

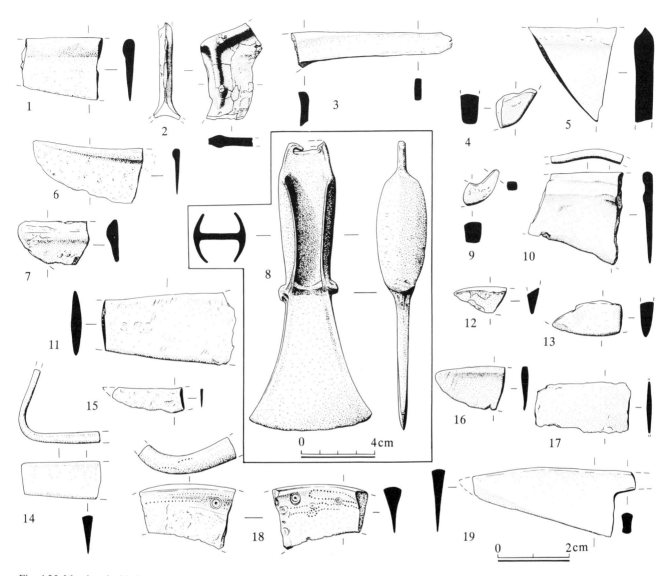

Fig. 4.25 Metalwork. Blades and scrap from Monte Ingino and Monte Ansciano. From Monte Ansciano: 4, 5, 8, 9, 10, 12, 13, 16, 17

networks, already three millennia or more old, were well developed and linked the coasts, mountains and inland plateaux together. As already remarked (section 3.2), the Gubbio Basin was not central to these processes in the Neolithic. The Bronze Age networks represented a great expansion in exchange activity, with the advent of new materials available, most notably metals, that were actively demanded by even the most remote communities. These new processes drew the Gubbio Basin into contact with the rest of central Italy.

Demand for metals from the Colline Metallifere of western Tuscany and from the Alps formed a major stimulus to the populations of central Italy. Stylistic traits from the Po Valley and central Europe as well as from the

south and eastern Mediterranean were shared in the context of a vigorous and rapidly changing industry. In the same context, a vibrant network of trade in metals and more exotic materials developed.

A study of the site of Frattesina in the Po Valley gives a measure of the materials potentially available in these late Bronze Age societies and the degree to which the Gubbio Basin was involved. There are grades of participation ranging from access to the commonplace and to the highly exotic. At Frattesina, there is evidence for the production not only of ceramics, but also of metals (including moulds and crucibles), glass, horn and bone (Bellintani 1984; Bietti Sestieri 1981). Artefacts in all these materials have been found on Monte Ingino and, except

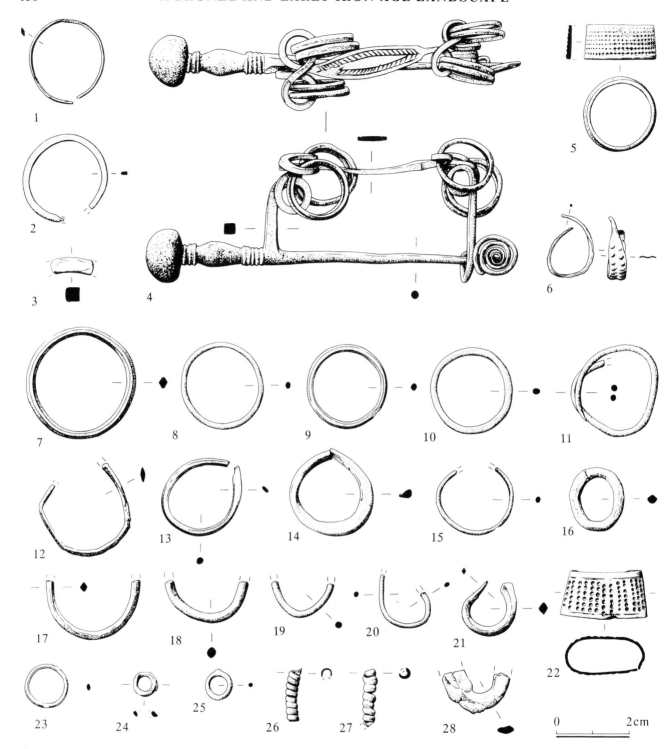

Fig. 4.26 Metalwork. 4. Late fibula from Monte Ansciano. Rings and spirals from Monte Ingino and Monte Ansciano. From Monte Ansciano: 1, 2, 3, 5, 6

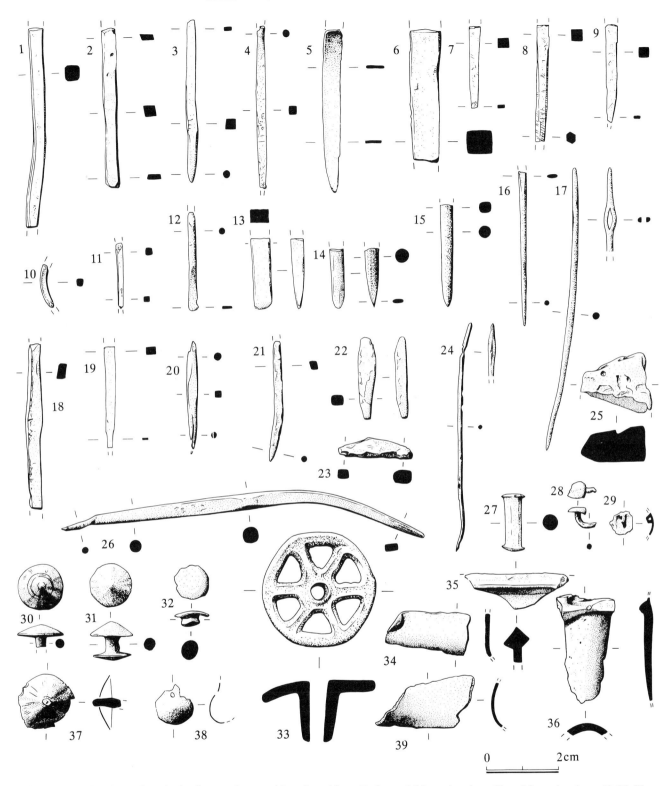

Fig. 4.27 Metalwork. Tools and miscellaneous bronze objects from Monte Ingino and Monte Ansciano. From Monte Ansciano: 18–26, 32, 34–37, 39

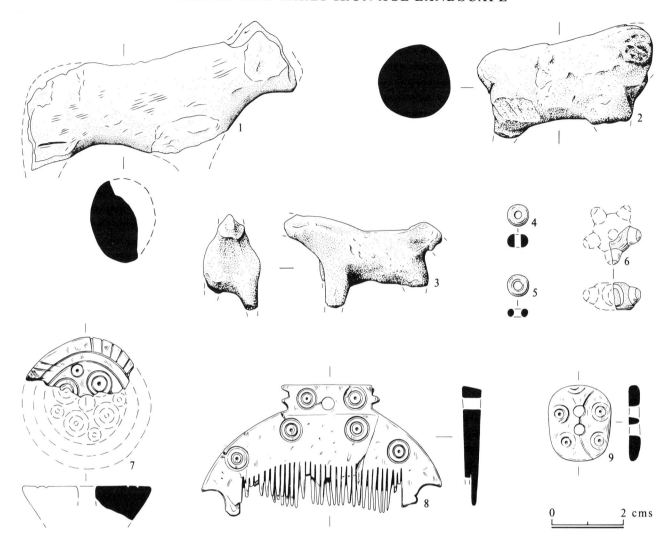

Fig. 4.28 Decorative items from Monte Ingino: 1–3 Clay figurines; 5–6 Glass beads; 7 Bone pin-head; 8 Bone comb; 9 Bone button

for glass, there is indirect evidence for their manufacture on the site. Glass beads (Fig. 4.28, 4–6) were most probably imported from a production centre such as Frattesina itself. Other more exotic materials such as elephant ivory, ostrich shell and amber were also worked on at Frattesina. Of these only amber has been found at Gubbio and then in the earlier levels (1300–1200 BC). Objects worked in precious metals such as gold appear in the Late Bronze Age not far from Gubbio at Gualdo Tadino (Peroni 1963c) and in the Po Valley at Borgo Panigale (Bologna) (Catarsi Dall'Aglio 1976: 262–3). Such finds were completely absent from Gubbio, but Gualdo Tadino is located sufficiently close to Gubbio to suggest that Gubbio was not excluded from the exchange of more luxury products. On the other hand, a possibly significant difference between Frattesina and the Gubbio

sites is that whereas there are fairly strong stylistic similarities between the combs found at Frattesina and that found on Monte Ingino, the former were made out of ivory and the latter from bone. At the very least, the upland populations around Gubbio were more conservative in their consumption and especially disposal of rich materials. The discoveries from Monte Ingino fill one more link in the exchange networks already proposed by Bietti Sestieri (1984b: 220) that connect a site such as Frattesina, a centre of surplus production and export, to sites as diverse as Pianello, Timmari, Allumiere and humble Monte Ingino, by the discovery of glass beads, bone combs and bone/horn pin-heads.

Explaining the presence of the exchange goods in the great range of archaeological contexts in which they are found is less easy than identifying their presence. Transhumant systems are traditionally seen as one of the major forces behind the mobility of the Bronze Age communities of Italy. Forced to make long seasonal journeys from coastal plain to mountain pasture and back again, a high proportion of the Bronze Age communities must have had wide-ranging social contacts over extensive geographic zones. Well-defined routes linking upland and lowland coast and river valley are known historically and were most probably in prehistoric times essential elements in a system that linked all the communities together on a regular and basic economic level.

That more elaborate and prestigious exchange activities became associated with the more mundane should come as no surprise. Inter-territorial movements of whole communities at seasonal intervals into areas that may have been considered buffer, even liminal, zones might have emphasised the need for active exchange of gifts, valuables and basic trade. Whilst we cannot envisage market centres amongst the Late Bronze Age communities of the Apennines, the seasonal movements and enforced social intercourse required by shepherds moving into liminal terrain, may have enabled even ritualised exchange, especially when the slaughter and exchange of animals stimulated it.

In the Final Bronze Age, societies may have become more settled, accompanied by a more permanent presence in upland areas such as the Gubbio Basin. Control of upland areas such as Monte Ingino and Monte Ansciano by at least components of the full society would then have become more important. In time, the verticality of the local terrain could have been exploited by local populations without the necessity of large-scale movement.

5 RITUAL PROCESS AND THE IRON AGE STATE

5.1 Rituals without texts

5.1.1 The analysis of Iguvine state formation

The analysis of the development of the state in the valley of Gubbio represents an interdisciplinary challenge. The challenge will be faced in the following chapter from three directions that emphasise the primacy of the archaeological evidence. Firstly, the local archaeological context will be presented (section 5.1). This is overwhelmingly ritual and therefore needs to be considered within the ambit of other ritualised landscapes. Secondly, the single (if of seven parts), elaborate, ambiguous and, most probably ritual, text will be examined, employing a radical critique which abandons the received tradition in favour of a less arcane, indeed deritualised, approach (section 5.2). Finally, the socio-political situation of the Gubbio valley in the first millennium BC is compared and contrasted with neighbouring areas of Umbria, the Marche, North Eastern Etruria and Samnium (section 5.3).

5.1.2 Pre-state ritual

The study of the past by archaeologists has uncovered some societies arranged principally as ritualised landscapes. The earliest of these are the ritual landscapes of the European Neolithic which have been recorded in contexts as diverse as Wessex (Renfrew 1973) and Malta (Bonanno et al. 1990). The societies concerned may not have made a conceptual division between the ritual and the domestic, but the outside observer can readily distinguish the difference in context between ephemeral flint scatters (Gardiner 1984) or small round houses (Malone et al. 1988) and the elaborate megalithic monuments of life and death rituals.

The appearance of sanctuaries in the first millennium BC in the eastern Mediterranean has, by now, been accepted as an archaeological symptom of state formation. The practice of delimiting 'ritual' spaces, and of depositing large quantities of metalwork within them is, for de Polignac (1984) and Snodgrass (1980) the surest sign of the emergence of the *polis* in the eighth century BC. In a similar vein, Cherry (1986) has suggested that, in Crete, peak sanctuaries appear at the same time as the Old Palaces, and indeed that the palaces deliberately encouraged ritual activity at such sites as a form of social control.

The Gubbio Valley in the central part of the first millennium BC (*c.* 600–400 BC) is primarily a ritual landscape, but as will be developed below, not a landscape that fits easily into the categories defined above. As introduced above (section 4.3), by the eighth century BC, domestic activities of the human populations of the Gubbio Valley appear to have been concentrated on the colluvial slopes close to the medieval and modern city of Gubbio. The limited evidence available from Sant' Agostino and the rescue excavations of the Superintendency in the town suggests insubstantial buildings with little differentiation of wealth and accumulation of power, although Roncalli (1988: 402) appears to make rather more of the same information. Evidence for ritual deposition in graves is also low key. Until the fourth century BC there is very little evidence of any settlement outside this area. A few finds from antiquarian collections[1] and a spearhead found during survey suggest the possibility of cemeteries and associated subsidiary settlements at Torre Calzolari and Branca to the south, most probably in the topographically distinct positions still occupied today. Recent excavations have uncovered part of a sixth century (?) chariot burial (Stopponi 1991) associated with the Gubbio area, but this find does not compare with those elsewhere in central Italy at the same time. Even in the fifth century BC, imported items such as Attic Red Figure are rare (Manconi 1991). The total evidence currently available suggests a lack of investment in domestic structures or mortuary display.

The upper reaches of the landscape appear in contrast to have been systematically marked out by simple ritual sites (Fig. 5.1). Bearing in mind the advice of some archaeologists that ritual must be carefully identified (Renfrew 1985: 3), it is important to justify this contrast. The sites can be distinguished as ritual by the repetitive act of making distinctive offerings of bronze figurines on simply prepared and demarcated surfaces above the

---

[1] Housed in the museum at Perugia in the Bellucci collection: Torre Calzolari: pugnale di ferro (Inventario Bellucci: Bianco 428), Branca: frammento di fibula (Inventario Bellucci: Giallo 3555). Roncalli also records pendants, bracelets and other fibulae (1988: 402).

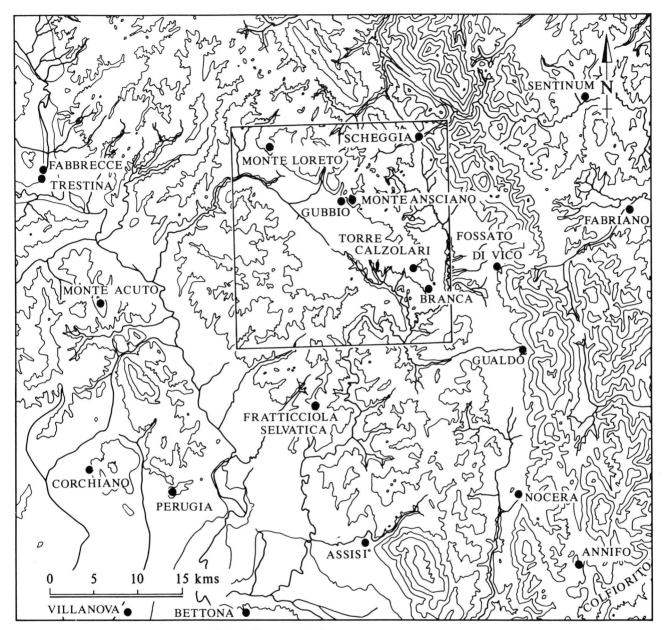

Fig. 5.1 Pre-Roman sites of north-east Umbria (including sanctuaries)

limestone bedrock in peak locations. In addition, the votive objects, although highly schematic, show clear signs of expressive gesture and action. These are cult activities, if simple in their form and articulation.

The northern and southern edges of the valley, particularly the north dominated by its escarpment, were the focus of these simple sanctuaries. Two are known only from surface finds (Monte Loreto, Fratticciola Selvatica (Colonna 1970: 87, n. 208; 105, n. 322)) and one from a single find in the excavation of Monte Ingino (Meloni pers. comm.). One (Monte Ansciano) has been the subject

of systematic excavation (Stoddart and Whitley 1988). It is from this site that more precise structural and chronological information can be established.

The ritual landscape of the Gubbio Valley does not fit easily into either of the two models most familiar to archaeologists. It bears no relation to the 'ritual landscape' of tombs, henges and megaliths that the British prehistorian understands by this term. Equally, it does not quite correspond to the classical idea of a ritual landscape associated with the *polis*, with its hierarchy of small rural shrines and major urban and extra-urban sanctuaries, and hierarchy of deities to which each sanctuary could have been assigned. It is thus difficult to characterise, but there is no reason to associate it with 'state formation' as the term is commonly understood. There are certainly very few other signs that a 'state' was emerging in the Gubbio area around the sixth century BC, and without state formation there cannot be a bounded language system defined as Umbrian (section 5.2). Survey around and excavation within the town itself has revealed little or no signs of urban life in Gubbio in the sixth, fifth and fourth centuries BC. Settlement in and around Gubbio remained no more than a scatter of hamlets on the slopes of Monte Ingino and Monte Ansciano until perhaps as late as Roman Republican times. The distribution of almond rim pottery, most readily dated to the immediately pre-Roman period, is mainly restricted to a halo around the later city of Gubbio (Fig. 5.10). This suggests manuring executed by an agglomeration of population at the foot of Monte Ingino and Monte Ansciano, but not intensification on a highly developed scale to support an expanding state. There are no signs that writing was being used before the time of the Iguvine Tables, which could have been incised as late as the first century BC (section 5.2).

Moreover a closer examination of the Minoan and Archaic Greek examples casts doubt on the simple equation between formalised ritual activity and the formation of a state. Peatfield (1983, 1990) has pointed out that Minoan peak sanctuaries appear several generations in advance of the emergence of the earliest palaces on Crete. Early Minoan peak sanctuaries, like Umbrian ones, are simple affairs. An imposing natural rock formation or false peak is chosen as a focus for cult, in front of which terracotta votive offerings are deposited. Sophisticated architecture, with ashlar masonry, comes in later, and represents the later integration of peak sanctuary cult within the palatial system. Peatfield also notes that there are far fewer palaces than peak sanctuaries, but many more peak sanctuaries than the *tholos* tombs which had characterised the Early Minoan period. He argues that the peak sanctuaries represent an intermediate stage of social integration, regional groupings halfway between the purely kin-based societies whose ritual focus was the tholos tomb, and state societies centred on the palaces.

Elsewhere in the Mediterranean, there are many examples which show that peak sanctuaries are an exception to the rule that sanctuaries signify states. In Dark Age and Archaic Attica, the sanctuary of Zeus on Mount Hymettus, a simple open-air altar on a mountaintop, has votive deposits which go back to the tenth century BC (Langdon 1976), well before the eighth-century revolution. In Ancient Israel, the popularity of cults on hilltops preceded the creation of a strong Israelite state by David and Solomon (I Samuel 9: 12–25; 10: 5–10; Peatfield 1990: 130).

Peak sanctuaries may then be not so much a symptom of the emergence of the state but of the development of a rather different kind of social formation. We lack a good theory that would describe the relationship between kinds of cult practice and kinds of society (Renfrew 1985). More importantly perhaps we lack a good social model for the kind of society which produces peak sanctuaries, but it would have to fulfil at least three criteria. It would have to (a) be a regional, territorial grouping; (b) possess a sense of community beyond that provided by kinship; and (c) lack any centre of state power. The notion of the 'chiefdom' does not really fulfil any of these criteria.

Recent work in the Gubbio Valley and in the rest of Umbria allows a re-analysis of inter-relationship between social formation and ritual landscape. There has generally been little theoretical treatment of Umbrian ritual sites. Indeed, until recently scholars have had to rescue what they can from the generalised provenances of antiquarian collections. Roncalli (1991) has recently distinguished two schools of study of Umbrian bronzes, the main ritual artefacts of these sanctuaries: the antiquarian or aesthetic interpretation of the individual object, above all in terms of their Umbrian or Etruscan affinities and a typological stylistic classification with the aims of recovering centres of distribution and workshops. To this can now gradually be added a third: the contextualised study of the artefacts with the aim of recovering the ritual and social processes.

Previous work on votive deposits has made two principal interpretations. The first by scholars working in the more developed areas of Umbria has envisaged them as expressions of aristocratic power on major transit routes (for example Bonomi Ponzi 1991: 59). The subject matter of the figurines, domestic animals and warriors, is seen as a representation of the basis of aristocratic power. In turn, the religious pantheon was based on the same socio-economic criteria. The second interpretation favoured by those working in less developed regions is that the sanctuaries were foci of pastoral populations presumably on a seasonal basis (for example Monacchi 1986: 80–1). The simple material culture found in these sanctuaries and their generally high altitude is seen to reflect the lifestyle of the pilgrims. The separation between these two extremes is probably artificial since they represent the range of sanctuary use that was ultimately dependent on the local socio-political context. A full appreciation of the socio-political context for central Italy must await section 5.3. For now, an interpretative map of the ritual landscape of Gubbio can be attempted.

The ritual landscape of Gubbio was not complex in spite of expectations that might be raised by traditional interpretations of the Iguvine Tables (for further discussion see section 5.2). At present there is no evidence to contradict the view that the simple sanctuary organisation unearthed at Monte Ansciano was also the pattern at the three other sites known simply from surface artefacts (see above). It is conceivable that Monte Ansciano represents the lowest level in a hierarchy of ritual order and that excavations of the few higher peaks such as Monte Foce will find a different order of complexity. Whilst these remain possibilities, it is probable that the same simple ground preparation and votive deposits will be detected by further research.

On Monte Ansciano, the one excavated sanctuary in the Gubbio area, the Bronze Age midden enclosed by its drystone wall (section 4.3) was capped by a drystone platform, in the course of the sixth century BC (Fig. 5.2).[1] The degree of deliberate intent in choosing a Bronze Age enclosure for a ritual platform will be discussed further below. It is, though, clear that there would have been a relatively insubstantial and yet clearly ancient earthwork visible to the sixth century populations of the area in a landscape otherwise dominated by natural forms. Parallel walls, composed of lines of limestone slabs, were built up against the Bronze Age wall. An outer face of marginally better quality was then constructed on both limestone and sandstone. Finally the triangular gap between the sixth century and the Late Bronze Age constructions was filled with rubble and redeposited material. Outside this area the platform was simply constructed of dumps of limestone. The overall finished construction was an extension of the summit of the hill in a style completely lacking architectural sophistication. The term sanctuary should not imply any complexity. The final design has a certain coherence, but the work could easily have been cumulative. The construction of the parallel walls could have taken place over some period of time, responding to the needs of the cult practice and would have required very little mobilisation of manpower and certainly no major centralisation of authority.

The activity on this platform was equally lacking in structure and sophistication. Sixty-five schematic bronze figurines common in the Umbrian region (Colonna 1970) were found in a scatter on this drystone surface. The distribution of the figurines may easily have suffered disturbance since their original deposition, but they still retained a fairly tight spread around the summit area (Fig. 5.3). The figurines are all anthropomorphic with differing levels of schematisation (Figs. 5.4–5.8). Most represent schematic gestures of raised arms that can be interpreted as an expression of prayer. The definite exceptions are warrior figures which remain a minority of the total (Fig. 5.6). Otherwise the figurines can be clearly distinguished into male (Figs. 5.4–5.5) and female (Fig. 5.7) on the basis of clear male anatomical details and female clothing. The figurines were associated with 169 nails of varying size and head and a few fragments of decorated terracotta

(Fig. 5.9). This implies the presence of either an insubstantial wooden structure or even a natural grove of trees to which the figurines and small decorative details were applied. The distribution of nails was broadly similar to that of the figurines and some may have been used to secure the votive offerings to a wooden structure, be it natural or artificial. No datable post holes have been discovered, but the most probable solution is some form of screen decorated with a display of votive objects in terracotta and bronze.

The most intensive phases of ritual activity on this site appear to have been between the late sixth century and the third century BC. The style of the figurines, the most frequent ritual artefacts, is archaicised and traditionally placed within this time bracket (Colonna 1970). However, given that the context is ritual and their form schematic a longer persistence of an archaic form cannot be ruled out. Data at present considered anomalous could, in time, provide proof of a longer period of manufacture. For instance, the inventory records of schematic bronze finds from Szombathely in Hungary (Szilgyi 1989), a site only founded in the first century AD, suggest that care must be taken of purely stylistic dating. However finds outside Italy (Colonna 1970: 200; Adam 1984: 177, n.265) could clearly have been taken there at a much later date.

Several artefacts on Monte Ansciano allow a more precise dating. The deposition of figurines certainly post-dates an elaborate bronze and iron fibula of the ninth/eighth century. The lack of exact parallels suggests a unique and probably ritual artefact (Fig. 4.26, 4). A further iron fibula, dated to the sixth century, is probably contemporary with the main ritual use of the site (Guzzo 1972: Type IX, 2). Coins of the Umbrian and Roman Republican period and lamp fragments of the Imperial Roman period suggest that some ritualised activity continued, even after figurines ceased to form part of the ritual. If the deposition of figurines was restricted to as short a period as two hundred years, and if an approximately representative number of figurines was recovered during the excavation[2], we are dealing with a sanctuary with a very low rate of activity.

Two recent excavations of comparable sites to those of Monte Ansciano enlarge this perspective of the sanctuary. The sites of Monte Acuto (Cenciaioli 1991) and Pasticcetto di Magione (Bruschetti 1988, 1989) lie to the south-east between Gubbio and Lake Trasimene in similarly upland locations (Fig. 5.1). Even if one allows for the thin topsoil and the exposed nature of Monte Ansciano to weather and previous unofficial excavations, the material culture

---

[1] Following Colonna's stylistic dating of the Esquiline group of figurines.

[2] Metal detector activity has increased in recent years and Monte Ansciano is a very exposed position. The largest figurines may have been selectively sampled.

Fig. 5.2 Plan of the sanctuary of Monte Ansciano

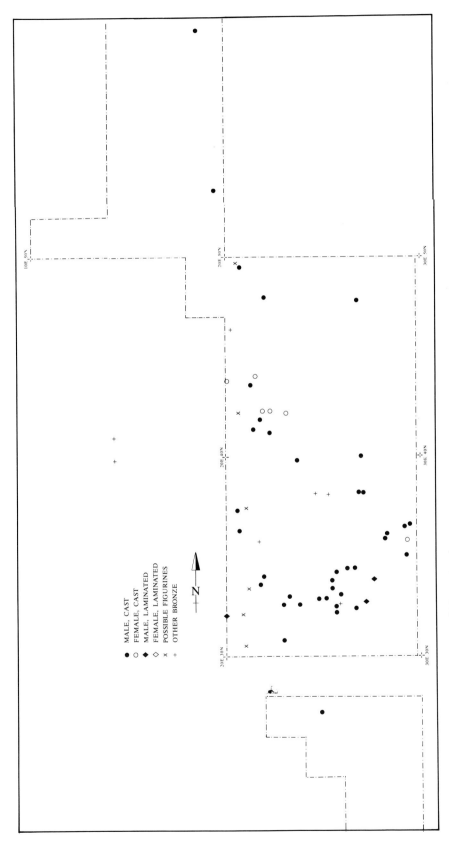

Fig. 5.3 Distribution of figurines on the site of Monte Ansciano

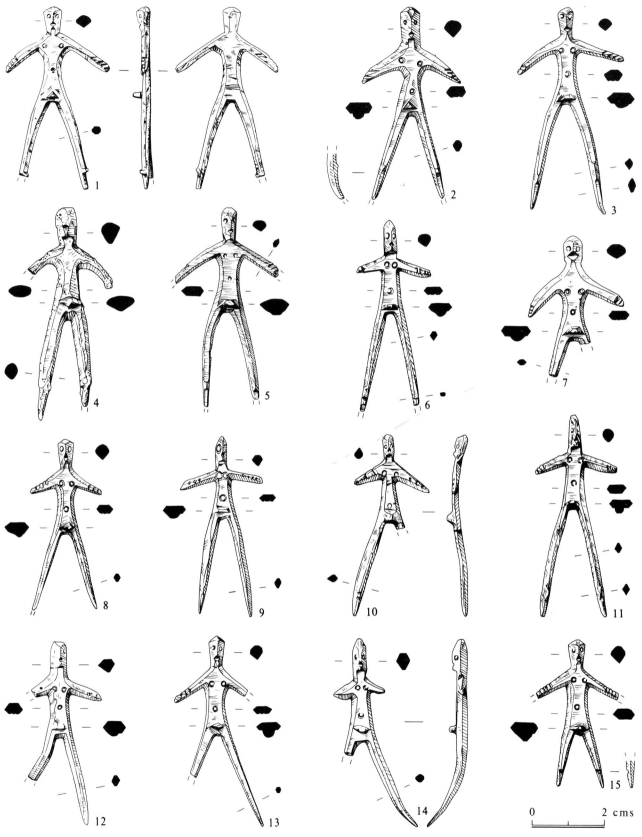

Fig. 5.4 Archaic figurines from Monte Ansciano: male examples

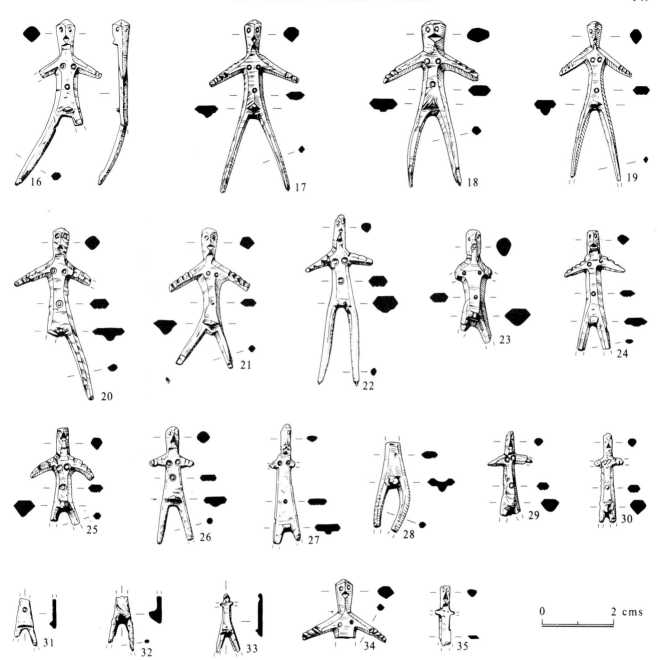

Fig. 5.5 Archaic figurines from Monte Ansciano: male examples

from the Gubbio sanctuary is indeed modest. Monte Acuto has produced 1,600 figurines and Pasticcetto di Magione 600. That the contrast is not simply a product of preservation is also suggested by the greater variety of form and subject matter of figurines from the two other excavated sites. The Pasticcetto site contained a more elaborate female form of the *Vöcklabruck* type (Colonna 1970: 88ff.), as well as animals and anatomical parts. The

Monte Acuto site also had animals and a miniature situla. In both these cases a small enclosure that survived largely intact contained the votive finds, whereas the Monte Ansciano site consisted simply of a drystone platform.

The ritual artefacts placed on the platform of Monte Ansciano must have been at the lowest level of the ritual hierarchy. All the bronze figurines are classed by Colonna as schematic (Colonna 1970: 85ff.). On many sites, the

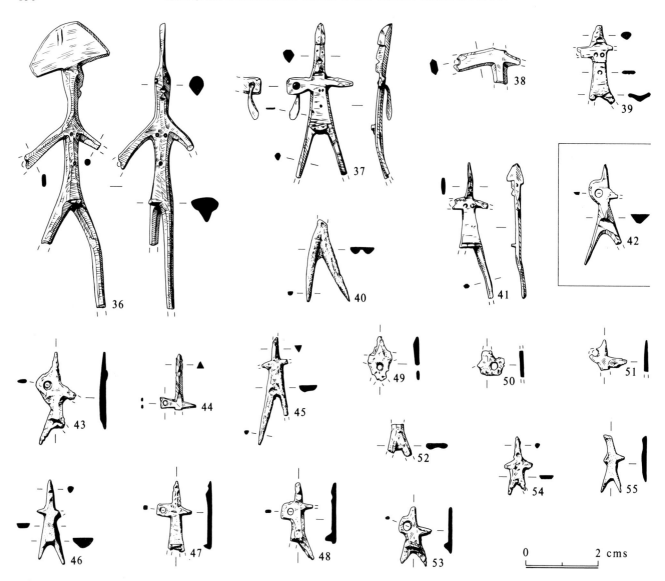

Fig. 5.6 Archaic figurines from Monte Ansciano and field survey (n. 42): warrior examples

figurines of the Esquiline group (Colonna 1970: 103–5) form a small component of the overall assemblage. At Gubbio they form virtually the complete assemblage. One figurine (Fig. 5.6, 36) can be attributed to the stylistically more sophisticated *Gruppo Foligno* (Colonna 1970: 96–100) made up of attacking Mars figurines (*Marte in assalto*) and two others (Fig. 5.6, 37, 41) loosely to the less sophisticated attacking Mars figurines of the *Nocera Umbra* group (Colonna 1970: 100–3).

The distribution of these figurines shows the widespread nature of the cult. The Esquiline figurines are named after a deposit in Rome, but have also been found at Foligno, Ancarano, Gualdo Tadino, San Severino Marche, Pievetorina, Orvieto, Carsoli and Fratticciola Selvatica

(Colonna 1970: 103–5). More recent research has identified the same types from Monte Acuto, (Cenciaioli 1991), Bettona (Scarpignato 1989) and Magione (loc. Pasticcetto) (Bruschetti 1989). The most schematic examples on Monte Ansciano (Fig. 5.6, 43–55) have good parallels from Grotta Bella (Monacchi 1988, Tav. XXXV). Relatively sure provenances of the *Foligno* figurines are from Amelia, Foligno, Gualdo Tadino, Calvi dell'Umbria and Collazzone. The *Nocera Umbra* group has poor provenance, with the exception of recent finds such as Grotta Bella (Monacchi 1988). The general distribution covers the Apennines and the Umbrian region, with significant outliers as far south as Rome. Although these ritual objects could have a different meaning in different contexts,

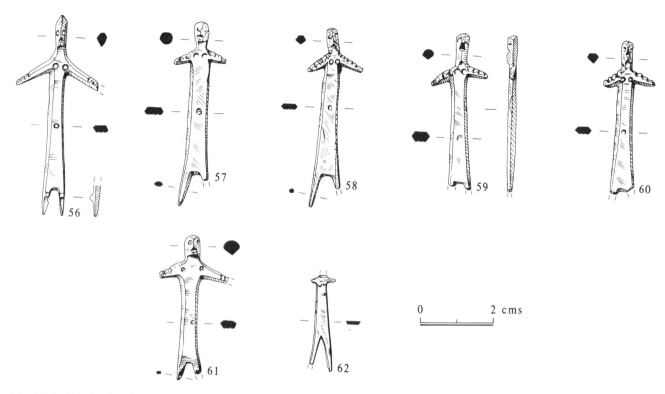

Fig. 5.7 Archaic figurines from Monte Ansciano: female examples.

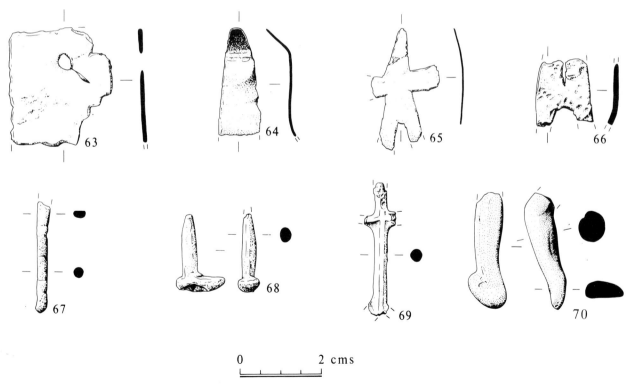

Fig. 5.8 Archaic figurines from Monte Ansciano: miscellaneous examples

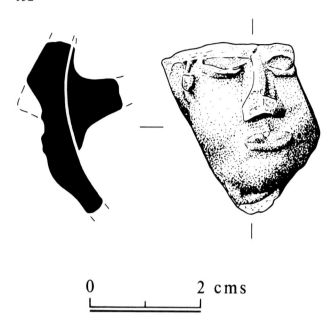

0   2 cms

Fig. 5.9 Archaic terracotta head

it is a reasonable assumption that their use in upland sanctuaries was broadly similar.

What was therefore the nature of the ritual landscape present at Gubbio? Of Renfrew's four categories of anthropological information (1985: 12–13), we only have one to aid our interpretation: the study of the material remains of cult practices. Depictions of these practices were not part of the cultural repertoire. Verbal testimony of ritual in written form has plausibly to await the inscribing of the Gubbio tablets.

The construction of the ritual landscape appears principally to have involved the strengthening of certain elements, the prominent features, of the natural landscape. The choice of the high points that demarcate the natural boundaries of the Gubbio Basin appear to be no coincidence. In addition to this, no attempt appears to have been made to place sanctuaries so as to break the natural order of the landscape. Given that this was a pre-urban society this is not surprising. The scale of investment was small and suggests no major central intervention or inegalitarian access to the rites concerned. In addition to this, participation appears to have been low key, especially considering the timescale over which it could have taken place.

A more difficult question to tackle is the question of ritual continuity. It is clear that the Bronze Age remains would have been visible to the practitioners of the rituals of the Archaic period. However, the two modern excavations of Archaic sanctuaries outside Gubbio discussed above do not record earlier deposits. On the other hand,

the distribution of proto-historic sites and upland sanctuaries is often very similar and in at least two well-documented, but rather different, cases – those of Spoleto (De Angelis and Manconi 1983) and Grotta Bella (Monacchi 1988) – there is evidence of re-occupation. The first case is a low hill of about 450 m within a contemporary population centre whereas the second is a cave (530 m above sea level) on the side of a mountain some 8 km from the nearest contemporary population centre. The heritage of the Bronze Age was not rich in the manner of the Greek, but the Archaic populations could have searched for legitimation of their rites even in a modest past, 'regaining time' in a pattern repeated in many other societies (Bradley 1987).

5.1.3 Synthesis

The picture can only become clear once two other sources of evidence are linked to the local pattern of Gubbio: the literary evidence of the Iguvine tablets (section 5.2) and the broader regional picture of ritual, settlement and society in contemporary central Italy (section 5.3). The traditional reading of the Iguvine Tables rejected by Wilkins (section 5.2) has superficially many attractions. It suggests an elaborate ideology for a well-defined political group characterised by (1) the setting out of a *templum* for the practice of structured rituals; (2) the clear distinction of aliens from citizens; and (3) implications for the spatial geography of the dependent territory. A whole branch of speculative topographical (not strictly archaeological) studies has developed from tenuous philological roots. Although material evidence may still be discovered for these theories by archaeological research, the likelihood is not very great.

5.2 The Iguvine Tables: problems in the interpretation of ritual text

5.2.1 Introduction

Gubbio is well known in modern times for the so-called Iguvine Tables, a set of seven inscribed bronzes (Plate 5.1). According to surviving accounts, they were discovered in 1444 in the neighbourhood of Gubbio. Evidence about their discovery is anecdotal only. They seem to have been discovered together in one deposit, and various find sites are given including the neighbouring Roman Temple of Jupiter and the local Roman theatre. The bronzes were subsequently acquired by the Comune of Gubbio, and have long been given pride of place in the Palazzo dei Consoli where they remain on view. Some sources claim that there were originally nine discovered and that two

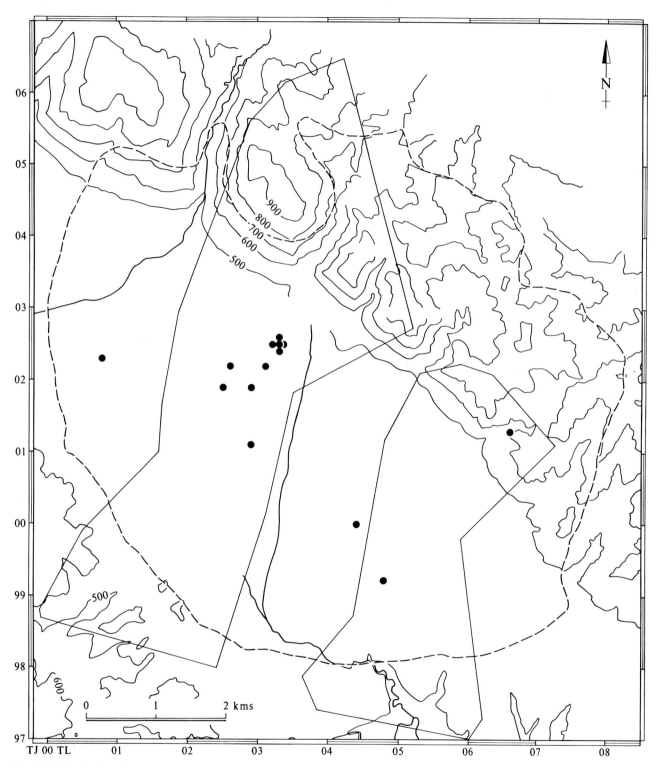

Fig. 5.10 Distribution of late Iron Age almond rims

Plate 5.1 The Iguvine Tables

have since been lost. No records exist of any text other than what has survived on the extant seven bronzes.[1] These seven bronzes constitute the major ancient linguistic evidence which is relevant to Iguvium. Specific literary references by classical authors to Iguvium are sparse, while a small number of short inscriptions from the vicinity add little to the epigraphic evidence.

If we accept the now conventional interpretation that the bronzes contain a ritual text, and if we date the composition of the text somewhere within the latter phases of the Roman Republic, then the bronzes should rank as a most exciting source for the reconstruction of ritual thought and practice in peninsular Italy of this period. Devoto (1974: 3) maintains that the bronzes are 'the most important ritual text of all classical antiquity. We possess nothing comparable either in Latin or in Greek; to find parallels we must have recourse to literatures of the near and far East' (my translation from the Italian).

5.2.2 Preliminary

Major editions of the Tables go back well into the nineteenth century (Aufrecht and Kirchhoff 1849–51; Bréal 1875; Bücheler 1883; von Planta 1892–7; Blumenthal 1931; Devoto 1937; 1948 (revised 1974); Poultney 1959; Prosdocimi 1978a; 1984). Other whole or partial accounts occur in other works devoted to Italic languages in general (e.g. Bottiglioni 1954; Buck 1979; Ernout 1961; Kent 1926; Meillet 1948; Pisani 1964; Vetter 1953). Although these studies differ from each other substantially, often surprisingly in major details, they can be taken together as sharing and developing basic assumptions and as forming the established tradition of scholarship on the Tables. By and large their general approach and a majority selection of their findings are accepted by

---

[1] For reasons of space I leave aside in this study any discussion of the *authenticity* of the bronzes. There is however some evidence which might be construed as suggesting at the least a medieval antiquarian influence upon their manufacture.

Italic/Indo-European philologists. At the risk of injustice to their considerable divergences, these and related authors will be grouped together as 'the traditional interpretation'.

5.2.2.i The bronzes

The seven bronzes do not themselves appear to be numbered or identified in any external way as being members of a set, sequential or otherwise; nor is there evidence for the original size of the set. The traditional numbering of the extant group of bronzes from I to VII is based upon internal analysis of the text (Lepsius 1833).

The seven sheets of bronze are rectangular in general shape, and in size fall into four classifications. Their dimensions are given by Prosdocimi (1984) as follows (values rounded here):

Tables III and IV	400 mm high × 275 mm wide
Table V	530 mm high × 350 mm wide
Tables I and II	650 mm high × 380 mm wide
Tables VI and VII	860 mm high × 565 mm wide

5.2.2.ii The inscriptions

Tables I, II, V, VI and VII are inscribed on both surfaces (traditionally designated a and b); III and IV on one side only. Tables I, II, III, IV, Va and Vb (first seven lines only) are all inscribed in what is usually described as a local script (sometimes termed Umbrian)[1] which runs from right to left and is closely related to Etruscan script, though with some important differences. Tables Vb (lines 8 onwards) and VI and VII are inscribed in a Roman alphabet (sometimes called Latin script) running from left to right. Generally speaking where two sides are engraved, the relationship is 'page-like', that is to say the table is turned on its vertical axis to read the obverse. Table I is an exception. Here the bronze has to be rotated horizontally to read the obverse. Much is made of these textual arrangements by most commentators. I do not myself see any necessary significance since the various surfaces of the bronzes could clearly be inscribed at separate and unrelated times, and quite conceivably without consultation or understanding of the reverse. Supposition of textual continuity and discontinuity both within the area of a side, and across sides, must necessarily rest primarily upon the interpretation of the text. There has been plentiful speculation on the possibility of different 'hands' in the engraving of the text but caution should be exercised in attributing too much weight to such analyses.

On the whole the script is clear and the letters readily distinguished. Elements of the text, normally taken by commentators as words, are mostly separated by a colon in the Umbrian script, and by a single stop at mid line height in the Roman. Some of these separators are deemed to be absent, resulting either in spaces or in the supposed running-together of 'words'. There is also some evidence for the alteration and addition of letters and separators.

5.2.3 Dating

5.2.3.i 'External'

The analysis of scripts in general suggests a third-century or early second-century BC date for the Umbrian script,[2] and a second- to first-century BC date, possibly post-Sullan, for the Roman (Wilkins forthcoming). The conclusion has to be that at best stylistic study of script can only give us a very approximate *terminus post quem* for the incising of the bronzes. Allowing a margin of up to fifty years for the conservative influences of style-preservation and archaisation, a guesstimate would give later limits of mid second-century BC for the Umbrian, and of late first century BC for the Roman.[3]

5.2.3.ii 'Internal'

By internal dating here I mean the assignment of the entire sequence of composition and inscription, seen as a whole episode and however internally complex itself, to an overall historical period.[4]

We have what appear to be a few external references made in the text. For instance both Tables I and II contain similar phrases occurring at the conclusion of a side, respectively: **kvestre:tie:usaie:svesu vuvçis titis teteies:** (Ib 45); and **kvestretie usaçe svesu vueçis ti teteies** (IIa 44). The second of these is squeezed into a small vertical space running up the bottom left-hand margin of the text. This latter position strongly suggests an addition to the text. In the first example there are no separators or spaces from **svesu** to **teteies**, where there is a final separator, while the

---

[1] The term *Umbrian* is used indiscriminately by some both as a label for the Etruscan-related script, and as a generic title for the language in which the texts are deemed to be written. The first usage is innocuous enough, if restricted as an identifier for the script. The second however opens up a number of complex areas of debate, and makes assumptions about the status and local and genetic affinities of the textual material. See further below, e.g. 5.2.5.v.

[2] See Maggiani 1984 for a recent study of Etruscan script parallels.

[3] Parallels with Roman examples on orthographical and possibly phonological points, such as the gemination of vowels, need to be handled with great care. Various inconsistent practices seem to occur on the bronzes.

[4] The traditional approach devotes much space to the reconstruction of internal phases within the text of the bronzes. I am unconvinced by these, and am not concerned with them here.

second example is written entirely without any kind of breaks. The division into words is the work of modern editors. If the office of quaestor is indicated by **kvestretie** (possibly meaning something like 'in the quaestorship of . . .'), and the sequence **vueçis ti teteies** is perhaps his name (maybe 'Lucius Teteius Titi filius') then the document is perhaps dated and/or authenticated by reference to an office which is of Roman provenance. The misdivision of **kvestre:tie:** in the first passage may on this interpretation indicate that the incisor did not understand the word, or that he only recognised the **kvestre** portion of it. (It could also indicate a more overtly grammatical tradition which separated off from the word elements which it judged to be suffixes). The word **kvestur** occurs also at Va 23. The running-together of words in both examples might indicate a similar unfamiliarity, or it may equally well reflect an inscriber trained in a diverse epigraphic tradition which did not use word-separators. Quaestors as financial officers both of *municipia* and *collegia* are well attested under the later Roman Republic. *Municipia* are commonplace after the end of the Social War in 89 BC, and *collegia* are refounded under Augustus. Iguvium is referred to by Cicero *pro Balbo*, 47 as a *civitas foederata*, and by Livy 45; 43, 9 as the place of exile to which the Illyrian king, Gentius, and his family were sent after Illyrian piracy was terminated by Rome in 168 BC. Iguvium would in any case have probably possessed *municipium* status with full Roman citizenship as from 89 BC.

Some other external references appear to be to Roman or Roman-related coinage. The word **numer** which may be related to Latin *nummus* occurs three times during the (Umbrian script) passage Va 17–21. Quantities are normally interpreted as one (no qualifier), two (**tupler**) and three (**tripler**). In the Roman text on surface Vb, four separate repetitions occur of *a.VI*, – which would appear to be a standard abbreviation for the Roman coin, the *as*. There is one case of *p.IIII* which on the same basis would be the abbreviation for Latin *pondo* for a measure of weight. The passage contains other presumed quantity or money formulae attached to the word (perhaps an abbreviation) *uef* which is itself obscure. The use of Roman coins would indicate Roman commercial values, though there is some debate concerning how low or high these would plausibly be. It may be that the 'devaluation' after the Social War may be critical. Before it, one to three *nummi* may be presumed to be a modest but still useful sum; after it, probably extremely trivial or even derisory. Conversely before the war, six asses, if the amount is a fine or penalty as frequently assumed, might be high; after it, still worth mentioning, but very much more manageable. This might mean that Va makes better sense before the war, and Vb after it.

Against these arguments, however, it has to be stressed that it would be well in character for a text of ritual, legal or other formal type, to specify either a ludicrously high fine, or a ludicrously low one. The first case would be deliberate, and the excessive amount would be written in to underscore the supreme status and dignity of the tasks and other matters being described, and the awesome consequences of any shortcoming in performance. The second case could arise in one of two ways: the first of these is the inverse of the argument just given, namely that a ludicrously small amount would be quoted to emphasise disconnection from and contempt for the values of the everyday world; the second of these is more probable and has to do with the passage of time. In this case, what might well have been a commonsense value written in the original text of a formal document, would remain unchanged with the passage even of centuries, because of the strong tendency of such texts both to preserve archaic language in general, and to fossilise other aspects of the text, precisely because the text does not have a practical commonsense relation with the real contemporary world. These tendencies should not be underestimated. The final conclusion would therefore be that the reconstruction of real-world values ascribed to such monetary statements as may occur, cannot be pressed into the service of an argument on dating.

What these monetary sums *may* indicate, however, is another *terminus post quem* for the composition of the relevant passages of text. Provided the figures belong to an original draft and were not perhaps incorporated later as an update (this could happen before incision on the bronze and would therefore leave no physical trace), then the composition of the text relates to a society which is familiar with Roman or Roman-related coinage of these denominations. The inclusion of an official with Roman title, the *quaestor,* suggests a *terminus post quem* for the composition of these passages of the Tables when Iguvium would be sufficiently absorbed within the general Roman administrative ambit. This would possibly be mid-third century BC after the Samnitic wars, and before the advent of Hannibal.

It could be further argued however that Iguvium's status at that time is more likely technically to be that of *socius*, which would not necessarily imply such close absorption. If we move the date to post 89 BC when full citizenship was extended over a wide area of Italy which would certainly have included Iguvium, then we definitely have sufficient conditions, but this may be too late. General loyalty of the area during the Hannibalic invasion would seem to indicate that local sentiment was not prepared to gamble against Rome. Also the later Social War was concerned primarily with the south, and may not directly of itself have brought any comprehensive changes to central Umbria. This leaves the second century BC as an attractive solution. At this time both the cultural and political boundaries are likely to have been still fluid, at least in effect if not in legal status. Nearby Perugia is still sufficiently Etruscan to maintain strong cultural links north-eastward with Iguvium, while at the same time there would remain persistent rivalry between Oscan and Roman ambitions. Iguvium can be seen as at a possible meeting point for these competing forces.

5.2.4 The traditional reading

It has become accepted practice in the scholarly tradition to provide translations. In the earlier editions these are usually into classical Latin, although this is most often an academic exercise which strives to follow the original word by word as faithfully as possible, rather than any attempt to write a continuous Latin version of the whole. This emphasis can have some bizarre results. In the case of Devoto 1937 (published during the Fascist era), the whole edition including all the commentary is written in an academic Latin. The post-war editions have recognised a need to provide something a little more accessible. Poultney 1959 translates into English. Devoto 1974 and Prosdocimi 1978a and 1984 translate into modern Italian.

These interpretations of the Tables depend *inter alia* on the recognition of parallel sections between the passages in Umbrian script and those in Roman. Generally speaking, these parallelisms are hypothesised between passages of Tables I and VI/VII, with the Roman text normally being interpreted as in some sense giving a fuller version of the content handled by the Umbrian passages. Several but not all commentators also conclude that the composition of the parallel Roman versions is later in date. I shall follow the convention now common in this scholarship of using **bold** type for quotations from the text in Umbrian script and *italic* for those from that in the Roman.[1]

5.2.4 i Summary of traditional reading

The bronzes are commonly interpreted as containing text on the following topics:

Ia–Ib 9/VIa 1–VIb 47
Purification ceremony. Double sacrifices at each of three gates (*treblanir*, *tesenocir*, *uehier*) and single sacrifices at each of two groves (*iouiu*, *coredier*). Animals to be sacrificed are oxen, sows, sucking-pigs, ewe lambs and bullocks. Deities invoked are mostly Jupiter and Mars with various epithets, such as *grabouie*. Other words taken as deities are (taking the Roman form in each case)

trebo iouie, *fiso sansie*, *uofione*, *tefrei ioui*, *honde serfi*. Auspices are to be taken (*aueis aseriater*) with specific birds being detailed in the Roman version, namely *parfa curnase peiqu peica* – identifications include owl, rook, woodpecker and magpie. A subsidiary passage is frequently read as giving spatial specifications of some kind, which some interpret as the setting-out of a sacred area or *templum*. The text is given of extensive prayers which are to be offered on behalf of *ocre fisiu* (interpreted as the arx, the sacred centre) and *tota iiouina* (interpreted as the Iguvine state), and for the *poplo* (people or people-under-arms) of the state.

Ib 10–44/VIb 48–VIIa
Purification ceremony (lustratio). Banishment of aliens and enemies (three times). Walking round the boundary (three times). Cursing of enemies. Auspices to be taken. Invocation of deities, and sacrifices. Words taken as deities include: *serfe martie*, *prestota serfia*, *tursa serfia*, *fisoui sansi*, and *tursa iouia*. Sacrificial animals are pigs, calves and heifers. Localities are thought to be mentioned: *acesoniame*, *fondlire*, *rubine*, and *traf sahatam*. Text of extensive prayers on behalf of the *poplo* and the *tota iiouina*. Table I carries the 'authentication' of the **kvestre** magistracy.

IIa 1–14
Ceremony to correct 'adverse auspices' (Devoto 1974) or failed ritual of some kind. Commentators have difficulty with the obscurity of the passage. **vestiçe saçe, iuvepatre, speture, ahtu iuvip, ahtu marti** and possibly **açetus** may be deities. Pig, ox, and sheep are specified.

IIa 15–45
Ceremony of the dog (**Huntia**). Obscure. Taken by Prosdocimi (1978a) as supplementary to the main lustratio. The ritual is seen as associated with the crops and infernal deities. Auspices are to be taken. Instructions for the sacrifice of the dog to **hunte iuvie**.

IIb
Ceremony to accompany the collection of tithes. Ten (possibly family) names are listed: **atiieřiate, klaverniie, kureiate, satanes, peieřiate, talenate, museiate, iuieskane, kaselate, peraznanie**. Pig, goat and calf are to be sacrificed to **iuvepatre**.

---

[1] Forms are quoted for the most part as they occur in the text, with the usual conventions of *ç* for Umbrian ꝺ, and *ř* for Umbrian ꟼ. Ʂ in examples from the Roman script represents the grave-accented *s* of the original.

III–IV

Obscure ritual under the direction of an official called the **uhtur** which is compared by some with Latin *auctor*. Both Devoto and Prosdocimi base their fragmentary interpretation around a central term **puni**. For Devoto (e.g. 1974: 99) **puni** is 'drink' and the ceremony is the sacrifice of the 'jar' (**huntak**). Prosdocimi (1978a) is convinced that **puni** is equivalent to the Latin *mola salsa* (a mixture of grains and salt reported by Latin authors as sprinkled on victims at sacrifices) and sees the ceremony as the ritual of its preparation, preferring to see this passage as only part of a greater and more complex whole.

Va–Vb 7

Decrees of the brotherhood concerning the duties, rewards and liabilities of the presiding brother, **ařfertur**, who officiates at the various ceremonies. Beside officiating, the presiding brother is held responsible for all proper preparations for each ceremony and for securing the presence of necessary personnel. He is responsible for the preparation of the brothers' subsequent supper, and at that supper it may be determined whether he has carried out his duties without fault. In the case of irregularities, the brothers have the power to fix the penalty at whatever level they deem fit.

Vb 8–18

Contract between the brotherhood and two sub-groups, the Claverni and the Casilate. A formula is stated whereby the groups named provide grain in return for pork and goatmeat from the brotherhood.

VIIb 1–4

A further short section thought by some to deal with a ceremony involving the ritual pursuit of heifers (?), and proposing a fine of 300 asses for shortcomings of the officiating brother.

The translations offered are remarkably precise and specific, as for example: '. . . When that in which he shall have placed the fire is carried to the sacrifices, he who will have the ritual staff shall carry it; the same shall carry what is to be burnt on his right shoulder . . . As soon as they will have said this, then he who will have the ritual staff shall say: "Forward, march, Iguvines."' (from VIb 48ff., translated by Pulgram 1978).

Textual work on the bronzes to date suffers from a degree of uncritical optimism and a self-confirmatory climate that is quite astounding. The plain fact is that even by the admission of existing commentators, large areas of the text are completely, or virtually completely, obscure. The most resistant are probably III and IV, and II in that

order. While the other bronzes have passages where it is easier to establish what a likely subject-matter may be, they also all contain a large number of passages, both short and long, which again are totally obscure. In the face of difficulties of this order, it is ludicrous to offer detailed continuous translations. These translations commonly draw no distinctions between the well-grounded and the poorly grounded, between the plausible and the highly speculative.

5.2.5 *The traditional paradigm and the Indo-European model*

It is not easy to establish a set of criteria that can validate the translations in a properly differentiated way. In other words, it is difficult to grade the results against a scale of acceptability. This in turn makes it hard to make reliable use of such results for archaeological, historical and sociological reconstruction. This is my dominant concern in the criticism which follows.

The approach exemplified in the traditional interpretation is based upon a long history of investigation of the texts (Devoto 1937; Prosdocimi 1984). Significantly, and not without a tinge of nostalgia, this tradition sees the essential framework as set out in a definitive way at the early stage. The 'golden age' of the scholarship according to Devoto (1974: 6) is the period from about 1850 to 1880 (Aufrecht and Kirchhoff 1849–51), expanded by Bréal (1875) and Bücheler (1883). According to Devoto, this group of works effectively set the agenda for some fifty years until the elaboration of Devoto's work itself in the 1930s. Prosdocimi (1978a) takes the same viewpoint when he refers with great respect to Devoto's *Tavole Iguvine* (1937) as 'closing a cycle'. What comes after, he says, can only be 'accademismi, bizantesimi, regressi'. His own work (which would then seem to be begging a justification) is to be seen as a 'rifondazione' of interpretations and methods, presumably of those which are already current (Prosdocimi 1978a: 592).

5.2.5.i *Primacy of the text*

The traditional paradigm, like any paradigm, requires explicit justification. This, for the most part, it does not receive. This omission is partly attributable to the general scholarly climate of the late nineteenth century which did not demand explicit models. It is also partly attributable to the overwhelming dominance of the Indo-European model. This latter dependence would in any case have made the finer delineation of model parameters largely redundant. Much the same can be said, for example, of other related scholarship of the late nineteenth and early twentieth century, as for instance traditional work upon the Etruscan and Oscan texts.

Most commentaries on the Tables have essentially two principal areas of interest. The first is an account of the discovery and scholarship of the bronzes, largely from a narrative antiquarian viewpoint, which contains few critical elements. The second is the text itself, commentary, translation and associated indices and appendices. Some editions do not offer any section devoted to contextual, analytical and methodological issues and their theoretical justification. Others, the more modern, contain peripheral treatments of topics such as socio-political structure (Prosdocimi 1984; Devoto 1974; Poultney 1959; Pfiffig 1964), but the comment is derived from the reading of the text, and is secondary to it. The reading of the text is seen as primary and essentially unconditioned.

5.2.5.ii The etymological method

In the vast majority of cases, any given reading of the text of the bronzes is achieved by a process of constructing etymological equations with forms in known languages. These in turn derive their validity and authority from the Indo-European model of language relationship. It is inevitable, therefore, that any discussion such as this has to concern itself with the validity of this methodology (Wilkins forthcoming).[1]

5.2.5.iii The Indo-European (IE) model

I am focusing primarily upon aspects of the IE model, which lend authority to this use of etymological equations, as commonly exploited by the Iguvine commentators. My emphasis and the driving consideration behind my critical comments is the whole issue of models of language-relationship and language-contact, and their relative applicability to the urbanising communities of peninsular Italy in the second half of the first millennium BC. Such issues substantially compromise the IE theory as a model for language relationship and contact in the particular context of the interpretation of the Iguvine bronzes.

The model that lends its authority to the etymological method is the neogrammarian model of the IE family of languages. This is the theory which has formed the basis of the greatest part of the work on the languages (and so-called dialects) of ancient Italy, as indeed it has of the greatest part of the work on the earlier historical development of European languages in general. To a degree which is perhaps unexpected, and in spite of its almost universal acceptance in these areas of scholarship, the assumptions underlying the neogrammarian model remain largely implicit and are not supported by a

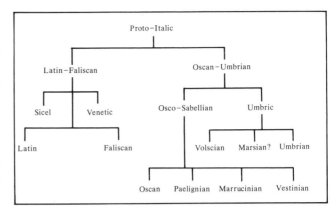

Fig. 5.11 Tree showing hypothesised relationship between Italic languages (Poultney 1958)

well-developed body of theoretical or systematic justification.[2]

5.2.5.iv The genetic language-tree

The dominant and central notion of the IE model is that of genetic relationship within a family of languages. The concept of genetic relationship is most usually thought of, and expressed diagrammatically, as a simple, rather unsophisticated, two-dimensional language-tree. Poultney's diagram (Fig. 5.11) is a good example. All those languages which can be shown to qualify for membership of the IE family are arranged upon a tree of parental relationship. It is important to note that the tree models genetic relationship only, and this is thought of as evidenced in characteristic typological family groupings. Languages, or their families, can only be attached at specific branching points (nodes) of the tree. Languages which do not satisfy the criteria (as conventionally for instance Etruscan, Basque, Hungarian, Finnish) cannot be attached, and are reckoned to be unrelated to the IE family.

One of the faults of such trees as utilised in standard IE scholarship is that they conceal differing levels of hierarchy and abstraction. For example, here there are three levels of proto-groups represented above the level of individual languages, with Proto-Indo-European (PIE) itself still beyond. PIE itself is the root of a larger tree, of which this subtree is assumed to be a subsection. The assumed hierarchy then includes at least the following levels:

[1] I am especially concerned here with the use of hypothetical etymological equations *as an heuristic tool* for the interpretation of otherwise obscure passages of text.
[2] Anderson 1973: 2, says with refreshing candour, 'Most of the notions in historical linguistics are not yet sufficiently well formulated to invite methods of testing. They appear in the guise of explanation of change but are still in the infant stage'.

PIE   Proto-Indo-European
PGA   Proto-Groupings (high level), e.g. Proto-Italic
PGB   Proto-Groupings (intermediate level), e.g. Oscan-
         Umbrian
PGC   Proto-Groupings (localised level), e.g. Osco-Sabellian
L   Individual Languages, e.g. Latin

The major split hypothesised here for ancient Italy is between Oscan-Umbrian and Latin-Faliscan. These are seen as descended from a superordinate Proto-group called Proto-Italic.

Hypothesised relationships of this kind in historical linguistics may be read in one of two ways. Generally the existing scholarship is ambivalent between the two. First, the tree may be read from the root in an historical sense. The immediate implication here would be that a given language is the factual result of an historical evolution from PIE (or in this case, Proto-Italic) along a given path through the historically intermediate stages represented by the various levels of Proto-Groups. This reading, the ontological interpretation, sees PIE (or Proto-Italic, as the case may be) as a real language (or group of languages or dialects) that was existent once, and necessarily has to grant reality also to the various Proto-Group sub-stages. In this historical sense, the tree can then be read almost directly as a geographical evolutive map of the historical process of the diffusion/progressive generation of languages.

Secondly, there is an abstract, or formal, reading. According to this approach, the links and pathways indicated by the tree are nothing more than a formal and abstract model useful for stating the relationships thought to obtain between the various languages. In its purest version this approach would wish to distance itself from any historical or historicist implications whatsoever. PIE and the Proto-Groups become merely theoretical devices for expressing linguistic relationship, without any direct or eventual real-world counterparts.

While I sympathise with the motivation that wishes to preserve a tight formality unmuddied by the need to accommodate the unpredictable irregularity of archaeological and historical input, I think that the second position, the formal reading, is implausible and untenable. In practice, it is almost impossible to preserve the purity of the position, and there are substantive and clear reasons for this. Any model of general genetic type carries with it inevitable expectations of historical genetic processes. It is essentially evolutive, and evolution implies a real time-dimension, and indeed a real-time dimension. Also it is difficult to see much point in the use of a model which implies real evolutive processes, if we excise these processes. After all, if a genetic model does not model evolutive

relationships of parentage and offspring through time, it is hard to see what it does model.

I conclude therefore that the formal position amounts to special pleading. It is an attempt to rescue IE theory, and to insulate the theory from inconvenient data and counter-examples – or more pertinently, from their absence.[1]

5.2.5.v The IE model in the context of an urbanising Italy

Diachronic

My first point concerns generalities of linguistic change over chronological time. Perhaps one important fundamental is the realisation that there is no *a priori* requirement that all phases of linguistic development and/or evolution throughout human history should be generically the same. The period of linguistic development, for instance, represented by urbanising ancient Italy of the first millennium BC is contextually unique. This can hardly be over-emphasised. By contrast, the standard IE model, with its very strong universalising and formalising tendency, seeks universals to demonstrate the absolute validity of its laws. This search tends to collapse particular phases of development which are in themselves generically utterly diverse, as, for example, urbanising Italy compared with the development of Romance Europe, or the development of second-millennium BC Anatolia compared with the growth of a redistributive society in Crete in the same millennium, into a kind of generalised amalgam of uniform data. Word-forms from one or the other, taken quite indiscriminately, are all combined, most often with a cavalier insensitivity both as to underlying sociological parameters, as to historical and cultural distance, and as to the need to demonstrate basic criteria of comparability.

The IE model emphasises the notion familiar to the late nineteenth century of the well-defined national language of an evolved and established nation-state. First millennium BC Italy, by contrast, is a period of transition from tribal to state society. National languages in this sense are only in a process of first formation. Parallels for linguistic pattern and usage are needed as much from tribal as state society. There is absolutely no correlation between the pattern of archaeological and historical evidence for urbanisation and the language names of Poultney's tree. No evidence exists of advanced urban structures for most of these. There is thus a very serious mismatch of model to evidence (Wilkins 1990).

---

[1] If we were to require, in a general Popperian sense, that the model be sufficiently well characterised as to permit the specification of counter-examples, it is difficult to imagine how we should recognise a counter-example to, say, Proto-Italic.

The reconstruction of the linguistic 'pre-constructs', the proto-groupings, is also weak and inapposite. Unlike the hypothesised separate languages, for which some inscriptional evidence can be pressed into play, there is no tangible evidence whatsoever for these stages. Groupings such as Poultney's Oscan-Umbrian are totally abstract, and furthermore constitute an abstraction demanded exclusively by the basic architecture of the theory. Without such abstractions, and more pertinently, without such abstractions as Proto-Italic, it would be impossible to connect the individual languages onto the IE family tree, and therefore ultimately formalise a relationship with PIE itself. PIE of course is the final abstraction.

Apart, however, from the problem of the abstract status of these constructs, and from the fact that we have no evidence that anyone anywhere ever spoke or wrote, say, Oscan-Umbrian, the hypothesisation of these proto-stages meshes very poorly with the evidence for Italic prehistory. To underpin the abstract pre-constructs of IE theory, we need to hypothesise societies which are likely to have sufficiently well-delineated public language systems, to possess the educational and cultural systems for their secure establishment, and similar systems to ensure their cultural survival and transmission over long periods of time, and through all the vicissitudes of spatial dissemination. The further back we push the IE abstractions, the worse and more compound the difficulties become. Proto-Italic requires a more (and not less) centralised and higher-organised set of social structures than a more limited regional Oscan-Umbrian. But the only societies capable of such organisation and control are necessarily state societies[1], and of these there is no archaeological trace at a sufficiently early date. On the contrary, Bronze Age Italy is peopled by evolved tribal societies (section 4.4). The standard IE model used to appear to harmonise extraordinarily well with the assumptions of the migration/invasion school of European prehistory at a time when such models were also popular in the archaeological literature. Indigenous models now predominate for central Italy. The archaeological pattern of a large number of communities developing in varying directions and at varying pace, changing only towards the end of the first millennium BC to centralised control, is quite the reverse (section 5.3) (see Wilkins 1991) of that proposed by IE models.

Synchronic

It is true that the IE theory is not normally seen as a synchronic model. Ironically, however, one could say that the only point of contact that IE theory has with archaeological and historical reality, is essentially a synchronic contact. The typical IE tree (Fig. 5.11) has some leaves (in most cases, the terminating point of a branch) which represent individual attested languages, for example Latin.

A tree such as Poultney's gives equal status to a whole collection of Italic languages – Latin, Faliscan, Sicel, Venetic, Volscian, Umbrian, Oscan, Paelignian, Marrucinian and Vestinian. No differentiation is made between them, and the unwary could be forgiven for concluding that we possess a wide range of evidence to back up these classifications and language names. Nothing, however, could be further from the truth. The factual situation is that the linguistic evidence for ancient Italy is extremely patchy. For some of these labels, such as Sicel or Vestinian, the linguistic evidence varies from pitifully small to non-existent, and what does exist is difficult to interpret and classify. For Oscan, by contrast, there are well over two hundred well-preserved inscriptions. Umbrian, by contrast again, although well-represented by the Iguvine Tables themselves (over 4,000 words), has only a small number of very short other inscriptions.

The vast bulk of all inscriptional material for early Italy belongs to one of three groupings only, Etruscan (which is not permitted to figure in IE accounts), Oscan and Latin. (I group Umbrian here under Oscan. It has a close affinity with Oscan and is probably better seen as a 'northern Oscan'.) For the first millennium BC Etruscan and then Oscan are statistically the better-attested languages. For the linguistic prehistory of Italy, it should also be noted that although altogether Latin has overwhelmingly the absolutely largest number of all surviving inscriptions, it is interesting that proportionately few fall in the Republican period, and the vast bulk are of Imperial date (see Wilkins 1990).

The IE model has no way of dealing directly with what is the predominant characteristic of the Italic material, and that is its fragmented state. Bits of text are the norm, but there is no way in which bits of text can be attached directly to the IE model. The invention of superordinate language systems simply to mediate the associating together of a few isolated inscriptions, or partial inscriptions, is clearly an absurd and bad practice.

Other problems of systematic inconsistency and ambiguity between synchronic and diachronic approaches concern the status of the labels which are attached to the tree either at node or leaf. Entities of differing status are attached without distinction, for example supposedly

---

[1] Renfrew's proposal, therefore (Renfrew 1987), of localised acculturation, cultural interactions and exchanges is a move in the wrong direction (viz., towards smaller, unrelated and less organised groupings), and only introduces further abstraction into the general model.

historical languages on the one hand, and various stages of abstract pre-groupings on the other. Entities of either type are also ambiguous as to their synchronic status. On the one hand a label such as Umbrian clearly has some relation or other to the small extant set of texts which were composed and inscribed in a given time phase. This is undeniably primarily a synchronic reference. On the other hand there is strong implication that it is not a given set of texts which is being attached to the tree, but more precisely the evolution of a whole putative language-system, presumably ranging over a long period of real time – for which the texts would be mere confirmatory evidence. There is a sense, therefore, in which the IE model wishes to have it both ways.

The upshot of all this is confusion. On the one hand, it turns out that the apparently more concrete entities, real attested language texts, for which a reasonably precise context of date and location can sometimes be worked out, can only be related to the IE tree through the elaboration of highly abstract (and highly debatable) reconstructed descriptions which cannot be located in time and space. These descriptions, in their search for complete grammars from evidence which is not adequate for such hypothetical constructs, inevitably have the effect of flattening the profile of the data which do exist. They obscure such information as can be gleaned as to time and location. On the other hand, the totally abstract entities such as proto-Italic which enjoy a bogus factual backing by virtue of their undifferentiated mode of attachment to the tree, require necessarily also to be related to real synchronic times and diachronic periods, but prove totally incapable of being located anywhere in time or space. Many other issues follow from this confusion.

The genetic model has one predominant emphasis, and that is upon genetic parentage. In general, the only relationship between two languages that can be directly modelled is that of evolution from a common ancestor (most usually in Italic studies requiring reconstruction). Thus, if we wish to connect Oscan and Umbrian, we are compelled to invent an ancestor, Oscan-Umbrian. If we wish to relate Latin with Oscan-Umbrian we must invent an ancestor, proto-Italic. Traditional IE analysis gives us no satisfactory way of discussing any direct relationship between say Latin and Oscan. Perhaps even more importantly, there is no theoretically developed framework for discussing relationships between historically neigh-bouring languages which are well attested, say Latin and Etruscan, or Oscan and Etruscan. On the contrary, the IE model has the effect of emphasising the separateness of such languages. The model tells us nothing about the internal configuration of linguistic geography that might or might not prevail at any given time. Since an intensity

of contact between the societies behind these three languages is probably a fairly uncontroversial assumption, this seems a strange and unsatisfactory method of approach.

Dialects and borrowing
The genetic model is commonly associated with a number of ancillary and auxiliary concepts which might be said to cover the 'sideways', and to some extent synchronic, relationships of language. Prominent among these are the concepts of dialect and borrowing. Virtually by definition, these models deliver better results in historically later contexts involving long-established urban societies. A majority of dialectal models are theoretically early linguistic versions of core-and-periphery relationships, either inter-preted literally or metaphorically. In the case of borrowing between languages, the assumption has to be a minimum of two culturally contiguous languages of somehow comparable status.

Neither of these sub-models works satisfactorily for early Italic texts. In general the base assumptions do not fit. Dialectal interpretations among recent commentators are relatively sparse. In spite of the Romanocentric assumptions which older titles such as that of Conway 1897 and of Vetter 1953 unfortunately imply (both speaking of 'Italic dialects'), there is no sense in which the totality of the Italic material can be explained by a dialect sub-model, which is clearly inappropriate to the evidence. Each of the three better-documented state languages – Etruscan, Oscan and Latin – offers difficulties. Etruscan (which is of course not included by the normal comparativist literature), although prolific in inscriptional material, has a strange profile. With rare and uncertain exception, virtually all the material has direct or indirect ritual or religious association. It may well be that this is the result of the configuration of negative evidence, or it is perfectly conceivable that the language only ever existed as an instrument of ritual activity, and without developing any of the many other parameters of usage which are so familiar to us to-day. Either way we have no obvious basis for the reconstruction of normative as opposed to divergent classes of material. Oscan has a more widely represented profile, but the sample is statistically too small to be reasonably certain of this kind of classification. Latin, for its part, has a large range of material, but very little of it is pre-Imperial, and this sample again is far too small for a soundly and broadly based piece of work.

The case with the sub-model of borrowing between languages is more serious, at least for our immediate purpose, namely that of the validation of interpretations of the Iguvine Tables, simply because this sub-model is used extensively by the Iguvine commentators. For borrowing to make sense as a model, however, we must require a reasonable archaeological and historical comparability both of the respective language systems between which borrowing is deemed to take place, and of the degree and breadth of linguistic sophistication likely in the respective societies. Type and degree of literacy is obviously a prime axis here, since it is likely that borrowings presuppose the contact of literate groups or sub-groups. One might also desire a minimum specification for the sort of avenues and mechanisms by which such borrowings are deemed to have taken place in the social and economic conditions likely to be prevailing at the time. In other words, the concept needs to have some archaeological and historical plausibility. It is not at all certain that such conditions can be met for the majority of loans suggested.

5.2.6 Suggestions for a revised paradigm

5.2.6.i Early urbanised societies and language boundaries

A start must be made with the context and related assumptions. All the inscriptional material from Italic linguistic prehistory is characteristically the product of urbanised state society. Much of it is possibly from urbanised states which are themselves only relative newcomers to this stage of development: early urbanised state societies. There is no material evidence for tribal, pre-urban or proto-urban societies developing and using writing systems, nor are there any clear parallels for such a phenomenon from anthropological literature.

Having said that, one should be careful not to see the whole phenomenon of urbanisation as somehow unitary, uniform, linear or irreversible. The process of urbanisation 'has phases and cycles, not all of which run at even speed, and not all of which run their full course' (Wilkins 1990: 68). The processes of urbanisation are plural, hybrid and complicated. Furthermore, writing is a potential element of this plurality. The framework has to allow just as much for urbanised societies which do not develop and use writing, as indeed for ones which use writing in what seem very partial and strangely limited ways.

The whole of the 'language industry' (the proliferation of scripts, grammars, dictionaries, effectively modern linguistics itself) is entirely, precisely and exclusively the artefact of urban state society.[1] The concept of a language as a constant, independent and permanent structure with a clear cultural identity, with hard and discernible edges, and with all the inevitable concomitants of national, ethnic or group identity and identification, is also the invention of urban state society. These are state languages (Wilkins 1990: 57f.).

The implication of all this for our immediate model is that this whole set of transitions which constitute ur-

banisation are in process during the period covered by Italic linguistic prehistory. It follows that areas, settlements and social groupings in general will vary enormously as to the degree to which they participate or are affected by this set of transitions. If in conventional 'progress' terms, there is a 'dash for urbanisation', then there will be leaders and laggards, while there will be both entire zones and minor pockets which are untouched (section 5.3). A theory of linguistic relationship is needed which can relate the inscriptional evidence to the socio-political map.

Some appreciation of 'the pre-urban linguistic backdrop' (Wilkins 1990: 63, 68) is fundamental. Any proposed model will need to incorporate as integral components, therefore, a whole range of ideas on the likely specification of language systems at a late tribal and early pre-urban state of development. The use and structuralisation of human language will be seen as developing from that which is essentially fluid to that which is essentially fixed. A contextual model of language relationship will give preference to comparisons with material from other linguistic sources within Italy, and particularly from neighbouring geographical areas. To accommodate these comparisons the model will need to develop various notions of communal, interlocking, unedged and side-by-side language and script shared learned development.

This is obviously a crude outline model, but it would suggest that state language formation will be at very different stages in differing political and geographical locations. In any comparison of linguistic materials like must be compared with like. Dating from archaeological context is clearly crucial to underpin internal methods of script and morphological analysis, while attributions as to political and geographical origin pose obvious and complex orders of difficulty.

5.2.6.ii Types of literacy

The sociological changes discussed above are often formulated in terms of 'literacy'. Discussions tend to utilise distinctions such as 'oral' versus 'literate'. It is characteristic of a majority of these models that a unitary literacy, which is a literal literacy of letter-learning, or alphabeticisation, is given a very powerful instrumental role as agent of change, becoming the virtually automatic harbinger of productivity and efficiency, as well as of an enhanced quality of intellectual life for the successfully trained.

---

[1] While treatises on grammatical and etymological points have a long history within urban states, dictionaries, by contrast, constitute a particularly recent phenomenon (essentially seventeenth century onwards). They form an aspect of the structuralisation of language form which is still visibly active.

Other recent studies, however, have laid stress on the complex nature of literacy, with some authors preferring to think in terms of different literacies or different types of literacy (Stoddart and Whitley 1988a). At the same time there has been some movement away from these early models which are seen as historicist in their emphasis on the great and single agencies of once-and-for-all change (of which the coming of literacy would clearly be one) toward models which emphasise the varied and complex interaction of many aspects of continuity and gradual change.

My own sympathies are with the revised models. There would seem on investigation to be many types of literacy which develop in differing societies, of which the stock case of alphabeticisation, especially as identified with educational systems and 'schooling', is only one variant. Important again is the literacy of special language systems within society. These special-case languages are also very much the hallmark of urban state societies, and will characteristically be related to specialised skills and sections of the populace, sometimes numerically very small. Equally important, is the notion of partial or incomplete literacies. This is important, whether on a state scale, or at a personal level. For antiquity, and for our revised paradigm, a wide range of possible types of literacy must be addressed which may develop or partially develop in the societies under study.[1]

5.2.6.iii Ritual language

Ritual language inhabits literally a world of its own. This is true both of spoken and written ritual language in all its forms. If we wish to assume that a given extant document falls within the range of ritual text, then we have no option but to try to assemble an adequate understanding of the world in which the text will have been created and used. Ritual text in this way is at a considerable remove from literary text. It is not simply, as commentators on the Iguvine Tables often seem to presuppose, some special minor case of literary text with odd repetitions and formulae. It is important to realise that a ritual text meshes in a quite particular manner with the social and symbolic assumptions of the society to which it relates. It is a truism that ritual language is heavily laden and imbued with both overt and covert symbolism. For the linguistic aspects of ritual, Bloch 1974 still provides a useful starting-point. Bloch argues that 'such symbols in ritual cannot be understood without a prior study of the nature of the communication medium of ritual in which they are embedded; and that once this has been done we find that symbols cannot anymore be understood as units of meaning simply on the Saussurian signifier/signified model, however subtly this model is handled.'

I would add that the 'intellectualist' tradition of western rationalism can also be an impediment to the interpretation of ritual language. This tradition looks for translations and explanations, where perhaps translations mean very little, and where there are no explanations. The problem here is that translations and explanations imply equivalences to, and relationships with, constructs in the modern 'interpreting' culture which are outside the original 'subject' culture which historically produced the text under examination. Inevitably therefore there are bound to be distortions. Most often ritual language and thought is essentially self-contained and circumscribed, and has very little if any truly 'outside' equivalence. The case is, however, not absolute, and the possibility of a range of partial equivalences will depend upon the extent to which the interpreting and subject cultures share an historical community or alignment. This is particularly relevant to the interpretation of the Iguvine bronzes, and of Italic/Etruscan/Roman ritual in general.

A further point is that ritual language inhabits a specialised domain even within the subject culture and within the whole context of the practice and evolution of the social uses of language. Ritual language, as used for example in ritual ceremonies, liturgies, hymns and prayers, can be seen to have its own domain, and within that domain, its own rules. Ritual uses of language deliberately restrict themselves to a tightly limited set of patterns. This is not so much an impoverished form of language, it is rather an area of deliberate 'linguistic engineering'. In ritual, constraints are not limited simply to the 'surface' and visible aspects of what is often called 'style', such as formulaic repetitions, restricted and specialised lexis, archaisms, syncopated syntax, reduced morphological range and abrupt transitions.

Much more importantly, the capacity of the language for formulating and transmitting concepts, by comparison with non-ritual language, is deliberately disabled and skewed. We cannot and should not presume that any supposed 'ordinary' inter-personal relationships of everyday communication apply at all. This is not the same as saying that ceremonies involving ritual language have no meaning. On the contrary they are full of symbolic meaning for those who inhabit and have 'knowledge' of the shared symbolic world. They will however frequently appear as meaningless 'mumbo-jumbo' to those who do not. Even

---

[1] Special-case languages and sub-languages are particularly important to the understanding of the complexity of the historical development of literacy. These are characteristically restricted to experts, whose training is long, intensive and highly selective. They will frequently 'inhabit' a world apart, which is of great conceptual and symbolic status. The specialist languages of pure mathematics and formal logic are standard examples. More important for our immediate discussion is the reserved linguistic world of professional ritual, with its public contact points of liturgy and popular theology.

for the 'initiated', such texts may employ deliberately obscure or even meaningless formulae as direct instruments of the ritual. This point applies with obvious and particular force to the interpretation of texts which are already obscure because of a general poverty of understanding of the normative non-ritual language usages of the subject culture.

The argument so far applies both to oral and written usages, and to a majority of contexts. In the particular context, however, of urbanised societies, the processes that produce the kind of written ritual texts which may possibly survive until the modern period, are particularly important. The writing of a ritual text occurs within a specialised real and symbolic context within the 'professional' world of the 'ritual specialists' itself. Especially in early urbanised society, it is likely that this inner reserve will have its own peculiar procedures and its own personnel.

In such an early context, ideas either of publication or of communication to persons outside the 'professional' ritual world are questionable and probably inappropriate. At this early and very restricted stage of literacy, the motivation of the priesthood which displays any document would not be the publication of a liturgy for indiscriminate unauthorised reading (which would expose their reserved expertise) but to emphasise the supreme status and powers of the priesthood by demonstrating its complete ownership and mastery over dark and immanent powers, and in particular over their special language, the mystic art of holy writing. The text would probably not therefore be designed to be read or to be directly intelligible to the 'lay' person. On the contrary, various steps might well be taken to make quite sure that it remained unintelligible. These might include the insertion of deliberately obscure or nonsense passages. Here there is a conscious manipulative intention to deceive outsiders and thereby protect a mystery of great 'holiness'. Similarly there may be deliberate corruption or encoding of the script, even something as simple as hanging the text upside-down! (It follows therefore that hanging perforations on the bottom edge of the text of the Iguvine bronzes, far from indicating hanging after the text ceased to be understood, may deliberately have been designed as an obstacle to any direct reading or understanding.)

This extreme 'apartheid' of ritual text may well be more characteristic of certain early periods of development. Equally, however, one should be careful of concluding that such characteristics remain in some definitional sense necessarily primitive. Some particular urban states may for one reason or another adhere to such a typology of ritual much longer than others. In other urbanising contexts, a wider literacy and the development of literature may rapidly reduce the status of the priests/experts as the sole possessors of written words. In this latter case, the

evolution of a different kind of ritual text is likely, something which arises more from literary and philosophical interests, than from the narrower preoccupations of the earlier priests themselves. In this latter context, the priests/experts will themselves very likely be involved with a wider circle of writers and thinkers in the new development of literature. This situation could well produce literary versions which authors imagined were equivalent to the liturgies of traditional practising priests, and lead eventually (with feedback influence upon priestly literatures themselves) to a liturgical literature in which the priests themselves again participate. These developments would lead towards the evolution of a written theology. The extent and speed of such developments are functions of the type and speed of the dissemination of literacy itself in the society, and of the degree to which closed ritual structures become assimilated more widely.

This last point introduces the important possibility of a typological or time/development dimension, somewhere upon which it may be necessary to place a given ritual text. Not all ritual texts are the same in some trivial sense, nor do they emanate from a society that is similarly placed, chronologically or in any other sense, as to the development of overt ritual language systems, and of liturgy and theology. Texts from heavily ritualised (not necessarily chronologically early) periods of development are likely to be characterised by their composition in a literate isolation or relative isolation. At the other end of the scale texts arising from periods of wider development of literacy and especially literature will have a feedback and reciprocal relationship with the sophistication of contemporary literature. These are likely to reflect more elaborate devices of periodic structure and rhetorical routines, and altogether to evince an overt and self-conscious self-publicising awareness of their own genre. Priests/experts are also likely in these societies to have a quite different set of approaches from the heavily retentive attitudes outlined above. In this more 'evolved' model of public ritual language, the priests/experts would have a distinct and overt public-consumption dimension.

5.2.7 *Towards an interpretation of the Iguvine Tables*

5.2.7.i *Primacy of the context*

Analysis of the text should be context-led. We therefore need to start by establishing as accurately as we can, the interpretative context which will govern and order any subsequent textual analysis. My procedure is therefore the reverse of the traditional, which, where it considers context, seeks to deduce it from the text. We may encapsulate the question to be explored as: 'What sort of an artefact do we take the bronzes to be?' A good starting point is the material upon which the inscriptions are written, and the general issue of whether a definition of ritual context is plausible.

5.2.7.ii The bronzes: ritual or not?

One starting point is to ask whether the use of bronze is significant. Bronze objects were admittedly numerous in antiquity. The phenomenal output of the workshops of Etruria, for example, is evidenced from several sources, and Vulci for instance was legendary in this respect. It is likely that the small numbers of bronzes surviving from antiquity to the present day are but a tiny proportion of those originally produced. The principal reason for this would have been the recycling of the metal during antiquity itself and since. It is relevant also that bronze was employed both on the one hand for coinage (an official state usage) and on the other hand for some versions of domestic objects (which might seem to argue a more utilitarian value).

We should probably not hasten to conclude that bronze was commonplace and, although an expensive resource, essentially utilitarian in application. On the contrary, it is doubtful whether the usage was ever predominantly utilitarian, or that it percolated indiscriminately throughout all the levels of society. It has to be remembered that coins, most especially historically early versions, have more to do with the authority and wealth of the state than with our modern preconceptions of commercial currency and practical utility. Similarly, domestic objects made of bronze are quite likely to have had a restricted context or special significance. A more plausible conclusion might be that in most instances the paramount importance of bronze was as a marker of high status, prestige and authority. It is also reasonable to suppose that the bigger the artefact and the greater the quantity of bronze used, the more likely that this is to be the case. This is clearly relevant in particular to the Iguvine bronzes.

It should also be remembered that bronze was an impressive physical medium for all kinds of status statements. Our modern impression of ancient bronzes, even where they survive in excellent condition and have not been the victim of so-called 'bronze disease', is often that of dull unattractive objects. Where they carry an inscription, this dullness can also make them difficult to read. In antiquity however bronzes were likely to have been kept highly polished, and oxidisation of the surface was prevented by a virtually continual process of polishing. When polished in this way, the brilliance of the surface is quite startling, having a lustre very similar to gold. This difference between the polished and unpolished surfaces is well demonstrated to anyone who has ever wondered how

on earth anyone ever saw themselves in an Etruscan bronze mirror!

The conclusion so far that the Iguvine examples are likely to be artefacts carrying associations of high status and indeed of state authority, is reinforced by the small number of direct comparanda. In general the number of comparable bronze inscriptions surviving from antiquity is small. In the late Republic and the Augustan era, there are even fewer. The contrast with the large number of inscriptions surviving on monumental stone is marked. While this may be due to melting down in the intervening millennia, it is also plausible to suppose that bronze would never have been the regular material for 'run-of-the-mill' state inscriptions. There is some evidence to suggest that in the context of a document of state authority, bronze generally had a particularly solemn and ritual association. The kind of evidence required is something that will give indications, preferably un-self-conscious, of contemporary attitudes and values.

Rome's famous and legendary Twelve Tables provide a good example from a less tightly defined period. It is not important to debate whether the supposedly fifth century originals of these documents ever existed and were in fact lost in the sack of Rome by the Gauls. What matters is that late Republicans firmly believed in them, and showed great respect for the surviving textual tradition which they believed represented the original text. The Twelve Tables were also centrally established in the educational system. Cicero relates proudly how he had learnt to recite them by heart as a schoolboy, and how he can still quote from them as an adult. From the very widespread references in Latin literature, we can deduce that Cicero in this instance was no particular exception for his background. From the fragments of text quoted by many writers, it is clear that the Tables contained very little of what today is classified as ritual, being devoted largely to a law code, and even then to one covering what we might regard as relatively minor areas of litigation.

The story that they contained the traditional laws of the Roman forefathers, and that the codification of the lawcode upon these monumental records was a concession that had to be wrung from the ruling aristocracy, is significant. The manner in which the ruling aristocracy, we are told, persisted in trying to keep knowledge of these laws to themselves (in spite of the inequity that people could be prosecuted and punished for infringement without knowing what they were infringing) has distinct ritual overtones. Reconstructing purely on general grounds (and without specific reference to the problematic recon-struction of this early stage of Rome's hypothetical development) one could say that this reluctance points to the well-known ritual phenomenon of the existence of a body of secret knowledge which was reserved to those who had privileged access to it. This reserved knowledge might well then represent a mystery which was the jealous preserve of a 'college' of 'priests' or other high-status specialists. (I will use priest here as a convenient generic for a whole range of possible high-status specialists). Legal expertise in particular might well be reserved in this way, and could be some kind of 'priestly' or specialist preserve. We could then hypothesise that it would be the case that only the priestly elder or specialist could communicate any part of this knowledge, such as a judicial ruling, and then only in the first instance to a suitably placed representative of the state, perhaps an aristocratic elder.

Another possible implication is that this type of literacy would be the sole prerogative of the priests and that both the majority of the aristocracy, and probably the totality of the remaining people would be illiterate in this special restricted language. Making a suitably edited version of a lawcode fixed, visible and available would not therefore carry any immediate risk of many persons being able to read or make use of the lawcode. The real risk for the priests would have been the making public of their reserved knowledge, and that would in any case not be a real risk if they were currently enjoying virtually exclusive access to this specialised type of literacy. The publication of the lawcode therefore would not necessarily imply the existence of persons literate enough to read and make use of it, but would necessarily greatly enhance the status of the law-experts whoever they were, by this impressive public demonstration of their extensive expertise. The notion of publication being forced by a demand for literate access is then clearly out of period.

If this mini-reconstruction has any plausibility, then we are very much in the realm of a ritual document, especially for the attitudes of the educated of the late Republic. Irrespective of the reconstruction, the single most significant fact is that Livy and his contemporaries regarded the Tables with ritual respect, and that they therefore *expected* them to have been written on bronze. Other examples of early laws reportedly inscribed upon bronze are the *lex Furia Pinaria* of 472 (reportedly incised on a bronze column) and the *lex Icilia de Aventino publicando* of 456 (reportedly inscribed on a bronze stele). These confirm the same set of expectations in the later sources who mention them.

Direct comparanda from surviving bronze inscriptions from the last centuries of the Republic and the Augustan period include the Tabula Bantina, a legal inscription found near Bantia, bearing a local law in Oscan; the Tabula Hebana from Magliano which interestingly records state honours conferred upon Germanicus after his death;

and the Tablet of Agnone, a small bronze tablet from Samnite territory (Molise) (some 280 mm × 165 mm). The tablet has brackets and chain fitted to enable its hanging, and display at a local sanctuary is reckoned to be a possibility. The reading of the Oscan inscription on the latter is however disputed. Devoto (1974) sees the inscription as primarily topographical rather than ritual, while Pisani (1964) sees a possible parallel with the Stations of the Cross. In spite of the apparent occurrence of names of deities, the text remains obscure and it is difficult to develop a precise parallel with the Gubbio bronzes.

Among more general parallels for the use of bronze for monumental state inscriptions, there is the *Monumentum Ancyranum*, a provincial stone version of bronze texts which were originally set up in Rome. Suetonius states that Octavian (who took the name *Augustus* specifically for its ritual overtones) desired a record of his achievements (his *res gestae*) to be engraved on two bronze tablets and erected outside his mausoleum in Rome. In the event, these original bronzes do not survive. Copies of the text were, however, made and set up in a number of the Roman provinces. The Monumentum Ancyranum, discovered in 1555, contains the majority of the text and a Greek translation and comes from a mosque at Ancyra (Galatia), formerly a temple of Rome and Augustus. The text, very much in the style of a Roman triumph, details Augustus' public honours, monies spent from his own pocket on state matters, his victories and conquests, and a grand perorative statement which summarises his public image. It is probably not irrelevant that Romulus himself was popularly supposed to have left behind an inscription detailing his own *res gestae*.

As with the possibly mythical Twelve Tables, so too here the significant point is that bronze is singled out not so much just to enhance the authority of state ritual, but above all as the expected medium for grand symbolic statements on behalf of or directly issued by the state itself. Following this line of argument it is reasonable to conclude that the Iguvine bronzes are most likely to constitute important state documents, whatever the precise analysis of the text. It follows also and axiomatically that the bronzes were intended for prominent public exhibition. The notion favoured by some of the commentators that some or all of the tablets amount to a private archive (of the collegium or brotherhood) stowed away from the public gaze, is therefore extremely implausible. This is of course not to deny the quite separate point that the composed texts as finally inscribed on the bronze might themselves emanate from earlier archives. That is a separate matter. In any case even the keeping of archives would imply a relatively stable linguistic and literate culture established over a length of time, at least within the ambit of the social structures of the college itself, and this is an assumption that needs separate exploration and justification.

A parallel consideration is that if the Iguvine bronzes represent a grand symbolic statement by the state, then they are perhaps on a surprisingly magnificent scale for a modest-sized civitas foederata or municipium. The physical size of the statement made would perhaps at first sight be better in proportion with a larger-scale established city. This might in turn suggest that the real archetype of the Iguvine bronzes lies somewhere distant in a larger urbanised centre, and that the surviving texts represent a model which has been specially adapted and imported for internal political reasons. Alternatively if the Tables are truly 'home-grown', then their magnificence would suggest some specialised, long-established, ritual importance for ancient Iguvium.

5.2.7.iii Expectations as to the content of the bronzes

Having established that the bronzes are likely to have been incised with the particular purpose of making an important public representation, on behalf of the state itself, or on behalf of some group which had or sought an important place in the local hierarchy, and that we might plausibly assign a ritual status in general to this statement, we then move to considering what kind of a statement or statements might be placed upon such a prominent medium. For a majority of the commentators, this has become self-evident. Poultney (1959: 1) may be taken as typical: 'The tablets contain instructions for the religious ceremonies of a college of priests known as the Atiedian Brothers who flourished in Iguvium during the period of the Roman Republic.' For what is presumably supposed to be an unexceptionable and innocent generalisation, the inaccuracies are disturbing. The only references to the **fratru: atiieřiu** (for example IIa, 21), come from the bronzes themselves. There is no mention of a *collegium*, and the 'Brothers' are not mentioned at all on Tables I, IV, VI and VIIa. More interesting is the assumption that these texts contain 'instructions'. Conway (1897) speaks of regulations. This is based linguistically upon the large number of forms in the Tables ending in -*tu* which is interpreted as an imperative form. It is not, however, self-evident under what circumstances the priesthood would authorise the written composition of such 'regulations', nor for whose benefit they would be composed. Who would be the intended audience, or in terms of literacy types, who would be expected to be able to read or make use of such a document? The trained priest within the collegium would not need further instruction, while those outside the collegium would by definition lack the training to make use of such a document. The commentators do not suggest any valid comparanda for such an 'order of service', and lay themselves open to the suspicion, as they do frequently, that they, consciously or unconsciously, are too much conditioned by their own Christian and Jewish backgrounds, in which the types and distribution of literacy are utterly diverse from this period of antiquity. If such a set of documents would make sense in the context of priestly archives, there remains the further issue of why such documents should be engraved upon bronze for display.

What distinctions can be made out within the group of bronzes? The starting point has to be the physical evidence, and the available contextual information. Many of the commentators have remarked on the heterogeneity of the bronzes (although they then proceed to treat them quite happily as some sort of textual unity). Physically, the bronzes fall into four distinct groups (one group having only one member). In the conventional numbering, these are:

Tables I and II	physically similar in mould and dimensions
Tables III and IV	physically similar in dimensions
Table V	physically unique
Tables VI and VII	physically similar in mould and dimensions

There are various obvious possibilities here, some of which have received comment in the literature. First, there is no reason to suppose that the bronzes originally belonged together in any sense, or that they represent the totality of the bronzes cast. (This is a general point, separate from the historical problem of the 'missing' two bronzes). They may represent random survivors of an unknown number of original categories, and of a larger number of bronzes. Equally there is no reason to suppose that they all belong to one and the same period of casting. It is plausible, for instance, that III and IV, and V, respectively, belong to quite distinct production phases from each other, and from the rest of the bronzes.

The situation with regard to text is different again. A distributive analysis of the texts (without recourse to equations or translations) shows that I, VI and VIIa are related in content. II, while similar to I in many ways, cannot be included in the same group. V is isolated (both scripts, and also each from the other). III and IV are possibly the most isolated, depending upon the precise method of analysis adopted. VIIb is separate again.

From the combination of this evidence, all of which is available without the uncertainties of textual interpretation, it is clear that it is inadequate practice to treat the bronzes as some sort of textual unity. On the contrary, the configuration of such evidence allows many other hypotheses. One possibility is a random grouping of bronzes which survived from different original contexts, and that they were perhaps brought together and hidden to rescue them from destruction, perhaps when the local Temple of Jupiter was threatened. Another approach would be to try to relate the differential relationships of physical characteristics and textual content more directly to one context of production and to the intentions of the producers at that time. In other words, there may be something inherently significant about the 'job-lot' nature of both the pieces of bronze and of the pieces of text. This promising approach will be addressed below.

First, let us return to the nature of the texts inscribed upon the bronzes. Although the commentators treat the bronzes as a group, the interpretations they do in fact provide, cover documents of different categories. According to the traditional interpretation, I is some kind of running order for a ceremony couched in a rather summary form, while VI and VIIa contain an amplified version of the same ceremony, a kind of complete order of service, together with the text of prayers. II contains specifications for other ceremonies, which are variously identified, couched again in a summary style but with many areas of obscurity. III and IV are generally thought to constitute one continuous text for a ceremony, but the text is so obscure that we should reject all the interpretations offered, and candidly admit that a valid overall interpretation cannot be achieved. V is quite different, containing variously, records of decrees concerning the role and conduct of the office of *adfertor*, and a separate section with contract details for supply and disposal of food. VIIb appears to be an odd isolated paragraph of text, concerned with further duties of the *fratricus*.

A problem with this diversity is finding comparanda for monumental application. V and VIIb, by virtue of their juridical nature, make some sense as published documents, with parallels in legal monumenta, although there is still the residual problem of a rationale for the separate paragraphs Vb, 8f., and VIIb. It is more difficult to make a valid case for comparanda, however, in the case of the publication of the running order of a ceremony as a monumental document. Several commentators refer to other priestly collegia known to us from Roman sources, notably the collegium of the haruspices, and that of the Arval Brethren. The haruspices are attractive as a parallel because of their acknowledged expertise in bird-watching and the taking of auspices, and the Fratres Arvales are attractive because Varro in particular tells us that their peculiar speciality was ceremonies for the purification and fertility of the fields (the key ritual word is *arva*, also

apparently found frequently in the Tables). There is a strong association with the dea Dia and thence with Ceres. There are difficulties, however, in using these particular collegia to provide some kind of direct parallel with the Tables. It is true that there is evidence to support the contention that collegia did regularly produce proper statements concerning their ritual activities. In fact, it can be argued that the proper publishing of the successful accomplishment of a ritual came to be regarded as a vital and integral part of the ceremony itself. That is to say, the ritual was not finally complete and valid, until it had been properly recorded. Unfortunately, however, the only such records to survive in any usable form are the *Acta Fratrum Arvalium*. There are various points of interest here. The Acta are Augustan and Imperial. No records survive for the Republican period. Secondly, the Acta do not record orders or instructions for the conduct of services, but, by their rehearsal of the fine details of the ritual, the vital fact that the ceremony on this occasion was carried out with ritual correctness. Thirdly, however strong their supposed original connection with the fertility of the fields, in fact the principal recorded business of the Arval Brethren under the Empire was the welfare of members of the Imperial household, and the ritual propriety of ceremonies connected with them. One cannot rule out deliberate archaising with the name Arvalis, and the story which Livy tells of the link with Romulus. In other words, the felt connection with Romulus and the special word for 'fields' are both part of the 'hallowing mechanism' for giving credibility to the priesthood which Augustus designed for the ritual accreditation of the new imperial family.

There are two fairly clear ways out of the dilemma just outlined. If the document is inappropriate as a monumental publication, one solution is to change the interpretation which is causing the anomaly. Since the 'instructional' nature is based upon the forms in -tu, it may be that they need to be re-interpreted, or re-assessed formally. The other solution is to hypothesise a context which fits the observed evidence.

5.2.7.iv What do the texts result from?

I should like to suggest a concept of the text which is closely related to the new model I have proposed (5.2.6) for linguistic development in the peninsula of Italy during this general period. The model thinks in terms of a gradual development in a range of linguistic structures from fluid to fixed, and from less defined to more defined, the principal agency of change being the structuralisation processes engineered by urbanising society. The model also thinks in terms of a development of both script and language that may variously be communal and interlocking at one end of the developmental bandwidth to unedged and side-by-side at the other.

Against such a shifting and varied background, one would expect that the earlier texts to appear, or those appearing in areas which are marginal to the mainstream urbanising process, might reflect various halfway stages towards full and discrete structuralisation. Language boundaries would not be finally formed, and the cross-utilisation of both words and forms across nascent boundaries could be quite extensive. The model gives preference, for instance, to comparisons with material from other linguistic sources within Italy, and particularly from neighbouring geographical areas within Italy. Such areas would include, for example, the Greek-speaking areas of Magna Graecia, and other smaller pockets of Greek speakers. It would also and quite necessarily include Etruria and all its zones of influence. The model is resistant on the other hand to giving status to comparisons with word-forms which are derived totally outside the ambit of the developing Italic communities, unless some valid archaeological and sociological reconstructions can be adduced which would show how these cultural links might have taken place, and give some reason for believing in their general historical plausibility.

The halfway stage of some early texts could therefore take many different forms. A useful image is the *palimpsest*. This is defined as a single resultant surface (or text) which incorporates within itself not so much actual underlying layers, but fragmentary evidence for earlier layers of linguistic structuralisation. In other words the resultant text is seen as a likely carrier of fragmentary information concerning the linguistic developments which have characterised this general area, in terms of geography, social structures and literate structures. Incidentally this is a preferable model for textual analysis not only because it accommodates the general linguistic model proposed, but also because it leaves room for a wider range of explanations that are not strictly related to that model, but are based upon other types of linguistic development, such as a textual tradition in the classical sense.

One advantage of the palimpsest proposal is that it removes the compulsion imposed by the IE model of fixed languages, to construct a complete local language system as a principal and central axis of the analysis. Too often in the past these have been painfully thin and of dubious validity. In fact the new model opens the door to a much wider range of possibilities. What are conventionally considered separate languages in their later clear manifestations, may result from periods of mixed, shared or side-by-side development. Such a framework gives an easy location for the development also of shared or partially shared ritual symbolism and practices. These would naturally be very closely associated with the linguistic gradations and shifts both of form and practice. The framework then gives a natural explanation for terms and words which are shared. These can result from periods of associated ritual development. Obvious examples from the Tables would be **arva**, supposedly the key ritual word for the fields, and **vinu**.

5.2.7.v The content of the Tables

Before the final synthesis, I should perhaps summarise briefly how I see the main contents of the bronzes. Fuller discussion appears in Wilkins (forthcoming). As one exception to this, and to give an example of appropriate argumentation, I have incorporated a fuller treatment of the *templum* issue.

Tables I, VI and VIIa are textually related. This can be demonstrated by distributive and frequency patterns. They probably describe one ceremony and that ceremony has to do with the fertility of the fields (section 6.2). Analogous ceremonies known from Roman sources would be the *lustratio agrorum* and the *ambarvalia*. From parallels discussed above, these texts do not contain instructions for this ceremony, but it is likely that they record the successful and duly ritual enactment of the ritual. The monumentally recorded text is the final act of the ritual itself.

There is mention of the taking of the auspices by studying the flight of certain birds, but again it is most unlikely that we have instructions for the same. The detail in VI on this topic is therefore most probably concerned with the public demonstration that the ritual was properly carried out.

I cannot agree that the text contains instructions for the laying out of a *templum*, the ritual demarcation of the area within which the flight of certain birds should be observed. There is even less evidence for Devoto's very precise geographical layout of the same in terms of the actual topography of Gubbio. This explanation has many devotees (Devoto 1974; Costantini 1970; Micalizzi 1988).

Some commentators (dominated by Devoto) take a passage starting at Table VIa, 8 as specifying the setting-out of a *templum*. The parallel cited here is with Varro *de lingua latina* vi, 53 and vii, 8. The trouble is that in neither passage is Varro really concerned primarily with the setting out of the *templum*. His interest is that of the antiquarian linguist. In the first passage he is concerned with words connected with *fari* 'to speak', and in the second with correlates of *tueri* (which he connects etymologically with *templum*) 'to look at'. In both passages he mentions the fact that the augurs would speak aloud certain words when performing the ritual of laying out the *templum*, but he is at pains in the second passage to stress that the words vary from place to place (*concipitur verbis non isdem usque quaque*) and he lays no particular emphasis on spoken words as vitally important or defining parameters of the ceremony. In the Table passage neither the word *templum* nor any recognisable correlate occurs. Instead commentators attempt to construct a link between the Iguvine word *uerfale* (for which they propose a connection with Latin *verbum* 'word') and *templum*, the idea being that a *templum* is something pre-eminently defined by words, *uerfale* being something presumably like 'the word-defined space'. This is a tortuous line of reasoning. It is prompted not by any plausible demonstration of a cultural parallel, but by a disproportionate reliance upon a tenuous etymological connection.

Tables VI and VII contain also the text of prayers and hymns which formed part of the ceremony. It would be an intrinsic part of the ritual that these should be recorded to demonstrate that they *had been properly performed*.

Tables II, III and IV are obscure.

Tables V and VIIb are regulatory ordinances promulgated at specific times for the proper and due management of the Brotherhood of the Atiedii.

5.2.8 A final synthesis

We might hypothesise as follows. Classical Iguvium, the find-site of the bronzes, was a sanctuary town serving north-east Umbria. By the term *sanctuary town* I mean an urbanising city of modest proportions, whose raison d'être is predominantly ritual, but did not produce ritual structures on the scale of Samnium or indeed some other parts of Umbria (section 5.3). Iguvium represents the institutionalised and institutionalising centre of a ritual valley,[1] and was so perceived in living memory. However, the material archaeological evidence for rituals is one shared by many other valleys in Umbria (section 5.1), as noted also historically (Cicero, *De Divinatione*, I: 94).

The scale of the bronzes, both their physical size, and their extravagant use of precious and high status material, suggests that they need to be linked with a state society of some established importance, and are intended for display to enhance that importance. Since by the earliest datings for the bronzes Iguvium would have fallen within Rome's ambit in an allied status or in much closer incorporation, it is implausible to suppose a political role of any importance in the later Republic for Iguvium (section 5.2). A preferable solution is that Iguvium is important *ritually*. It is likely that for Rome the utility of such a sanctuary town would be at its highest value when Rome had the greatest need of its specialised function, both as a

symbolic force, and as a stabilising and mediating focus in an area where conflicting urbanising and tribal interests could cause trouble. This points to the fourth and third centuries BC. Interestingly such a policy may have been successful, since the general area remained loyal even through the temptations of the Hannibalic invasion.

The fourth to third centuries are also the most likely for the diffusion of some kind of literacy into this area. This is plausible among a set of influences exerted by the more advanced neighbours to west and south, and would be mediated by the type of mechanisms and contacts hypothesised earlier, for example by the extension of priestly and aristocratic systems of administration and education. The advent of this restricted literacy would fit well with the process of the institutionalisation of Iguvium's ritual function and would help to reinforce it.

Having said that, there are difficulties with dates as early as this, even for the supposedly earlier of the actual texts which have survived. We might rather propose that the publishing of documents on bronze is essentially an Augustan phenomenon, most probably belonging to a date in the last decades of the BC period. This gives the best explanation of the available evidence, and makes good sense in terms of the proposed model. Interestingly, this coincides chronologically with the archaeological evidence for the monumentalisation of the Roman town of Gubbio (section 6.1).

The key to the suggestion is the decision of Augustus that the ritual traditions of Rome needed to be strengthened by the re-establishment of what were seen as her major state rites. To this effect the Auguraculum was rebuilt, various priestly *collegia* were re-established and others given new investment or encouragement. The two most important events for the interpretation of the phenomenon of the Iguvine bronzes was the re-establishment of the collegium of the Fratres Arvales, and the investment made in the school of haruspices at Caere. The new era of Rome was celebrated in the staging of magnificent games, the Ludi Saeculares – an important state ritual to celebrate the new *saeculum* – in 17 BC.

Apart from these very obvious associations with the rituals referred to in the Iguvine Tables, the next salient parallel is the publishing of state rites immediately after the event, both to provide the proper and essential conclusion of the rite itself, and as a public guarantee by

---

[1] The strong connection between Umbria in general and bird-divination is well exemplified in Cicero, *De Divinatione*, 1, 92: '*Phryges autem et Pisidae et Cilices et Arabum natio avium significationibus plurimum obtemperant, quod idem factitatum in Umbria accepimus*', where Umbria is not only explicitly connected with eastern parallels, but *facitatum* implies established practice. See also CIL XI 5824, *L. Venturius Rufio avispex extispicus sacerdos publicus et privatus*, which is provenanced from Gubbio.

the state and by the presiding ministrants, that all had been properly (*rite*) executed. If some of the Iguvine tables are not instructions, but a due and properly ritual celebration of a major local ceremony, perhaps even not without some ritual significance for Rome itself, then we have a very attractive basic setting for committing to bronze of, say as a minimum, Tables VI and VIIa.

The moves at Rome were obviously part of Augustus' general plan to give his new regime ritual authority. How genuine the idea of re-establishment of these institutions may or may not have been, is clearly a point for the cynical to doubt. Cicero, it is true, comments on the disuse into which Rome's traditional rituals had fallen, which would seem to argue at least for their continuing reality. There are problems, however, with the analysis of his attitude, which is perhaps more that of the armchair philosopher (his work, *De Divinatione*, is not a field exploration of the current practices of divination, but essentially a translation of a Greek philosophical work on the nature of prophecy). There is a sense in which the Arval Brethren in particular may be essentially a Roman urban invention. It is also fairly obvious that all these re-vamped, re-invented or freshly invented rituals at Rome were very much the new erudite city person's view of what an original agrarian ritual would have been like. They probably do not constitute usable evidence here for the real ritual history of what went on in the developing period of the urbanisation of Italy.

How does Iguvium fit into this part of the picture? One can imagine that the Augustan moves might well be seized on as the perfect occasion to try and re-establish also what was seen as Iguvium's traditional ritual significance. This would give very strong motivation for the expense and commitment of the publishing on bronze of the Iguvine documents.

There remains the need to explain the particular collection of surviving texts. The texts are heterogeneous or, more bluntly, a job lot. It is tempting to suggest a fairly random batch of texts emanating from various periods of composition, that happened to be what was available for transcription onto bronze, at the time that the decision was taken. The inscriptional 'hands' on this premise would be no more than the copying of the scripts as they existed on the various 'originals'.

Equally, however, there may well have been a tradition of published rituals in Iguvium, of which some earlier stone and bronze examples still survived at this time. These might then be combined with some newer transcriptions to form the surviving group. A weakness of this more historical explanation, however, is that the surviving texts show a greater range of scripts (probably archaising) than they do of language change in the traditional philological sense.

There does not appear to be evidence for a textual tradition in the conventional sense. It is however perfectly plausible that there might have been continuity of ritual significance from a period long before urbanisation without continuity of the precise rituals themselves which the proposed model rejects. The texts do nevertheless contain a palimpsest of information which still needs to be decoded.

5.3 Text and context: the regional setting[1]

The Iguvine Tables mark the transition between oral and written history. Yet they represent a frustrating, ambiguous set of texts (section 5.2). These ritual artefacts can be analysed internally along linguistic lines, but the precise archaeological context which might make sense of their use is missing. The ritual context has already been examined (section 5.1). It is critical now to set the texts in a wider Umbrian setting.

The traditional view is that of the ancient authors, where the archaeological evidence only provides incidental information. One school of archaeologists, both ancient and modern (Mommsen 1903: 111–15; Coli 1964: 159; Bonomi Ponzi 1991a) have echoed the views of Pliny (*Natural History*, III: 112), Dionysius of Halicarnassus (I, 19, 1) and Florus (I, XII, 17) that the Umbrians were a distinct and ancient people whose origins can be traced deep into prehistory. The ancient authors are employed to lay the cultural ground rules and the geographical framework. This reliance on the testimony of the ancient authors sometimes leads to a distressing tendency to impose a *polis*-like structure (Coli 1964: 143) upon the evidence. Gubbio is assumed to be, or at least to be in a state of becoming, a city-state, like any other in the Mediterranean, until proven otherwise. Such interpretations run counter to most modern theoretical research which points to a multiplicity of local models for state formation (see section 5.2). Moreover these concepts of remote antiquity do not accord with the evidence of the material culture from Gubbio and beyond, evidence which suggests a highly inter-connected network of social and political relationships within the Bronze Age linking the territories of the later Etruscan city-states to much of the rest of central Italy.

What is the wider political context (Fig. 5.12) into which the Iguvine Tables fit? Was there the competitive pressure to produce rapid state formation in the mountain-locked valley of Gubbio. The most highly advanced Etruscan polity in the region, Chiusi, was distant. Etruscan communities closer to Gubbio, such as Perugia, and even

---

[1] This section is based on an updated synthesis of Stoddart (1987) and a paper presented by Simon Stoddart at Princeton University in April 1991.

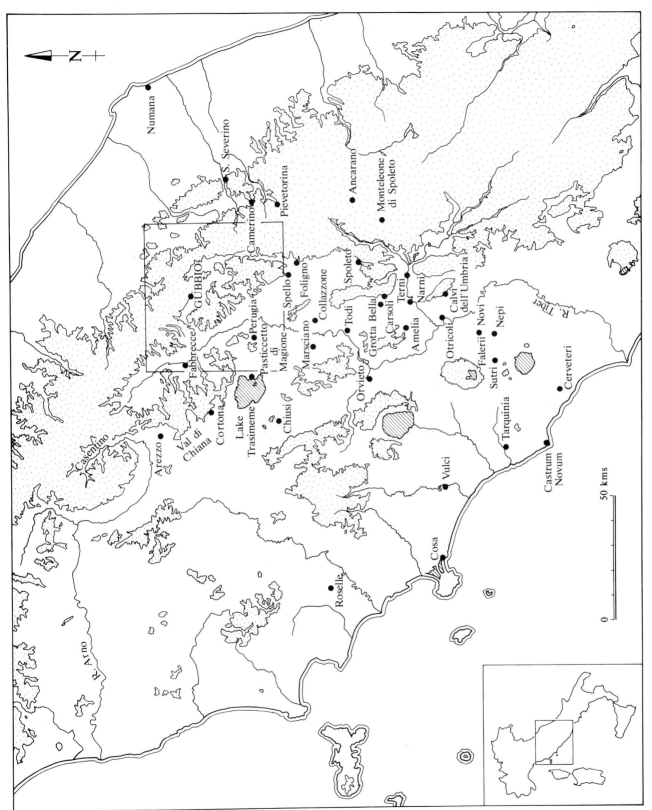

Fig. 5.12 Central Italy in the pre-Roman period

some further away, such as Arezzo, were simply retarded. Developments in the Apennines to the east and the south-east, particularly marked at Colfiorito, were the products of distinctly different circumstances and too distant to have provided the necessary political pressure. Developments in the Upper Tiber Valley do not appear to have amounted to more powerful developments than Gubbio, despite the high quality and the artistic merit of the material that was discovered in these areas.

In the territory of Chiusi (and its satellites), the distribution of burial finds, the relative wealth of grave goods and the onomastic use of inscriptions (Bianchi Bandinelli 1925; Stoddart and Whitley 1988a) demonstrates the presence of an élite with increasing territorial control from the middle of the seventh century BC. The distance from Chiusi to Gubbio (65 km) and the topographical barriers between the two centres (Lake Trasimene, Upper Tiber Valley) are, though, considerable. The political interests of Chiusi were, furthermore, directed more on a north–south axis, governed in part by the easier topographical constraints of the tectonic valleys of this part of Etruria and in part by the greater political opportunities in the Po valley to the north.

The centre of Cortona, further north, is much more difficult to define in terms of its political power. Recent excavations in the heart of the medieval city have finally proved a late Villanovan origin (late eighth century) for the centre (Trotta 1990). The early tombs of Camucia and Sodo located near to the valley bottom of the Val di Chiana show the development of the local élite in the succeeding centuries, presumably still housed domestically within the topographical area of the medieval city. In spite of these important finds the main evidence for the city is substantially later than Chiusi (Neppi Modena 1977).

The city of Arezzo, further north in the Val di Chiana, was very undeveloped in the Archaic period and even failed to have an economic impact even on its immediate hinterland (Stoddart 1979–80). One part of this hinterland, the Casentino, shared with the Gubbio Basin some aspects of ritual organisation in an upland landscape, but lacked a significant population centre. Scholars who have studied the city directly have had great difficulty in substantiating a major tradition of formal burial within the city limits (Bocci Pacini 1975). The importance of the city increased in the post-Archaic period quite considerably, but again its political influence was not directed east towards the relatively marginal Apennines.

The intervening area of the Upper Tiber Valley (that is lying between Gubbio and the Val di Chiana) has been stressed recently as an important power centre following the re-interpretation of the seventh century BC burial finds from Fabbrecce and Trestina (Pellegrini 1902; Sensi 1985). These finds appear, however, to be symbols of a fluid political authority that did not develop rapidly into a state organised society. Thus although the Tiber Valley is immediately to the west of Gubbio, it would not have provided a challenge to the local authority of the populations from Gubbio. A similar interpretation can be given to the contemporary burials of the Marche (for example Fabriano) (Landolfi 1988).

Perugia, to the south-west, although now provided with a clear Late Bronze Age and Villanovan origin (Cenciaioli 1990; Feruglio 1990), remained very much a frontier zone (Stoddart 1990) up until at least 500 BC; a number of epigraphic and iconographic details suggest that Perugia was first, in the seventh century, the target (Stopponi 1991: 77) and then, in the late sixth century, the departure point (Torelli 1985: Fig. 53) for raids executed by more stratified societies on their neighbours. Other epigraphic information, which indicates family links between Orvieto and Perugia, might also suggest Perugia to be a frontier area ready to absorb the energies of surplus kin and freedmen liberated from their humble origins. Stepping ahead of our argument, it is appropriate to point out that it was only in the Roman period that epigraphic evidence is found for Perugia and other cities (Arezzo and Cortona) supplying surplus kin for Gubbio (section 6.1).

Finds of the eighth to seventh century from the modern town centre of Perugia and the nearby suburbs (Monteluce, Palazzone, Pieve di Campo) imply that a number of settlements existed on the hills of Perugia, but the complexities of urban archaeology prevent more substantive conclusions (Stopponi 1991: 76). Exploitation of the local territory, as measured by the distribution of rich burials was extremely restricted. Only a few late Archaic burials are known from outside the city limits at Castel San Mariano di Corciano (Höckman 1982), San Valentino di Marsciano and Villanova. These combined facts suggest a fluidity of political power that was still not fully centralised. This underdevelopment is corroborated by the fact that only one Archaic inscription (from the second half of the sixth century BC) is recorded. It was only from the fifth century BC that Perugia can be described as urbanised (Stopponi 1991: 79). A temple, indicated by late Archaic antefixes (Andren 1940: Plate 88, no. 313) was constructed in the town around 500 BC, representing a new, centralised religious authority, an authority that did not as yet threaten to displace the dispersed rural cults described in section 5.1 above. It is clear that by the fourth century BC Perugia had emerged as a powerful centre, at least as measured by the prosperity of its cemeteries. But the expansion of Rome prevented Perugia from developing as a major political power in its own right, though Perugia's economic vibrancy was relatively unaffected. It is only from the third century BC that rural settlement increased in the territory of Perugia as indicated indirectly by numerous cemeteries. The lack of political development of Perugia, combined with the topographical barriers between Perugia and Gubbio, would have militated against major political pressure being brought against Gubbio prior to the fourth century BC.

In the rest of Umbria, in the seventh century BC, there were trends towards territorial consolidation (Roncalli 1988; Bonomi Ponzi 1991a). These included the concentration of population in submountain areas (of which Gubbio is one example) and cemeteries (which are virtually missing from Gubbio). In certain areas, there were rich graves of a proto-élite, known principally from tombs. These show some differentiation along lines of sex, but no complicated social hierarchy; females are buried with ornaments and males with chariots, bronze and iron armour (helmet and shield) and weapons (spear and sword). These inhumations, which in the most elaborate cases involve stone circles and tumuli, reached a peak in the sixth century BC (for example Fabriano, Gualdo Tadino, Spello). There is also evidence of widespread contacts, principally with other central Italian areas, to provide the exotic and luxury goods. Only limited traces of this phenomenon have been found at Gubbio (section 5.1).

In the sixth to fifth centuries BC (Bonomi Ponzi 1991a), evidence for different trajectories of socio-political development became much more apparent. Upland areas in the main Apennine range were covered with a defensive chain of fortified positions, best known from Colfiorito, but also from Camerino and Amelia. In particular, recent work[1] on the pass of Colfiorito has uncovered a complex of defended hillforts and rich cemeteries which reached its climax in the sixth century BC. The inhabitants of these forts were placed at points of strategic importance on the passes through the Apennines. They were thus more than able to accumulate wealth, and more than willing to dispose of it in rich graves such as those found at Annifo di Foligno and Colfiorito di Foligno (Bonomi Ponzi 1991b). These highly developed communities must be seen in the context not only of commerce with Etruria, but also in the context of the increasing prosperity of the Picene populations of the Adriatic coast (Landolfi 1988). The self-contained Valley of Gubbio was in no position to control such movement of people and goods.

A new pattern of funerary display by other elements of a proto-élite occurred in new areas such as Todi, Monteleone di Spoleto, the Colfiorito plateau itself and within the Marche at Pitino di San Severino and Numana. Gubbio has produced some fleeting evidence of this type

in the form of an unpublished chariot burial and at least one provenanced example of Red Figure pottery (Manconi 1991). This was also the period of the construction of sanctuaries. The majority of the sanctuaries were of the type described in detail for Gubbio (section 5.1), located in the uplands on hills, passes or in caves. However the minority were urban sanctuaries of greater structural sophistication in areas of more developed socio-political complexity such as Todi, Amelia, Spoleto and Terni. There is no evidence that Gubbio was involved in that type of sanctuary organisation. By the fourth century BC, other signs of urbanisation are found in the construction of polygonal walls at Spoleto and Amelia (De Angelis and Manconi 1983). Claims of antiquity have been made for polygonal wall structures on the flanks of Monte Foce (Pagliari 1920), but there is no substantive proof at this stage.

Both external and internal pressures towards state formation were missing in the marginal agricultural regime of the upland Apennine Valley of Gubbio. Upland and lowland resources are present within a very small horizontal distance in a manner that enables self-contained sufficiency in the absence of other demands. Although Gubbio was not entirely isolated from networks of prestige present in central Italy, as a sixth century chariot burial illustrates (Stopponi 1991), access to such symbols of power were on a much reduced scale. Even in the fifth century BC, it is rare to find imported items. Gubbio did not have to change.

External political pressures were missing until the impact of a much more powerful entity: Rome. For instance, the coinage of Gubbio, dated generally to the first decades of the third century BC (Catalli 1989), belonged to a period of mounting Roman pressure. The Iguvine Tables, if dated, quite plausibly, to the first century BC, fit within the political context of an expanding Roman state, a state which was becoming an empire. Even if the term empire was not applied by the Romans themselves until later, on a cross-cultural basis many of the elements were already being put into place during this period (see Alcock 1989).

The advance of Rome is well recorded in textual sources (Harris 1971), since it represents a phase of military activity which dominates our sample of political action; this gives a fineness of chronology that is lacking from the generalised archaeological framework. The missing component is, of course, the reaction of locals, such as the inhabitants of Iguvium. The only measure of this process is the Iguvine Tables themselves which cannot

[1] By the Soprintendenza Archeologica per l'Umbria.

be detached from an increasingly Romanised political context.

A process of mounting pressure on north-east Umbria can be noted in pages of Livy (*Histories*, IX–XXXI) starting in the period between 300 and 250 BC. The first phase of intensive activity was between 311 and 308 BC. In 310 BC, the north-eastern Etruscan cities of Perugia, Cortona and Arezzo were defeated, followed by the defeat of an Umbrian army and the surrender of the garrison at Perugia. All this activity was on the southern and western margins of the territory of Gubbio and must have had a profound effect on the political attitudes of the inhabitants who would, almost certainly, have lacked the means to counter this threat.

A second phase of intense Roman activity took place between 302 and 293 BC. In 303 BC, there was a military expedition to Umbria, followed in 299 BC by the founding of *colonia* in southern Umbria. There is evidence that the undefined Umbrians joined the Etruscans to form an alliance against Rome in 296 BC. The pressure on Gubbio reached a climax with the Sentinum campaign of 295 BC where Iguvium was caught between the devastation of Chiusi to the west and the defeat of the Gallic army and allies to the east. Sentinum is separated from the Gubbio Valley only by the Valley of Gualdo Tadino. Iguvium was left in a highly vulnerable political position. By 280 the Umbrians in general were surrounded by the allies or subjects of Rome. By 266 BC, the northern Umbrians (Harris 1971) had acknowledged this irresistible pressure and surrendered.

The military records recorded in great annalistic detail by Livy are, of course, only a fragmentary indication, partial symptoms, of the longer-term processes studied in this volume. The longer-term strategies of the Romans are marked by more substantial material evidence. Before the military pressure, during the course of the fourth century BC, Roman and Faliscan imports replaced Etruscan imports of pottery within the Umbrian area (Bonomi Ponzi 1991a: 61). During the period of military pressure, it is clear that varied strategies were adopted by the Romans according to the political structure of the opposing forces. In some circumstances, *coloniae* were inserted to provide the focus of political authority under direct Roman control. Colonies close to Rome were often inserted directly into existing towns such as Nepi (383 BC) and Sutri or on new ground at Falerii Novi in 241 BC. As the political frontier advanced and communications became more distant, strategic boundary areas were frequently exploited to deflect the preceding centralised political authority. Castrum Novum was inserted in 264 BC on the boundary between the rival Etruscan territories of Cerveteri

and Tarquinia. The famous colony of Cosa was similarly placed in 273 BC on the boundary of the rival Etruscan territories of Vulci and Roselle. This pattern established close to Rome and on the Tyrrhenian coast was mirrored further inland in the Umbrian heartland. The first colonies were placed within communities at Spoleto in 241 BC and at Narni in 299 BC. Others were placed on the communication routes up the Via Flaminia and into the uplands of the Apennines (Fulginae, Interamna, Plestia and Tadinum). The last named, Tadinum or modern Gualdo Tadino controlled the valley immediately to the east of Gubbio.

The most important material change on Iguvium was undoubtedly the construction of the Via Flaminia itself, 'the one road for the date of which we have explicit literary evidence' (Harris 1971: 162). This was built by C. Flaminius in his censorship in 220. It ran through Umbria by the modern towns of Gualdo Tadino, Fossato di Vico and Scheggia, and so came very close to Gubbio itself. The Romans' reason for building this road probably had little to do with Gubbio, and more to do with establishing a good system of military communications from Rome to the Adriatic and the lands north of the Apennines. Nonetheless its effect on Iguvium was profound, since the road effectively removed Gubbio from the relative isolation it had enjoyed until then.

A second major strategy implemented by the Romans was to work through the local élite. It is this strategy that appears to have been adopted in the case of Gubbio. Since this was not a military option, it is less visible in the textual records. However, there is the clear mention of Gubbio entering a *foedus* with Rome in common with Camerino (Cicero, *Pro Balbo:* 36). The major material reference of this relationship is the Iguvine Tables. The *longue durée* described in the preceding pages demonstrates that the inhabitants of the Gubbio area had no substantial past recorded in material form. The only means of substantiating that insubstantial past based on oral tradition was to give it a material reality in a valuable material: bronze. Hence the Iguvine Tables.

The sanctuary status of the city of Iguvium was, however, very different from that of a contemporary society located on a different flank of Roman expansionist endeavour: the Samnites. The city of Iguvium could not have drawn on a territory much larger than the immediate valley area, because of the presence of Perugia to the south, guarding against contact with the vast majority of the neighbouring societies of similar socio-political development, loosely classified as Umbrian. No trace of the material culture appropriate to large sanctuaries has been found within the city. The temple of Jupiter which was most probably located outside the city walls has proved to be very elusive. Even in the Augustan period (section 6.1), the munificence of the city was only suitable for a small local centre.

The situation in Samnium provides a well documented comparison with Umbria, and more specifically Gubbio. In some respects there are similarities. The Samnites have been extensively recorded in their capacity as military rivals to Rome (Salmon 1967), if with greater success than their Umbrian counterparts. They occupied a mountainous Apennine area which had a profoundly ritualistic aspect to it (La Regina 1976). Part of the area has been subject to a landscape study (Barker 1977). In other respects there are profound differences. The sanctuaries of Samnium are on a different scale, comprising major investment in construction. Furthermore these investments in ritual date to the pre-Roman period. A complementary component of the these substantial ritual sites was the construction of defensive enclosures in most cases not originally intended as permanent population centres (La Regina 1989: 373–4).

A good example of a Samnite centre which combines the defensive and ritual, is Pietrabbondante (La Regina 1980a). The area is dominated by the summit of Monte Saraceno (1,212 m above sea level) fortified in the fourth century BC, but not used after the third century BC. To the south, in loc. Troccola at 600 m above sea level, is the necropolis which was used from the fifth century BC until the abandonment of the fortification. At this point, a third location, Calcatello (966 m above sea level) was developed as one of the most important Samnite sanctua-

ries, at the meeting point of local routeways. This ritual complex combined an Ionic temple with a theatre, of a size which must have drawn on the whole territory for their congregations. After the Social War (90 BC) the ritual functions of the centre were transferred to a local *municipium* and the buildings were re-employed for other uses including burial by the later Roman period. It was only in the Roman period that urbanisation took place (La Regina 1980b: 35)

Despite the greater elaboration of Samnite sanctuaries, there is nothing in either the Samnite or the Umbrian evidence to suggest that urbanised city-states had developed before the Roman conquest. Indeed we would like to suggest that the Samnite and Iguvine cases are variations on a broadly similar strategy. In both cases some kind of territorial polity had emerged which made use of sanctuaries, and which created a particular kind of ritual landscape. The differences lie in terms of spatial geography and munificence of material culture. Gubbio was a modest population centre without major investment in material culture. Pietrabbondante lacked the nucleation of population, but was extravagant in ritualised material investment. Moreover, there is nothing in the Iguvine Tables themselves that contradicts this picture of a less developed, and less urbanised polity that cannot be called a state (section 5.2). Iguvine society was part of a pattern of political and territorial organisation common to the upland areas of Italy, outside the ambit of Rome, Etruria and the Greek colonies to the south.

6   IMPERIAL INCORPORATION: THE ADVENT OF ROME

6.1 The city

6.1.1 The historical setting for the city from documentary sources

It is not surprising that Umbria fills so insignificant a place in Roman annals

(Frank 1914: 69)

This verdict on the importance of Umbria during the Republic follows a discussion of ritual cursing in the Iguvine Tables, which was interpreted as displaying the exceptional paranoia and disunity of the Umbrian peoples. Although in reality the Umbrians were probably no less unified than the Samnites, the hostility and geographical proximity of the Samnites to the Romans and their consequent political impact on Rome, ensured frequent appearances in the most prominent documentary sources, the Roman annals. An unfortunate consequence of Umbria's less hostile relations with Rome, for the present study, is that relatively little can be learnt of Umbria's development during the Republic from the scanty records of Roman foreign policy alone. Some essential facts can, nevertheless, be gleaned.

The third century BC witnessed two fundamental actions by the Romans in Umbria: in 290 BC a Roman army defeated allied Gauls and Samnites at Sentinum; and in about 220 BC the Via Flaminia was driven through the Apennines to the east of Iguvium. The increasing influence of Rome in this century may have led Gubbio to accept a *foedus*, as is suggested in Cicero (*Pro Balbo:* 36), but this is unlikely to have been on the favourable terms agreed with Camerinum (Harris 1971: 105).

On those rare occasions when Gubbio is mentioned by classical authors, the text is often corrupt. For instance, the exile of the Illyrian King Gentius (169 BC) to Gubbio after the refusal of Spoleto to receive him (Livy, XLV: 43) is based on the emendation of *igiturvium* to *Iguvium*. If this emendation is correct, then it is possible to infer that some inhabitants of Gubbio were eager to please Rome, which in turn considered the town to be trustworthy.

Gubbio's position during the Social War is historically unknown, although the mention of the town in two fragments of Sisenna show that it was not inactive. One inhabitant of Gubbio, M. Annius Appius, was probably a client of Marius (Harris 1971: 195). Harris also argues convincingly (1971: 236–50) that the enrolment of Gubbio within the Clustumina tribe, along with several other small Umbrian towns, was a punitive measure, designed to hinder the political advancement of individuals and, consequently reduce urban patronage in those centres. Despite this possible punishment, it is after the Social War that Gubbio is most likely to have gained its municipal status. During the Civil War, Caesar records that he sent troops to occupy Gubbio, and that they were well received (Caesar, *Bellum Civile*, I: 12).

This paucity of documentary evidence relating to the development of Gubbio and its relations with Rome is not adequate to gain a reasonable understanding of the process of change in the area. In order to develop a broader understanding of the town's social and political history, the archaeological evidence must be employed.

6.1.2 The archaeological evidence

6.1.2.i Introduction: conformity to an urban ideal?

Gubbio still boasts two impressive standing monuments, a mausoleum (Fig. 6.1) and a fine theatre (Plate 6.1), which indicate a certain level of wealth for the Roman *municipium*. Neither monument would seem out of place in Spoleto, Assisi, or any other central Italian Roman town (Fig. 6.4), and they reveal the existence of an élite willing to patronise the town in a Roman way, with buildings in a Roman style. An interesting inscription (Borman 1901: 5,820) provides the name of one member of this élite, Gnaeus Satrius Rufus, who paid for the restoration of another monumental structure (the temple of Diana) and for the roofing and flooring of a basilica, which quite possibly formed part of the theatre complex. The Roman urbanisation of Gubbio is not, however, only visible in the public monuments; well constructed and decorated urban houses (*domus*) from the same period

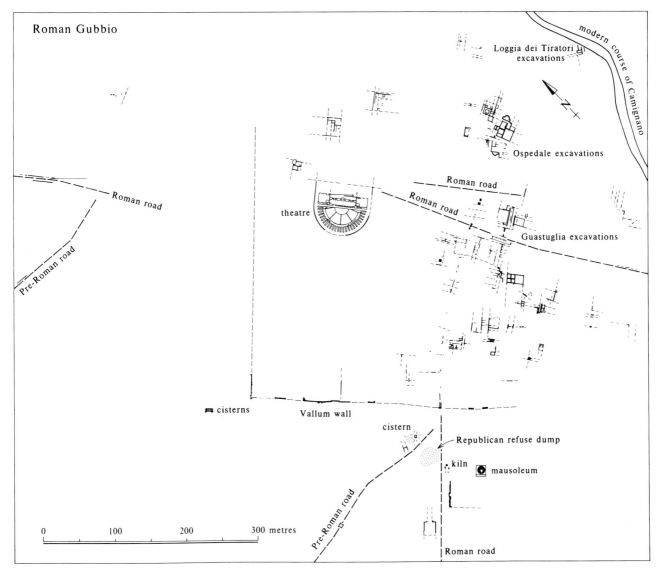

Roman Gubbio

Fig. 6.1 Detailed map of Roman Gubbio

have also been excavated. Such excavations, carried out by the Soprintendenza Archeologica dell'Umbria, demonstrate that a Roman urban ideal was being aimed at and achieved in late Republican/early Imperial Gubbio. In the first century BC the upper class at Gubbio may have taken pride in a distinguished Umbrian past, as exemplified by the Iguvine Tables (section 5.2), but they were not willing to compromise on the comforts of a Roman present.

6.1.2.ii Urban history and development

Despite topographical reconstructions based on readings of the Iguvine Tables (Costantini 1970), we have little

archaeological evidence for the size, nature or exact position of pre-Roman Gubbio. The most probable location of the Umbrian centre, established by piecing together the available evidence, is under the medieval city (section 5.1).

After the difficulty of documenting the nature of Iron Age and Umbrian Gubbio, the explosion of evidence in the Roman period is quite striking. It should, however, be emphasised that the archaeological evidence for the Roman period has for the most part been from rescue excavations, few of which have yet been published in any detail. Further research and publication over the next few years should greatly enhance and clarify the current picture, for which reason a detailed reconstruction, similar

Plate 6.1 Roman theatre

to those carried out for better known Roman centres (Meiggs 1973; Jongman 1988), will not be attempted.

Probably by the end of the second century BC, buildings were being constructed in a Roman style immediately to the south of the Umbrian settlement. This development took place on previously unoccupied land, within an area demarcated by an unimpressive boundary wall cr *vallum*, which provided a symbolic, but not defensive, separation from the cemeteries and fields beyond (Fig. 6.1). From the first these structures have a Roman, and sometimes wealthy appearance; their walls are built of small limestone blocks bonded with mortar and decorated with painted wall plaster, while floors are of *cocciopesto* or adorned with mosaic pavements.

The early Roman town displayed wealth in both private and public buildings. The Ortacci site *domus*, for example has the plan of a Pompeian house, complete with peristyle. Of slightly later date, but still from the first century BC, are the remains of a second *domus*, discovered to the north of the theatre, which produced an *opus vermicellum emblema* (a fine inset mosaic roundel) depicting Odysseus and Scylla. Several prestigious burials and a number of rural sites can be considered to be contemporary with this urban development. Among the most notable burials are the mausoleum, and a second/first century BC grave, from Fontevole to the west of the town, which included a bronze funerary bed (Bonomi Ponzi 1990). Within the surrounding countryside most Roman settlements, including the five substantial rural villas, can be shown to date from this period, which represents the main phase of rural expansion (section 6.2).

At the same time as the construction of the private dwellings, the town was also being provided with all the amenities which might be expected in Roman Italy. The theatre is by far the best studied and preserved of these urban embellishments. It is estimated to have had a capacity of 6,000 people (Gaggiotti *et al.* 1980: 181) and was probably constructed in the mid first century BC along with most of the private buildings in the Guastuglia area. In addition to this a basilica was probably added to the *scaena*, and was completed in the Augustan period through the patronage of Gnaeus Satrius Rufus. This covered area, which was considered to be a necessary part of a theatre complex (Vitruvius, *De Re Architectura*, V: 9), was clearly started at an earlier date, since the recorded benefaction was only of the roof and floor. In addition to these monuments, there was an amphitheatre in the north-west quarter of the town; a baths complex, probably public, which developed on the Ortacci site; and at least two temples, which were partly excavated to the east of the theatre (Borman 1901: 5809). Whether these temples or another unexcavated one formed an integral part of a monumental theatre complex, similar to the one at Spello, can, at present, only be hypothesised. The temple of Diana, recorded in the Gnaeus Satrius Rufus inscription, may also have been located near the theatre, if he were concentrating his resources on the restoration and completion of one monumental public space.

6.1.2.iii The internal organisation of the urban area

It is only possible to make a tentative assessment of the internal organisation of the urban area, since excavations have necessarily followed rescue and redevelopment priorities (Manconi 1982–3). The monumental core of the town is well defined within the south-west corner of the area enclosed by the *vallum*. The prominence of the theatre complex suggests an overall organisation of the public buildings, the planning of which was aided by the relatively unconstricted nature of the site. In this respect the situation at Gubbio contrasts markedly with the topographical contraints on urban development at Spoleto and Assisi.

While the most impressive urban houses may have clustered to the north-east of the theatre, many of those in the Guastuglia area also display a notable level of wealth. Although some planning clearly took place in the monumental area, the main urban development is not on a wholly regular alignment, with, perhaps, both an imposed grid and pre-existing road alignments being followed (Fig. 6.1). There is also some evidence that the town was in part arranged in terraces on the hillside of Monte Ingino above the level of the plain (Manconi *et al.* 1991)

6.1.2.iv Later development of the Roman town

The development of the town after its first-century BC to first-century AD heyday is once again poorly documented archaeologically. Although many of the houses have levels datable into the fourth century AD, little new building, either private or public appears to have been undertaken, while mosaics from earlier centuries were patched and reused, rather than replaced. The one later building inscription that we have (Borman 1901: 5926) records the construction of a Christian basilica, and at some period the baths in Via Ortacci were also converted to that use. By the third century AD, the town seems to have stagnated, as, it might be argued, had the countryside (section 6.2). Only the requirements of a new religion were still being catered for.

6.1.2.v The cemeteries

Aedificas monumentum meum, quemadmodum te iussi? . . . praeterea ut sint in fronte pedes centum, in agrum pedes ducenti.
(Petronius, *Satyricon*, 71)

In recent years research and rescue excavations undertaken by the Umbrian Soprintendenza around the outskirts of Gubbio have uncovered many hundreds of burials (Figs. 6.2 and 6.3). These lay thickly around the town and along the major roads out of the town. In particular, excavations have been undertaken at San Biagio, at Fontevole and along the Vittorina, a road which ran east towards the Via Flaminia. Even some 2 km from the town in this direction the cemeteries continue, although at this distance the burials form less a cemetery, than a ribbon one tomb wide following the road (Fig. 6.3).

The cemeteries that have been discovered can be interpreted in terms of the Roman social attitude to death. The locations of cemetery areas appear to have been determined by one legal principle – exclusion from the urban area, at Gubbio defined by the *vallum*. Apart from this constraint, the clear tendency was to place the burials on prominent, accessible, well-travelled routes out of the town. Beyond this, although different locations tend to have been favoured at different times, no strictly designated areas for the placing of burials can be identified.

Literary evidence can assist in the more detailed interpretation of the funerary evidence at Gubbio. The Roman author Petronius wrote a parody of a planned funeral, that of the wealthy freedman Trimalchio in the Satyricon, which can provide particular insights into certain social attitudes to burial. Trimalchio is concerned about the size of his funerary monument, its decoration, its future protection and more generally about the people who might pass the monument, read the inscription and

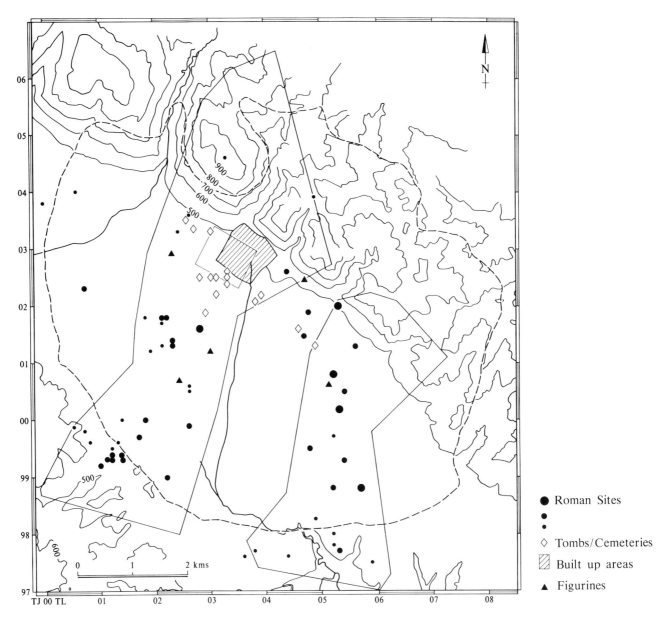

Fig. 6.2 General map of environs with suburban villas, cemeteries and figurines

realise the importance of the person buried. This, together with the proposed iconography, reveals a rather unsubtle attitude towards the public display of wealth and social position in death. It could be argued that the fluid nature of Roman society, as exemplified in the changed socio-political circumstances of Gubbio in the first century BC, with rootless slaves receiving freedom and gaining wealth and power, demanded the legitimisation and display of social position in death. Such ostentatious display would be unnecessary in a stratified society with a longer history of development, but less internal social mobility. Trimalchio had been a slave, was a successful freedman, and had to

leave a monument for posterity to underline this achievement.

Viewed from this perspective it may be no coincidence that over half of the funerary inscriptions from Gubbio record freedmen, a phenomenon which is common to a number of other Umbrian centres as well. The social instability suggested here is, in many ways, similar to that argued by Hopkins (1983) for the senatorial class at Rome, where the composition of the Senate was continually changing. The major difference between the freedmen of Gubbio and the senators of Rome in this case is the level of the social hierarchy on which the changes occur.

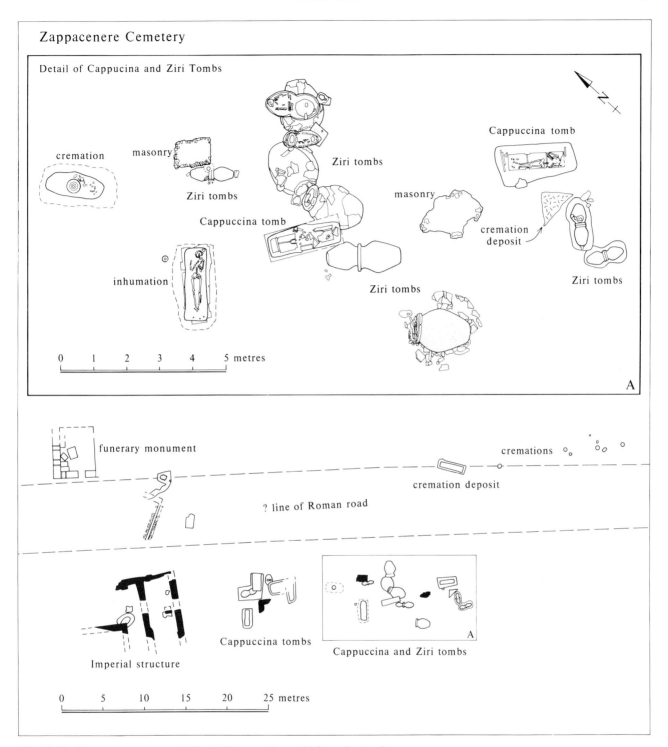

Fig. 6.3 The Zappacenere cemetery (with detail): cremation and inhumation tombs

Funerary inscriptions at Gubbio have, for the most part, a short text, which is frequently entirely spent on recording the name of the deceased and dimensions of the grave plot. This second feature may reflect overcrowding or high prices in prime cemetery areas, rendering a larger plot a status symbol, as is certainly the case with enclosures such as that surrounding the mausoleum at Gubbio. It could also reveal, however, a preoccupation with the future disturbance of remains, guarded against by Trimalchio both by employing a freedman caretaker, and having a large gardened enclosure. The disturbance of burials was of sufficient concern to Romans for it to have been a criminal act (*violatio sepulcri*), partly, doubtless, because common Roman belief included a notion that the spirit of the departed (*manes*) remained to some extent conscious and near its burial place. This belief is taken to extremes in the provision, often seen at Gubbio along the Vittorina, of vertical lead pipes above burials, down which offerings to the dead could be poured. Although not demonstrated at Gubbio, it has been shown in other excavations that the position of individual graves was marked on the surface by stones, pottery sherds or amphorae (Jovio 1987). While such definition could stop unintentional disturbance, the reservation of a designated area, recorded on stone, might also give peace from encroachment, and provide room for funerary ceremonies and feasts.

The burial practices of Roman Gubbio were numerous, if, for the most part, simple. At the top of the hierarchy are the mausolea, which were imposing both in structure and location. The mausoleum still visible just south of Gubbio, which can be stylistically dated to the early Augustan period, had ashlar masonry, of which only the chamber lining and doorway remain, around a concrete core, and stood within a large walled enclosure. This wall, which probably defined the boundary of a funerary garden, also enclosed other concentrations of earlier ceramic material, probably representing graves conveniently disregarded for the construction of the mausoleum complex. It is unfortunate that we cannot relate this important structure to any known individual or family, but it is worth noting that even the largest of tomb complexes, one that swallowed earlier burials, could not guarantee immortality for a name. Other mausolea and funerary monuments did exist in the environs of Gubbio, such as the one recently uncovered by the Soprintendenza on the Vittorina (Fig. 6.3). This was a slightly less impressive ashlar structure, and while doubtless dominating the road, was in a less important position. Fragments of a further important funerary monument are now to be found built into a house at San Felicissimo. This may be associated with the *villa rustica* lying just to the north. Our two examples of *in situ* mausolea suggest that there was

no one area laid aside for wealthy burials outside the walls, just as there was no one area within the walls for wealthy residences.

So far the most systematically excavated cemetery at Gubbio has been the Vittorina necropolis of early Imperial (first century to second century AD) date. Here, the most common burial technique was cremation, with the remains contained in a variety of ceramic vessels, although inhumation – under tiles (*tombe alla cappuccina*), in *amphorae* and in *dolia* – was also frequently encountered. Later burials have been identified at San Felicissimo and on the west side of Gubbio at Fonte Arcano. Most of the earlier burials were accompanied by ceramic material, although the lack of published data renders any serious analysis impossible.

As the difference between cremation and inhumation in Roman burial techniques appears to be an index of chronological rather than social significance, the material poverty of many cremations cannot necessarily identify them as lower class burials. It could, indeed, be argued that less effort was spent on the disposal of a corpse by inhumation, than cremation, which demanded the construction of a pyre, whether grave-goods were included or not. With inhumations it is possibly those in reused transport or storage vessels which indicate a low social class, but even they are found on road frontages, occasionally with lead feeder-pipes. In the absence of *columbaria*, or other alternatives, we appear to lack evidence for the burial practices of the lowest classes, both servile and free, of the population of Gubbio.

6.1.3 *Population: numbers and composition*

Through archaeological investigation, some impression is gained of the private houses and monuments of a small Roman town, but this is a landscape without figures, a culture without people. To understand the significance of the archaeological evidence we must attempt to reconstruct the size and composition of the population. In contrast to the later medieval period, there are no census records (Chapter 7) and neither the *annona* at Rome, nor other sources of population statistics for Italy provide much assistance (Patterson 1987). Without access to recorded population figures, there remain three alternative ways of estimating the size of the population: from the capacity of the theatre; from the urban area; and by interpolation from the medieval census reports, on the assumption that, all things being equal, the hinterland might support a similar population size on a premodern technological base.

Each approach has significant drawbacks. The extrapolation of population size from theatre capacity depends upon estimates both of that capacity – judged to be in the region of 6,000 people (Gaggiotti *et al.* 1980: 181) – and of the percentage of the population of the town and *territorium* – which it also served – that it was constructed to hold.

The second method is more commonly used and is based on ethnographic parallels. For Gubbio the work in this vein was undertaken by Colonnesi (1973) who estimated 200 inhabitants per hectare, following a similar figure given by Beloch (1898) for Pompeii. She thus arrived at a figure of between 4,000 and 5,000 from the 23 urban hectares of the Roman city of Gubbio. The Pompeii evidence has, however, recently been questioned and the population estimate cut, in one case by half from 15–20,000 to 7–7,500 (Russell 1977). This dramatic change is perhaps an over-reaction to the growing realisation that the urban areas of Roman towns were not uniformly residential, but included areas of gardens, public monuments and open spaces (Jashemski 1979).

The census figures for the Comune of Gubbio between the sixteenth and eighteenth centuries reveal a remarkably stable population of about 20,000, of whom between 5,000 and 6,000 lived in the city. This stability of population size suggests that these numbers approached the hinterland's carrying capacity for a pre-industrial society. Were this economic capacity to be considered the determining factor, and the important socio-economic differences between the Roman and late medieval periods to be disregarded, then a possible level of population is provided.

These different approaches all point to a surprisingly similar level of population, even allowing for the doubt inherent in each technique. On these grounds it is possible to suggest 5,000 inhabitants as an upper limit for the population of the urban area, and up to 15,000 for the *territorium*, at least during the most prosperous periods of the Roman Empire. Even if inaccurate, this figure can at least provide a background against which to consider wider evidence for demography, economy and lifestyle.

Any work on the composition of the population of Iguvium and its change through time must necessarily be tentative in its conclusions. Our starting point, the pre-Roman town, is still of unknown size and composition (section 5.1). There is little evidence for the names of local Umbrian families; our only sources are the Iguvine Tables (section 5.2) and a passage from Cicero's *Pro Balbo* (XX: 46) which records Marcus Annius Appius as coming from Gubbio. Such limited evidence does not provide a good base from which to build. Even in the Roman municipal period, despite our hypothesised urban population of 5,000 for some 400 years, there are under 130 inscriptions published (Borman 1901). Even these are unlikely to provide a cross section of local Roman society, since, as

discussed above, certain social groups were more anxious to record their *fama* in stone than others.

The reconstruction of the social composition of the population, nevertheless, depends entirely on inscription evidence, with all its uncertainties. A few dedicatory inscriptions record wealthy locals. Some of these were *ingenui* (of free stock), although at least one, T. Vivius Carmogenes, was of servile stock, if not a freedman himself. Funerary inscriptions also record women and children and although there exists no direct epigraphical evidence for slaves, their presence too is demanded to provide an origin for the freedmen who dominate the record. This dominance in funerary inscriptions of two to one cannot be used to estimate the proportion of freedmen in society, since we do not fully understand the social pressures which led to the production of funerary epigraphy, although they seem to have influenced freedmen more than *ingenui*. Equally difficult is the estimation of slave numbers from freedmen numbers, since not all freedmen would have been successful enough to have afforded memorials, and not all slaves could have stood the same chance of being freed–manumission for unskilled and agricultural slaves, in particular, may have been unusual. What can be said is that freedmen played an important role in Gubbio and that slaves, although archaeologically invisible, must have been sufficiently numerous to produce them.

The sudden building expansion of the last century BC, in both urban and rural areas, might suggest a major influx of new settlers at that period. It should be possible to establish the background of important citizens from the study of *Gens* names on inscriptions. Gubbio's first recorded Roman citizen, Marcus Annius Appius, does not appear to have been part of a major recorded *Gens*. The lack of evidence for distinctive, accredited local *Gens* names, makes it difficult to establish a local origin for recorded citizens. Some later *Gens* names from Gubbio are, however, recorded in earlier Etruscan centres or appear to be of Etruscan form. This link would seem to be supported by the appearance at Gubbio of two members of the *Gens* Cutu, famous for its tomb at Perugia. The presence of this family at Gubbio clearly dates at least to the Social War, since they are inscribed in the Clustumina tribe. The work of Schulze (1904) on the origins of names indicates that other major Gubbio families are also recorded in Arezzo, Cortona and Perugia. For example, two of the three known quattuorviri, Volcacius and Satrius, Iavolenus who rebuilt the temple to Mars Cyprius, Vistilius, and the Pisentii, the second most commonly recorded *Gens*, all fall into this category.

There are three possible explanations for this pattern: a common kinship system to northern Etruria and Umbria that cut across the perceived political boundaries; an adoption of Etruscan names by local people in Gubbio at some earlier period; or an influx of north Etruscan families into Gubbio, possibly to exploit the expanding economic opportunities of the last centuries BC (sections 5.1 and 5.3).

Some impression of the composition of the middle classes may also be gained from the epigraphy, with the important caveat that freedmen were more likely than *ingenui* to express their social position by leaving a monument. Of the ninety-four funerary inscriptions, the status of the deceased is known in sixty, of which forty-one are *liberti* – a ratio of two to one. Of the remaining thirty-four, fifteen have Greek names, indicative if not of certain freedman status, at least of servile ancestry. The comparison of these figures with those of other Umbrian towns reveals interesting variations. At Assisi the proportion of freedman to *ingenui* is roughly equal, whereas at Spello the situation is the reverse of Gubbio with far more *ingenui* recorded than *liberti*. These differences may relate to the previous socio-economic history and subsequent development of each centre with, for example, the colonial background of Spello being significant.

6.1.4 The urban economy

After a tentative study of the town's physical structures, its population and their burials, it is appropriate to consider the economic system within which they all functioned. The prosperity of Gubbio, and indeed many Umbrian towns, can be gauged by the wealth both of urban and rural buildings, and the material culture found associated with them. The prosperity of the first century BC to first century AD was common to the whole region. Similar expansions within urban and, where investigated, rural settlement, are identifiable in the centres of Assisi and Spello.

Skilled artisans were doubtless brought to Gubbio to assist in the construction and decoration of the town's buildings, but most of the construction materials themselves were local, with very little imported stone. More easily transported luxuries, such as the funerary bed from the gravegoods at Fontevole, the mosaic emblema from the recently excavated *domus*, and the intaglio found on field survey were clearly imported. Some forms of tableware and fine foods (wine, olive oil and *garum*) were also imported on a much larger scale and these even reached the smaller villas of the countryside, such as that excavated at San Marco (section 6.2). Given the remote location of Gubbio, in the Apennines, far from water transport, the quantity of staples both imported and exported must

have been very low. The general economic pattern would seem to be a closed productive system, with imported luxuries and services. It is consequently reasonable to ask, whether such a system could produce wealth.

If the model proposed is primarily of a subsistence farming economy, then the function of the local town and, indeed, the reason for its existence might be questioned. Clearly, however, it fulfilled a function as a central place for administration, entertainment and ritual, which uses are evidenced by the theatre, temples, baths and amphitheatre. In addition, however, excavations and inscriptions provide some evidence for services and production located in and around the town. Inscriptions record two doctors, an ointment-maker and a wool-worker, while ritual services were provided by L. Veturius Rufio, an auger, diviner, public and private priest (Borman 1901). Evidence for the local production of goods is provided by the excavation of two kiln sites at San Biagio and at the Vittorina cemetery, which appear to have served both the local, domestic market and the specialist, gravegoods market (Cipollone 1988). This production activity, although located outside the urban area, presumably to reduce the risk of fire, was an urban phenomenon. The only literary evidence, of even tangential relevance to the economy of Gubbio, is a passage from the Elder Pliny, which records that the Iguvines sold a herb extract on the *Via Flaminia*. This can scarcely be considered a foundation of the regional economy.

In addition to services, the town provided a population centre and market for local produce. Many of the poorer residents may have laboured, at least seasonally, on rural estates, while others probably worked land in the heavily manured, but lightly settled, area around the town (section 6.2), in a similar way to that proposed for the House of Menander at Pompeii (Ling 1984).

Evidence for the central market function of the town was found on one of the richest rural sites, which lay close to Gubbio. The discovery of a marble weight amongst the surface finds suggests that market gardening may have been practised, linked to the requirements of the urban economy.

There can be little doubt, given the landscape, local resources and survey evidence (section 6.2), that the economy of Roman Gubbio had an agricultural and pastoral base. This upland economy would have been internally integrated, but unable to launch heavy produce into a wider market, because of transport constraints. The production of wool in such upland economic systems could, however, have been as important as in the medieval period (Chapter 7). Umbria, with its abundant high pastures and drove roads, certainly had suitable terrain and there is support from literary evidence as well. A

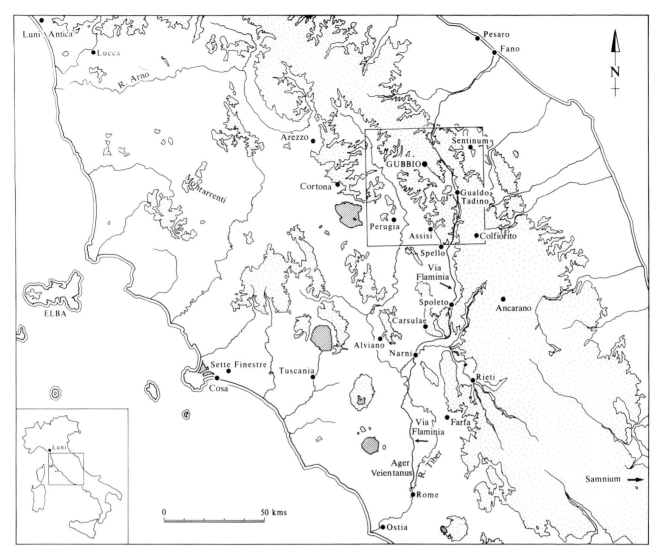

Fig. 6.4 Central Italy in the Roman period

breed of sheep called the Umbrian is recorded by Pliny the Elder (*Historia Naturalis*, VIII, LXXV); a famous cheese came from Umbria (*Historia Naturalis*, II: 240–2); and Varro records the delivery of a flock of sheep from 'furthest Umbria' to southern Italy (*de Agricultura*, II, IX; 6). The inscriptions provide supporting evidence. There is the mention of the *lanarius* (wool-worker), and in addition the *Gens* Fullonia (fuller) is the most commonly recorded, comprising both free and freed members. Although none of the inscriptions relating to this *Gens* records a profession, at some point the name must have been descriptive.

The evidence from the *territorium* of Gubbio, more fully covered in the next section (section 6.2) provides some complementary information. The excavation of the Roman structure at San Marco, suggests the presence of

sheep herding and household cloth production. A pastoral emphasis, however, might not be expected from a lowland settlement of this type. More important is the location, by survey, of upland settlements, some of considerable wealth, and occasionally in village form. To these must be added the evidence for dispersed ritual organisation in the Roman period. Some ritual sites in pastoral locations originally occupied in the pre-Roman period produce evidence for re-occupation, both locally (Monte Ansciano), and generally in Umbria (Manconi *et al.* 1981: 372). Furthermore some of the clay figurines found on the valley floor can be seen as illustrative of the surplus exports to be expected from this upland economy: a sheep and a fleece (Fig 6.14, 5).

6.2 The Roman countryside

Rura cano rurisque deos
                Tibullus (II, Poem 1, line 37)

6.2.1 Introduction: the study of Roman countrysides

The study of towns divorced from their rural hinterlands, or linked only to that urban phenomenon the luxury villa, has traditionally dominated Roman archaeology in Italy, as, to a similar extent, tombs have dominated Etruscan archaeology. Recently, however, an orthodoxy has developed, based on the tenet that neither town nor country can be understood in isolation (Potter 1987; Dyson 1992). A clear example of the danger of studying either one alone can be seen at Luni Antica in Liguria, where the fortunes of the marble quarries and port are a fundamental determinant of local land exploitation (Ward-Perkins *et al.* 1986). The inherent difficulty of isolating urban and rural themes can also be seen in these two sections, where it is frequently necessary to transgress the *pomoerium* (the ritual boundary of a Roman town).

In the Roman world both town and *territorium* were necessary parts of local economic and social systems and that symbiotic unit was, in turn, a part of the wider Imperial network. In some areas of the Empire the system itself determined land exploitation: the supplying of Rome with produce was a major economic driving force in some areas of Africa and Spain, with the army playing a similar role for some of the northern provinces. Within Italy too, regions and estates that were well located to supply Rome, such as the Ager Veientanus (Kahane *et al.* 1968) and the villas at Colle Plinio and Alviano on the navigable Tiber (Ministero 1983), appear to have had rather different fortunes from those without the benefits of proximity, or enhanced access, to this main market.

The work of archaeologists on both excavations and surveys in different regions of Italy has begun to produce an impression of the Roman landscape as a more balanced entity than previously believed. Except in unusual circumstances, the luxurious *villae maretimae* are relegated to a position of less dominance than that formerly occupied. Even in cases where work continues to address itself to the villa, as at Settefinestre (Carandini 1985), the methodology and aims have become more sophisticated, eschewing the purely artistic/architectural bias traditionally associated with such studies.

6.2.2 Roman rural images and idylls

The Roman countryside has always suffered from images; some Roman poets, in particular Horace, Virgil and Tibullus, idealised a life of rural simplicity, which they portrayed as being a desirable and practical alternative to life in Rome. In his letters Pliny (Sherwin-White 1966) painted a tranquil picture of his villa existence, while the agricultural writers offered principally theoretical advice to educated land owners on how best to run their estates. The contemporary literary impressions of the Roman countryside to have survived, therefore, are highly idealised, or constrained by convention – the productive estate, or the Good Life.

Traditionally archaeologists have bolstered this ideal view of the landscape by concentrating their efforts on uncovering the non-productive areas of large, wealthy villas. Mosaic floors, painted wall plaster and fine objects became the excavated image of rural Italy and complimented well the poetic images and indeed the artistic images from Roman frescos on rural themes, such as those in Livia's house on the Palatine (Ling 1991).

More recently the image chosen by some ancient historians, in part as a reaction to the idealism detailed above, has been that of the slave-based, exploitative production system, which is frequently considered a prerequisite for the villa economy (Hopkins 1984). While direct literary evidence is found to support this view in the political, rather than poetical, details of Tiberius Gracchus' journey through Etruria, this does not alter the impression of a town- and villa-dominated landscape, but adds an unpleasant slant to it.

In neither extreme image of rural life do the increasingly detailed results of most archaeological surveys willingly fit. The number and variety of surface material concentrations and the surprising level of wealth encountered at many of them (as measured by fine pottery and imported amphorae), together with the consideration that somebody was working the heavy soils with limited technology, lead to an unhappy union of both images.

6.2.3 Context of research

The Gubbio Project provided an excellent opportunity to study – through both survey and excavation – the changes in landscape exploitation and economy in a relatively isolated, upland valley. Since the development of field survey in archaeology as a major research tool, the most impressive results in Italy have been achieved on rich agricultural plains, as in the south Etruria survey (Potter 1979), recently continued at Tuscania (Barker and Rasmussen 1988). While such surveys have produced very full, if still incomplete, records of settlement location and date, the realisation has grown that land exploitation and development in Roman Italy was very much dependent on geographical and geological variables. As a consequence of this, extrapolation from coastal plains to upland valleys is increasingly difficult to justify. Regional differences in taphonomy and geomorphology also call for research methodologies tailored to the needs of the different landscapes (Chapter 1 and section 2.1).

Some workers have been undertaking survey in more difficult, and materially less rewarding, upland areas, such as the Molise Project (Barker *et al.* 1978), Montarrenti (Barker 1983; Barker and Symonds 1984), Farfa (Moreland 1986, 1987) and, more recently, Rieti and Rascino. Study of the main landscape and settlement types in the Gubbio Valley is more likely to find acceptable comparisons in such similar environments, than in the coastal plains, and it is to the growing interest in regional settlement variation that the Gubbio data are able to add significant results.

Visibility and sampling problems encountered on the valley floor, the eroding hill slopes, and the grass covered hill tops made the collection, comparison and interpretation of data difficult. A particular problem for the Roman period was the heavy colluviation and alluviation on the northern side of the valley, where both the main road to the *Via Flaminia* ran and, it might be suggested, the optimal sites for villa locations would lie. In many areas the paucity of finds, particularly those of a chronologically indicative nature, was an unwelcome surprise, so that at the end of the Project, all circumscribed concentrations could be placed on one map (Fig. 6.5), with but little scope for detailing chronological sequence. Details of site chronology will be considered later, first must be considered the purpose, method and parameters of definitions.

The aim of the survey for the Roman period was to study the landuse of the *territorium* of the *municipium* of Iguvium and its change through time. The extent and boundaries of the *territorium* have never been clarified, but with the circumscribed nature of the terrain must have included the whole valley floor as well as many upland, pastoral areas.

Classification of the concentrations of Roman date had to be undertaken, and since the nature of these concentrations appeared to be so different from those of other published surveys, a simple system was adopted which took more account of the nature of the material found, than the area covered by it. While it is not intended to deny the importance of concentration size, current landuse and geomorphology conspired to obscure it in too many cases to leave a meaningful sample. As in all site categorisations the precise parameters, except for simple presence/absence categories, are too vague for truly scientific minds:

Grade 1: Large farm/Villa Large area covered by building stone, tile and pottery, signs of architectural distinction (for example mosaics, box tiles or column materials).

Grade 2: Farm Small area covered by building stone, tile and pottery.

Grade 3: Shed Very small area covered with tile, sometimes some stone, sometimes some pot, although often neither.

Grade 4: Village A number of small, discrete, scatters, similar to Grade 2 or 3 sites, in very close proximity to one another, with none displaying exceptional size or wealth.

This simple approach, while easy to use in the field, is incapable of identifying unique site uses, so, for example, the village site at the top of Monte Loreto might, were it excavated, prove to be an upland sanctuary site, although in all aspects other than location it corresponds to the Grade 4 site definition.

Archaeological survey, as initially developed and employed in Italy, is able to produce maps of site locations; at Gubbio it was hoped to do far more by employing detailed recording methods to isolate all minor variations in what is usually given the blanket name 'background noise'. The study of this off-site material reveals in part how much of the landscape was exploited in Roman times, but alone is still unable to present the complete picture, since if associated with manured areas, then it relates to arable not pastoral or arboreal exploitation.

Using these results, the interpretative system was expanded to attribute finds to cemeteries and manuring spreads, when ratios of fine to coarseware pottery were unusual, or material was spread, without concentrations, over large areas (Stoddart and Whitehead 1991). In the immediate environs of the town, and along the modern Vittorina, the evidence to justify the cemetery category has been strengthened by Soprintendenza excavations (Fig. 6.5).

Despite the alluviation, taphonomy and poor visibility, however, the five years of survey in the Gubbio Valley produced more material attributable to the Roman period than to any other. With standing remains to testify to Gubbio's Roman past, this evidence for exploitation of the valley in that period came as less of a surprise than its obvious poverty. Recent agricultural activity has, however, reduced many concentrations of cultural material to little more than amorphous spreads of badly broken and degraded fragments of tile and pottery. The main exception to this rule was in the area directly to the south of Gubbio, where pottery dumps and cemetery areas provided a wide range of respectably preserved ceramics, despite continual cultivation in that zone. Concentrations of Roman material were, nevertheless, found throughout the valley in all environmental and geological zones represented within

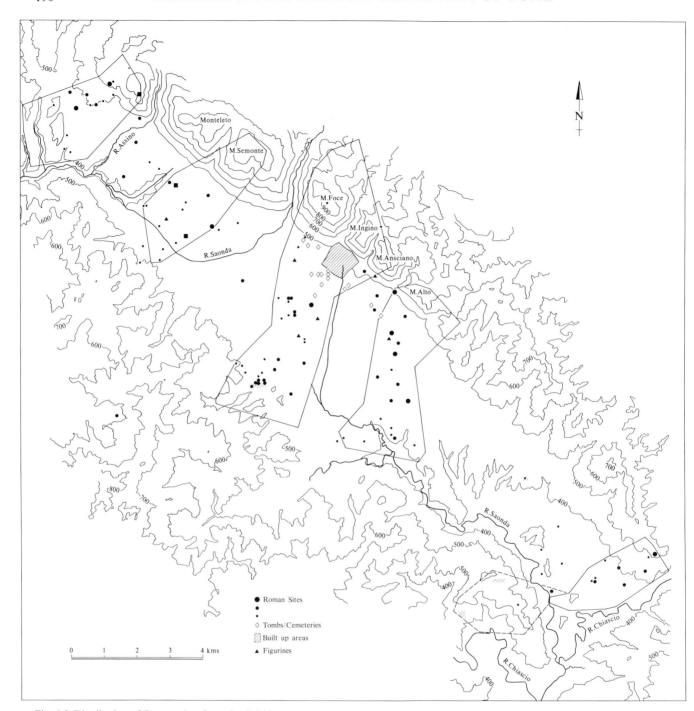

Fig. 6.5 Distribution of Roman sites from the Gubbio survey

the survey area. The adaptability shown by this ubiquity is only equalled and not surpassed by the early-modern settlement pattern.

6.2.4 Distribution patterns, chronologies and explanations

At this stage, we must consider what can be expected from such incomplete survey data and the distribution maps produced from them. A map on its own (Fig. 6.5) is of limited use without an understanding of the factors that influenced the variable survival and retrieval of remains. In an ideal world an attempt could be made to understand the factors and reasoning which lead to the selection of one site over another for a settlement location. Despite the limitations of the Gubbio data, they are sufficient to show that the application of a model developed in a south Etrurian context would be wholly inappropriate. This is not merely a factor of the greater material wealth of many south Etrurian sites, but also of disparate chronological and economic development within the areas, caused in part by the greater influence of Rome on Etruria.

From the study of the survey material it emerges that the great preponderance of datable objects are from the second half of the first century BC and the first century AD, rather than earlier and later periods. This peak is marked materially by a few sherds of *Vernice Nera* (Fig. 6.12, 1–3), later Dressel 1 and Dressel 2–4 *amphora* sherds and a comparative wealth of fragments of *Terra Sigillata Italica* (Fig 6.12, 4, 16). Where forms of earlier dates do occur, such as the almond rim they are primarily in dump or manure locations around Gubbio and by revealing their penetration of local pottery assemblages, make more marked their absence from rural sites. The indication of agricultural exploitation of the town's immediate surroundings at an early date is however of independent interest. This absence of early material on sites where it might be expected to be found if present would suggest that the arable exploitation of much of the valley began in the first half of first century BC, well after the construction of the *Via Flaminia* and comparable developments elsewhere in Italy. The alternative hypothesis, that earlier ceramic forms, while reaching the valley did not penetrate the agricultural hinterland seems unlikely from the study of later evidence and the excavated sample from San Marco. The settlement explosion into the landscape, which could be linked to the late Republican developments around the theatre (section 6.1), might relate to the deduction of an unrecorded colony or other large immigration that would have increased the requirement for food and thereby land. This pattern of a late Republican/early Imperial expansion in both rural and urban settlement is surprisingly different from that recorded in Samnium

(Lloyd 1991), where a reduction in occupied sites recorded between the *Vernice Nera* and *Terra Sigillata Italica* periods is interpreted as being caused by the agglomeration of small estates.

Less neatly documented is the date of the abandonment of the rural settlements after the early Imperial boom. Sherds of characteristically later material, such as African oil amphorae and African Red Slip, were very rarely found in the survey, either on settlements or surrounding the town. As historical evidence suggests that the town continued to be inhabited throughout the Roman period, the dearth of later material surrounding it can not be indicative of desertion. If distinctive later material is rarely found around Gubbio, then this could indicate a change in trade patterns, rather than settlement ones. Even on sites where later material is present, such as the sherd at San Marco, it is likely, as in this case, to be the only evidence of later occupation. Before, therefore, using any datable pottery categorically, the probability of presence of a particular type must be considered. In the Gubbio Valley the absence of *Terra Sigillata Italica*, given its usual frequency and the proximity of Arezzo, from any site may suggest that it was not occupied during the late Republican/early Imperial period; the absence of later materials, however, cannot be considered indicative of abandonment, as the material, or any known substitute, is too scarce (see Millet 1991 for similar argument in Spain). Few sites have produced surface material of the second and third centuries AD, while at San Marco the second century material was only uncovered, and then in tiny quantities, during excavation.

From the nature of the material, therefore, arguments based upon the settlement pattern other than during the first century BC or first century AD are insupportable and, although continuity of some settlement is provable, changes in settlement pattern or landuse can not be postulated from the available evidence.

The interpretation of scatters of cultural material found during survey can only be made through comparison with the excavation of similar scatters in similar locations. Workers in Umbria benefit from a collation of results from excavations of rural sites produced by the Soprintendenza (Ministero 1983). Although these results, primarily from rescue excavations, are not biased towards the *pars urbana* of *villae* they still over-represent the large rural complex, as, doubtless, archaeologists were not alerted except for obvious masonry walls and solid flooring. The data collected do, nonetheless, provide some comparative background context for the Grade 1 sites encountered during the Gubbio survey, as well as forming a useful handbook of locally occurring pottery forms. This is particularly important as local coarseware forms are not

Plate 6.2 San Marco Romano under excavation

to small Roman rural settlements, combined with the absence of an adequate local coarse pottery corpus that rendered necessary the excavation of a typical Grade 2 site.

In 1987, an excavation team of eight spent a month in sampling concentration 326 (San Marco Romano – SMR) (Plate 6.2), located on an alluvial fan on the valley floor some 4 km south-east of the town of Gubbio. This site was chosen as being representative, in terms both of extent and material recovered from surface collection, of one of the most common settlement types identified during the survey. It lay on a site slightly elevated from the surrounding heavy, but fertile, fields. Although no well was located during the excavations, and *dolia* were only fragmentary, a modern stream lies less than 100 m to the west and numerous land drains, including one of Roman date (Fig. 6.9), would suggest an adequate and at times overabundant water supply. Although no Roman road has been identified near the site, access was probably by tracks (*strade bianche*) similar to those serving the area today.

The detailed surface collection of the site had revealed the presence of building rubble (stone and tile), local coarsewares, datable finewares, lamps, *amphorae, dolia* and even an illegible coin, spread over an area of some 3,000 m². A sample, totalling some 107 m², was excavated in an attempt either to extend or corroborate the somewhat restricted chronologies of such sites, and to provide direct evidence for the economic system within which they functioned. The excavation, of what turned out to be a complex, multi-phase Roman farmyard, did increase the quantity and variety in all of the above categories of finds, as well as producing limited later material, modest structural remains and floral and faunal evidence.

The buildings had a sequence, which could be divided into some four phases, ranging from the late Republic to the third century AD (Figs. 6.6–6.8). The main structure, enclosed by wall 88, comprised a barn or stall, while other masonry remains probably relate to farm outbuildings, with no part identifiable as having been used for human habitation. The surviving wall footings were constructed of unmortared stone and reused *tegolae* with a number of post holes identified, including one at the entrance to the main structure. From the evidence of a dense clay/mud layer overlying the main rooftile collapse levels, the walls above the footings seem most likely to have been of timber supporting *pisé*. The materials used in the construction of the wall's footings included reused tiles, limestone, both rolled and quarried, and sandstone, possibly from outcrops on the south side of the valley.

The floor, of beaten earth, accumulated a large deposit of pottery sherds, bones and other rubbish during occupation, which deposit was finally sealed by tiles from

in the core Romano-Etruscan tradition, as categorised by Dyson at Cosa (Dyson 1976), and seldom have clear comparables among better studied assemblages. The excavation of kilns dating to the first two centuries AD at Vittorina to the east of Gubbio and the publication of the ceramic evidence (Cipollone 1988) has gone some way to improve matters.

The difficulty of interpreting surface scatters increases as their size and wealth, in terms of material finds, decreases. The category of farm (Grade 2), or hut (Grade 3), are, despite their common occurrence, traditionally understudied and, thus, difficult to study by survey alone. Although 94% of scatters interpreted as sites connected with farming in the Gubbio survey were below the villa standard, no locally or even regionally excavated and published comparable examples could be found. It was this dearth of any interpretative framework for medium

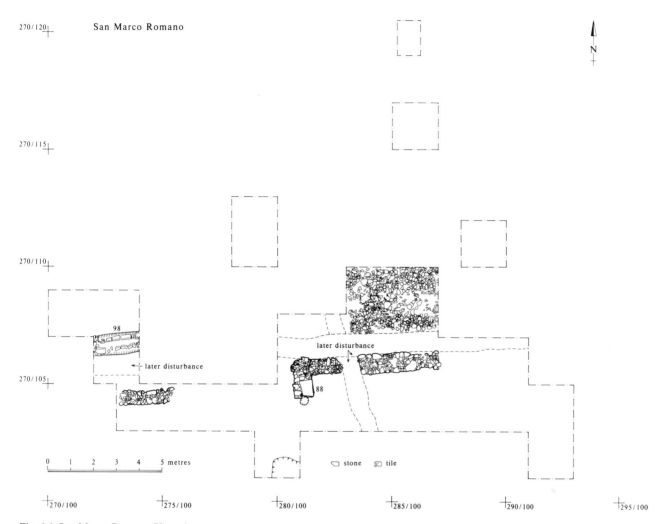

Fig. 6.6 San Marco Romano Phase 1

the collapsed roof. To the north of this structure lay a cobbled area, again rich in ceramic finds, which this time displayed more deliberate placing, with a possible attempt to infill gaps, although it is recognised that brushing or water action would produce the same pattern of sherd accumulation in voids in a cobbled surface.

There was no significant stratigraphy associated with the main structure, where all datable material was of first-century BC to first-century AD date. In contrast to this was the situation in the spatially more restricted western part of the site. Here was unearthed a complex stratigraphy with the lowest level being of large, heavy, paving blocks, possibly the floor of a pig sty, over which was laid a crushed tile floor, bedded on horizontally laid tegolae. This floor was in turn cut by a series of post holes and pipes, which formed the latest identifiable phase. Although the disturbance of earlier levels by later is

indisputable, the presence of a sherd of second-century African Red Slip pottery in a low-lying context might suggest a third-century date for the final timber structure, with which no datable finds are associated. The simple nature of this final, timber, phase might be considered an index of the poverty into which the coloni, now aceramic, had sunk, or equally of the low status of the building, perhaps merely a logistic location following estate agglomeration. In either case the character of the site had certainly altered by the third century.

Other excavated remains included virtually ploughed-out walls towards what once formed the crest of the hill, shallow pits and a well-constructed, tegola lined drain, filled with tile fragments (Fig. 6.9).

If the concept of 'standard of living' has any validity in a Roman context, then that of the inhabitants of San Marco during the early Imperial period would seem to be

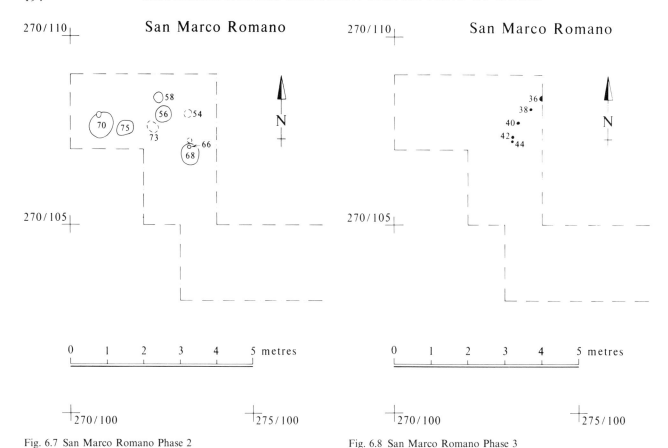

Fig. 6.7 San Marco Romano Phase 2

Fig. 6.8 San Marco Romano Phase 3

surprisingly high. The evidence of material remains suggest not a purely subsistence economy, but one where a productive surplus enabled the inhabitants to link in to the imperial trade network. Some pottery is of a very coarse nature, but by far the greatest proportion is competently manufactured in a variety of forms, which would suggest specialisation of production, as evidenced at the Vittorina kilns (Cipollone 1988), rather than Peacock's household production (Peacock 1982). Even more telling is the presence, if hardly abundance, of fine and specialist pottery, such as lamps (Fig. 6.12, 19–22), 'incensarii' (Fig. 6.12, 1–3) and *amphorae*. Numerically, the most common fineware in the excavated contexts, although it does not survive well in the ploughzone, is *Parete Sottile* (Fig. 6.12, 3 and 5–15) which, although presenting a great variety of forms, is entirely of local production with very close comparables at Vittorina, although fewer from Cosa (Marabini Moeus 1973). Both *Vernice Nera* (Fig. 6.12, 1–2) and *Terra Sigillata Italica* (Fig. 6.12, 4 and 17) are of local/regional and central Italian production and the proximity of Arezzo is to be noted in relation to the latter. The *amphorae* and African

Red Slip (ARS) spread the evidence of an active trade network further to southern Italy (Dressel I and II–IV), North Africa (ARS and African Amphorae) and the Iberian Peninsula (Dressel VII–XI).

The coinage that would be a necessary prerequisite for any integrated trade network was evidenced on the site by four identifiable examples, ranging in date from 3 AD to about 150 AD. The small number is less of a surprise than it might have been in an urban or later Imperial context (Reece 1984) and combined with the evidence of imports might support a model of surplus production and exchange within a monetary economic network. This is a pattern which is corroborated by the surface finds on other sites both within the valley and elsewhere in Umbria. The evidence from Alviano and Colle Plinio (Ministero 1983), for example, both impressive villas with access to markets at Rome, fully supports the evidence from Gubbio and, indeed, underlines the scarcity of later, predominantly African, imports to even wealthy areas of Umbria.

Of more fundamental importance to the study of the Gubbio landscape is an understanding of the productive

San Marco Romano

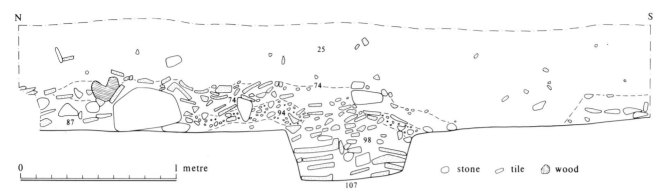

Fig. 6.9 Section through drainage ditches and associated features of San Marco Romano

systems which operated there and enabled, through surplus, economic integration. Roman site publications are often poorly provided with floral and faunal studies and even when produced these tend to indicate a paucity of such material on Roman sites (Carandini 1985). In this case SMR is no exception. The floral remains were so poorly preserved that only two cereals and their associated chaff fragments were identifiable, representing free-threshing and hulled wheat (Giorgi pers. comm.). There is no evidence for olives, grapes, or indeed for the exploitation of wild fruits, as was evidenced on the Neolithic site (section 3.2).

The faunal sample (Clark pers. comm.), although small in terms of minimum number of individuals, did produce evidence for the exploitation of a number of species. Ovicaprids, with goat certainly represented, formed the most common fauna, with the age profile – most deaths occurring at over 36 months – suggesting that they were kept for wool/milk. The production of wool, at least for domestic use, if not the market, is incidentally evidenced by the presence of a loom weight and bone needles (Fig. 6.10, 6 and 7), on site, although butchery marks on the bones confirm that the production of meat was also a consideration.

Although the ovicaprids were numerically most important, other domestic animals were also exploited, with equid and large bovid for transport and traction and pig also represented. The bird bones recovered could be either domestic or wild, so that the exploitation of wild animals is evidenced only by the presence of roe deer in the sample. Roe have a fringe woodland habitat, and this could suggest hunting in the upland environment and peripheral scrub, rather than on the cultivated plain (Corbet and Southern 1977). Thus, while the range of exploited species

is quite broad, in terms of absolute numbers it equates to far fewer than one individual per year of site occupation.

The excavation supplied, therefore, data against which to test the theories being proposed as models of the functioning of an upland pastoral and agricultural economy. This evidence, from a medium-sized farm, however, can help only indirectly with the interpretation of the lower grade scatters. These are clearly not of the same nature as that excavated, being characterised by very little pottery but a small concentration of tile, with, in some cases, building stone. Once again, no other excavated examples are forthcoming and interpretation could vary from poor farms through slave dwellings to pigsties and tool sheds. No excavation of such a site was possible, and in any case a great deal of variation would be anticipated within the class.

The excavation also provided little assistance with regard to some troublesome historical questions. Two in particular elude any approach from the available data: the system of landholding around Iguvium and the composition of the workforce. San Marco Romano may produce imports and fine pottery, but it is not possible to categorically state that the farmer was the owner rather than a bailiff, tenant, or, in the later Empire, *colonus*, occupying the site. Equally the property may have been subject to different tenure systems at different periods of its history.

The slave problem also remains. Tiberius Gracchus' celebrated journey through Etruria and vision of slave-worked *latefundia* and the numbers involved in Sparticus' agroslave army suggest a large rural slave population. Pliny, however, seems to suggest that chained slave gangs were not used in Umbria, whatever the case elsewhere (Pliny, *Epistolae*, III; 19). The British School at Rome

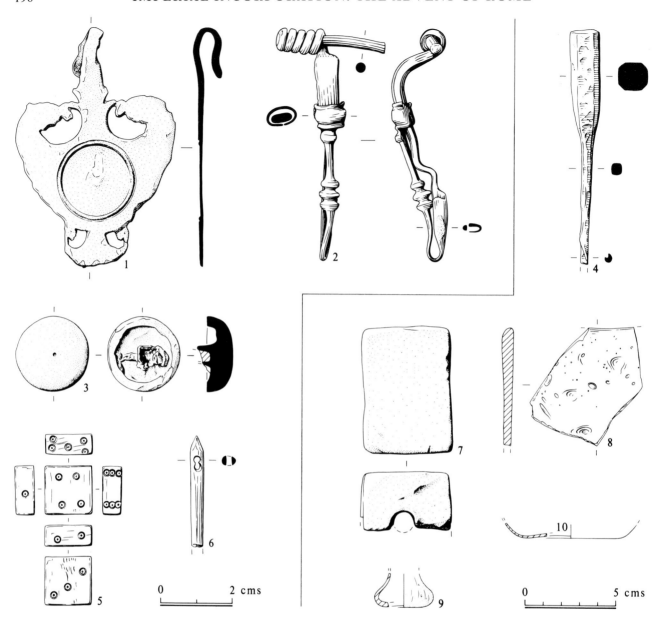

Fig. 6.10 San Marco Romano: small finds in bronze, iron, bone, terracotta and glass. 1 Bronze pendant; 2 Bronze brooch; 3 Bronze mount; 4 Iron awl; 5 Bone die; 6 Bone needle; 7 Terracotta loomweight; 8 Glass window pane fragment; 9 Glass vessel fragment; 10 Glass bowl base

South Etruria Survey may be put forward as evidence of exaggeration on Tiberius Gracchus' part, as his trip corresponded with a period of expansion of small farms, not at all suggestive of our concept of slave dwellings (Potter 1979). This is not to argue that slaves were an unimportant part of the rural economy, but merely to stress that archaeologically they are invisible or nearly so. All of the evidence from the San Marco excavation would suggest a free family farm, but there is no accepted way of recognising slave dwellings. Small uniform rooms are what have been chosen as indicative of servile use by Carandini in the Settefinestre excavations (Carandini 1985) and a similar interpretation was made at Torre Annunziata near Pompeii. There is no evidence, however, that rural slaves would have had specific buildings designed for them, indeed Varro advises estate owners that in some cases their slaves should sleep in the agricultural buildings (Varro, *Rerum Rusticarum*, I: xiii, 1–2).

6.2.5 *A model for upland settlement*

Having ordered the data resulting from both the survey and excavation, they can be used to form and test theories relating to the development of upland landscape exploitation. Initially the determining variables in settlement location can be considered. Four main factors might be identified, of which one or more may be relevant in each individual case:

(1) Purely economic – the site was judged by the settler to be the most suitable available for his economic/ productive needs and to offer the greatest prospect of a tradeable surplus for the least work. This would, logically, determine the location of Neolithic villages.

(2) Political – at the end of the Republic large tracts of land were taken from their occupiers and distributed, often after centuriation, to army veterans and loyal supporters (Keppie 1983). Locally this took place at Spello, and distribution, if not centuriation, took place near Assisi, where Propertius suffered its consequences (Propertius). In such circumstances a veteran would be restricted in locating his buildings to within either his plot, or an accessible local town.

(3) Social/aesthetic – many, and in particular the larger, country residences were located so as to benefit from surrounding views and good communications to Rome or other major centres.

(4) Environment – within a defined area, a site might be located for its aspect, following Cato and Varro: south- or east-facing; near a water supply; away from stagnant water or swampland (Cato I: 3).

In determining the cause of site locations on the ground, it is likely that the economic/environmental factors are going to be of primary importance at the lower end of the settlement hierarchy, with social and aesthetic reasons being of importance only at the upper end, when economic practicality is not paramount. Thus the most inappropriate location for a villa is that of the Villa Jovis on Capri, constructed for the Emperor Tiberius (Sear 1982: 88–91).

From a study of aerial photographs, all available textual evidence and the survey results, there is no proof that the Gubbio Valley was ever centuriated, although the extension of settlement in the first century BC might be taken as implying a settler influx.

If it is accepted that the determinants of settlement location at Gubbio are most probably utilitarian and economic, then these can be studied in individual landscape segments:

(1) The environs of the town – as mentioned above this area was agriculturally exploited before most of the plain was settled, and the dense manure scatters, with material from all periods, would suggest that exploitation from the town continued into at least the later Roman period. Such direct exploitation would tend to explain the scarcity of larger sites in the immediate environs of the town, which with the market so close might be thought to provide prime locations.

(2) The valley floor – the largest and wealthiest sites located were on the valley floor or alluvial/colluvial slopes, and within easy reach of Gubbio. If all sites started at a similar level originally, then it could be the special suitability of the location that led to the success and development of these particular sites. One site near the town produced possible evidence for cash-cropping and market gardening, in the form of a polished stone weight. The plain is, however, most suitable for arable farming and it is assumed that, except on the heaviest Pleistocene terraces and clay deposits, which lie uncultivated even today, this was the main function of lowland sites. Having said that, the faunal and floral evidence from San Marco Romano is unequivocally that of a mixed arable and pastoral farm.

(3) The third location is the upland areas of hill, mountain and pasture, where survey was most hampered by visibility problems, although eroding patches and small ploughed fields permitted vestigial traces of settlement to be located. As argued when considering the urban economy, sheep provide a useful sideline in upland environments and may, considering Gubbio's later history (Chapter 7), and the demand for cloth in the Roman world, have been of great economic significance then. Certainly an important transhumance route from the Marche to the south is known to pass through the Gubbio Valley.

The discrete nature of most Roman rural settlement in the survey area makes groupings of scatters – Grade 4 sites – a noteworthy occurrence. Within such groups the individual scatters are smaller than those of Grade 2 farms, but display a good range of finds and, where finewares are present, these show that occupation of all parts was simultaneous. The position of these 'villages' is of interest, as they lie on marginal land, or in positions where upland and lowland environments can both be exploited. While without any comparable sites having been excavated, their interpretation remains in doubt, the distinct bias towards marginal locations could suggest a primarily pastoral basis to their economy.

6.2.6 Gubbio industry, trade and economy

The consideration of Roman economics is particularly prone to anachronistic reasoning. In particular the idea of balancing books sits unhappily in a Roman context, where an area's wealth may be based on either the exploitation of natural resources, which in Gubbio today are agriculture, cement production and tourism, or on the patronage of wealthy local individuals with broadly based financial resources, such as the patronage of Pliny at Como. A mixture of the two is also possible, but for Roman Gubbio neither seems to have been particularly applicable. Gubbio did not produce a major senatorial family and nor were its products easy to distribute, there being no inexpensive means of transport for bulk goods. As already demonstrated, however, local consumption included both what was produced locally and luxuries from further afield.

Most agricultural staples were locally produced, with the exception of oil, wine and garum, the evidence for which is in the amphora fragments recovered from both San Marco and a number of other survey sites. Building materials, both in the town and countryside are primarily of local origin, although once again, the presence of coloured *tesserae* and cut marble on a few sites suggests the importation of luxury materials and perhaps skills. Most of the pottery recovered during the survey was of local production and the Vittorina kilns clearly illustrate this. Although some finewares and in particular *Parete Sottile* are local products, others are clearly imported. There has been no evidence found for glass production at Gubbio, and yet several vessels are recorded from San Marco, while the cornelian intaglio depicting Mars holding a Victory, found during the survey, clearly originated outside the valley (Fig. 6.13, 7).

In each case the material remains demonstrate the inclusion of the Iguvine city-state into the Roman sphere of influence and its economic integration, if on a small scale, into a larger system. The pattern presented is remarkably consistent, with staples and bulk materials being produced locally, but high value and worked luxury goods being imported. From the finds made during the project it is not possible to say whether this integration was more fundamental than that which existed with the Etruscan world (section 5.3), but the penetration of imported materials into the countryside is more obvious than before. Just as buildings of a Roman character are introduced to the town on a grand scale, so the amphora evidence from rural sites suggests that Roman taste in fine wine and, later, olive oil and fish sauce (garum) was being catered for in the *territorium*. This is despite the inaccessability of the upland Umbrian valley, the impracticality of

the container vessels for anything other than water transport and the fact that alternative local sources of wine and oil were certainly available. There appears to be an active choice at work, selecting imported goods as an alternative to local products. This is not to say that most wine or oil was imported. Indeed San Marco provided fragments of some fifteen identifiable wine amphorae (Dressel Ib and II–IV) during the first two centuries of its habitation, an amount which could not have quenched an Iguvine thirst.

Without better evidence, it must be suggested that what wealth was produced in Gubbio, was based on the rearing of livestock, primarily sheep, both for their wool, and their meat value, following transportation on the hoof to the markets at Rome. The evidence for an important pastoral side to the economy is admittedly limited, but nonetheless present in every aspect of study in the project, even that of ritual.

6.2.7 Rural ritual systems

> Nam veneror, seu stipes
> habet desertus in agris
> seu vetus in trivio
> florida serta lapis;
>
> Tibullus.1, 11–12

Religious manifestation within the urban area of Gubbio appears to have taken a traditionally Roman form, with temples, statues, altars and other trappings of formal religion. Two sets of data recovered from non-urban contexts, however, suggest that rural ritual observance may have been as deeply embedded as is suggested by the above quotation.

The first set of finds is a series of terracotta figurines, found on the surface during survey apparently unassociated with other material or topographical variable (Fig 6.14). That such objects, which closely resemble tile fragments, were recovered at all reflects the detail of the survey, but the number remaining in the ploughzone of the valley must be very high indeed. To interpret these contextless finds, for which no comparables from either survey or excavation have been found, one must turn to literature.

It is something of a commonplace to argue that while official religion in its urban context grew increasingly decadent and politicised, private and rural religion continued unaffected. Certainly it was the *pagani* who would ultimately be so difficult to convert to Christianity, as their beliefs had never ceased to be of daily importance. The urban dweller could blame the Emperor or ruling faction if the *horrea* were empty, but the farmer was in no way cushioned from the harsher realities of nature.

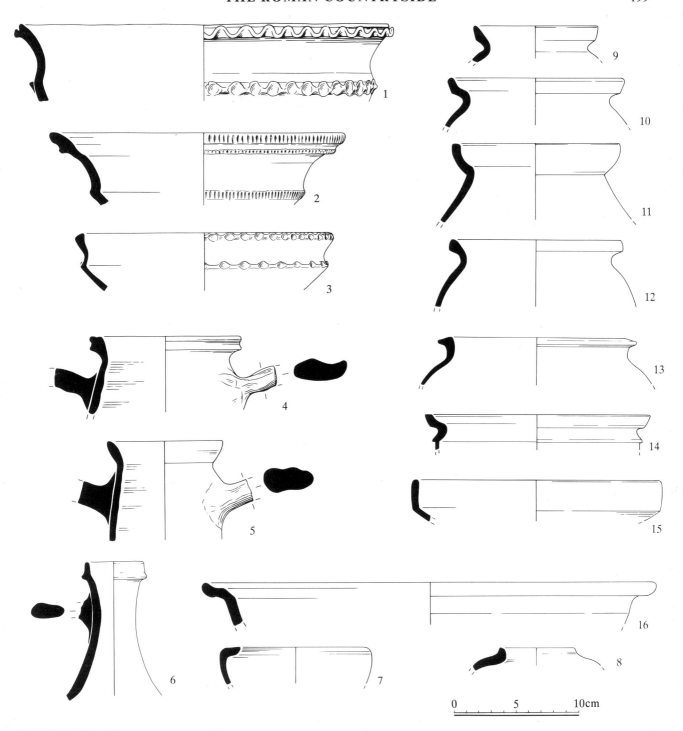

Fig. 6.11 San Marco Romano: coarse ceramic types. 1–3 Carinated bowls with impressed decoration; 4–5 *Anforette*; 6 Flagon; 7–8 Ink bottles; 9–14 jars; 15 Bowl; 16 Basin

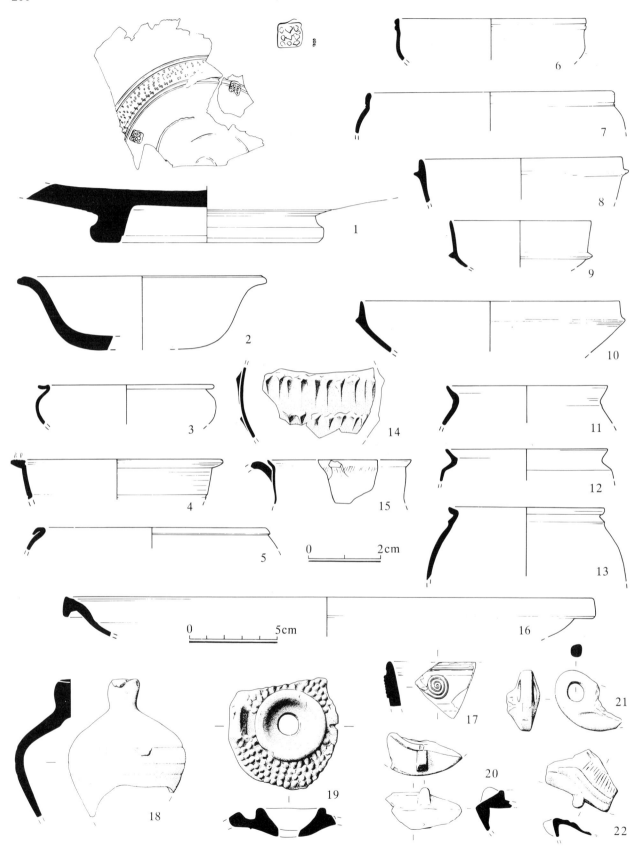

Fig. 6.12 San Marco Romano: Finewares and lamp fragments. 1–2 Vernice Nera; 3–15 Parete sottile; 16–17 Terra sigillata italica; 18 Flask; 19–22 Lamp fragments

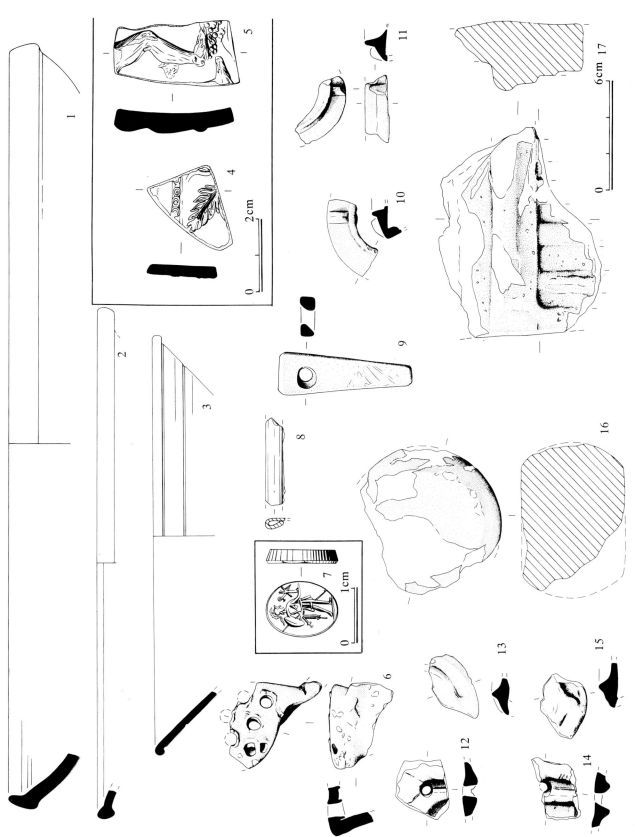

Fig. 6.13 Survey (except 10–15): Roman ceramic forms and small finds. 1–2 African Red Slip; 3–5 Terra sigillata italica; 6 Milk strainer? 7 Cornelian intaglio; 8 Glass rim; 9 Whetstone; 10–15 Lamp fragments from Monte Ansciano excavation; 16 Polished stone weight; 17 Architectural fragment

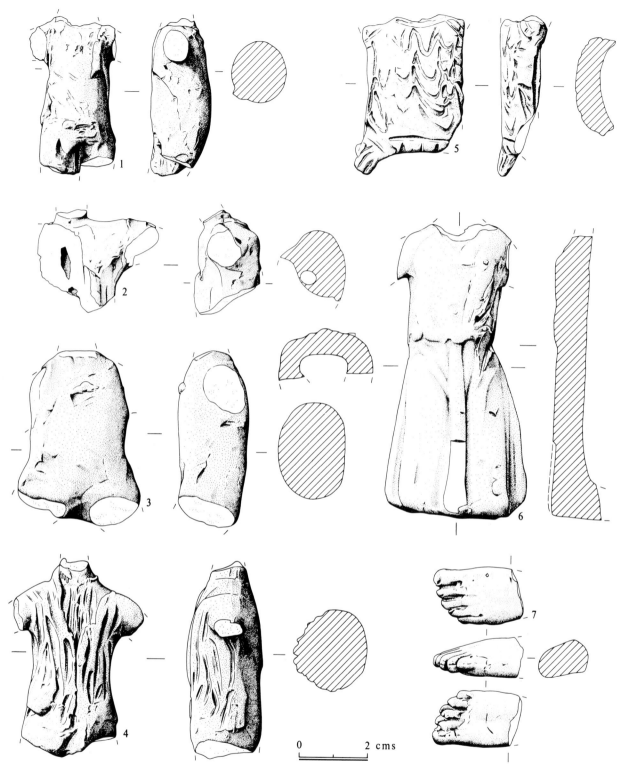

0   2 cms

Fig. 6.14 Terracotta figurines from the valley

To develop a system of powerful and potentially harmful spirits (*numina*) and then to placate them was an attempt to take control of the environment. The complexity of the system became such, however, that the sex and function of many *numina* became forgotten, while others were doubtless never known. Thus it is that Cato proposes the formula 'si deus, si dea es' when a wood requires thinning and a protective spirit is assumed, but unidentified (Cato, CXXXIX). Despite the urban bias of most Roman literature a number of primarily rural festivals are documented, as are the names of some improbable spirits, such as Stercutius, who is concerned with manure, Spiniensis, with thorns, and Robigus, with rust or mildew. This very range of rural gods and spirits combined with the dearth of detail concerning them, makes a positive equation of any one with the material record difficult. The presence of figurines, however, may point to a connection with the Paganalia, or Sementiva, a major festival, held in January to celebrate the sowing. As part of this festival, along with the garlanding of oxen, sacrifice and prayers, figurines (*oscilla*) are recorded as being hung from trees. Given the absence of similar finds from other surveys, it would have to be added that regional variation could make figurines more important in some areas than others, and indeed that a purely local, unrecorded ritual cannot be ruled out. In this context it should be noted that one village in the Gubbio Valley still hosts an annual tripe festival.

If the above interpretation is correct, then the figurines are connected to ritual associated with arable farming. Even more difficult to interpret are the finds of Roman date from the mountain top excavations at Monte Ansciano. After the main phases of sanctuary activity and deposit of the bronze figurines (section 5.1), the frequency of artefacts would suggest sporadic deposition – the products of picnics and the like. While this is adequate to explain the few Roman coins recovered, it is insufficient when considering the numerous small fragments of cups and lamps, which were also recovered in the upper levels. If sporadic deposition is ruled out as an explanation, then half-parallels, at least, are to be found in Umbria for continuity in upland Iron Age ritual sites, such as Gualdo Tadino, where a small temple is constructed; Ancarano, where loomweights come from the peripheral areas and coins from the centre; and Colfiorito, where small agricultural structures are built. It may be that Ancarano offers an explanation, even if not itself a ritual site, in the presence of materials connected with wool-working. Just as the agricultural plain had a ritual system, partly illustrated by the figurines, so the pastoral uplands had rituals, such as the *Parilia*, in which lustral bonfires are of importance, and these unexpected finds may relate to such a festival.

6.2.8 Conclusion – altered images?

The development of landscapes and the towns within them is not determined by any one political, environmental or ritual factor, but by the interaction of all of these over long timescales. The results from Gubbio show again that one simplified model of Roman rural settlement development and decline cannot be transposed from one region to another. Furthermore, environmental adaptation within a complex economic system means more than the exploitation of marginal areas and production or importation of a surplus.

Having cast off the poetic, artistic and historical images of the countryside, we are left with complexity and regional variation. The Roman landscape around Gubbio differs from that recorded in other areas of Italy both in its settlement history and ritual manifestations. To isolate the one most significant variable in creating this record at Gubbio one could again look at Cato's advice for choosing a farm site: access to markets, either by sea, road or river is stressed (Cato, 1.3). Gubbio lacked all three.

7 THE MEDIEVAL PERIOD

7.1 Introduction

The visible material culture of Gubbio today is dominated by the impressive remains of the medieval city (Micalizzi 1988). In this volume, which has as its theme the spatial study of material culture, it would be inexcusable to ignore this record, even if the major focus of this volume has been on prehistory, broadly defined.

Unfortunately, the archaeological research undertaken by the Gubbio Project uncovered little of securely medieval date. On Monte Ingino, the medieval levels had already been excavated (Meloni 1987) and little can be added here (Fig. 4.10) to what has already been reported in that volume (Flavell *et al.* 1987). On Monte Ansciano, two burial pits of late medieval date (325 ± 35 BP in radiocarbon years, producing a 2 date range of 1454–1650 AD cal (Q-3222)) and 280 ± 50 BP in radiocarbon years, producing a 2 σ date range of 1469–1955 AD cal (BM 2503) were cut into the sixth-century BC ritual platform. On the same mountain peak, a Lombardic strap end (Fig. 7.1) was found during systematic plotting of metal detector anomalies. The other excavations did not include medieval levels. Other archaeological work by the Superintendencies and further bodies is gradually establishing the layout of the city in the medieval period (Manconi *et al.* 1991), but is not reported here.

More surprisingly, the landscape survey detected very little that cannot be understood from the existing settlement patterns. Manuring scatters were detected around the medieval city, but in very few other locations in the valley. A few rural settlements were discovered in the valley bottom, but the vast majority of medieval settlement must still be occupied today. Since the objectives of the project were primarily prehistoric, no strategy was developed to date the phases of occupation of these sites even though some probably date to at least the Roman period (established in at least one instance). A major methodological hindrance was the poor knowledge of locally diagnostic medieval coarsewares. In summary, the increased understanding of the medieval landscape would require a complementary study of vernacular architecture, cartography and associated material culture.

For now, the best evidence of the spatial landscape of

Fig. 7.1 Lombardic strap end

Gubbio is available from the written sources supplemented by some initial analysis of early cartography (section 2.3). These sources are considered in more detail elsewhere (Menichetti 1987; Micalizzi 1988), but the aim here has been to follow through the themes of demography, agricultural production, commerce and spatial organisation which have been the focus of earlier chapters.

7.2 The political background

Gubbio was already in the Byzantine period part of the *Pentapoli Annonaria* together with the cities of Urbino, Fossombrone, Jesi and Cagli (Menichetti 1987: 27). Gubbio became strategically important as a staging post on the corridor between Rome and Ravenna which avoided direct use of the Flaminia (Micalizzi 1988: 39). It was also, though, a collecting point for exiles from papal Rome, given its liminal position of remoteness and isolation (Partner 1972: 60).

Geographically and politically Gubbio became a free comune at the beginning of the twelfth century. Urbanisation began at the same stage, initiated by the feudal lords of the various castles in its well-defined natural territory. By degrees, the comune became an urban centre which was, in time, backed by legal authority (Menichetti 1987: 47). The political situation that influenced the eleventh and twelfth centuries was that of simple control and defence by the feudal lords of their own castle, territory and dependents. There were many frontier wars between these same nobles, in support of either the papal or imperial allegiance, allegiances which became points of political and economic reference in moments of need.

The political climate gradually changed from one dominated by noble families to an increasing participation of a wider citizen body. Gubbio had already towards the middle of the twelfth century incorporated the newly emerging bourgeoisie, made up of merchants, artisans and professionals in the political administration originally run by nobles. Tensions, however, remained, particularly in nominations for the election of the new magistrate, the *Podestà* who had initially represented only the noble class (Menichetti 1987: 48). Later still, popular representatives were added to the administration of the comune who elected their representative, the *Capitano del Popolo*.

This historical period was characterised by various alliances with the Pope (Guelf) and with the Emperor (Ghibelline), as small comunes like Gubbio attempted to retain independence. At first Gubbio was Ghibelline, even if Menichetti (1987) considers her Guelf by the beginning of the thirteenth century. Gubbio was most probably Ghibelline for the best part of the thirteenth century, even if on several occasions she made pragmatic alliances with Guelf cities to achieve military and territorial objectives. In that century, the population of Gubbio expanded greatly, accompanied by a major agricultural expansion, so that Gubbio became an economic and military rival even to cities larger than her, such as Perugia and Spoleto (Menichetti 1987: 56).

At the beginning of the fourteenth century, Gubbio expelled the Ghibellines and became Guelf (Menichetti 1987: 65). For many years, Gubbio was governed by *Podestà* and consuls, particularly those belonging to the Gabrielli family. Fourteenth-century Italy continued to be affected by the continuing struggle between Pope and Emperor, directed towards regaining control over lost cities and territories. The Pope entrusted Albornoz (Menichetti 1987: 93) with this task which was only partly successful. This action had some affect on Gubbio, since aristocratic individuals from other cities were inserted as leading political figures, but the popular-aristocratic government headed by the Gabrielli family was also important (Menichetti 1987: 106). Gubbio was in fact governed towards the end of the fourteenth century by Bishop Gabriele di Necciolo, a member of the Gabrielli family, who sought to defend Gubbio from external foreign control, maintaining her relative independence from the neighbouring lordships. The period of his government was quiet until his death in autumn 1383, which, combined with the onset of famine, led to the handing over of Gubbio by ten nobles of the city to Count Antonio da Montefeltro on 29 March 1384 (Menichetti 1987: 131–4).

From this moment until 28 April 1631, the comune of Gubbio became part of the wider political network of the Dukedom of Urbino. The Montefeltro state has been described as 'a grid thrown across the Apennine passes' where the Gubbio Basin was one of the few fertile agricultural, as well as strategic, regions (Partner 1972: 431). The figures of the consuls, the Podestà and Captain of the People became mere executors of orders from Urbino. Gubbio passed effectively from the position of free and independent city to a position subject to external *signorile* control (typical of the control of other noble families of the period such as the Malatesta, the Medici and the Gonzaga), first by the Montefeltro and then by the della Rovere, another noble family of Urbino (Menichetti 1987).

The *signorile* period lasted until 1631, that is until the death of the last of the della Rovere family, Francesco Maria II, who left the Dukedom of Urbino to the Pope. Gubbio, therefore, belonged to the papal state from 1631 until the unification of Italy in 1860, that is, always under external political control.

7.3 Demography

Gubbio, as already discussed (section 2.3), underwent phases of low and high population, most marked by major demographic increase in the first half of the fourteenth century. This increase was halted by the 1348 plague. A new demographic increase occurred towards the end of the fifteenth century, with some setbacks brought about by the plagues of 1530 and 1623. The seventeenth century was a period of disturbance. Foreign invasions, war and famine had a negative effect on the population levels. The first precise population figures are available in the sixteenth century (Menichetti 1987: 302–4) and become more frequent in the eighteenth and nineteenth centuries (Table 7.1).

7.4 Agriculture

The agricultural system, as always, was profoundly influenced by demography. Agricultural production in the feudal period was regulated by trusted dependents of the feudal lord. This regulation comprised both the lands of the immediate neighbourhood of the castle and those of the much larger *pars* some distance from the castle, which was divided into small holdings worked by the *plebes* of the castle. This *curtense* (manorial) system began to change towards the end of the thirteenth century, as

Table 7.1. *Population figures for Gubbio and territory*

Year		Population
1591	City	5,780
	Territory	14,132
1605	City	5,200
	Territory	14,520
1788	City and Territory	20,299
1853	City and Territory	25,661
1897	City and Territory	27,364

concessions were made to the peasantry in the form of new agrarian pacts (Allegrucci 1980: 14). The first agrarian contracts in Gubbio date to the first years of the eleventh century (Cenci 1915: 64) and are called *di livello e di Enfiteusi*. The enfiteusi, the most widespread (generally seven-year) contract of the period, envisaged the concession of ground by the landowner to the farmer in exchange for a rent paid with agricultural products (grain, wine and so on).

The continuous demographic increase pressed the landowners to cultivate the maximum amount of ground to satisfy the demand of the urban market. The new landowning class, made up of notaries, artisans, professionals and so on, introduced a new type of contract, *ad Laboritium* (Allegrucci 1980: 98–101). This contract consisted of an agreement by the landowner to cede his lands to the farmer, who had to work the land at his expense, while the costs of seed and other material were shared. At the end of the agricultural year, the products of the harvest were divided in a proportion that generally favoured the landowner. This type of agrarian contract present in Gubbio from the first years of the fourteenth century (Archivio Statale Gubbio, Fondo Notarile, Prot. 14, C.40v., 41r), was still in use until a few years ago; confirmation of the agricultural stagnation that affected Gubbio until the first years of the 1900s. Other types of contract, *Cottimo* and *Affitto*, were found together with those already mentioned, although with much lower frequency (Allegrucci 1980: 102).

There were also contracts which only regulated animal husbandry. The *Soccida* which concerned cows, sheep and pigs, required that the costs of purchase and rearing should be equally divided as should offspring and secondary products (Archivio Vescovile Gubbio, M.2, C.30v, 31r). These contracts of *Laboritium* and of *Soccida* show clearly the the equal division of landowners' capital and farmers' labour with similar rules applying to the fruits of the labour, although these were rarely respected. In this way the landowner could live in the city (pursuing other

activities) and receive the agricultural products that ensured subsistence autonomy and the selling of surplus.

An interesting related study is that of the water mill, since these were essential for agricultural production. In the period of control by the Montefeltro dukes, these were frequently under ducal control. This control was not just a matter of ownership, but also allowed the control of grain which could be purchased at the moment of milling and avoid dispersal in areas outside the political territory of Gubbio (Allegrucci 1980: 98). This economic control was also confirmed with ducal edicts that forbade the selling of agricultural products outside the local market under the threat of heavy penalties (Allegrucci 1980: 265–6).

7.5 Commerce

To write accurately of commerce in the medieval period at Gubbio is difficult given the lack of study to date. Certainly one can be certain that Gubbio had, above all in the fourteenth century, a notable commercial life, regulated in terms of imports by the *Ordine della Gabella*. This controlled with great detail every type of merchandise that entered the city, assigning to it, according to type, a tax, the *Gabella* (Archivio Statale Gubbio, Ordine della Gabella vol. 1). As regards exports, the most exported product from the thirteenth century was certainly wool. Pottery, even though produced in a small-scale artisan way (Menichetti 1987: 143), served not only a local market, but was also sold in part in other Italian cities. The few studies do not permit any more detailed models of production and distribution, particularly since most attention has been devoted to Mastro Giorgio (Mazzatinti 1931; von Falke 1934; Fiocci and Gherardi 1985).

7.6 Military defence

The territory of Gubbio, from the thirteenth century, included both the modern territory of the *comune* and the territories of the modern *comuni* of Cantiano, Scheggia, Costacciaro and Pergola (ceded in the fourteenth century). These boundaries were defended by a system of castles, towers and keeps at a considerable distance from the city walls (Menichetti 1979: 295).

The first documents that speak of the construction of castles in the territory of Gubbio date to 1097 (Menichetti 1979: 80–8). They were the property of feudal nobles, bishops and monastic communities and were placed both on the summits of hills and in strategic points from which roads, rivers and boundaries could be controlled, thus protecting the territory with a defensive belt (Menichetti 1979: xi). Only the castles which had a Captain, a castellan and soldiers had a defensive role and were used militarily;

CASTLES IN ACTIVE USE

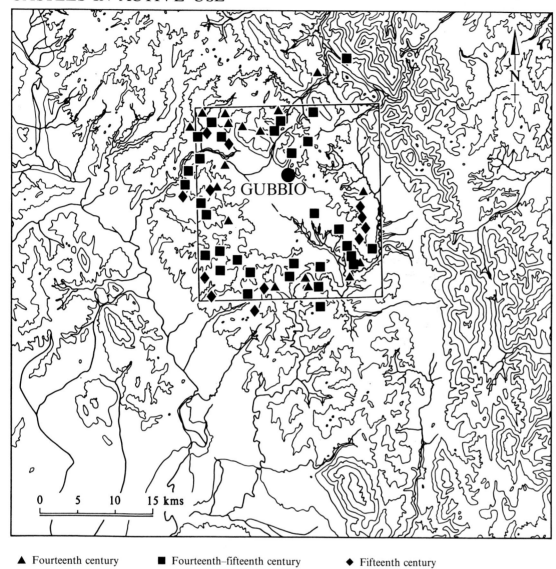

▲ Fourteenth century   ■ Fourteenth–fifteenth century   ◆ Fifteenth century

Fig. 7.2 Changing distribution of castles in the political territory of Gubbio

the others were residential (Menichetti 1979; xiv). In some cases, in periods of serious military threat, these structures proved inadequate and private palaces were also fortified (Menichetti 1979: 295).

Castles were subject to considerable alteration over time; some were destroyed and others reconstructed; others, once their defensive function was finished, were abandoned. The dated distribution of castles (Fig. 7.2) gives an accurate impression of the political landscape in any one phase of Gubbio's history. There were dangerous phases, such as during the ducal period when certain castles were altered and others were constructed particularly on the boundaries facing Perugia and the Duchy of Spoleto to the south and east, since the territory of Gubbio was the first defence of the duchy (Menichetti 1979, xii; Micalizzi 1988, 151). In fact, the Montefeltro regime re-used some of these castles that were already in existence. On the other hand they dismantled some of those placed to the north-east which had once defended the territory against Montefeltro pressure. In time, these structures for defence and visual control lost their utility and many were destroyed. Of the various castles cited by Menichetti, only about fifteen remain in good condition today (Menichetti 1979: xii).

8 THE LONG-TERM TRAJECTORY OF AN INTERMONTANE POLITY: COLONISATION, FORMATION AND INCORPORATION

The aim of this volume has been to contribute to the understanding of the long-term development of an isolated upland valley in the Apennines of central Italy. The analysis has followed an approach currently styled in archaeological circles as Braudelian, or more correctly, in the style of the Annales school (Bintliff 1991; Knapp 1992; Delano Smith 1992). This approach is particularly appropriate to a valley like that of Gubbio which has not always been recorded by written texts. Within Italy, for most periods, archaeological research has concentrated on the rapid socio-political developments of the coastal zones where written texts have had a certain primacy. This volume is one of a number of current attempts by archaeologists (Barker 1991) and historians (Wickham 1988) to provide the complementary evidence from relatively remote mountainous areas.

Practice and theory are too often firmly divided into separate camps. This is sometimes an explicit theoretical statement, but, more frequently, a worrying artificial division between fieldwork and interpretation. Processual archaeology has a good record in rejecting the separation of practice and theory through the exercise of fieldwork. In the same tradition, the current study has aimed to link a field project to a set of achievable objectives which allow the interpretation of a human landscape. Post-processual archaeology has appropriated the term contextual archaeology. This volume has aimed to show that contexts can also be provided by long-term processes. This said, the current volume is less a platform for a new general theory of socio-political development, than the implementation of a set of models to elucidate the development of one valley.

The developments elucidated in the Gubbio Valley form a process that started with the first colonisation of the area in the Palaeolithic and continued with the first permanent settlements in the Neolithic. They led to the formation of the first signs of regional identity in the Bronze Age and to the inscription of that identity on bronze in the first century BC, at the very moment of absorption into the wider political entity of Rome. The last millennium has included phases of separate identity, but each of these has been successively dominated by politically strong external forces (Table 8.1). In these circumstances, symbols from the past, such as the Iguvine Tables (Chapter 5) and the Festa dei Ceri, the modern festival of 15 May, whose origins are perceived to have great antiquity (Bower 1897), have assumed great importance.

The sweep of archaeological history has unfolded within a well-defined geographical unit (Chapter 2) with three principal components: altitude, verticality and well-demarcated boundaries. The geography of the regions surrounding Gubbio was much more diverse, and lacked the clear natural boundaries which have given Gubbio an almost in-built natural identity. The natural boundaries of the Gubbio Basin always contained the potential for political appropriation. However, political power, ultimately dependent on the mobilisation of local resources, was rarely great enough to construct rigid barriers on those natural limits. In the sixth century BC they were strengthened by flimsy ritual monuments. In the eleventh century AD they were fortified by military monuments, at the one moment when natural boundaries corresponded to political reality.

In concluding this volume, a number of dimensions of long-term development will be reviewed. The primary dimension is the organisation of space, both ritual and domestic. All other dimensions derive from this: demography, style and politics. Together they form interlinked cycles of development, that interweave one with one another, granting the valley a distinction out of proportion to its relative isolation.

8.1 The organisation of space

The first occupation of the valley dates to the Middle Palaeolithic (120,000–80,000 BC), with surviving evidence restricted to relict river terraces (Chapters 2 and 3). The

Table 8.1. *Summary of the long-term trends of political status of Gubbio. Short-lived political events are ignored*

Approximate Date BC/AD	Period	Characteristics	Status
120,000–80,000	Middle Palaeolithic	Small bands of hunter-gatherers at extreme of territorial range	Pre-state society
40,000–8000	Upper Palaeolithic	Intermittent seasonal bands of hunter-gatherers	Pre-state society
8000–5000	Epi-Palaeolithic	Intermittent seasonal bands of hunter-gatherers	Pre-state society
5000–2000	Neolithic	First permanent settlement in small clearings on alluvial fans on northern flanks of valley Mixed agriculture and hunting/gathering	Autonomous, Pre-state society
2000–1700	Early Bronze Age	Limited settlement occupation of valley bottom	? Pre-state society
1700–1300	Middle Bronze Age	Hilltop seasonal settlement occupation Pastoral emphasis	Part of inter-regional network Pre-state society
1300–900	Late Bronze Age	Loosely nucleated settlement on upland and colluvial landscape, central to valley More permanent occupation based on mixed agriculture	Part of inter-regional network Greater local autonomy Pre-state society
900–400	Iron Age	Nucleated settlement central to valley. Some incipient social ranking	Some local autonomy Pre-state society
400–200	'Umbrian'	Nucleated settlement central to valley Very limited rural settlement	Local autonomy? Independent city-state?
200 BC–400 AD	Roman	Monumental city central to valley Extensive rural settlement until 200 AD	Part of wider empire Politically subordinate
400 AD–550 AD	?	Urban decline? Rural decline	Political vacuum
550 AD–750 AD	Byzantine		Politically subordinate
750 AD–1100 AD	?	Political vacuum	
1100 AD–1384 AD	Free Comune	Urban and rural expansion Fortification of boundaries	Independent city-state
1384 AD–1631 AD	Urbino	Cyclical economic and demographic development Re-organised fortification of new boundaries	Part of wider state Politically subordinate
1631 AD–1866 AD	Papal	Cyclical economic and demographic development	Part of wider state Politically subordinate
1866 AD–Present	Italy	Cyclical economic and demographic development	Part of wider state Politically subordinate

finds from these terraces most probably represented logistical activities at the territorial limits of mobile hunter-gathering groups. The primary foraging and resource zones of contemporary populations were in more lowland districts and along more direct routes, favoured by migrating animals, such as the Upper Tiber Valley to the west and the Chiascio Valley to the east. The Gubbio Basin was a peripheral area. This was the constant picture for millennia. Change did, though, gradually take place. By the Upper Palaeolithic, there is tentative evidence of an expansion of activity onto alluvial fans and even some of the lower hills, particularly at the confluences of river basins to the south-east. The main focus of activity within the valley was not centrally placed, but skewed towards the south-east, the lower and more open landscapes, and drawn into the wider inter-regional systems of central Italy.

A more articulated organisation of space took place in the Neolithic (late sixth millennium BC). Permanent settlement was concentrated on the prime fertile and well-watered soils of the alluvial fans at low altitude. These were sites well placed to practise horticulture and small-scale cereal cultivation, but not too distant from logistical locations for hunting and other resource procurement.

Such logistical locations have been detected on the heavier Pleistocene soils and even upland locations above 500 m. For biogeographical reasons similar to those which governed the colonisation of the smaller Mediterranean islands, the Gubbio Basin only became a viable, relatively self-contained unit once agriculture was practised.

This agro-settlement potential was strengthened by the intensification of agriculture in the second millennium BC. In the Bronze Age, the local populations gradually switched from the lowland landscape of the Neolithic to upland settlements, concentrated in the central point of the valley, a zone that was never again abandoned as the key settlement location. The choice of this central position was influenced by local topography rather than any prescient Christaller design. It is here that the limestone hills rise to an apex commanding excellent visibility of the surrounding terrain just above the springline and in easy reach of fertile alluvial soils (section 4.1). Initially (about 1400–1200 BC), this central location was occupied by one, probably seasonal, site placed so as to control access through a gorge to the mountainous north as much as to the lowland and upland landscape to the south. Within a few hundred years (about 1100 BC), a single site had become an interrelated system of sites (section 4.1). This central, south-facing point also allowed control of both the uplands and the Valley of Gubbio now devoid of rival settlement. The trend of these earlier phases was increasing control of the uplands, without sacrificing access to the lowlands, following patterns seen in other upland landscapes of central Italy, such as Liguria and Molise.

By the eighth century BC, only the lowland constituent of this co-operating system of sites appears to have remained. Apart from a few subsidiary settlements, this central place was where domestic activities were concentrated until the Roman period. The implications for agriculture were long travel times to and from a loose agglomeration of settlement in the central part of the valley. During this period, however, the upper part of the landscape was explicitly ritualised, strengthening natural features in the landscape and, in some cases, perhaps deliberately re-occupying visible, if modest, monuments of the Bronze Age.

From the third and second century BC, the landscape was rapidly colonised by dispersed settlement, administered from the emerging urban centre of Gubbio. A network of farmsteads and, more rarely, villages, was regularly distributed in the landscape with some ribbon development along road communications. From the full Roman period up to the present day there have been cycles of expansion and retraction from the permanent urban settlement centrally placed in the valley. At times of socio-political stress, defence became an important consideration, both centrally at Gubbio, and on the margins of the territory, acting as havens of safety and ideological points of reference for those farming the local terrain. In the modern period, a phase of agricultural retraction is coming to an end under the dual impact of EEC grants and the purchase of second homes in Umbria.

8.2 Demography

On the timescale that we are measuring change, population levels in the Valley of Gubbio are notable for long periods of tranquil equilibrium, broken rarely by rapid and dynamic change. At the time of first colonisation, Gubbio was almost certainly part of the wider territory of a band or group of bands of hunter-gatherers, opportunistically entering the valley principally from the two major communication routes to the south-east and the north-west. One can estimate an average population as low as 25, with a high rate of interchange with competing and allied groups. As a self-contained valley, the Gubbio Basin probably lacked the mobility, and hence rapid replacement and biomass, of migratory resources. The average population probably increased throughout the Upper Palaeolithic, but it was with the Neolithic that demographic growth accelerated again to reach a new plateau, determined this time by the availability of light well-drained soils on the alluvial fans. Contemporaneity is difficult to prove, but several clearings, amounting to perhaps a hundred people in total is a realistic estimate. Even at this stage, the Gubbio Basin was probably not a self-contained biological unit and would have been very dependent on neighbouring areas not so much for subsistence resources, but to maintain biological viability. The Early Bronze Age is indistinguishable demographically from the Neolithic and, if the level of activity measured by material culture is taken literally, could even have represented a decline.

The Middle Bronze Age represents the start of a new and more vibrant demographic cycle. At first (about 1400 BC) population levels were probably only those of the Neolithic, but during the Later Bronze Age there was a notable surge in demographic levels, by the standards of previous millennia. It is conceivable that five hundred or, seasonally, even a thousand people were concentrated around the central hilltops of the Gubbio Valley. It is noticeable that even in the Late Bronze Age, population levels continued to depend greatly on intermittent contributions from outside the natural territory.

During the early first millennium BC, a new plateau of population was reached that most probably varied only very little until the dramatic effect of incorporation in the Roman political and economic system. It should be noted that the short-lived period of state formation which may have occurred prior to the Roman period, had very little visible effect on population levels. It was the new phenomenon of the Roman town that created a population explosion. It is estimated (section 6.1) that up to 20,000 people were present in the valley, of which 5,000 could have been located in the town.

A decline in the late Antique period, perhaps even to levels approaching those of the first millennium BC was replaced by gradual improvement throughout the early medieval period. Documentary sources reveal fluctuations due to disease, famine and economic recession, not detectable in the *longue durée* of preceding prehistory. By the sixteenth century, a new plateau slightly above the Roman had been reached which lasted almost up to the present day.

8.3 Style

In the Palaeolithic, the Gubbio Valley remained part of a much wider stylistic/technological network of material culture. The surviving repertoire is restricted to simple stone artefacts and is indistinguishable from the rest of central Italy or indeed much of southern Europe.

The diffuse nature of the style networks continued into the Neolithic in spite of the addition of pottery to the surviving record. The excavated site of San Marco is part of a poorly known Italian style group, generally classified as Impressed–Sasso–Fiorano. Within this poor state of knowledge, it is difficult to measure the originality of the stylistic elements. One indication of the isolated nature of the Gubbio Valley is, though, the lack of painted, or even slipped pottery styles which form a major component of other more coastal groups. The Neolithic site of San Marco gives the appearance of a frontier site in a remote valley, connected by only the most infrequent social contact, perhaps demographically determined, with the rest of the Neolithic world. It is possible that the San Marco site of the late sixth millennium is one of the first settlements in the upland zone. One or two millennia later, in the developed Neolithic, polished stone axes of various stones, attest to the more sophisticated stylistic and exchange links of a materially richer society.

In the Bronze Age, Gubbio was fully incorporated into the stylistic networks of central Italy. The scale of these networks was on a very broad scale. The position of Gubbio on the watershed between the east and west coasts of Italy, made it ideally placed to be part of the broad clinal distributions of the period. Through time, a more local stylistic component developed. The supposedly earlier Apennine styles were shared with the whole of central Italy, but variability was perhaps highest in the Marche region of which Gubbio was part. In the sub-Apennine, a similar wide style zone was maintained with contacts even beyond central Italy, although some distinctive handles were most visible from the Marche region. In the Protovillanovan period, a more regional style developed based principally on the area between Monte Cetona and Pianello in the Marche, but these are subtle distinctions, compared with the overriding similarity of styles in all forms of material culture throughout the Italian peninsula.

In the succeeding period of the first millennium BC, there was a continual process of standardisation of material culture and their accompanying styles. However, this process did not lead to a clear demarcation from surrounding areas. A contributing factor was the slow development (section 5.3) of state formation in the area, which retarded the elaboration of local identity in material culture and language (section 5.2). In the early Iron Age, Latial pottery styles appear to be dominant. In the immediately pre-Roman period, there were also almond rims, ultimately of Etruscan derivation. The most famous elements of material culture from this period, presumably of local production, were the Iguvine Tables; yet the medium – bronze – and the style of the lettering, link Gubbio to the rest of central Italy. At the close of the millennium, as Gubbio entered the Roman orbit, standardisation took on new levels of rigour within a much broader range of material culture (Stoddart and Whitehead 1987). Unlike some Etruscan areas, there does not appear to have been any powerful local stylistic tradition. Elsewhere, this can usually be perceived in the local coarsewares of the Roman period.

Knowledge of the late classical period and early medieval period is depressingly scanty. Some early medieval sculpture indicates the presence of contacts. However, similar stylistic patterns re-emerged during the medieval period reaching a new climax in the Renaissance through the manufacture of faïence ceramics. The pottery of Mastro Giorgio is illustrative of this very process and for the first time attached to the hand of a named person. Mastro Giorgio was an individual master of the Renaissance, but very much embedded within the contemporary cultural milieu of Urbino and Deruta (Wilson 1987: 103). Giorgio di Pietro was born in Lombardy about 1465–70 and moved to Gubbio around 1490. By 1498, he had received the citizenship of Gubbio and was exempted taxes. He thus became irrevocably linked to the city of Gubbio. Yet, the products of this famous workshop were linked stylistically to both Deruta to the south and the Marche to the east, in a manner strikingly reminiscent of preceding patterns of material culture.

The Gubbio area was thus never a zone of sharply defined boundaries of material culture. One very brief pre-Roman period of independent state formation, with a greater potential for display in material culture, was quickly interrupted by the cultural uniformity of the Roman Empire. The one exceptional artefact group, the Iguvine Tables, was inextricably linked to external political and cultural forces (section 5.2). The later medieval comune was one of a number of polities competing on roughly equal terms. Stylistic identity can perhaps then for the first time be detected in artists such as Oderisi.

8.4 Politics

The driving forces behind many of the trends outlined above was initially economic and subsequently political. During the Palaeolithic, upland Umbria was a spatial buffer zone occasionally visited by mobile groups lacking any form of central organisation. Later prehistoric groups (from the Neolithic until at least the Apennine Bronze Age) were probably located in a similarly uncentralised environment controlled more by concerns of agricultural and pastoral territory than social ranking and individual advancement. Political independence was the long term trend of this early period, but this was accompanied by a lack of centralised political control.

By the Late Bronze Age the pressure of an expanding population, stronger territorial identity and economic diversity focused spatially on the centre of the valley, created a new political atmosphere. It is in this context that one would expect the growth of aspiring local families and the growth of a local élite. This development, if present, was masked in funerary ritual by the cremation ideology. There were tentative signs of a proto-élite, viewed through burial in the middle of the first millennium, but this development does not appear to have been sustained. A fleeting period, which combined centralisation and political independence may have immediately preceded the Roman take-over. A comparable period was not to recur until the free comune of the Middle Ages.

The Roman take-over was the critical threshold in the development of the valley. From this moment, settlement hierarchy and clearly defined political boundaries became constant. Under external political control for the majority of this period, Gubbio nevertheless managed to retain a degree of local political identity. This well-defined region survives today as one of the largest communal territories in the local administration of the Italian peninsula.

8.5 The ritual landscape

The most distinctive feature of the Gubbio Valley is the florescence of ritual activity in the first millennium BC which continued into the Roman period. Even without

the Iguvine Tables, ritual provides a distinctive attribute of this upland valley. Ritualisation was part of a profound cycle of historical development, consciously recalled by the present-day *feste* of the modern town.

By contrast, the early development of the valley is marked by an absence of demarcated ritual. Ritual activity cannot be separated from domestic activity. Whole Neolithic vessels may have been deliberately placed in the ditch of the settlement of San Marco, but they do not represent any elaborate ritual performance. The upland settlements of the Bronze Age on Monte Ingino, Monte Ansciano and nearby were primarily domestic, even if it is difficult to separate the patterns of periodic consumption completely from the ritual sphere.

In the middle of the first millennium BC, the valley took on a new ritualised appearance. Domestic activity was restricted primarily to the nucleated settlement of Gubbio. The upland landscape was covered with simple ritual sites, many of which re-occupied Bronze Age settlements. Ritual was pervasive but low key, requiring little investment of manpower or resources. Only on the eve, or at the very moment, of Romanisation, was an elaborate investment made in bronze: the Iguvine Tables.

The Roman period brought a new phase of ritual activity. This was in part the ritual of monuments, primarily concentrated in the city itself. It was also the ritual of rural life, denoted in the Gubbio landscape by figurines found scattered in the landscape. There was also a lingering use of some of the upland sanctuaries of the late first millennium.

8.6 Achievements and avenues for future research

The research in the Gubbio Valley set out to be interdisciplinary and all-embracing. Environmental work has been carried out in three different national traditions. Surface survey has been combined with selective excavation. The study remains one of few within central Italy that has sought to give balance to all periods within a complete landscape, if with particular areas of selective emphasis. Some achievements are quantifiable. Some figures reflect the neglect elsewhere. The Gubbio Valley has amongst the largest number of radiocarbon dates (23) for one small territory in Italy and 15% of the published radiocarbon dates for archaeological sites from central Italy (Skeates pers. comm.). There is only one other date from the region of Umbria. Other figures indicate the strengths of the evidence. The valley has produced one of the largest prehistoric faunal collections (16,000 identified fragments) from Italy. Other figures demonstrate the physical remoteness and low economic potential of the region. The finds of Greek pottery would excite no art historian. The number of Roman sites would not fire the imagination of an ancient historian. This volume has attempted to identify and quantify the nature of the sample, be it seven unique bronze tablets or 145,000 sherds of Bronze Age pottery.

Inevitably there are, though, avenues for future analysis and further fieldwork. Perhaps three areas for further fieldwork can be briefly defined. Firstly, the alluvial fans spreading out from the limestone escarpment hold great potential for more detailed work. These provide a Neolithic landscape that is preserved substantially intact, in conjunction with good environmental data. Additional excavation and survey would bring great rewards. Secondly, watching briefs on the colluvial deposits of the northern edge of the valley and on construction in the urban centre would, in time, bring greater knowledge of first millennium BC settlement, and elucidate more effectively the character of local state formation. Finally, although the Roman landscape is impoverished by Mediterranean standards, the study of the unusual village clusters would provide knowledge of a class of classical site rarely found in more lowland topography.

8.7 Conclusion

It is appropriate to return to the initial paradox, the elaboration of the Iguvine Tables in a valley that retained a determined prehistory until the medieval period. The problem is solved by treating these bronze tablets as simply another artefact, by providing the archaeological perspective, and demystifying the web of imagination that has been woven around them. The bronze tablets represent a moment of glory, under Roman (Augustan) inspiration, which was a brief episode in the long-term development of the Gubbio Valley. Methodologically, the problem is comparable to that of the early medieval period (Moreland 1992) where the ritual texts of monastic origin have been mystified in a similar manner. By presenting the archaeological framework first, the written script is placed in appropriate perspective. Texts add details, but do not determine the script.

BIBLIOGRAPHY

Adam, A-M. 1984. *Bronzes etrusques et italiques*. Paris, Bibliothèque Nationale – Département des Monnaies, Médailles et Antiques.

Adams, R. McC. 1965. *Land behind Baghdad: a history of settlement on the Diyala Plain*. Chicago, University of Chicago Press.

Alcock, S. E. 1989. Archaeology and imperialism: Roman expansion and the Greek city, *Journal of Mediterranean Archaeology* 2 (1): 87–135.

Alessio, M., Bella, F. and Cortesi, C. 1964. University of Rome carbon–14 dates II. *Radiocarbon*, 6: 77–90.

Alessio, M., Bella, F., Improta, S. *et al.* 1973. University of Rome carbon–14 dates X, *Radiocarbon*, 15: 165–78.

1975. University of Rome carbon–14 dates XIII, *Radiocarbon*, 17, 313–27.

Alessio, M., Allegri, L., Bella, F. *et al.* 1978a. University of Rome carbon–14 dates XV, *Radiocarbon*, 20: 68–78.

1978b. University of Rome carbon–14 dates XVI, *Radiocarbon*, 20: 79–104.

Alessio, M., Allegri, L., Bella, F. *et al.* 1986. ^{14}C datings, geochemical features, faunistic and pollen analyses of the uppermost 10 m core from valle di Castiglione (Rome, Italy), *Geologica Romana*, 25: 287–308.

Allegrucci, F. 1980. *L'Economia agraria dell'Eugubino tra XI secolo e devoluzione dello Stato Roveresco*. University of Urbino, unpublished tesi di laurea.

1982. La Caccia a Gubbio nel XV secolo. *Proposte e ricerche. Rivista di Storia dell'agricoltura e delle società rurali Marchigiane*, 9: 94–102.

Ambrosetti, P., Carboni, M.G., Conti, M.A. *et al.* 1978. Evoluzione paleogeografica e tettonica dei bacini tosco–laziali–abruzzesi nel Pliocene e nel Pleistocene Inferiore, *Memorie della Società Geologica Italiana*, 19: 573–80.

1988. Il Pliocene ed il Pleistocene Inferiore del bacino del Fiume Tevere nell'Umbria meridionale, *Geografia Fisica Dinamica Quaternaria*, 10: 10–33.

Ambrosetti, P., Carraro, F., Deiana, G. and Dramis, F., 1982. Il sollevamento dell'Italia centrale tra il Pleistocene Inferiore ed il Pleistocene Medio. In *Progetto Finalizzato 'Geodinamica', Contributi conclusivi per la realizzazione della Carta Neotettonica d'Italia*, vol. 2. Rome, Consiglio Nazionale delle Ricerche, pp. 219–23.

Ammerman, A. J. and Butler, J. J. 1978. Report on excavations at Monte Leoni: a bronze age settlement in the Parma valley, *Helinium*, 18: 126–66.

Ampolo, C., 1980. Le condizioni materiali della produzione. Agricoltura e paesaggio agrario, *Dialoghi di Archeologia*, 2: 15–46.

Andren, A. 1940. Architectural terracottas from Etrusco-Italic temples, *Acta Instituti Romani Regni Sueciae*, 4°, 6.

Ashby, T. 1927. *The Roman campagna in classical times*. London, Benn.

Aufrecht, S. Th. and Kirchhoff, A. 1849–51. *Die umbrischen Sprachdenkmäler*. Berlin, Dümmler.

Bally, A. W., Burbi, L., Cooper, C. and Ghelardoni, R. 1986. Balanced sections and seismic reflection profiles across the central Apennines, *Memorie della Società Geologica Italiana* 35: 257–310.

Barfield, L. in press. The Bronze Age of northern Italy. In Mathers, C. and Stoddart, S. (eds.), *Development and decline in the Mediterranean Bronze Age*. Sheffield, John Collis Publications.

Barker, G. 1972. The conditions of cultural and economic growth in the Bronze Age of central Italy, *Proceedings of the Prehistoric Society*, 38: 170–208.

1975. Prehistoric territories in central Italy. In Higgs, E. (ed.), *Palaeoeconomy*. Cambridge, Cambridge University Press, pp. 111–75.

1976. Animal husbandry at Narce. In Potter, T. (ed.), *A Faliscan town in south Etruria*. London, British School at Rome, pp. 295–307.

1977. The archaeology of Samnite settlement in Molise, *Antiquity*, 51: 20–4.

1981a. Excavations at Monte Covolo, Villnuova sul Clisi, Brescia (1972-1973): The animal bones, site catchment and discussion of the prehistoric economy, *Annali del Museo di Gavardo*, 13: 41–69.

1981b. *Landscape and society: Prehistoric central Italy*. London, Academic Press.

1983. The Montarrenti survey, 1982, *Archeologia Medievale*, 10: 339.

1985. *Prehistoric farming in Europe*. Cambridge, Cambridge University Press.

1988. Archaeology and the Etruscan countryside, *Antiquity*, 62: 772–85.

1991. Two valleys, one valley: an *Annaliste* perspective. In Bintliff, J. (ed.), *The Annales School and archaeology*. Leicester, Leicester University Press, pp. 34–56.

in preparation. *Mediterranean landscape change: the archaeology and history of the Biferno Valley*.

Barker, G. W. W., Biagi, P., Castelletti, L., Cremaschi, M. and Nisbet, R. 1987. Sussistenza, economia ed ambiente nel neolitico dell'Italia settentrionale. In Atti della XXVI Riunione Scientifica. *Il neolitico in Italia.* Florence, 7–10 November 1985. Florence, Istituto Italiano di Preistoria e Protostoria, pp. 103–18.

Barker, G. and Lloyd, J. (eds.) 1991. *Roman landscapes. Archaeological survey in the Mediterranean region.* (Archaeological Monographs of the British School at Rome, 2) London, British School at Rome.

Barker G. W., Lloyd, J. and Webley, D. 1978. A classical landscape in Molise. *Papers of the British School at Rome,* 46: 35–51.

Barker, G. and Rasmussen, T. 1988. The archaeology of an Etruscan Polis: A preliminary report on the Tuscania project, *Papers of the British School at Rome,* 43: 25–42.

Barker, G. and Stoddart, S. in press. The Bronze Age of central Italy. In Mathers, C. and Stoddart, S. (eds.), *Development and decline in the Mediterranean Bronze Age.* Sheffield, John Collis Publications.

Barker, G. and Symonds, J. 1984. The Montarrenti survey, 1982–3, *Archeologia Medievale* 11: 278–89.

Barnaba, P. F. 1958. Geologia dei Monti di Gubbio, *Bollettino della Società Geologica Italiana,* 77 (3): 39–70.

Barra Incardona, A. 1976. Timmari–La necropoli. In Soprintendenza archeologica della Basilicata. *Il Museo Nazionale Ridola di Matera.* Matera, Edizioni Meta, pp. 94–6.

Barrett, J. C. 1991. Towards an archaeology of ritual. In Garwood, P., Skeates, R. and Toms, J. (eds.), *Sacred and profane: Proceedings of a conference on archaeology, ritual and religion.* Oxford, Oxford University Committee for Archaeology, pp. 1–9.

Batterink, M. *et al.,* 1982. *Landevaluatie en enige traditionele landbouwsystemen in West-Europa en in de tropen.* Landbouw Hogeschool, Wageningen.

Beard, M. and Crawford, M.H. 1985. *Rome in the Late Republic: problems and interpretations.* London, Duckworth.

Bell, M. 1982. The effects of land-use and climate on valley sedimentation. In Harding, A. F. (ed.), *Climatic change in later prehistory.* Edinburgh, Edinburgh University Press, 127–42.

Bellintani, G. F. 1984. (reprinted from 1973). I manufatti enei e la tecnologia del bronzo nella stazione pre-protostorica di Frattesina di Fratta Polesine, *Padusa,* 20 (1–4): 105–28.

Beloch, G. 1898. Le città dell'Italia antica, *Atene e Roma,* 1 (6): 257–78.

Berggren, K. 1984. Un tentativo di spiegare la cultura 'Protovillanoviana'. In Forsberg, S. and Thomasson, B. F. (eds.), San Giovenale. Materiale e problemi. Atti del simposio all'Istituto Svedese di studi classici a Roma. 6 aprile 1983, *Acta Instituti Romani Regni Sueciae,* 4°, 41: 61–4.

Bertolani Marchetti, D., Accorsi, C. A., Pelosio, G. and Raffi, S. 1979. Palynology and stratigraphy of the Plio-Pleistocene sequence of the Stirione River (northern Italy), *Pollen et Spores,* 21: 149–67.

Betzler, P. 1974. *Die Fibeln in Süddeutschland, Österreich und der Schweiz I. (Urnenfelderzeitliche Typen)* (Prähistorische

Bronzefunde, Abteilung XIV, Band 3). Munich, C. H. Beck'sche Verlagsbuchhandlung.

Bianchi Bandinelli, R. 1925. Clusium: richerche archeologiche e topografiche su Chiusi e il suo territorio in età etrusca, *Monumenti Antichi,* 30: 210–578.

Biancofiore, F. and Toti, O. 1973. *Monte Rovello. Testimonianze dei Micenei nel Lazio.* (Incunabula Graeca LIII) Rome, Edizioni dell'Ateneo.

Bietti, A. 1990. The late upper palaeolithic in Italy: an overview, *Journal of World Prehistory,* 4 (1): 95–155.

Bietti Sestieri, A. M. 1973. The metal industry of continental Italy, 13th to the 11th century BC, and its connection with the Aegean, *Proceedings of the Prehistoric Society,* 39: 383–424.

1975–80. Lo scavo dell'abitato protostorico di Frattesina di Fratta Polesine (Rovigo), *Bullettino di Paletnologia,* n.s. 24 (82): 221–56.

1976. Contributo allo studio delle forme di scambio della tarda età del bronzo nell'Italia continentale, *Dialoghi d'Archeologia,* 9–10 (1–2): 201–41.

1981. Economy and society in Italy between the Late Bronze Age and early Iron Age. In Barker, G. and Hodges, R. (eds.), *Archaeology and Italian society. Prehistoric, Roman and medieval studies.* (Papers in Italian archaeology, II) (BAR International Series, 102) Oxford, British Archaeological Reports, pp. 133–55.

1984a. Central and southern Italy in the Late Bronze Age. In Hackens, N. T. and Holloway, R. R. (eds.), *Crossroads of the Mediterranean. Papers delivered at the Haffenreffer Museum of Anthropology, Brown University, May 8–10, 1981.* (Archeologia Translantica, II – Publications d'histoire de l'art et d'archéologie de l'université catholique de Louvain, 38) Providence, Brown University, pp. 55–122.

1984b. (reprint from 1975) Elementi per lo studio dell'abitato protostorico di Frattesina di Fratta Polesine (Rovigo), *Padusa,* 20, (1–4): 209–22.

Bintliff, J. (ed.), 1991. *The Annales School and archaeology.* Leicester, Leicester University Press.

Biondi, E. 1982. Analisi e storia dell'ambiente. In *La città della carta. Ambiente, società e cultura nella storia di Fabriano.* Comune di Fabriano, Arte Grafiche Iesine, pp. 21–116.

Biondi, E., Allegrezza, M. and Taffetani, F. 1990. Carta della vegetazione del Bacino di Gubbio, *Webbia. Raccolta di scritti botanici. Rivista internazionale di sistematica e fitogeografia,* 44 (2): 197–216.

Blanton, R. E., Kowaleski, S., Feinman, G. and Appel, J. 1982. Monte Alban's hinterland: Part 1. The central and southern parts of the valley of Oaxaca. *Memoir of the Museum of Anthropology, The University of Michigan,* 15.

Blumenthal, A. 1931. *Die Iguvinische Tafeln.* Stuttgart.

Boccaletti, M., Calamita, F., Centamore, E., Deiana, G. and Dramis, F. 1983. The Umbria-Marche Apennines: an example of thrust and wrenching tectonics in a model of ensialic Neogenic–Quaternary deformation, *Bollettino della Società Geologica Italiana,* 102 (4): 581–92.

Boccaletti, M., Calamita, F., Centamore, E. *et al.* 1986. Evoluzione dell'appennino tosco-umbro-marchigiano durante il Neogene, *Giornale di Geologia*, 48 (1–2): 227–33.

Bocci Pacini, P. 1975. Appunti su Arezzo arcaica, *Studi Etruschi*, 43: 47–70.

Boerma, 1986. Internal Report. Geografisch instituut, University of Utrecht.

Bonanno, A., Gouder, T., Malone, C. and Stoddart, S. 1990. Monuments in an island society: the Maltese context, *World Archaeology*, 22 (2): 190–205.

Bonatti, E. 1963. Stratigrafia pollinica dei sedimenti postglaciali di Baccano, lago craterico del Lazio, *Atti della società Toscana di Scienze Naturali*, Ser. A. 70: 40–8.

1966. North Mediterranean climate during the last Wurm glaciation, *Nature*, 209: 984–5.

1970. Pollen sequence in the lake sediments. In G. E. Hutchinson (ed.), Ianula. An account of the history and development of the Lago di Monterosi, Latium, Italy, *Transactions of the American Philosophical Society*, 60 (4): 26–31.

Bonomi Ponzi, L. 1970. Il ripostiglio di Contigliano, *Bullettino di Paletnologia Italiana*, 79: 95–156.

1985a. Topographic survey of the Colfiorito di Foligno plateau: a contribution towards the study of the population in the territory of the Plestini. In Malone, C. and Stoddart, S. (eds.), *Papers in Italian archaeology IV. The Cambridge conference. Part 1: The human landscape.* (BAR International Series, 243). Oxford, British Archaeological Reports, pp. 201–38.

1985b. Il territorio di Nocera in età protostorica. In Menichelli, A. M. and Rossi, N. (eds.), *Il territorio nocerino tra protostoria e altomedioevo.* Florence, Centro Di, pp. 26–33.

1990. Gubbio: loc. Fontevole. Kline di bronzo. In Corbucci, M. P. and Pettine, S. (eds.), *Antichità dall'Umbria a Leningrado.* Perugia, Electa Editori Umbri, pp. 297–323.

1991a. Gli Umbri: territorio, cultura e società. In Corbucci, M. P. and Pettine, S. (eds.), *Antichità dall'Umbria a New York.* Perugia, Electa Editori Umbri, pp. 51–61.

1991b. Tombe principesche dell'altipiano plestino. In Corbucci, M. P. and Pettine, S. (eds.), *Antichità dall'Umbria a New York.* Perugia, Electa Editori Umbri, pp. 143–70.

Bordes, F. 1961. Typologie du Paléolithique Ancien et Moyen, *Publications de l'Institut de Préhistoire de l'Université de Bordeaux, Memoire 1.*

Borman, E. 1901. *Corpus Inscriptionum Latinarum*, vol. XI, 2, 1. Berlin, George Reimer.

Bos, R. G. H. and Sevink, J. 1975. Introduction of gradational and geomorphic features in descriptions of soils, *Journal of Soil Science*, 26 (3): 223–33.

Bottema, S. 1975. The interpretation of pollen spectra from prehistoric settlements (with special attention to Luguliflorae), *Paleohistoria*, 17: 17–35.

Bottiglioni, G. 1954. *Manuale dei Dialetti Italici, Osco, Umbro, e dialetti minori; grammatica, testi, glossario con note etimologiche.* Bologna, Università di Bologna.

Bower, H. M. 1897. *The elevation and procession of the Ceri at Gubbio. An account of the ceremonies together with some suggestions as to their origin and an appendix consisting of the Iguvine lustration in English.* London, David Nutt-Folk-Lore Society.

Bradley, R. 1984. *The social foundations of prehistoric Britain. Themes and variations in the archaeology of power.* London, Longman.

1987. Time regained: the creation of continuity, *Journal of the British Archaeological Association*, 140; 1–17.

1990. *The passage of arms. An archaeological analysis of prehistoric hoards and votive deposits.* Cambridge, Cambridge University Press.

Braudel, F. 1972. *The Mediterranean in the age of Philip II.* London, Collins.

Bréal, M. 1875. *Les tables eugubines.* Paris.

Brusadin Laplace, D. 1984–7. Le necropoli protostoriche del Sasso di Furbara. Il Montorgano ed altri sepolcreti protovillanoviani, *Origini*, 13: 341–408.

Bruschetti, P. 1988. Magione (Perugia), *Studi Etruschi*, 54: 383–6.

1989. Il santuario di Pasticcetto di Magione e i votivi in bronzo. In Corbucci, M. P. and Pettine, S. (eds.), *Antichità dall'Umbria a Budapest e Cracovia.* Perugia, Electa Editori Umbri, pp. 113–22.

Büchler, F. 1883. *Umbrica.* Bonn.

Buck, C.D. 1979. *A Grammar of Oscan and Umbrian.* Hildesheim-New York, Georg Olms Verlag.

Bynon, T. 1977. *Historical Linguistics.* Cambridge, Cambridge University Press.

Calamita, F., Coltorti, M., Deiana, G., Dramis, F. and Pambianchi, G. 1982. Neotectonic evolution and geomorphology of the Cascia and Norcia depressions (Umbria-Marche Apennine), *Geografia Fisica Dinamica Quaternaria*, 5: 263–76.

Calamita, F. and Deiana, G. 1988. The arcuate shape of the Umbria-Marche-Sabina Apennines (central Italy), *Tectonophysics*, 146: 139–47.

Calderoni, G., Coltorti, M., Consoli, M. *et al.* 1989. Degradazione dei versanti e sedimentazione nei pressi di Borgiano (Appennino Marchigiano) nell'Olocene Recente, *Memorie della Società Geologica Italiana*, 42, 301–10.

Caloi, L. and Palombo, M. R. 1981. Analisi dei resti ossei. In Negroni Catacchio, N. (ed.), *Sorgenti della Nova. Una comunità protostorica e il suo territorio nell'Etruria meridionale.* (Catalogo della mostra). Rome, Consiglio delle Ricerche, 269–77.

1985. La fauna di Monte Rovello (XII–IX sec. a.C.). Origine delle forme domestiche – Elenco del materiale, *Notiziario dell'Associazione archeologica 'Adolfo Klitsche de la Grange' di Allumiere*, 7: 49–82.

Calzoni, U. 1928. I tipi di industria aurignazione nell'Umbria, Archivio per l'Anthropologia e la Etnologia, 58: 153–4.

1933. Cetona. L'abitato preistorico di Belverde sulla montagna di Cetona, *Notizie degli Scavi*, 1933: 45–102.

1936. Resti di un'abitato preistorico a Casa Carletti sulla montagna di Cetona, *Studi Etruschi*, 10: 329–39.

1939. Lo strato superiore delle 'Tane del Diavolo' presso Parrano (Orvieto), *Studi Etruschi*, 12: 225–32.

1954. *Le stazioni preistoriche della montagna di Cetona.*

Belverde I. Premessa. L'ambiente naturale. Topografia e scavi. (Quaderni di Studi Etruschi, 1). Florence, Olschki. 1962. *Le stazioni preistoriche della montagna di Cetona. Belverde II. La Ceramica.* (Quaderni di Studi Etruschi, 2). Florence, Olschki.

Cantalamessa, G., Centamore, E., Chiocchini, U. *et al.*. 1986a. Il Plio-Pleistocene delle Marche. In La geologia delle Marche, *Studi Geologici Camerti*, numero speciale: 61–81. 1986b. Il Miocene delle Marche. In La geologia delle Marche, *Studi Geologici Camerti*, numero speciale: 35–55.

Carancini, G. 1975. *Die Nadeln in Italien. Gli Spilloni nell'italia continentale.* (Prähistorische Bronzefunde, Abteilung XIII, Band 2). Munich, C. H. Beck'sche Verlagsbuchhandlung.

Carancini, G. L., Massetti, S. and Posi, F. 1986. Gli insediamenti perilacustri di età protostorica individuati nell'alveo dell'antico Lacus Velinus: dati e considerazioni. In Atti dell'incontro di Acquasparta 1985. *Gli insediamenti perilacustri dell'età del bronzo e della prima età del ferro: il caso dell'antico Lacus Velinus.* Palazzo Cesi, 15–17 November 1985. Perugia, Istituto di Archeologia, pp. 65–91.

Carancini, G. L., Massetti, S., Posi, F., Curci, P., and Dionisi, P. 1990. Seconda relazione sulle nuove ricerche di superficie eseguite nell'alveo dell'antico Lacus Velinus (TR-RI). In Carancini, G. L. (ed.), *Miscellanea Protostorica* (Archeologia Perusina, 6). Rome, Giorgio Bretschneider Editore, pp. 1–185.

Carandini, A. (ed.), 1985. *Settefinestre. Una villa schiavistica nell'Etruria Romana,* 3 vols. Modena, Panini.

Carandini, A. and Settis, S. 1979. *Schiavi e padroni nell'Etruria Romana.* Bari, De Donato.

Cassano, S. M. and Manfredini, A. 1978. Torrionaccio (Viterbo). Scavo di un abitato protostorico, *Notizie degli Scavi di Antichità*, 32: 1–382.

Catalli, F. 1989. Monetazione preromana in Umbria: le zecche di Tuder ed Iguvium. In Corbucci, M. P. and Pettine, S. (eds.), *Antichità dall'Umbria a Budapest e Cracovia.* Perugia, Electa Editori Umbri, pp. 140–52.

Catarsi Dall'Aglio, M. 1976. La stazione preistorica di Borgo Panigale-Bologna (Scavi 1950–1959). In *Atti della XIX Riunione Scientifica in Emilia e Romagna, 11–14 ottobre, 1975.* Florence, Istituto Italiano di Preistoria e Protostoria, pp. 243–66.

Catastro Bertoli, 1770. [Map of the central Gubbio valley]. Archivio dello Stato, Gubbio.

Cato. *De Agri Cultura.* (Translated 1979 by W. D. Hooper and W. D. Ash), Cambridge, Loeb ed.

Cattani, L. and Renault-Miskovsky, J. 1989. La réponse des végétations aux variations climatiques quaternaires autour des sites archéologiques du sud de la France et du nord-est de l'Italie, *Il Quaternario*, 2 (2): 147–70.

Cattuto, C. 1973. Carta e lineamenti geomorfologici del territorio di confluenza tra il T. Chiascio ed i torrenti Rasina e Saonda, *Geologica Romana*, 12: 105–24.

Cattuto, C. and Cavanna, F. 1971. Studi sulla idrogeologia del bacino del Fiume Chiascio: charattteristiche climatologiche, *Camera di Commercio, Industria, Artigianato e Agricoltura*

Quaderno, 22: 1–40.

Ceccanti, M. 1979. Tipologia delle anse 'ad ascia' dell'età del Bronzo della penisola italiana, *Rivista di Scienze Preistoriche*, 34 (1–2): 137–78.

Cecchelli, C. 1942. **Nota su alcuni resti** barbarici dello scavo di Gubbio, *Notizie degli Scavi alle Antichità* 68 (3): 359–67.

Celuzza, M. and Regoli, E. 1982. La valle d'Oro nel territorio di Cosa, *Dialoghi di Archeologia*, 4: 31–62.

Cencetti, C. 1990. Il Villafranchiano della 'riva umbra' del F. Tevere: elementi di geomorfologia e di neotettonica, *Bollettino della Società Geologica Italiana*, 109: 337–50.

Cenci, P. 1915. *Carte e diplomi di Gubbio dall'anno '900 al 1200.* Perugia, Unione Tipografica Cooperativa.

Cenciaioli, L. 1990. Perugia: l'insediamento protovillanoviano di Via Settevalli. In Corbucci, M. P. and Pettine, S. (eds.), *Antichità dall'Umbria a Leningrado.* Perugia, Electa Editori Umbri, pp. 83–92. 1991. Il santuario di Monte Acuto di Umbertide. In Corbucci, M. P. and Pettine, S. (eds.), *Antichità dall'Umbria a New York.* Perugia, Electa Editori Umbri, pp. 211–26.

Centamore, E., Chiocchini, M., Chiocchini, U. *et al.* 1979. *Note illustrative del foglio 301 Fabriano alla scala 1:50.000.* Rome, Servizio Geologico d'Italia.

Cherubini, G. 1984. Paesaggio agrario, insediamenti e attività silvo-pastorali sull montagna tosco-romagnola alla fine del medievo. In Anselmi, S. (ed.), *La montagna fra Toscana e Marche.* Milan, pp. 58–92.

Cherry, J. F. 1986. Polities and palaces: some problems in Minoan state formation. In Renfrew, C. and Cherry, J.F. (eds), *Peer polity interaction and socio-political change.* Cambridge, Cambridge University Press, pp. 19–45.

Chiesa, S., Chiocchini, M., Cremaschi, M., Ferraris, M., Floris, E. and Prosperi, L. 1988. Loess sedimentation and quaternary deposits in the Marche province. In Cremaschi, M. (ed), The Loess in northern and central Italy; a loess basin between the Alps and the Mediterranean region, *Quaderni Geodinamica Alpina e Quaternaria*, 1: 103–30.

Chisholm, M. 1962. *Rural settlement and land use.* London, Hutchinson.

Ciccacci, S., D'Alessandro, L., Dramis, F., Fredi, P. and Pambianchi, G. 1985. Geomorphological evolution and neotectonic evolution of the Umbria-Marche ridge, northern sector, *Studi Geologici Camerti*, 10: 7–15

Cipollone, M. 1988. Gubbio (Perugia). Officina ceramica di età imperiale in loc. Vittorina. Campagna di Scavo 1983, *Notizie degli Scavi*, 8 (38–9): 95–167.

Cipolloni, M. 1971. Insediamento protovillanoviano sulla vetta del Monte Cetona, *Origini*, 5: 149–91.

Cocchi Genick, D., Damiani, I., Macchiarola, I., Peroni, R., Poggiani Keller, R. and Vigliardi, A. 1991–2. L'Italia centro-meridionale. In Atti del Congresso L'età del bronzo in Italia nei secoli dal XVI al XIV a.C. Viareggio 26–30 ottobre, 1989, *Rassegna di Archeologia*, 10: 69–103.

Colasanti, A. 1925. *Gubbio.* Bergamo, Istituto Italiano d'Arti Grafiche.

Coles, G. M., Gilbertson, D. D. and Hunt, C. O. 1984. Soil

erosion and soil genesis in the Tuscan landscape: 1. morphological sequences of carbonate induration in slope deposits, *Archeologia Medievale*, 11: 289–95.

Coli, U. 1958. *Il Diritto Pubblico degli Umbri e le Tavole Eugubine*. Milan, Giuffre.

— 1964. L'organizzazione politica dell'Umbria preromana. In Problemi di storia e archeologia dell'Umbria. *Atti del primo convegno di Studi Umbri, 26–31 maggio, 1963*. Gubbio, Centro di Studi Umbri presso la Casa di Sant'Ubaldo in Gubbio, pp. 133–59.

Colini, G. A. 1914a. Necropoli del Pianello presso Genga (Ancona) e l'origine della civiltà del ferro in Italia, *Bullettino di Paletnologia italiana*, 39: 19–68.

— 1914b. Necropoli del Pianello presso Genga (Ancona) e l'origine della civiltà del ferro in Italia, *Bullettino di Paletnologia italiana*, 40: 121–63.

— 1916. Necropoli del Pianello presso Genga (Ancona) e l'origine della civiltà del ferro in Italia, *Bullettino di Paletnologia italiana*, 41: 48–70.

Collinge, N. E. 1985. *The Laws of Indo-European*. Amsterdam–Philadelphia, Benjamins.

Colonna, G. 1970. *Bronzi votivi umbro-sabellici a figura umana. I. periodo arcaico*. Florence, Sansoni.

— 1988. L'écriture dans l'Italie centrale a l'époque archaique. In *Revue de la société des élèves, anciens élèves et amis de la section des sciences religieuses de l'école Pratique des Hautes Études*, pp. 22–31.

Colonnesi, E. 1973. Le città dell'Umbria (VI Regio) nell'antichita, *Rivista Geografica Italiana*, 130–54.

Coltorti, M., 1981. Lo stato attuale delle conoscenze sul Pleistocene ed il Paleolitico Inferiore e Medio della regione marchigiana. In *Atti del I Convegno di Beni Ambientali e Culturali delle Marche, Numana 8–10 maggio 1981*. Pesaro, Paleane Editori, pp. 63–122.

— 1991. Modificazioni morfologiche oloceniche nelle piane alluvionali: alcuni esempi nei fiumi Misa, Cesano e Musone, *Geografia Fisica Dinamica Quaternaria*, 14 (1): 73–86.

Coltorti, M., and Dal Ri, L. 1985. The human impact on the landscape: some examples of the Adige Valley. In Malone, C. and Stoddart, S. (eds.), *Papers in Italian archaeology IV. The Cambridge Conference. Part 1: The human landscape*. (BAR International Series, 243). Oxford, British Archaeological Reports, pp. 105–34.

Coltorti, M. and Dramis, F. 1987. Sedimentological characteristics of stratified slope-waste deposits in the Umbria-Marche Apennines (central Italy) and their genetic implications. In Godard, A. and Rapp, A. (eds.), *Processus et mesure de l'érosion*. Paris, Centre National de Recherche Scientifique, 145–52.

— 1988. The significance of stratified slope-waste deposits in the Quaternary of Umbria-Marche Apennines, central Italy. *Zeitschrift für Geomorphologie*, 71: 59–70.

Coltorti, M., Dramis, F. and Pambianchi, G. 1983. Stratified slope-waste deposits in the Esino river basin (Umbria-Marche Apennines, central Italy) *Polarfoschung* 53: 59–66.

Coltorti, M. and Galdenzi, S. 1982. Geomorfologia del Complesso Carsico Grotta del Mezzogiorno (4 MA-AN) Frasassi (1 MA-AN) con riferimento ai motivi neotettonici dell'Anticlinale di M. Valmontagnana (Appennino Marchigiano), *Studi Geologici Camerti*, 7: 123–32.

Coltorti, M., Dramis, F., Gentili, B. and Pambianchi, G. 1991. Evoluzione geomorfologica delle piane alluvionali nelle Marche centro-meridionali, *Geografia Fisica Dinamica Quaternaria*, 14(1): 87–100.

Conti, M. A. and Girotti, O. 1977. Il Villafranchiano del Lago Tiberino, ramo sud-occidentale: schema stratigrafico e tettonico, *Geologica Romana*, 16: 67–80.

Conway, R. S. 1897. *The Italic Dialects*. Cambridge, Cambridge University Press.

Corbet, G. B. and Southern, H. N. 1977. *The handbook of British mammals*, 2nd edn. Oxford, Blackwell.

Cornell, T. 1991. The tyranny of the evidence: a discussion of the possible uses of literacy in Etruria and Latium in the archaic age. In Literacy in the Roman World, *Journal of Roman Archaeology, Supplementary series*, 3: 7–33.

Corrado, G. 1984. I boschi del bacino di Gubbio, *Umbria Economica*, 5 (4): 37–55.

Costantini, F. 1970. Ipotesi sulla topografia dell'antica Gubbio, *Atti e Memorie dell'Accademia Toscana di Scienze e Lettere "La Colombaria"* 35: 51–73.

Cremaschi, M., 1977. *Palaeosols and Vetusols in the central Po plain (northern Italy). A study in Quaternary geology and soil development*. Milan, Edizioni Unicopli.

— 1979. Unità litostratigrafiche e pedostratigrafiche nei terreni quaternari pedeappenninici: loess e paleosuoli tra il fiume Taro ed il torrente Sillar, *Geografica Fisicale e Dinamica Quaternaria*, 1: 4–22.

Cruise, G. M. 1991. Environmental change and human impact in the upper mountain zone of the Ligurian Apennines: the last 5000 years. In Maggi, R., Nisbet, R. and Barker, G. (eds.), Atti della Tavola rotonda internazionale. Archeologia della pastorizia nell'Europea meridionale, *Rivista di Studi Liguri*, 57 (1–4): 175–94.

Cuda, M. T. 1990. Il bronzo medio appenninico. In Martini, F. and Sarti, L. (eds.), *La preistoria del Monte Cetona. Materiali e documenti per una guida del Museo Civico per la preistoria del Monte Cetona*. Florence, All'Insegna del Giglio, pp. 165–70.

De Angelis, M. C. 1979. Il bronzo finale in Umbria e Toscana interna. In Atti della XXI Riunione Scientifica. Il bronzo finale in Italia. Florence, 21–23 October, 1977. Florence, Istituto Italiano di Preistoria e Protostoria, pp. 221–47.

— 1990. Casa Carletti. In Martini, F. and Sarti, L. (eds.), *La preistoria del Monte Cetona. Materiali e documenti per una guida del Museo Civico per la preistoria del Monte Cetona*. Florence, All'Insegna del Giglio, pp. 88–90.

De Angelis, M. C. and Manconi, D. 1983. I ritrovamenti archeologici sul Colle S. Elia. In Banca Populare di Spoleto (ed.), *La rocca di Spoleto. Studi per la storia e la rinascita*. Spoleto, Banca Populare di Spoleto, pp. 19–32.

De Angelis d'Ossat, G. 1971. Concezioni e imprese urbanistiche nell'Umbria del trecento. In *Storia e arte in Umbria nell'età comunale.* Atti del VI Convegno di Studi Umbri, Gubbio, 26–30 maggio 1968. Parte Seconda. Perugia, Centro di Studi Umbri – Casa di Sant'Ubaldo, pp. 837–54.

De Feyter, A. J., Koopmann, A., Colenaar, N. and Van Der Ende, C. 1986. Detachment tectonics and sedimentation, Umbro-Marchean Apennines, Italy, *Bollettino Società Geologica Italiana*, 105: 65–85.

De Feyter, A. J. and Menichetti, M., 1986. Backthrusting in forelimbs of rootless anticline with examples from the Umbro-Marchean Apennines, Italy, *Memorie Società Geologica Italiana*, 35: 357–70.

Delano Smith, C. 1992. The Annales for archaeology? *Antiquity*, 66: 539–42.

Delpino, F. and Fugazzola Delpino, M. A. 1979. Il ripostiglio del Rimessone. In Atti della XXI Riunione Scientifica dell'Istituto Italiano di Preistoria e Protostoria. *Il Bronzo Finale*. Florence, Instituto Italiano di Preistoria e Protostoria, pp. 425–52.

Demangeot, J., 1965. *Geomorphologie des Abruzzes adriatiques.* Memoires et Documentations du Centre National Recherche Scientifique. Paris, Centre National de Recherche Scientifique.

De Min, M. 1986. La necropoli protostorica di Frattesina di Fratta Polesine, *Dialoghi di Archeologia*, 4 (2): 277–82.

De Min, M. and Bietti Sestieri, A. M. 1984. I ritrovamenti protostorici di Montagnana: elementi di confronto con l'abitato di Frattesina, *Padusa*, 20 (1–4): 397–411.

de Polignac, F. 1984. *La naissance de la cité grecque.* Paris, Editions de la Découverte.

D'Ercole, V. 1986. Prima campagna di scavo alle 'Paludi di Celano'. In Atti dell'incontro di Acquasparta 1985. *Gli insediamenti perilacustri dell'età del bronzo e della prima età del ferro: il caso dell'antico Lacus Velinus.* Palazzo Cesi, 15–17 novembre 1985. Perugia, Istituto di Archeologia, pp. 317–43.

Desplanques, H. 1969. *Champagnes ombriennes.* Paris, Centre National de Recherche Scientifique.

Devoto, G. 1937. *Tabulae Iguvinae*, 1st edn. Rome.
1940. *Tabulae Iguvinae*, 2nd edn. Rome.
1974. *Le Tavole di Gubbio.* (reprinted and revised from 1948). Florence, Sansoni.

Doorenbos, J. and Kassam, A. H. 1979. *Yield response to water.* (FAO irrigation and drainage paper, 33). Rome, Food and Agriculture Organisation.

Duchaufour, P. 1977. *Pedologie.* Paris, Masson and Cie.
1982. *Pedology.* London, Allen and Unwin.

Dupré Theseider, E. 1971. Il cardinale Albornoz in Umbria. In *Storia e arte in Umbria nell'età comunale.* Atti del VI Convegno di Studi Umbri, Gubbio, 26–30 maggio 1968. Parte Seconda. Perugia, Centro di Studi Umbri – Casa di Sant'Ubaldo, pp. 609–40.

Dury G. H. 1970. *Rivers and river terraces.* Edinburgh, Macmillan.

Dyson, S. L. 1976. Cosa: the utlitarian pottery. *Memoirs of the American Academy at Rome*, 33.
1978. Settlement patterns in the Ager Cosanus: the Wesleyan University Survey, 1974–6, *Journal of Field Archaeology*, 5:

251–68.
1992. *Community and society in Roman Italy.* Baltimore–London, Johns Hopkins University Press.

Elter, P., Giglia, G., Tongiorgi, M. and Trevisan, L. 1975. Tensional and compressional areas in the recent (Tortonian to present) evolution of northern Apennines, *Bollettino di Geofisica Teorica ed Applicata*, 17: 3–19.

Engstrand, L. G. 1965. Stockholm natural radiocarbon measurements VI, *Radiocarbon*, 7, 257–90.
1967. Stockholm natural radiocarbon measurements VII, *Radiocarbon*, 9: 387–438.

Ernout, A. 1961. *Le dialecte ombrien.* Paris, C. Klincksieck.

FAO. 1974. *Soil map of the world.* Paris, Food and Agriculture Organisation.

FAO. 1976. *A framework for land evaluation.* (Soils bulletin, 32). Rome, Food and Agriculture Organisation.

FAO. 1977. *Guidelines for soil profile description.* Rome, Food and Agriculture Organisation.

FAO. 1983. *Guidelines for rainfed agriculture.* (Soils bulletin, 52). Rome, Food and Agriculture Organisation.

Ferrara, G., Fornaca-Rinaldi, G. and Tongiorgi, E. 1961. Carbon–14 dating in Pisa – II, *Radiocarbon*, 3: 99–104.

Feruglio, A. E. 1990. Perugia: le testimonianze di tipo villanoviano. In Corbucci, M. P. and Pettine, S. (eds.), *Antichità dall'Umbria a Leningrado.* Perugia, Electa Editori Umbri, pp. 92–102.

Finke, P. A. and Sewuster, R. J. E. 1987. *A soil survey and land evaluation in a bronze age context for the central Gubbio valley.* Amsterdam, Department for Physical Geography and Soil Science, University of Amsterdam.

Fiocco, C. and Gherardi, G. 1985. Produzione istoriata nella bottega di Maestro Giorgio di Gubbio: un piatto del Maestro del Giudizio di Paride al Museo del Vino di Torgiano, *Faenza*, 71: 297–302.

Flannery, K. V. 1976. *The early Mesoamerican village.* New York, Academic Press.

Flavell, P., Malone, C. A. T. and Stoddart, S. K. F. 1987. Nota preliminare sui nuovi scavi a Monte Ingino – 1983 e 1984. In Meloni, G. (ed.), *La rocca posteriore sul Monte Ingino di Gubbio.* (Campagne di scavo 1975–77). Florence–Perugia, 'La Nuova Italia' Editrice – Regione dell'Umbria, pp. 313–32.

Follieri, M., Magri, D. and Sadori, L. 1988. 250,000-year pollen record from the Valle di Castiglione (Rome), *Pollen et Spores*, 30: 329–56.

Francheschini, G. 1970. *Montefeltro.* Urbino, Dall'Oglio Editore.
1971. Gubbio dal comune alla signoria dei Montefeltro. In *Storia e arte in Umbria nell'età comunale.* Atti del VI Convegno di Studi Umbri, Gubbio, 26–30 maggio 1968. Parte Seconda. Perugia, Centro di Studi Umbri–Casa di Sant'Ubaldo, pp. 363–395.

Frank, A. H. E. 1969. Pollen stratigraphy of the Lake of Vico (central Italy), *Palaeogeography, palaeoclimatology, palaeoecology*, 6: 67–85.

Frank, T. 1914. *Roman Imperialism.* New York, Macmillan.

Fugazzola Delpino, M. A. 1976. *Testimonianze di cultura apenninica nel Lazio.* Florence, Sansoni Editore.

Gaffney, C., Gaffney, V. and Tingle, M. 1985. Settlement, economy or behaviour? Micro-regional land use models and the interpretation of surface artefact patterns. In Haselgrove, C., Millett, M. and Smith, I. (eds.), *Archaeology from the ploughsoil. Studies in the collection and interpretation of field survey data*. University of Sheffield, Department of Archaeology and Prehistory, pp. 95–107.

Gaggiotti, M., Manconi, D., Mercando, L. and Verzar, M. 1980. *Umbria Marche* (Guide archeologiche Laterza). Bari, Laterza.

Galiberti, A. 1982. Il palaeolitico inferiore della Toscana e dell'Umbria. In *Atti della XXIII Riunione Scientifica. Il paleolitico inferiore in Italia*. Florence, Istituto Italiano di Preistoria e Protostoria, pp. 147–63.

Galli, E. 1944–5. Gubbio. Statua marmorea maschile, *Notizie degli Scavi alle Antichità*, 69–70 (5–6): 1–6.

1948. Scoperte di tombe romane e Genestrelle, *Notizie degli Scavi alle Antichità*, 73 (2): 46–56.

Gamble, C. 1982. Animal husbandry, population and urbanisation. In Renfrew, C. and Wagstaff, M. (eds.), *An island polity: The archaeology of exploitation*. Cambridge, Cambridge University Press, pp. 161–71.

Gardiner, J. 1984. Lithic distributions and Neolithic settlement patterns in central southern England. In Bradley, R. and Gardiner, J. (eds.), *Neolithic studies*. (BAR British Series, 113) Oxford, British Archaeological Reports, pp. 15–40.

Garwood, P. 1991. Ritual tradition and the reconstitution of society. In Garwood, P., Skeates, R. and Toms, J. (eds.), *Sacred and profane: Proceedings of a conference on archaeology, ritual and religion*. Oxford, Oxford University Committee for Archaeology, 10–32.

Gejvall, N. G. 1967. Esame del materiale osteologico. In Östenberg, C. E. Luni sul Mignone e problemi della preistoria d'Italia, *Acta Instituti Romani Regni Sueciae*, 4°, 25: 2263–76.

GEMINA. 1963. *Ligniti e torbe dell'Italia continentale*. Turin, ILTE Editori.

Ghelli, G. M. and Bartoli, C. 1760–1769. *Catasto Ghelliano*. Unpublished survey. Gubbio, Archivio Storico.

Gilbertson, D. D. and Hunt, C. O. 1987. An outline and synthesis of the geoarchaeological development of the southern Montagnola Senese, Tuscany, *Archeologia Medievale*, 14, 349–408.

Gimbutas, M. 1970. Proto-Indo-European culture: the Kurgan culture during the fifth, fourth and third millennium BC, Indo-European and Indo-Europeans, 55–97.

1977. The first wave of Eurasian steppe pastoralists into Copper Age Europe, *Journal of Indo-European Studies*, 5 (4): 277–339.

Giovagnoli, E. 1932. *Gubbio nella storia e nell'arte*. Città di Castello, Società Anonima Tipografica 'Leonardo da Vinci'.

Gowlett, J. A. J., Hedges, R. E. M., Law, I. A. and Perry, C. 1987. Radiocarbon dates from the Oxford AMS system: archaeometry datelist 5, *Archaeometry*, 29: 125–55.

Grant, A. 1982. The use of tooth wear as a guide to the age of domestic ungulates. In Wilson, B., Grigson, C. and Payne, S. (eds.), *Ageing and sexing animal bones from archaeological*

sites. (BAR British Series 109). Oxford, British Archaeological Reports, pp. 91–108.

Gregori, L. 1988. Il 'bacino di Bastardo': genesi ed evoluzione nel quadro della tettonica recente, *Bollettino Società Geologica Italiana*, 107: 141–51.

Grifoni Cremonesi, R. 1987. Il neolitico della Toscana e dell'Umbria. In Atti della XXVI Riunione Scientifica. *Il neolitico in Italia*. Florence, 7–10 November 1985. Florence, Istituto Italiano di Preistoria e Protostoria, pp. 229–37.

Gruppo Nazionale di Geografia Fisica e Geomorfologia 1982. Geomorfologia del territorio di Febbio tra il Monte Cusna ed il Fiume Secchia (Appennino Emiliano), *Geografia Fisica Dinamica Quaternaria*, 5: 285–360.

1986. Ricerche geomorfologiche nell'alta val di Peio (Gruppo del Cevedale), *Geografia Fisica Dinamica Quaternaria*, 9: 137–91.

Guzzo, P. G. 1972. *Le fibule in Etruria dal VI al I secolo*. (Studi e materiali di Etruscologia e antichità italiche, 11). Florence, Sansoni Editore.

Harding, J. 1986. In Malone, C. and Stoddart, S. *Provisional report – 1985 season – Gubbio project*. Unpublished report.

Harris, E. C. 1989. *Principles of archaeological stratigraphy*, 2nd edn. New York, Academic Press.

Harris, R. 1980. *The language-makers*. London, Duckworth.

1981. *The language myth*. London, Duckworth.

1986. *The origin of writing*. London, Duckworth.

Harris, W. V. 1971. *Rome in Etruria and Umbria*. Oxford, Clarendon Press.

1989. *Ancient literacy*. Cambridge MA, Harvard University Press.

Havelock, E. A. 1982. The literate revolution in Greece and its consequences. Princeton NJ, Princeton University Press.

Hedges, R. E. M., Housley, R. A., Law, I. A. and Bronk, C. R. 1990. Radiocarbon dates from the Oxford AMS system: archaeometry datelist 10, *Archaeometry*, 32 (1): 101–8.

Higgs, E. S. (ed.), 1975. Palaeoeconomy. Cambridge, Cambridge University Press.

Higgs, E. and Vita-Finzi, C. 1970. Prehistoric economy in the Mount Carmel area of Palestine: Site catchment analysis, *Proceedings of the Prehistoric Society*, 36: 1–37.

Höckmann, U. 1982. *Die Bronzen aus dem Fürstengrab von Castel San Mariano bei Perugia. Staatliche Antikensammlungen München. Katalog der Bronzen*, vol. 1. Munich.

Hodder, I. and Orton, C. 1976. *Spatial analysis in archaeology*. Cambridge, Cambridge University Press.

Hooke, R. LeB. 1967. Processes on arid-region alluvial fans, *Journal of Geology*, 75: 438–60.

Hopkins, K. 1983. *Death and renewal*. (Sociological Studies in Roman History, 2). Cambridge, Cambridge University Press.

1984. *Conquerors and slaves*. Cambridge, Cambridge University Press.

Housley, R. 1986. The plant remains from Gubbio 1984: a preliminary report. In Malone, C. and Stoddart, S. *Provisional report – 1985 season – Gubbio project*. Unpublished report.

Hunt, C. 1988. Environmental studies. In Barker, G. and

Rasmussen, T. (eds.), The archaeology of an Etruscan Polis: a preliminary report on the Tuscania project (1986 and 1987 seasons). *Papers of the British School at Rome*, 56: 34–7.

1992:15,000–7500 BP. Climate and palaeohydrology in the latest Pleistocene and early Holocene in central Italy, *Program and Abstracts of the 8th International Palynological Congress at Aix-en-Provence, 6–12 September, 1992*: 68. *Quaternary Science Reviews.*

in preparation. Environmental work. In Barker, G. (ed.), *Mediterranean landscape change: the archaeology and history of the Biferno Valley.*.

Hunt, C. and Eisner, W. R. 1991. Palynology of the Mezzaluna core. In Voorrips, A., Loving, S. H. and Kamermans, H. (eds.), *The Agro Pontino Survey Project.* (Studies in Praeen Protohistorie, 6). Amsterdam, University of Amsterdam, pp. 49–59.

Hunt, C., Gilbertson, D. D. and Donohue, R. E. 1992. Palaeobiological evidence for late Holocene soil erosion in the Montagnola Senese, Tuscany, Italy. In Bell, M. and Boardman, J. (eds.), *Past and present soil erosion: Archaeological and geographical perspectives.* Oxford, Oxbow Monograph 22, pp. 163–74.

Hunt, C., Malone, C., Sevink, J. and Stoddart, S. 1990. Environment, soils and early agriculture in Apennine central Italy, *World Archaeology*, 22 (1): 34–44.

Irti, U. 1981. Testimonianze dell'età del bronzo ad Ortucchio (Fucino), *Atti della Società Toscana di Scienze Naturali, Memorie, Serie A*, 88: 261–86.

Jankowsky, K. R. 1968. *The neogrammarians.* Washington.

Jashemski, W. F. 1979. *The gardens of Pompeii, Herculaneum and the villas destroyed by Vesuvius.* New York, New Rochelle.

Jongman, W. 1988. *The economy and society of Pompeii.* (Dutch Monographs on Ancient History and Archaeology, 4). Amsterdam, J. C. Gieben.

Jovio, S. 1987. *Sub Ascia: una necropoli romana a Nave.* Modena, Panini.

Kahane, A., Murray-Threipland, L. and Ward-Perkins, J. B. 1968. The Ager Veientanus, north and east of Veii, *Papers of the British School at Rome*, 36, 1–218.

Kassam, A. H., 1979. *Agro-climatic suitability for rainfed crops of winter barley, upland rice, ground nut, sugarcane, banana and oil palm in Africa.* Rome, Food and Agriculture Organisation.

Kelly, M. G. and Huntley, B. 1991. An 11,000-year record of vegetation and environment from Lago di Martignano, Latium, Italy, *Journal of Quaternary Science*, 6: 209–24.

Kent, R. G. 1920. Studies in the Iguvine Tables, *Classical Philology*, 15: 353–69.

1926. *The textual criticism of inscriptions.* Linguistic Society of America, Monograph 2.

Keppie, L. 1983. *Colonisation and veteran settlement in Italy 47–14 BC.* London, British School at Rome.

Kintigh, K. W. 1984. Measuring archaeological diversity by comparison with simulated assemblages, *American Antiquity*, 49: 44–54.

Klein, R. G. and Cruz-Uribe, K. 1984. *The analysis of animal bones from archaeological sites.* (Prehistoric Archeology and Ecology Series). Chicago, University of Chicago Press.

Knapp, A. B. (ed.), 1992. *Archaeology, Annales and ethnohistory.* Cambridge, Cambridge University Press.

Kukla, G. J., 1975. Pleistocene land-sea correlations: I, Europe, *Earth Science Review*, 13: 307–74.

Landolfi, M. 1988. I piceni. In Pugliese Caratelli, G. (ed.), *Italia Omnium terrarum alumna. La civiltà dei Veneti, Reti, Liguri, Celti, Piceni, Umbri, Latini, Campani e Iapigi.* Milan, Libri Scheiwiller, pp. 313–72.

Langdon, M. K. 1976. *A sanctuary of Zeus on Mt Hymettus.* Athens, American School of Classical Studies at Athens.

La Regina, A. 1976. Il Sannio. In Zanker, P. (ed.), *Hellenismus in Mittelitalien. Kolloquium in Göttingen vom 5. bis 9. Juni 1974.* Göttingen, Vandenhoeck and Ruprecht, pp. 219–48.

1980a. Pietrabbondante. In Gastaldi, P. (ed.), *Sannio. Pentri e Frentani dal VI al I sec. A.C.* (Catalogo della Mostra). Rome, De Luca, p. 131.

1980b. Introduzione: Dalle guerre sannitiche alla romanizzazione. In Gastaldi, P. (ed.), *Sannio. Pentri e Frentani dal VI al I sec. A.C.* (Catalogo della Mostra). Rome, De Luca, pp. 29–42.

1989. I Sanniti. In Pugliese Caratelli, G. (ed.), *Italia Omnium terrarum alumna. La civiltà dei Enotri, Choni, Ausoni, Sanniti, Lucani, Brettii, Sicani, Siculi, Elimi.* Milan, Libri Scheiwiller, pp. 299–432.

Leningrad. 1990. *Gens Antiquissima Italiae. Antichità dall'Umbria a Leningrado. Catalogo della mostra.* Perugia, Electa Editori Umbri.

Lepiksaar, J. 1975. Animal remains. In Hellström, P. Luni sul Mignone. The zone of the large Iron Age Building, *Acta Instituti Romani Regni Sueciae*, 4°, 27 (2) (2): 77–84.

Lepsius, R. L. 1833. *De Tabulis Eugubinis.* Bonn.

Ling, R. 1984. The insula of the Menander at Pompeii. Interim Report, *Antiquaries Journal*, 43: 34–57.

1991. *Roman painting.* Cambridge, Cambridge University Press.

Lipparini, T. 1939. I terrazzi fluviali delle Marche, *Giornale di Geologia*, 13: 5–22.

Lloyd, J. 1991. Farming the Highlands: Samnium and Arcadia in the Hellenistic and early Roman Imperial periods. In Barker, G. and Lloyd, J. (eds.), *Roman landscapes. Archaeological survey in the Mediterranean Region.* (Archaeological Monographs of the British School at Rome, 2). London, British School at Rome, pp. 180–93.

Lollini, D. 1956. L'abitato preistorico e protostorico di Ancona. (Nota preliminare), *Bullettino di Paletnologia*, 65: 237–62.

1979. Il bronzo finale nelle Marche, *Rivista di Scienze Preistoriche*, 34 (1–2): 179–215.

Lona, F. and Ricciardi, E. 1961. Studio pollinografico su una serie lacustre pleistocenica dell'Italia centrale (bacino di Gubbio, Perugia), *Pollen et Spores*, 3 (1): 93–100.

Loving, S. and Kammermans, H. 1991. Figures from flint: first analyses of lithic artifacts collected by the Agro Pontino survey. In Voorrips, A., Loving, S. H. and Kammermans,

H. (eds.), *The Agro Pontino survey project. Methods and preliminary results.* (Studies in Prae- en Protohistorie, 6). Amsterdam, University of Amsterdam, pp. 99–116.

Lowe, J. J. and Watson, C. 1992. Lateglacial and early Holocene pollen stratigraphy of the northern Apennines, *Program and Abstracts of the 8th International Palynological Congress at Aix-en-Provence, September 6–12, 1992:* 88.

Macnamara, E. 1976. The smallfinds. 1. The metalwork. In Potter, T. (ed.), *A Faliscan town in south Etruria.* London, British School at Rome, pp. 127–59.

Maggi, R. 1984. Aspetti del popolamento della Ligura orientale nell'età del bronzo: gli insediamenti d'altura. In *Deya Conference of Prehistory.* (BAR International Series, 229) Oxford, British Archaeological Reports, pp. 123–34.

—— (ed.), 1990a. *Archeologia dell'Appennino Ligure. Gli scavi del Castellaro di Uscio: Un insediamento di Crinale occupato dal neolitico alla conquista Romana.* (Collezione di Monografie preistoriche ed archeologiche, 8). Bordighera, Istituto Internazionale di Studi Liguri.

—— 1990b. Datazioni radiometriche. In Maggi, R. (ed.), 1990a. *Archeologia dell'Appennino Ligure. Gli scavi del Castellaro di Uscio: Un insediamento di Crinale occupato dal neolitico alla conquista Romana.* (Collezione di Monografie preistoriche ed archeologiche, 8). Bordighera, Istituto Internazionale di Studi Liguri, pp. 59–61.

Maggi, R. and Nisbet, R. 1990. Prehistoric pastoralism in Liguria. In Maggi, R., Nisbet, R. and Barker, G. (eds.), Atti della Tavola rotonda internazionale. Archeologia della pastorizia nell'Europea meridionale, *Rivista di Studi Liguri,* 56 (1–4): 265–96.

Maggiani, A. 1984. Iscrizioni iguvine e usi grafici nell'Etruria settentrionale. In Prosdocimi, A. L., *Le Tavole Iguvine I.* Florence, Olschki, pp. 217–37.

Mallory, J. P. 1989. *In search of the Indo-Europeans.* London, Thames and Hudson.

Malone, C. and Stoddart, S. 1984. Late Bronze Age settlement nucleation in Umbria, *Antiquity,* 58: 56–8.

—— 1986. The Gubbio project: The study of the formation of an intermontane polity, *Dialoghi di Archeologia,* 2: 201–8.

—— 1992. (With contributions from G. Barker, M. Coltorti, L. Costantini, J. Giorgi, G. Clark, J. Harding, C. Hunt, T. Reynolds and R. Skeates). Survey and excavation of the Neolithic site of San Marco, Gubbio (Perugia), Umbria. 1985–7, *Papers of the British School at Rome,* 60: 1–69.

Malone, C. A. T., Stoddart, S. K. F. and Trump, D. 1988. A house for the temple builders. Recent investigations on Gozo, Malta, *Antiquity,* 62: 297–301.

Manconi, D. 1982–3. Studi su Gubbio Romana, nuovi scavi a via degli Ortacci, *Annali della Facoltà di Lettere e Filosofia dell'Università di Perugia,* 20: 81–3.

—— 1991. Attic red-figured krater. In Corbucci, M. P and Pettine, S. (eds.), *Antichità dall'Umbria a New York.* Perugia, Electa Editori Umbri, pp. 324–28.

Manconi, D., Tomei, M. A. and Verzar, M. 1981. La situazione in Umbria dal III A.C. alla tarda antichità. In Giardina, A. and Schiavone, A. (eds.), *Società romana e produzione schiavistica,* vol. 1. Bari, Laterza, pp. 371–406.

Manconi, D., Venturini, G., Bernardi, M. and Cencaioli, L. 1991. Indagine archeologiche all'interno del Palazzo Ducale di Gubbio (PG). Nuove conoscenze sulla dinamica insediativa medievale e sull'urbanistica del sito, *Archeologia Medievale* 18: 429–76.

Mannoni, T. and Tizzoni, M. 1980. Lo scavo del Castellaro di Zignago (La Spezia), *Rivista di Scienze Preistoriche,* 35: 249–79.

Marabini Moeus, M. T. 1973. The Roman thin-walled pottery from Cosa, *Memoirs of the American Academy at Rome,* 32.

Marchesoni, V. 1959. Storia climatico forestale dell'Appennino umbro marchigiano, *Annali di Botanica,* 25: 459–97.

Martini, F. and Sarti, L. 1990a. S. Maria in Belverde. Scavi: Università di Siena, 1984–1988. In Martini, F. and Sarti, L. (eds.), *La preistoria del Monte Cetona. Materiali e documenti per una guida del Museo Civico per la preistoria del Monte Cetona.* Florence, All'Insegna del Giglio, pp. 92-5.

—— 1990b. Vetta del Monte Cetona. In Martini, F. and Sarti, L. (eds.), *La preistoria del Monte Cetona. Materiali e documenti per una guida del Museo Civico per la preistoria del Monte Cetona.* Florence, All'Insegna del Giglio, pp. 90–2.

—— 1991. Gli insediamenti neo-eneolitici nel territorio di Sesto Fiorentino e Prato. Primi risultati e prospettive di ricerca, *Studi e Materiali. Scienza dell'antichità in Toscana,* 6: 16–29.

Massaro, D. 1941. Di un culto di Marte a Gubbio, *Studi Etruschi,* 15: 391–3.

Matteini Chiari, M. 1979–80. La ricognizione per un'ipotesi di definizione territoriale: il territorio eugubino in età preromana. *Annali della facoltà di Lettere e Filosofia dell'Università di Perugia,* 13(3): 215–21.

Mazzatinti, G. 1931. Mastrogiorgio, *Il Vasari,* 4: 1–16, 105–22.

McVicar, J. and Stoddart, S. K. F. 1986. Computerising an archaeological excavation: the human factors. In *Proceedings of Computer applications in Archaeology Conference 1986.* Birmingham, University of Birmingham, pp. 225–7.

Meiggs, R. 1973. *Roman Ostia,* 2nd edn. Oxford, Clarendon Press.

Meillet, A. 1948. *Esquisse d'une histoire de la langue latine.* Paris.

Mellars, P. 1990. A major 'plateau' in the radiocarbon time-scale at *c.* 9650 b.p.: the evidence from Star Carr (North Yorkshire), *Antiquity,* 64 (245): 836–41.

Meloni, G. (ed.), 1987. *La Rocca posteriore sul Monte Ingino di Gubbio. (Campagne di Scavo 1975–1977).* Florence–Perugia, 'La Nuova Italia' Editrice – Regione dell'Umbria.

Menichetti, M. and Pialli, G. 1986. Geologia strutturale del Preappennino umbro tra i Monti di Gubbio e la catena del Monte Petrano – Monte Cucco, *Memorie della Società Geologica Italiana,* 35: 371–88.

Menichetti, P. L. 1979. *Castelli, palazzi fortificati, fortilizzi, torri di Gubbio dal secolo XI al XIV.* Città di Castello, Rubini e Petruzzi.

—— 1980. *Le Corporazioni delle arti e mestieri medievali di Gubbio.* Città di Castello, Rubini e Petruzzi.

—— 1987. *Storia di Gubbio dalle origini all'Unità d'Italia.* Città di Castello, Petruzzi.

Micalizzi, P. 1988. *Storia dell'architettura e dell'urbanistica di Gubbio.* Rome, Officina Edizioni.

Millet, M. 1991. Pottery population or supply patterns? The

Ager Tarraconensis approach. In Barker, G. and Lloyd, J. (eds.), *Roman landscapes. Archaeological survey in the Mediterranean region.* (Archaeological Monographs of the British School at Rome, 2) London, British School at Rome, pp. 18–26.

Ministero. 1983. Ministero per i beni culterali e ambientali Soprintendenza archeologica per l'Umbria. 1983. *Ville e insediamenti rustici di età Romana in Umbria.* Perugia, Editice Umbra cooperativa.

Mommsen, T. 1903. *Röm Geschichte.* Berlin, Weidmannsche Buchhandlung.

Monacchi, D. 1986. Resti della stipe votiva del Monte Subasio di Assisi (Colle S. Rufino), *Studi Etruschi,* 52: 77–89.

1988. Nota sulla stipe votiva di Grotta Bella (Terni), *Studi Etruschi,* 54: 75–99.

Moreland, J. 1986. Ricognizione nei dintorni di Farfa, 1985. Resoconto preliminare, *Archeologia Medievale,* 13: 333–43.

1987. The Farfa survey: a second interim report, *Archeologia Medievale,* 14: 409–18.

1992. Restoring the dialectic: settlement problems and documents in medieval central Italy. In Knapp, A. B. (ed.), *Archaeology, Annales and ethnohistory.* Cambridge, Cambridge University Press, pp. 112–29.

Moschella, P. 1939. Il teatro di Gubbio, *Dioniso. Bullettino dell'Istituto Nazionale del dramma antico,* 7(1): 13–15.

Müller Karpe, H. 1959. *Beiträge zur Chronologie der Urnenfeldzeit nördlich und südlich der Alpen.* (Römische-Germanische Forschungen, 22) Berlin.

Needham, S. P. and Sørensen, M. L. S. 1988. Runnymede refuse tip: a consideration of midden deposits and their formation. In Barrett, J. C. and Kinnes, I. A. (eds.), *The archaeology of context in the Neolithic and Bronze Age: recent trends.* Sheffield, John Collis Publications, pp. 113–26.

Negroni Catacchio, N. (ed.), 1981. *Sorgenti della Nova. Una comunità protostorica e il suo territorio nell'Etruria meridionale.* (Catalogo della mostra). Rome, Consiglio delle Ricerche.

Neppi Modena, A. 1977. *Cortona etrusca e romana nella storia e nell'arte.* (Accademia Toscana di Scienze e Lettere 'La Columbaria' Studi, 45). Florence, Olschki.

Nilsson T. 1989. *The Pleistocene.* D. Reidel Publishing Company.

Nuti, F. 1964. *Gubbio nell'antichità.* Florence, Tipografia dell'artiginiato.

Östenberg, C. E. 1967. Luni sul Mignone e problemi della preistoria d'Italia, *Acta Instituti Romani Regni Sueciae,* 4°, 25: 1–306.

Paganelli, A. 1956. Analisi pollinica dei depositi torbosi e lacustri del piano di Colfiorito, *Bollettino della società Eustachiana (Camerino),* 49: 79–91.

1958. Cicli forestali del piano montano dell'appennino umbro-marchigiano, *Nuovo giornale di botanica,* 65: 202–13.

Pagliari, V. 1885. *Età della pietra in Gubbio.* Florence.

1890. *Abitazioni avanti roccia e fortilizi preistorici in Italia.* Gubbio, Tipografia Romitelli.

1920. *La cittadella preistorica al M. Calvo presso Gubbio.* Gubbio, Scuola tipografica Oderisi.

Pallottino, M. 1947. *Etruscologia.* Milan, Hoepli.

Pannuti, S. 1969. Gli scavi di Grotta a Male presso L'Aquila, *Bullettino di Paletnologia Italiana,* 78 (20): 147–247.

Partner, P. 1972. *The lands of St Peter. The papal state in the Middle Ages and the early Renaissance.* London, Eyre Methuen.

Patterson, J. D. 1987. Crisis, what crisis? Rural change and urban development in Imperial Apennine Italy, *Papers of the British School at Rome,* 55: 115–46.

Peacock, D. P. S. 1982. *Pottery in the Roman world: an ethnoarchaeological approach.* London, Longman.

Pearson, G. W., Pilcher, J. R., Baille, M. G., Corbett, D. M. and Qua, F. 1986. High precision ^{14}C measurement of Irish oaks to show natural ^{14}C variations from AD 1840 to 5210 BC, *Radiocarbon* 28: 911–34.

Pease, A. S. (ed), 1963. *M. Tulli Ciceronis De Divinatione.* Darmstadt, Wissenschaftliche Buchgesellschaft.

(ed.), 1968. *M. Tulli Ciceronis De Natura Deorum.* Darmstadt, Wissenschaftliche Buchgesellschaft.

Peatfield, A. A. D. 1983. The topography of Minoan peak sanctuaries, *Annual of the British School at Athens,* 78: 273–79.

1990. Minoan peak sanctuaries: History and society, *Opuscula Atheniensia,* 18: 117–31.

Pecsi, M. 1970. *Problems of relief planation.* Budapest, Akadèmiai Kiadò.

Pellegrini, G. 1902. Scavi alla Villa di Fabbrecce, *Notizie degli Scavi di Antichità,* 1902: 479–94.

Perini, I. 1981. Bronzo. In Negroni Catacchio, N. (ed.), *Sorgenti della Nova. Una comunità protostorica e il suo territorio nell'Etruria Meridionale.* Rome, Consiglio Nazionale dell Richerche, pp. 435–7.

Peroni, R. 1960. Per una definizione dell'aspetto culturale 'subapenninico' come fase cronologica a sè stante, *Atti della Accademia Nazionale dei Lincei. Memorie. Classe di Scienze morali, storiche e filologiche,* 9: 1–253.

1963a. Dati di Scavo sul sepolcreto di Pianello di Genga, *Archäologischer Anzeiger,* 3: 361–403.

1963b. Monte Primo, *Inventaria Archeologica,* 3 (I, 7): 1–8.

1963c. Gualdo Tadino, *Inventaria Archeologica,* 3 (I, 6): 1–5.

1969. Per uno studio dell'economia di scambio in Italia nel quadro dell'ambiente culturale dei secoli intorno al mille a.C., *Parola del Passato,* 24: 134–60.

1980. (ed.) *Il bronzo finale in Italia.* (Materiali e Problemi, 1). Bari, De Donato.

Peroni, R., Carancini, G. L., Bergonzi, G., Lo Schiavo, F. and Von Eles, P. 1980. Per una definizione critica di facies locali: nuovi strumenti metodologici. In Peroni, R. (ed.), *Il bronzo finale in Italia.* Bari, De Donato, pp. 9–103.

Petronius. *Satyricon.* (Translated by M. Heseltine) Cambridge, Loeb edn.

Pfiffig, A. J. 1964. *Religio Iguvina. Philologische und Religionsgeschichtliche Studien zu den Tabulae Iguvinae.* (Österreichische Akademie der Wissenschaften Philosophisch Historische Klasse Denkschriften, 84). Vienna, Hermann Böhlaus Nachf.

Phillips, P. 1975. *Early farmers of West Mediterranean Europe.* London, Hutchinson.

Pisani, V. 1964. *Le lingue dell'Italia antica oltre il latino.* Turin,

Rosenberg and Sellier.

Placidi, C. 1978. Fauna. In Cassano, S. M. and Manfredini, A. Torrionaccio (Viterbo). Scavo di un abitato protostorico, *Notizie degli Scavi di Antichità*, 32: 270.

Poggiani Keller, R. and Figura, P. 1979. I tumuli e l'abitato di Crostoletto di Lamone (Prov. di Viterbo): nuovi risultati e precisazioni. In Atti della XXI Riunione Scientifica dell'Istituto Italiano di Preistoria e Protostoria. *Il bronzo finale*. Florence, 21–23 October 1977. Florence, Istituto Italiano di Preistoria e Protostoria, pp. 346–81.

Polizzi, S. 1908. L'epigrafe dell'antico theatro di Gubbio, *Rivista di Storia Antica*, 12 (1–2): 3–8.

Potter, T. 1979. *The changing landscape of south Etruria*. London, Paul Elek.

   1987. *Roman Italy*. London, British Museum Publications.

Poultney, J. W. 1959. *The bronze tables of Iguvium*. Baltimore, MD, American Philological Association.

Propertius. (Translated by H. E. Butler) Cambridge, Loeb edn.

Prosdocimi, A. L. 1978a. *Le Tavole di Gubbio*. Padua, Istituto di Glottologia. (Reprinted from Prosdocimi, A. L. 1978. L'Umbro. In Prosdocimi, A. L. (ed.), *Lingue e dialetti dell'Italia antica*. Rome, Biblioteca di Storia Patria.)

   1978b. L'Osco. In Prosdocimi, A.L. (ed.), *Lingue e dialetti dell'Italia antica*. Rome, Biblioteca di Storia Patria.

   1984. *Le Tavole Iguvine I*. Florence, Olschki.

Puglisi, S. M. 1956. Gli scavi nella Grotta del Mezzogiorno, *Bullettino di Paletnologia*, 65: 499–521.

   1959a. *La civiltà appenninica. Origine delle comunità pastorali in Italia*. Florence, Sansoni.

   1959b. La civiltà del Piceno dalla preistoria alla protostoria alla luce delle più recenti scoperte. In *Atti del primo convegno di Studi Etruschi*. Florence, Olschki, pp. 29–44.

Pulgram, E. 1978. *Italic, Latin, Italian*. Heidelberg, Winter.

Purseglove, J. W. 1972. *Tropical crops – Monocycletons*. London, Longman.

Raaflaub, K. A. (ed.), 1986. *Social struggles in Archaic Rome: new perspectives on the conflict of the orders*. California, University of California Press.

Radi, G. 1986. Le ricerche nel Fucino: notizie preliminari sull'insediamento di Trasacco. In Atti dell'incontro di Acquasparta 1985. *Gli insediamenti perilacustri dell'et del bronzo e della prima et del ferro: il caso dell'antico Lacus Velinus*. Palazzo Cesi, 15–17 novembre 1985. Perugia, Istituto di Archeologia, pp. 301–16.

Radmilli, A. M. 1977. *Storia dell'Abruzzo dalle origini all'età del bronzo*. Pisa, Giardini Editori.

Raffy, J. 1982. Orogènes et dislocation quaternaires du versant tyrrhénien des Abruzzes (Italie centrale), *Revue Geologie Dynamique Geographie Physique*, 23 (1): 55–72.

Ranghiasci Brancaleoni, F. 1857. *Giorgio da Gubbio e di alcuni suoi lavori in maiolica*. Pesaro, Nobili, A.

Reading, H. G. (ed), 1978. *Sedimentary environments and facies*. Oxford, Blackwell.

Reece, R. 1984. The use of Roman coinage, *Oxford Journal of Archaeology*, 3: 197–210.

Regione Umbria. 1956. *Riprese aerostereoscopiche bianche-nere*,

648, 650, 652, 654. Perugia.

   1976. *Riprese aerostereoscopiche colori*. 646–660, 686–692, 751–758, 793–796, 896–905, 1741–1747, 1750–1752, 1758–1768, 2044–2054, 2107–2110, 2112–2114, 4946–4949, 4980–4986. Perugia.

   1977 (revised edition). *Carta topografica regionale*. Sheets 123–V and 116–III. Perugia.

   1983. *Ortofotocarte*. Sheet numbers 300-30, 300-70, 300-80. Perugia.

Rellini, U. 1931. Le stazioni enee delle Marche di fase seriore e la civiltà italiana, *Monumenti Antichi*, 34: 129–280.

Renfrew, A. C. 1973. Monuments, mobilisation and social organisation in neolithic Wessex. In Renfrew, A. C. (ed.), *The explanation of culture change: models in prehistory. Proceedings of a meeting of the Research Seminar in Archaeology and Related Subjects held at the University of Sheffield*. London, Duckworth, pp. 539–58.

   1985. Towards a framework for the archaeology of cult practice. In Renfrew, A. C. (ed.), *The archaeology of cult. The sanctuary of Phylakopi*. (British School of Athens Supplement, 18). London, Thames and Hudson, pp. 11–26.

   1987. *Archaeology and language*. London, Jonathan Cape.

Renfrew, J. M. 1973. *Palaeoethobotany. The prehistoric food plants of the near East and Europe*. London, Duckworth.

Reposati, R. 1772. *Della Zecca di Gubbio e geste dei Duchi d'Urbino*. Bologna, Lelio della Volpe.

Reynolds, P. J. 1979. *Iron Age farm. The Butser experiment*. London, British Museum Publications.

   1981. Deadstock and livestock. In Mercer, R. (ed.), *Farming practice in British prehistory*. Edinburgh, Edinburgh University Press, pp. 97–122.

Riccardi, R., 1966. *Memoria illustrativa della carta della utilizzazione del suolo dell' Umbria*. Rome, Consiglio nazionale delle ricerche.

Robinson, S. W. 1988. Calibration algorithm. Unpublished computer program.

Roncalli, F. 1988. Gli Umbri. In Pugliese Caratelli, G. (ed.), *Italia Omnium terrarum alumna. La civiltà dei Veneti, Reti, Liguri, Celti, Piceni, Umbri, Latini, Campani e Iapigi*. Milan, Libri Scheiwiller, pp. 373–407.

   1991. I bronzetti umbri. In Corbucci, M. P. and Pettine, S. (eds.), *Antichità dall'Umbria a New York*. Perugia, Electa Editori Umbri, p. 187.

Rossi, D. 1980. Una ciotola protovillanoviana dall'abitato di Sorgenti della Nova. In Peroni, R. (ed.), *Il bronzo finale in Italia*. Bari, De Donato.

Russell, J. C. 1977. The population and mortality at Pompeii, *Bulletin of the International Committee on Urgent Anthropological and Ethnological Research*, 19: 107–14.

Säflund, G. 1939. Le terramare delle provincie di Modena, Reggio Emilia, Parma, Piacenza, *Acta Instituti Romani Regni Sueciae*, 7: 7–265.

Salmon, E. T. 1967. *Samnium and the Samnites*. Cambridge, Cambridge University Press.

Salzani, L. 1984 (reprint from 1973). Insediamento protoveneto di Mariconda (Melara–Rovigo), *Padusa*, 20 (1–4), 167–201.

Sanders, W. T., Parsons, J. and Santley, R. 1979. *The basin of Mexico: cultural ecology of a civilisation.* New York, Academic Press.

Sarti, L. 1990. Il territorio del Monte Cetona nell'età del bronzo. In Martini, F. and Sarti, L. (eds.), *La preistoria del Monte Cetona. Materiali e documenti per una guida del Museo Civico per la preistoria del Monte Cetona.* Florence, All'Insegna del Giglio, pp. 47–57.

Scarpignato, M. 1989. La stipe votiva di Bettona. In Corbucci, M. P. and Pettine, S. (eds.), *Antichità dall'Umbria a Budapest e Cracovia.* Perugia, Electa Editori Umbri, pp. 124–33.

Schomaker, M., and van Waveren, E. 1984. *A physiographic soil map of the Gubbio Basin, Umbria, Italy, scale 1:50,000.* Amsterdam, Department for Physical Geography and Soil Science, University of Amsterdam. Unpublished report.

Schulze, W. 1904. *Geschichte Lateinischer Eigennamen.* Berlin, Weidmannsche Buchhandlung.

Scullard, H. H. 1981. *Festivals and ceremonies of the Roman Republic.* London, Thames and Hudson.

Sear, F. 1982. *Roman Architecture.* London, Batsford.

Segre, A. G. 1990. Bacino quaternario di Rieti – Piediluco. In Carandini, G. (ed.), *Miscellanea protostorica.* (Archeologia Perusina 6). Rome, Giorgio Bretschneider Editore, pp. 177–83.

Sensi, L. 1985. *Itinerari Etruschi. 3. Umbria.* Milan, Gruppo Editoriale Electa.

Servizio Geologico d'Italia. 1952. *Carta geologica d'Italia. Foglio 116 'Gubbio' a scala 1:100.000.*

Sevink, J. 1985. Physiographic soil surveys and archaeology. In Malone, C. and Stoddart, S. (eds.) *Papers in Italian Archaeology IV. The Cambridge Conference. Part 1: The human landscape.* (BAR International series, 243), Oxford, British Archaeological Reports, pp. 41–52.

Sevink, J., Remmelzwaal, A. and Spaargaren, O. C. 1984. *The soils of southern Lazio and adjacent Campania.* Publicaties van het Fysisch Geografisch en Bodemkundig Laboratorium (38). Amsterdam, University of Amsterdam.

Sherwin-White, D. N. 1966. *The letters of Pliny: a historical and social connection.* Oxford, Clarendon Press.

Silver, I. 1969. (second edition) The ageing of domestic animals. In Brothwell, D. and Higgs, E. (eds.), *Science in Archaeology,* 2nd edn. London, Thames and Hudson, pp. 283–302.

Snodgrass, A. M. 1980. *Archaic Greece: The age of experiment.* London, Dent.

Sollevanti, F. 1972. Le cavità dei preappennini ed egli Appennini intorno alla zona di Gubbio, *Rassegna Speleologica Italiana,* 4 (2): 165–98.

Sorrentino, C. 1981. La Fauna. In Berggren, E. and Berggren, K. San Giovenale. Excavations in Area B. 1957–60, *Acta Instituti Romani Regni Sueciae,* 4°, 26 (2) (2): 58–64.

Spivey, N. and Stoddart, S. 1990. *Etruscan Italy.* London, Batsford.

Stefani, E. 1942. Scoperte varie di antichit dentro l'abitato e nell sue immediate vicinanze, *Notizie degli Scavi alle Antichità* 68 (3): 335–59.

Stoddart, S. K. F. 1979–80. Un periodo oscuro nel Casentino: la

validità del evidenza negativa? *Atti e Memorie dell'Accademia Petrarca di Lettere, Arti e Scienze,* 63, 197–232.

1987. *Complex polity formation in N. Etruria and Umbria. 1200–500 BC.* Cambridge University, unpublished PhD dissertation.

1990. The political landscape of Etruria, *The Journal of the Accordia Research Centre,* 1, 39–51.

in press. *Power and place in Etruria. The spatial dynamics of a Mediterranean civilisation.* Cambridge, Cambridge University Press.

Stoddart, S. K. F. and Whitehead, N. 1987. La ceramica del territorio di Gubbio prima di Mastro Giorgio, *Gubbio Arte,* 1987: 10–12.

1991. Cleaning the Iguvine stables: site and off-site analysis from a central Mediterranean perspective. In Schofield, J. (ed.), *The interpretation of artefact scatters.* Oxford, Oxbow, pp. 141–48.

Stoddart, S. K. F. and Whitley, J. 1988a. The social context of literacy in Archaic Greece and Etruria, *Antiquity,* 62 (237): 761–72.

1988b. 20. Gubbio, loc. Monte Ansciano (Perugia). *Studi Etruschi,* 65: 379–82.

Stopponi, S. 1991. Orvieto e Perugia etrusche. In Corbucci, M. P. and Pettine, S. (eds.), *Antichità dall'Umbria a New York.* Perugia, Electa Editori Umbri, pp. 75–84.

Street, B. V. 1984. *Literacy in theory and practice.* Cambridge, Cambridge University Press.

Stuiver, M. and Reimer, P. 1986. A computer program for radiocarbon age calibration, *Radiocarbon,* 28: 1022–30.

Szilágyi, J. G. 1989. Undici bronzetti schematici umbro-meridionali. In Corbucci, M. P. and Pettine, S. (eds.), *Antichità dall'Umbria a Budapest e Cracovia.* Perugia, Electa Editori Umbri, pp. 183–6.

Torelli, M. 1985. *L'arte degli Etruschi.* Bari, Laterza.

Trotta, A. 1990. Cortona: i rinvenimenti di Via Vagnotti. In Corbucci, M. P. and Pettine, S. (eds.), *Antichità dall'Umbria a Leningrado.* Perugia, Electa Editori Umbri, pp. 103–12.

Ugolini, F. 1859. *Storia dei conti e duchi d'Urbino.* Florence, Grazzini and Giannini.

Varro. *Rerum Rusticarum.* (Translated 1979 by W. D. Hooper, and W. D. Ash.) Cambridge, Loeb edn.

Verhoeven, A. A. A. 1991. Visibility factors affecting artifact recovery in the Agro Pontino Survey. In Voorrips, A., Loving, S. H. and Kammermans, H. (eds.), *The Agro Pontino survey project. Methods and preliminary results.* (Studies in Prae- en Protohistorie, 6). Amsterdam, University of Amsterdam, pp. 79–97.

Vetter, E. 1953. *Handbuch der italischen Dialekte.* Heidelberg, Winter.

Villa, G. M. 1942. Nuove ricerche sui terrazzi fluviali delle Marche, *Giornale di Geologia,* 16: 5–75.

Vink, A. P. A., 1975. *Land use in advancing agriculture.* Berlin–New York, Springer Verlag.

1983. *Landscape ecology and land use.* London, Longman.

Vita-Finzi, C. 1978. *Archaeological sites in their setting. Ancient peoples and places.* London, Thames and Hudson.

Viviani, G. C. 1967. Alcune cavità nei monti di Gubbio (Perugia), *Rassegna Speleologica Italiana*, 19 (2): 1–8.

Von Blumenthal, A. 1931. *Die iguvinischen Tafeln*. Stuttgart.

Von Eles Masi, P. 1986. *Le fibule dell'Italia settentrionale*. (Prähistoriche Bronzefunde, Abteilung XIV, Band 5). Munich, C. H. Beck'sche Verlagsbuchhandlung.

Von Falke, O. 1934. Der Majolikmaler Jacopo von Caffaggiolo, *Pantheon* 12: 111–16.

Von Planta, R. 1892–7. *Grammatik der oskisch-umbrischen Dialekte*. Strassburg, Trübner.

Wagner, C. 1990. Prehistoric pottery production. In Maggi, R. (ed.), *Archeologia dell'Appennino ligure. Gli scavi del Castellaro di Uscio: Un insediamento di Crinale occupato dal neolitico alla conquista Romana*. (Collezione di Monografie preistoriche ed archeologiche, 8). Bordighera, Istituto Internazionale di Studi Liguri, pp. 245–8.

Ward-Perkins, B., Mills, N., Gadd, D. and Delano-Smith, C. 1986. Luni and the Ager Lunensis: the rise and fall of a Roman town and its territory, *Papers of the British School at Rome* 54: 81–146.

Watts, W. A. 1985. A long pollen record from Lago di Monticchio, southern Italy: a preliminary account, *Journal of the Geological Society, London*, 142: 491–9.

Whitehouse, R. D. and Wilkins J. B. 1985. Magna Graecia before the Greeks: towards a reconciliation of the evidence. In Malone, C. and Stoddart, S. (eds.), *Papers in Italian archaeology IV. Part 3: Patterns in protohistory*. (BAR International Series, 245). Oxford, British Archaeological Reports, pp. 89–110.

1989. Greeks and natives in south-east Italy: approaches to the archaeological evidence. In Champion, T. (ed), *Centre and periphery*. London, Unwin Hyman, pp. 102–26.

Wickham, C. 1988. *The mountains and the city. The Tuscan Apennines in the early Middle Ages*. Oxford, Clarendon Press.

Wijmstra, T. A. 1978. Palynology of the first 30 metres of a 120 m deep section in northern Greece, *Acta Botanica Neerlandica*, 18: 511–17.

Wilkens, B. 1990. La fauna del villaggio del Colle dei Cappuccini, *Rassegna di Archeologia*, 9: 327–64.

Wilkins, J. B. 1990. Nation and language in Ancient Italy: problems of the linguistic evidence, *Accordia Research Papers*, 1: 53–72.

1991. Power and idea networks: theoretical notes on urbanisation in the early Mediterranean and Italy, *Papers of the Fourth Conference of Italian Archaeology*, 1: 221–30. Accordia Research Centre, University of London.

forthcoming. *Auspices and auguries: the Bronze Tables of Gubbio*, 2 vols. Accordia Specialist Studies on Italy, 4. Accordia Research Centre, University of London.

Wilson, T. 1987. *Ceramic art of the Italian Renaissance*. London, British Museum Publications.

Wobst, M. 1977. Stylistic behaviour and information exchange, *University of Michigan, Museum of Anthropology Anthropological Papers*, 61: 317–42.

Woillard, G. M. 1978. Grand Pile peat bog: a continuous pollen record for the last 140,000 years, *Quaternary Research*, 9: 2–21.

INDEX

232   **INDEX**

See also Caverna di Frasassi, Grotta del
   Mezzogiorno, Grotta delle Monache,
   Monte Santa Croce
Sentinum, *143*, 176, 178, *187*
seriation, 9
Serra Brunamonti (Gubbio), 44, 69
Serravallian, 19
Sette Finestre, *187*, 188, 196
settlement, 1, 20, 57, 67, 69, 73, 79–80, 81
   Roman, 180, 186, 188, *190*, 191–2, 197
shale, 62
sheep, 76, 91, 94, 187, 195, 196, 198
shepherds, 44
sickle gloss, 67, 76
sieving, 78
Sisenna, 178
site catchment analysis, 71, 81, 93
site exploitation territories, 90–4
slash and burn, 84
slaves, 182, 185, 188, 195
slope, 20, 22, 24, 25, 29, 33–4, 38, 42, 45, 57,
   67, 78–9, 189, 196
social war, 178
society, Roman, 182
soil
   degradation hazard, 86
   toxicities, 86
   suitability, *88*
   workability, 86, 89
soils, 5, 19–23, 24, 26, *27–8*, 29, *30*, 32, 35–6,
   38, 42, 57, 69, 72, 78–80, 83, 85, 188
   Acrisols, 33
   calcareous, 87
   Cambisols, 32–5
   decalcified top-, 87
   Fluvisols, 32–5
   Pleistocene, 210
   Regosols, 32–4
   Vertisols, 34
Solomon, King, 144
Sorgenti della Nova, *119*
   agriculture, 103–4
   bronzework, 125, 126
   pottery, 132
   social interpretation, 128
South Etruria survey, 1, 196
Spain, 188, 191, 195
Spartacus, 195
Spatial Analysis, 7
Spello, *173*, 175, 186, *187*, 198
spindle whorls, 114, *118*
Spineto (Frasassi, Sentino valley), 131
Spoleto, 152, *173*, 175, 176, 178, 181
springs, 37
spruce, 21, 57
SPSS/PC, 7
stadial, 59
state formation, 1, 5, 142
Stazione di Padule, 87
Sterpeto (Gubbio), 43
style, 13
sub-Apennine
   period, 9–11, 119
   style, 130, 131–2, 136, 211
subsistence, 76, 78, 80, 81, 193
survey, 4, 5, 11, 28, 34, 59, 65, 69, 72, 76, 81,
   186, 191–2, 196, 198
Sutri, *173*
Szombathely (Hungary), 145

Tables, Iguvine, 1, 144, 152, *154*, 155–72, 175,
   177, 178–9, 211, 212, 213
   dating:
      external, 155; internal, 155–7
   description, 155
   early history, 152, 154
   previous scholarship, 154–5, 158
   relationship to Indo-European, 158–60
   interpretation: new, 165–72; *templum*,
      170–1; traditional, 157–8
Tane del Diavolo (near Orvieto), *119*, 135
taphonomy, 189
Tarquinia, *173*, 176
technology, 83, 184, 188
tectonic, 17–19, 25, 60
Tegole, 192
temperature data, 37, 86
temples, 186, 198
   Temple of Diana (Gubbio), 178, 181
Terni, *119*, 130, *173*, 175
terraces (geomorphological), 20–1, *23*, 24–5,
   28–9, *32*, 32–4, 37, 45, 62, 63
terracotta, Archaic head, 152
Terramare, 125, 135
   bronzework, 126
   clay figurines, 135
Terra Sigillata Italica, 191, 195
Territorium, 185, 187–9
territory, 1, 79, 81, *82*, 83, 204, 206
Tertiary, 17
Thalictrum, 42
Thalweg, 20
theatre, Roman (Gubbio), 178, 181, 184, 186,
   191
thermophilous, 42
threshing, 79
thin section analysis, 74
Tiber, 4, 17, 24
   Upper, 174, 209
Tiberius, 196
Tibullus, 188
tile, 189, 192, 193
tillage, 79, 84
Timmari, 128, 140
Titonian, 19
Todi, *119*, 130, *173*, 175
Tolfa, *119*
Tomba alla cappucina, 184
tools
   Bronze Age, 83
   Neolithic, 74
   Palaeolithic, 59–67
Topino (Gubbio), 18, 25
topography, 1, 4, 28, 80, 83, 179, 181, 198
Toppello, bronzework, 109
Torre Annunziata, 196
Torre Calzolari (Gubbio), 79, 142, *143*
Torre Chiaruccia, *119*, 131
Torrionaccio, *119*
   agriculture, 103
   bone pinhead, 135
   bronzework, 125, 126
trade, 191, 193, 197
transect, 5, *6*, 67
transport, 186, 198
Trasimene, Lake, 145, *173*, 174
travertine, 20–1, 72
Tre Erici, 16
Trend Surface Analysis, 7

Trestina, *143*, 174
Tsuga, 38
turkey oak, 37
Tuscania, *187*, 188
Tuscany, 42
   western, 136
Type Diversity Analysis, 7, 9
typology, 11, *12*, 13, *14*, *15*, 16, 59, 73
Tyrrhenian, 18

Ulluzian, 63
Ulmus minor, 37
Umbelliferae, 42
Umbria, *2*, 3, 4, 17, 19, 59, 62, 67, 178–80,
   182, 185–7, 191, 195, 203
   north-east, 171
Umbrians, 172, 176, *209*
urbanisation, Roman, 178, 181, 185
Urbino, 204–5, *209*, 211

Valfabbrica, *119*
   bronzework, 106
Val di Chiana, *173*
vallum, 180–1
Varro, 104, 169, 187, 196
vegetation, 4, 5, 24–5, 36–58, 59, 72, 79, 81
Venchi, 44
Vernice Nera, 191, 195
Verucchio, *119*, 133
Vescovado, 4, 90–3, *107*, 108
Via Flaminia, 4, 178, 181, 186, *187*, 189, 191
Vibernum opalus, 37
villa
   Roman, 180, *182*, 188, 189, 191
   rustica, 184
Villa Dondana, 22
Villafranchian, 18–19
Villages, Roman, 189, 197, 213
Villa Jovis, 196
Villa Magna, 4
Villanova, *143*, 174
vines, 43, 44, 72, 84
violatio sepulcri, 184
Virgil, 188
Vistilius, 185
Vitruvius, 181
Vittorina cemeteries, 181, 184, 186, 189, 192,
   195, 198
Volcacius, 185
Volcanic, 45, 74
Vulci, 166, *173*, 176

wall plaster, 188
water mills, 43, 206
watershed, 3
weeds, 79
Wessex, 142
wheat, 79, 84–5, 195
willow, 44, 57
wine, 186, 198
wood, 80
woodland, 37–8, 43–5, 57–8, 60, 67, 72, 78,
   195, 203
wool, 76, 186, 195, 197, 206
Wurmian, 26

Zappacenere, 33, 87, *183*